MW01126773

Paul Grey, Rosemarie Little, Robin Macpherson, John Etty and Graham Goodlad

Cambridge IGCSE® and O Level

History

Option B: the 20th Century Coursebook

Second edition

CAMBRIDGE UNIVERSITY PRESS

CAMBRIDGE
UNIVERSITY PRESS

University Printing House, Cambridge CB2 8BS, United Kingdom

One Liberty Plaza, 20th Floor, New York, NY 10006, USA

477 Williamstown Road, Port Melbourne, VIC 3207, Australia

314–321, 3rd Floor, Plot 3, Splendor Forum, Jasola District Centre, New Delhi – 110025, India

79 Anson Road, #06–04/06, Singapore 079906

Cambridge University Press is part of the University of Cambridge.

It furthers the University's mission by disseminating knowledge in the pursuit of education, learning and research at the highest international levels of excellence.

Information on this title: www.cambridge.org/9781108439497

First published 2002
Second edition 2017
Current edition 2018

20 19 18 17 16 15 14 13 12 11 10 9 8 7 6 5 4

Printed in Malaysia by Vivar Printing

A catalogue record for this publication is available from the British Library

ISBN 978-1-108-43949-7 Paperback
ISBN 978-1-108-43950-3 Cambridge Elevate edition

Additional resources for this publication at www.cambridge.org/education

....

Contents

How to use this book

Studying history is not simply about memorising facts and dates. Instead, you have to investigate events by asking questions, considering different perspectives and evaluating the evidence you find. The Cambridge IGCSE® and O Level History courses encourage you to delve beyond simply asking 'what?', 'where?' and 'when?' to explore 'why?' and even 'what else might have happened?'

The first two chapters in this book are an introduction to the material, providing an overview of the 20th Century and the First World War. The rest of the book is divided into two sections: Core content and Depth studies. Section A: Core content addresses the seven Key Questions in turn. It is important that you learn and understand all of the material in this section. Section B covers four depth studies. You will only be studying one of the chapters in this section and your teacher will be able to tell you which one has been chosen.

It is important to read a variety of materials on a topic as well as the textbook. Additional reading is essential for enhancing your knowledge and enriching your learning experience. A good historian does not rely on a single source!

This book also contains a chapter which will help you to prepare for assessment. Here, the structure of the IGCSE and O Level assessments are discussed and the chapter will help you to familarise yourself with different types of questions and sources.

Coursebook features

This book contains a number of features to help you work through each of the topics.

Each Core content chapter begins with a set of **Focus points**: important points for you to consider as you work through the chapter.

Focus points

- What were the motives and aims of the Big Three at Versailles?
- Why did all the victors not get everything they wanted?
- What was the impact of the peace treaty on Germany up to 1923?
- What were the terms of the other peace treaties?
- Could the treaties be justified at the time?

Key term boxes explain the meaning of important terms from the text. You can also find the definitions of these terms in the **Glossary** at the back of the book.

KEY TERM

Pacifism: opposition to violence and war.

Each chapter contains multiple **Activities**. These are a mixture of individual and group tasks to help you develop your skills and practise applying your knowledge of a topic.

ACTIVITY P2.2

Look at Source P2C. Which countries suffered most during the First World War in terms of loss of life and injured survivors? Create a list of five in rank order and identify which alliance system each country belonged to – Allied Powers or Central Powers.

Top tip boxes provide helpful advice.

TOP TIP

Would *you* say that the 1914 system of alliances caused the war to break out, or did it just mean that once a war had started it was bound to get bigger and bigger? Similarly, did Russia's decision to mobilise in itself cause the war to break out? Just because one historian argues something doesn't mean they are automatically right. See if another historian says something different. Look at the evidence for yourself.

Fact file boxes contain useful background knowledge to enhance your understanding.

FACT FILE

The Maginot Line was built to avoid a surprise attack from Germany and to give the alarm if an attack happened. The government knew that it would take two to three weeks to mobilise the French Army and that the Line would give it valuable time in the event of an attack. It was made of fortifications, border guard posts and anti-tank rails. Not all parts of the Maginot Line were equally strong. You can see this in Sources 3G and 3H.

Check your understanding boxes contain questions that encourage you to reflect on what you have learned and to quickly check your understanding of the topic.

CHECK YOUR UNDERSTANDING 1.1

'Winning the peace' is an expression that means 'succeeding in the post-war period'. What circumstances in 1919 made this success so hard for the victors to achieve?

Each Core content and Depth study chapter ends with **Summary points**, a **Big Challenge** and **Exam-style questions**.

Summary points are a brief summary of the main points in the chapter to help you revise.

Summary points

- The USA reacted to the development of the Cold War by establishing a new policy of limiting Soviet expansion called containment.
- The first test of this policy was in the Korean War of 1950–1953. The North Koreans were pushed back but the UN forces led by the USA failed to make any further gains.

- The Cuban Missile Crisis was the closest threat to the USA. President Kennedy had to use skilful diplomacy to ensure a peaceful end to the conflict, but he had to allow Fidel Castro to remain in power.
- The war in Vietnam was a disaster for USA, and for containment. After US troops withdrew all of Vietnam came under communist control.

The Big Challenge is a short project that helps you to review and consolidate your learning of the chapter.

The Big Challenge

With a partner, review the structure and Covenant of the League of Nations:

- How could you make it more effective?
- If you were helping set up the League in the 1920s, how would you deal with the League's weaknesses?

You won't have to change everything: much of the work of the League's agencies was successful.

- Having completed your review, do you think that the League was doomed to fail from the start or was it undermined by later events?

Exam-style questions provide an opportunity to relate your learning to the formal assessment and practise writing longer answers.

Exam-style questions

1   How did Hitler go about revising the Treaty of Versailles between 1933 and 1936?

2   Was the Treaty of Versailles itself to blame for the outbreak of war in 1939 or was it the way it was implemented that was at fault?

3   '*Lebensraum* (living space) was the crucial factor in causing the war in 1939.' How far do you agree?

4   'Instead of causing the war, appeasement kept the peace for longer in the 1930s.' How far do you agree?

5   'The Second World War was inevitable after: a) 1936, b) 1938, c) March 1939.' For each of the three dates, explain to what extent you agree with the statement.

Introduction Part 1
What is the big picture of the 20th century?

People and history

Source P1A: Harry Patch during a ceremony in 2007 to remember those who fought and died in the First World War and the Second World War.

Source P1B: The gravestone that marks the burial place of Harry Patch.

Source P1C: Brezhnev as a political leader, receiving applause after giving a speech in October 1968.

Source P1D: Brezhnev signing a treaty in Vienna in 1979. Sitting at the same table and also signing is the US's president Carter.

Harry Patch (Sources P1A and P1B) and Leonid Ilyich Brezhnev (Sources P1C and P1D) never met. Their lives stretched across much of the 20th century and both became famous during their lifetimes.

Harry was not a king, politician, business leader, film star or great scientist; he was the son of a stonemason who worked as a plumber, an ordinary person who took part in extraordinary events. He was born in the UK in 1898 and lived for 111 years, 1 month, 1 week and 1 day. When he died in 2009 he was the last of the soldiers who had fought in the trenches during the First World War (1914–1918).

Leonid was born in 1906. His home was Russia, which was ruled by a **tsar**. While he was a boy, several members of the royal family were executed during a period of political violence and the survivors fled from the country. The huge country changed from being a

> ### KEY TERM
>
> **Tsar:** Russian word for emperor.

monarchy to being a communist state. Leonid, the son of a metal worker, went into politics. By the time of his death in 1982, he was the leader of the country, a superpower during the years of the Cold War (1945–1989). In the years that followed his death, that country changed again and broke apart into different, separate countries, something he could almost certainly never have expected. We will be turning to these topics in chapters 4 and 6.

In this book you will learn about the key developments and events that Leonid Brezhnev and Harry Patch both lived through between 1901 and 2000. Most of the people you meet in this story will be like Brezhnev, decision makers; you will see Brezhnev's name again (in chapter 6), but not Patch's. However, don't forget that in the background there are always a lot of people who, like Patch, had to live with the consequences of other, more powerful people's decisions.

This first chapter provides you with the 'big picture' of 20th-century history. Many of the issues identified here will affect your life as you make your way through the 21st century.

> ### ACTIVITY P1.1
>
> What do Sources P1A, P1B, P1C and P1D tell us about the 20th century? What issues do the four photographs raise?

Life and death

Let's start our big-picture overview of the century with matters of life and death.

Between 1901 and 2000 people lived longer, healthier lives than they had ever done before. Sources P1E, P1F and P1G provide evidence of these developments.

For all but the richest few in the more developed, industrialised countries in 1900, life expectancy was low. The improvements in life expectancy in all the world's regions have been dramatic. But as historians, you should think about what caused these developments and what they in turn caused. The improvements were largely the result of the development of cures for common diseases and reduction in infant mortality rates. However, you should note that the gap between the industrialised and developing worlds at the end of the century remained wide.

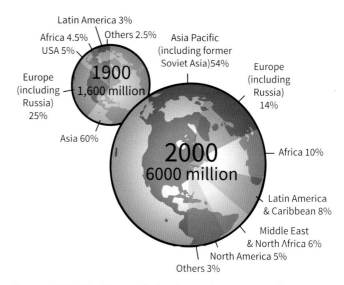

Source P1E: World population by region, 1900 and 2000.

> ### ACTIVITY P1.2
>
> Study Sources P1E and P1F. What would you expect the consequences of the changes in population to have been: would the increase put pressure on resources and drive the increase in technology? How would the political structures, which had been in place since the 18th and 19th centuries, cope? Would more people lead to more wars, more extreme politics and more revolutions? Write down a few predictions and later, when you have worked through the book, see how many were right. You might decide that the real causes of major events are the things going on in the background, not the decisions taken by individuals.

3

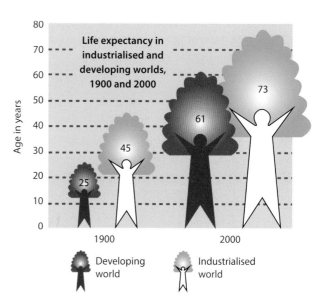

Source P1F: A graph showing life expectancy across the 20th century.

Wealth

World consumption rose from $1.5 trillion in 1900 to $4 trillion in 1950. It then grew rapidly to $12 trillion in 1975 and $24 trillion in 1998. However, the benefits have not been fairly distributed: poor countries have a much smaller share than they did in 1950. Recently, this has been combined with the increasing availability of mass media, allowing more people to see more of the world. Even where standards of living have risen, the fact of such differences in prosperity between different groups is now more visible than ever before.

ACTIVITY P1.3

What do you imagine the consequences of changing levels of wealth, continuing inequalities of wealth, and increasing media coverage have been or are now – or are likely to be soon?

Energy

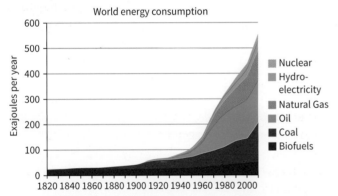

Source P1G: A graph showing the consumption of various forms of energy from 1820 to 2010.

Black gold

Today, oil is the world's biggest business. Until an alternative source of energy is found in sufficient quantity, the availability and price of oil will have far-reaching effects on the global economy.

The battlefields of the First World War (1914–1918), where Harry Patch fought, established the importance of oil when the internal combustion engine began to be used more than the horse and the coal-powered train. Germany's wish to have access to oil was a contributory

factor to the outbreak of the Second World War, and oil was vital to all sides during the course of that war. After it ended in 1945, there was a contest for control of oil between international companies and developing countries that were struggling to gain independence after decades, or in some cases, centuries of European rule. Oil was an issue both in the Iraqi invasion of Kuwait in 1990 and in the resulting international reaction, a topic we will look at in chapter 7. The United States, once the world's largest oil producer and still its largest consumer, has to import 60% of its oil supply today, weakening its position as a **Great Power**.

In the first decades of the 20th century, the oil business provided the industrialising world with a product called 'kerosene'. This was used in oil lamps. Gasoline (petrol) was then only a by-product and of little value. However, just when the invention of the light bulb seemed to mark the end of the oil lamp and the oil industry, a new era began with the development of the internal combustion engine powered by gasoline. The oil industry had a new market. In the 20th century, oil, together with natural gas, took the place of coal as the most important power source for the industrial world.

Oil is essential to our modern way of life. Oil (and natural gas) are the essential ingredients in fertiliser, on which world agriculture depends; oil makes it possible to transport food to the dependent megacities of the world; oil provides the plastics and chemicals that are the very foundations of your way of life.

ACTIVITY P1.4

What does Source P1G tell us about the modern world and sources of conflict? Would your familiar social order and civilisation collapse if the world's oil wells suddenly dried up?

The impact of industrialisation and growth

People had a far more destructive effect on the global environment in the 20th century than in all the thousands of years that preceded it.

- The release of chlorofluorocarbons (CFCs) into the atmosphere from the 1930s onwards caused holes in the ozone layer that protects the Earth from the Sun's ultraviolet radiation.

4

- About two-thirds of the effect of global warming comes from the emission of carbon dioxide from the burning of fossil fuels. Over half the total increase in carbon dioxide levels between 1750 and 1990 occurred after 1950.
- About half the world's tropical forests (which help slow climate change by absorbing carbon dioxide) were destroyed after 1950. About 75% of the clearance provided land for agriculture.

ACTIVITY P1.5

How many of the conflicts studied in this book were due to competition for resources? When you read about wars breaking out or peace treaties being signed, see what evidence there is that they were not just military and political affairs, but economic ones.

Who rules in the 20th century?

In 1901, the peoples of Western Europe and North America seemed to have every reason to greet the 20th century as the start of a new and happier era in the history of humankind. Science and technology were already improving their standard of living and they dominated the world with their trade, their finance and their military power. Most of the western hemisphere, the continent of Africa, the Indian subcontinent and much of Asia outside China had been either directly colonised by Europeans or deeply influenced by European culture. By the end of the century, much of this had changed!

European countries have lost their **empires** and therefore some of their importance. One of the factors that caused this was the cost involved in fighting two world wars: the First World War (1914–1918) and the Second World War (1939–1945). Europe (and several other parts of the world) saw periods of savage fighting during the 20th century. The economic power of Europe meant that relationships between individual European countries affected the rest of the world directly or indirectly. The existence of their empires translated European wars into world wars. Because European countries built up their industries, towns and empires at different speeds, the balance of power changed within the continent. Britain was the first to industrialise and during the 19th century was the most powerful of the group. By 1900, Germany had been developing and growing, and was seen by Britain not just as a competitor, but as a direct threat.

As the empires broke up in the second half of the century, the world's diplomatic and military picture changed. There were now new powers to consider. But also, with the decline of the old imperial powers – Germany, UK, France and others – the remaining two Great Powers, **USSR** (formerly Russia) and USA became even more important and were known as 'superpowers'. Now, every action by these two countries had consequences for everyone else.

Peaceful international relations proved very hard to achieve.

War and peace

We often take for granted the idea that countries and nations are the same thing, and also that there is something natural and permanent about them. For example, during the Second World War, one popular song declared that 'there'll always be an England'. In fact, all countries have come about through a process, and there is nothing inevitable about their make-up or their borders. One key issue over many centuries was the border between France and Germany. Although few historians would want to say that this was what the First World War and the Second World War were fought over, the fact is that countless wars had been fought over this issue, pushing the border one way and then the other, depending on who won. Also, countries tend to be collections of groups, not of individuals. In any population there are likely to be different religious groups, different social classes, different languages and dialects, and of course different genders. Inside each country the most powerful force holding together these diverse groups as they moved into the new century was that of 'nationalism'.

For a century the power of the state had increased. Improved communications enabled governments to increase their control over the administration, welfare and education of their citizens and allowed governments to force citizens to serve in their armies. As the power of

KEY TERMS

Empire: an area of territory usually comprising more than one country, ruled by a single monarch or government.

Great Powers: countries with considerable military, diplomatic and economic power and influence.

USSR: Union of Soviet Socialist Republics, also known as the Soviet Union.

5

the state increased, so did the sense of being a 'nation'. This could be seen in military parades and ceremonies, in anthems and flags and patriotic symbols. Pride in 'your' country created a sense of common dignity and purpose. As the new century developed, appealing to nationalist feelings was the most powerful way any government could mobilise its citizens in a cause, perhaps most importantly in war.

During the 20th century other political ideologies emerged. People could identify with others like them and form groups. The group they chose might indeed be a nation (for example, German nationalism), but it might instead be a social class (for example, the Marxist ideology of the **Soviet** Union), an ethnicity (different groups in the civil-rights, apartheid and decolonisation disputes and movements) or a religious faith (as we see today in various Muslim political parties and insurgencies). As you will see, any of these forces, and indeed others, might cause or prevent enormous political developments and wars. For one thing, people campaigning for change in their countries asked whose country it really was.

To people in 1900, the prospect of war, with all the destructive weapons that technology had made possible,

was truly terrible. The 19th century had seen a long period of peace in Europe and the idea of a new war, using new weapons, was looked on with concern. So much so that the leaders of Europe met in The Hague in 1899 to see what could be done to reduce the chances of war occurring. Another conference followed in 1907. A third such conference, scheduled for 1914, never took place. Talking and reaching agreement about weapons were overtaken by the start of the First World War in 1914. There was still the widespread belief that even if war was terrible, it remained the ultimate test of the fitness of a nation to survive.

Another key aspect of wars in the 20th century was not just who won and who lost but what happened next. We begin by examining the situation at the end of the First World War in chapters 1 and 2, and the war's longer-term consequences in chapter 3. But the aftermath of war is an important element in the later chapters as well. You may well come to conclude that however important winning a war might seem, 'winning the peace' is at least as important and just as hard.

KEY TERM

Soviet: Russian for 'council' or 'committee'.

Introduction Part 2
The First World War: 1914–1918

How did the First World War break out?

Historians still debate the key causes of the First World War (1914–1918) and who to blame for the catastrophe – as did people at the time. Source P2A is a map showing the **alliance** system in 1914; many blame this system for dragging the major powers into war because each government felt it had to stick by its agreement to support its alliance partner if it was attacked.

Others blame Germany for encouraging Austria-Hungary to declare war on Serbia, despite knowing that Serbia's **Slav** population would be supported by the Russian Empire. In fact, it was Austria-Hungary and then Russia that **mobilised** their armies first – Austria-Hungary because the challenge from Serbia already existed, Russia because the process was so cumbersome and took time.

TOP TIP

Would *you* say that the 1914 system of alliances caused the war to break out, or did it just mean that once a war had started it was bound to get bigger and bigger? Similarly, did Russia's decision to mobilise in itself cause the war to break out? Just because one historian argues something doesn't mean they are automatically right. See if another historian says something different. Look at the evidence for yourself.

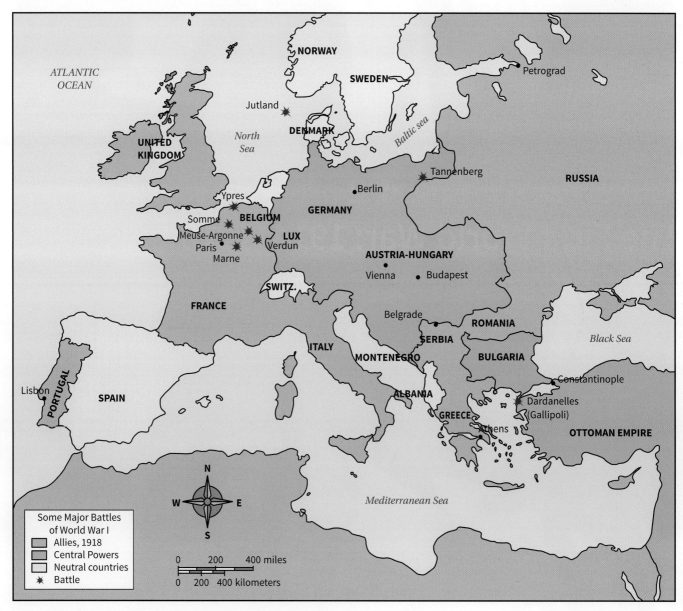

Source P2A: A map of Europe in 1914 showing the Allied Powers and the Central Powers – the two sides that fought each other in the First World War.

There were other causes too. Several European countries had developed large empires in Africa and Asia, while Germany had not. Strong feelings of nationalism encouraged competition with neighbouring countries. Another cause of that was the naval arms race between Germany and Britain, which created increasing tension and distrust. Ordinary citizens, military leaders and politicians expected some kind of war at some point. This expectation encouraged the German and Austro-Hungarian governments to take risks in 1914, risks that added more threats to the fragile European peace. There had not been a major European war for a hundred years, but in 1914 the tensions turned to war.

1914

28 June:	Archduke Franz Ferdinand and his wife from the Austro-Hungarian Empire were assassinated by a Serb nationalist, Gavrilo Princip.
28 July:	The Austrian government blamed the Serbs and declared war on Serbia. This was an opportunity for the Austrians to end Serbian nationalism once and for all. However, Serbia was bound by treaty with Russia. The Russian government announced a general mobilisation of its army in its defence.
1 August:	Germany, allied by treaty to Austria-Hungary, saw the mobilisation as an act of war against its friend and declared war on Russia.
3 August:	The German High Command had put in place the Schlieffen Plan to avoid war on two fronts against both France and Russia. This was now triggered. If France could be defeated quickly in six weeks, then German forces could turn east and take on the Russians. It would take the Russian army all that time to get ready.
4 August:	The German army started to move quickly through Belgium and France to reach Paris in six weeks. Belgium was a small country and its king asked Britain for help. Standing by the 1839 treaty that guaranteed Belgian neutrality, Britain declared war later on that day.

Source P2B: The sequence of events and decisions that led to the start of the First World War in Europe.

Tensions had been building in an area of Europe called the Balkans. In 1912 and 1913 there had been two localised wars in the area.

You can see in Source P2B the events and decisions that led to the First World War in Europe. Whatever historians might argue, the winners of the First World War in 1918 blamed the losers – Germany and the other **Central Powers** – for starting it.

ACTIVITY P2.1

Using Sources P2A and P2B, explain why the Central Powers would not want to fight a war on two fronts.

Europeans welcome war

The conflict began in 1914 and many thought it would be over by Christmas. It wasn't. It was more than four years before the guns fell silent. Back in August 1914, huge crowds welcomed the declarations of war in London, Paris, Berlin and St Petersburg. People across Europe saw it as a welcome opportunity to fight: some out of a sense of duty, some because of **patriotism**, and others to make things right. Europeans had been prepared for war by the first mass newspapers and by years of intense nationalism that placed country against country in bitter rivalry. It might well have been the most popular war in history when it started. A German politician looking back to the first weeks of war in 1914 said that the moment was like a 'ringing opening chord for an **immortal** song of sacrifice, loyalty and heroism'.

KEY TERMS

Alliance: a collection of two or more countries that agree to support the other/s if they are attacked by another country.

Slavs: a number of ethnic groups of people in eastern and south-eastern Europe. They and their languages (e.g. Russian, Polish, Czech, Serbian) are related and many (though not all) of them belong historically to the Orthodox Christian churches.

Mobilisation: describes all the various actions that need to be taken to prepare for war, not just by the soldiers and sailors but by the civilians as well.

Central Powers: refers to the German and Austro-Hungarian empires at the beginning of the First World War. The Ottoman Empire joined the Central Powers later in 1914 and in 1915, the Kingdom of Bulgaria also did so.

Patriotism: having strong support for your country.

Immortal: undying.

The First World War

In its scale and the way it was fought, the First World War was different from anything that had gone before. The slaughter was more terrible than anyone expected. No one has ever exactly calculated the numbers killed and wounded, but for four years about 5,000 men died on average every day, mostly from wounds inflicted by shellfire. Source P2C gives you the estimates of the dead and wounded from both sides. The intense warfare was not confined to land. From the start, the struggle at sea was fierce as each side tried to starve the other by **blockade**. Air space became a zone of combat for the first time. In 1914 the major powers had just over 100 planes each; by the end of the war air forces had grown enormously. The Royal Air Force had over 20,000 machines in 1918; but this was only one sign of the new importance of technology in war.

 KEY TERM

Blockade: a form of economic warfare where one country attempts to prevent goods being imported to its rival. The Royal Navy's blockade in the Great War also ensured that German ships could not get out of port.

ACTIVITY P2.2

Look at Source P2C. Which countries suffered most during the First World War in terms of loss of life and injured survivors? Create a list of five in rank order and identify which alliance system each country belonged to – Allied Powers or Central Powers.

ACTIVITY P2.3

The numbers in Source P2C are what is called 'raw data', which means they are numbers with minimum context. It would help to do some research to put them into context. Find out what the population of some of the different countries was at the time of the 1914–1918 war. Now calculate what percentage of that population the numbers of dead and wounded add up to in those cases. How different is your opinion of which countries suffered most now? Historians often use numbers, such as dates and statistics, in their analyses and arguments, and you definitely should too. But always remember: numbers don't tell their own story, they always need contextualising and interpreting, and different historians will interpret them differently.

Technology of death

Source P2C shows vast numbers: how did so many people die in four years of fighting? Movement on the battlefield was transformed. By 1914 petrol-driven engines were available in quantity and by 1918 trucks and tractors were as important as horses to the soldiers in the field.

Country	Dead	Wounded	Missing	Total
Australia	58,150	152,170	-	210,320
Austria-Hungary	922,000	3,600,000	855,283	5,377,283
Britain	658,700	2,032,150	359,150	3,050,000
Canada	56,500	149,700	-	206,200
Caribbean	1,000	3,000	-	4,000
France	1,359,000	4,200,000	361,650	5,920,650
Germany	1,600,000	4,065,000	103,000	5,768,000
Greece	5,000	21,000	1,000	27,000
India	43,200	65,175	5,875	114,250
Italy	689,000	959,100	-	1,424,660
Japan	300	907	3	1,210
New Zealand	16,130	40,750	-	56,880
Russia	1,700,000	5,000,000	-	6,700,000
South Africa	7,000	12,000	-	19,000
Turkey	250,000	400,000	-	650,000
USA	58,480	189,955	14,290	262,725

Source P2C: A list of countries involved in the First World War with the number of dead, wounded and missing.

Weapons got even more deadly. Soldiers were maimed or killed by poison gas, flame-throwers and tanks. Machine guns were developed that were capable of firing 600 rounds a minute; new field guns could fire three or four times a minute at ranges of 10,000 yards, and heavier guns could hit enemy targets six or seven miles away (Sources P2D and P2E show heavy field guns and the effect they had on the landscape). The scale of the battlefield, like the scale of dead and wounded, was so much bigger than ever before.

Source P2D: A photo of part of the Western Front in France in October 1917. Big field guns fired shells that scarred the landscape and turned the surface to mud during the winter months, making it impossible to advance any distance against the enemy.

Source P2E: Both sides had heavy field guns like this one to fire shells that scooped out holes in the landscape. Photo from October 1917.

CHECK YOUR UNDERSTANDING P2.1

Look at Sources P2D, P2E and P2F. What connects all of them? What other sources would you like to study to help you understand how so many people could be killed and injured?

On the Home Front, civilians suffered too. Poorer diet and the spread of disease became more common as the war went on and each side tried to starve the other into surrender using the naval blockade. Undernourishment and sickness hit children and older people more than the soldiers. The First World War killed civilians. On the Home Front, for the first time in warfare, death came by air. Source P2F shows you the results of one of the air raids carried out by the Germans using airships called Zeppelins. Airships made about 50 bombing raids on Britain during the First World War. These killed 557 and injured another 1,358 people. Aeroplanes carried out 27 raids resulting in 835 deaths.

Source P2F: A photograph of the morning after a Zeppelin raid on Surrey in the south of England on the 19th January 1915.

European war to global war

The First World War may have started as a European war but it soon spread. Japan and the Ottoman Empire joined in soon after the start; Japan on the side of the Allies; the Ottoman Empire joined the Central Powers. In 1915 and 1916, as stalemate developed, the search was on for new allies. Italy did not join her Triple Alliance partners but instead chose the Allied side in return for promises of Austrian and Ottoman land. Others soon joined in: Bulgaria joined the Central Powers in September 1915 and Romania joined the Allies in 1916. Greece followed Romania in 1917. In Europe only Spain, Switzerland, the Netherlands, Norway and Sweden remained neutral throughout the four-year struggle.

The war wasn't one struggle between only two sides; you might say that there was a collection of different wars, larger and smaller, all being fought at the same time. In the Middle East, the British, French, Russians and Arabs all fought in a war against the Ottoman Empire. In East Asia, the Japanese took the opportunity to strengthen their position in China. In Africa, there was fighting between different countries' colonies. Finally, in April 1917, the USA became an Associated Power of the Allies. The war had truly become world-wide.

FACT FILE

Additional allies

The two alliance systems in 1914 did not mean that all countries were on one side or the other. Some countries delayed their decisions until the war had started. Japan only joined the Allied Powers once Britain agreed that it could take Germany's Pacific territories – the Mariana, Caroline and Marshall Islands.

Romania joined the Allied Powers because the government wanted to take Transylvania – which had a largely Romanian population – from Austria-Hungary.

The Ottoman Empire joined the Central Powers because Germany wanted her as an ally. The Berlin-Baghdad Railway had been a joint German-Ottoman project and the Germans wanted to extend it further to give them easier access to its African colonies and to trade markets in India. To keep the Ottoman Empire from joining the Allied Powers, Germany encouraged Bulgaria to join the Central Powers.

Italy was a special case. At the start of the war, Italy was part of the Central Powers. However, Italy refused to commit troops arguing that the alliance was defensive and Austria-Hungary had been the aggressor in its attack on Serbia. Not only that, but Italy wanted Trentino, Fiume and Dalmatia – all in the Austro-Hungarian Empire. So, in April 1915 it joined the Allied Powers and by the Treaty of London was promised parts of South Tyrol and Dalmatia.

Stalemate on the battlefield

On the battlefield, the quick war that was expected never happened. Instead, both sides settled down to siege warfare on an unprecedented scale. Military operations were dominated by the huge killing power of modern

weapons. When human targets were not visible, the explosive force of modern artillery could destroy the unseen enemy.

You have seen two photos that partly explain why the war turned into a stalemate with miles of trenches stretching from the French coast to Switzerland. Another reason was that the land in France and Belgium is mostly very flat, and it was easy for machine gunners to fire a stream of bullets to deadly effect; the best way to take cover if you faced this was to dig a trench. Both sides had machine guns so both developed trench systems.

FACT FILE

Both sides in the war demonstrated an ability not only to kill and wound their enemies but to conscript and organise their own people. Governments took action that they would never do in peace time. For example, in 1916 the British government imposed **conscription** – men between the ages of 16 and 45 were made to join the military. To ensure soldiers were properly equipped the government managed the making and distribution of boots, uniforms, mess tins, water bottles, barbed wire, timber for building, picks, shovels, cooking utensils, sandbags and sacks. There never seemed to be enough weapons and ammunition.

Source P2G: Women working in a British munitions factory during the First World War.

Total war

The First World War was the first total war: whole societies were engaged in warfare. The mills, factories, mines and furnaces of Europe worked as never before. So did those of the USA and Japan. Everywhere, governments attempted to control materials, production and conscript labour: thousands of women filled the gaps in industry and farming that men had left when they joined the military. Much of this work was vital and dangerous as you can see in Source P2G. Whether a civilian or a soldier, both were vulnerable in the First World War.

KEY TERM

Conscription: compulsory military service.

FACT FILE
Male attitudes towards women restricted what work women could or couldn't do. Women had been working as servants for centuries. They had worked in factories since the Industrial Revolution. In 1914 many were also teachers, nurses or governesses looking after the children of those rich enough to pay for their services. When men became soldiers in 1914 there was a huge demand for munitions and these had to be made in factories by women. Some of them paid with their lives while handling high-explosive material.

Why did the Allies win and the Central Powers lose?

At the end of 1916, the German High Command concluded that Germany would lose the war because of the impact of the British blockade. It was preventing supplies getting to Germany. Something had to be done quickly. In German cities people were suffering; food riots and strikes were becoming more frequent. To turn the direction of the war, German submarines had to be used differently. If submarines could operate without restrictions and torpedo both Allied shipping and the shipping of neutral countries, like the USA, then Britain could be starved out of the war. Of course, if German submarines happened to sink any US (neutral) ships then this might bring the USA into the war on the Allied side.

On 31 January 1917, Germany gambled. The US government was informed that the following day unrestricted submarine warfare would begin. The German decision was a direct threat to US interests and the safety of its citizens. The German plan was this: if Great Britain could be defeated by starvation, this would force France to give in before American soldiers could arrive in large numbers from across the Atlantic.

For a couple of months it looked like the gamble might be successful, but on 6 April 1917 the USA declared war on Germany. The Allies could now be sure of eventual victory if they could hold on long enough for the US armies to reach France. That year did not go well for the Allies. The new **strategy** followed by German submarines sank many supply ships; and the battle of Passchendaele cost another 300,000 dead and wounded, while the battle line only moved about five miles. Exhausted, the French army was shaken by a series of mutinies. Then military and political discipline in the Russian Empire collapsed, a Bolshevik government seized power and sued for peace with the Germans. Even so, once the submarine campaign failed to defeat Great Britain, it was only a matter of time in 1918 before the extra American soldiers and resources arrived and would make a telling difference on the Western Front.

CHECK YOUR UNDERSTANDING P2.2

Is it accurate to say that the intervention of the USA: a) shortened the war and b) resulted in victory for the Allied Powers?

The Treaty of Brest-Litovsk

German hopes were raised by the news that the Russian Empire had pulled out of the war on the Eastern Front. The new Russian government led by Bolshevik

KEY TERM

Strategy: a plan intended to achieve an overall, long-term military aim.

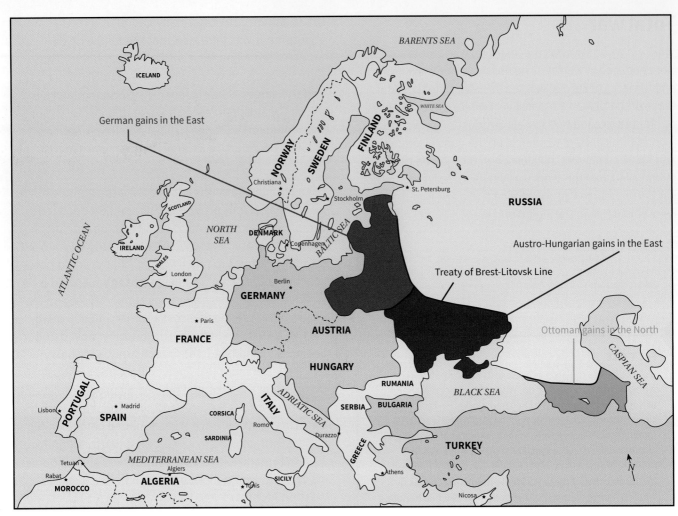

Source P2H: A map showing the territorial losses that Russia was forced to give up to the Central Powers in March 1918.

leader Lenin wanted an immediate **peace treaty** with Germany. In March 1918, the Treaty of Brest-Litovsk was signed. You can see in Source P2H that the terms were very harsh on Russia. The Russians lost one million square miles of territory to the Germans, and with it went both one-third of their population and also significant resources such as oil, coal and iron. Finally, the Germans demanded 6 billion German gold marks in **reparations**. Lenin and the Bolsheviks had to sign the treaty because the German and Austrian armies were making further advances into Russian territory. Following the peace in the East, Germans transferred thousands of soldiers to the Western Front. The Allies were afraid that the arrival of these troops would transform the military situation there.

What happened to Germany?

However, with US resources crossing the Atlantic to support the Allied Powers, the end for the German war effort was getting closer. A German Spring Offensive in 1918 led to a breakthrough and it looked as though victory was possible for the Germans, but the cost of the operation, in deaths, injuries and materials, exhausted the resources of the German army. The German army and navy and the people back home were at the limit of what they could take. **Desertions** multiplied as soldiers left their posts and headed home from the trenches. Sailors mutinied and refused to go to sea. The British blockade was hurting German civilians as well as soldiers by creating severe shortages of food, fuel and other essentials.

The German Supreme Army Command knew that defeat was not far away. On 29 September 1918 it told Kaiser Wilhelm II that the military situation was hopeless. Some believed that if, as head of state, he **abdicated**, the Allies could be persuaded to negotiate a peace settlement because the government could then argue that Germany was reforming and was no longer a threat to the allies.

Once the Kaiser had abdicated on 9 November, political power fell to German democratic politicians. Two days later, on 11 November, the **Armistice** to stop the fighting was signed. The German generals wanted to save their own honour and that of Germany so they made a plan to shift the blame for the military disaster onto civilians. In this way it would be the democratic politicians and new chancellor, Friedrich Ebert, who the German people would see as responsible for the dishonourable defeat. German people started to believe that their soldiers and generals had been 'stabbed in the back' by politicians, none of whom had sacrificed anything for four years because they had not joined the army. This judgement on Germany's new government was a myth but it was made all the more believable by four other facts about the end of the war:

- No foreign army had occupied any part of Germany during the four years of fighting and the German army had not been finally defeated in a battle.
- German citizens were angry that their king was no longer head of the government and had been forced to abdicate.
- German newspapers had not published any reports that the war was not going well for the Central Powers, so few (including relatively few soldiers) had any insight into the true state of affairs.
- Germans believed that the Armistice would lead to a fair peace because it was not a 'surrender', just an agreement to stop fighting. In fact, the terms of the Armistice were harsh. No one who read them could be in any doubt that Germany had come out of the war on the 'losing' side.

CHECK YOUR UNDERSTANDING P2.3

Do you agree with the view that it was soldiers and civilians that cost Germany the war, not its leaders?

In Source P2I you can see an artist's view of the signing of the Armistice. The terms under which the First World War ended underline that it was the Central Powers who 'lost' and the Allied Powers who were the victors. Among other demands the Armistice stated that:

- Hostilities will end at 11 am.
- There will be an immediate withdrawal of German troops from France and Belgium and this includes the provinces of Alsace and Lorraine that had been part of Germany since 1871.
- All German submarines must be surrendered.
- French, British and Italian prisoners of war must be released immediately. German prisoners of war will only be released after a peace treaty has been agreed.
- The following must be handed over to the Allied Powers: 25,000 machine guns, 1,700 aeroplanes and 5,000 trains.

So, as the guns fell silent on 11 November, what happened next? At 11 am there were a few examples of greetings exchanged between the two sides, but in general, reactions were muted. A British corporal reported: '… the Germans came from their trenches, bowed to us and then went away. That was it'. Unsurprisingly, the dominant feeling was one of silence and emptiness after 52 exhausting months of war. The Allied Powers had won the war, now could they win the peace?

 KEY TERMS

Peace treaty: a document that sets out what should happen after a war is over. It is signed by the victors and the losers.

Reparations: a kind of fine paid by an aggressor and intended to make up for loss or damage suffered by a victim.

Desertion: when soldiers leave their post, refuse to obey their officers and walk away from the front.

Abdicate (as head of state): when a king or emperor steps down or gives up the throne.

Armistice: an end of fighting as a prelude to peace negotiations.

Source P2I: The Armistice is signed in a railway carriage and peace broke out at 11 am on 11 November 1918. What strikes you about the scene as depicted here?

The situation in France

Of all the countries involved in the fighting on the Western Front, France suffered huge losses and devastation.

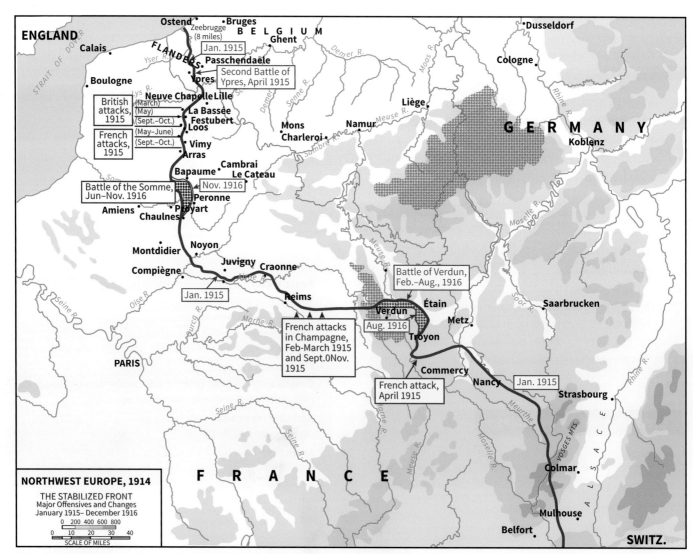

Figure P2J: This map shows the main battlefield locations on the Western Front. Note how much of the fighting took place on French soil.

The data on French casualties sums up the impact of the First World War on this one country:

- Around 1,400,000 of the soldiers were killed, an average of 893 deaths per day.
- More than 4,300,000 men were wounded, an average of 2745 per day; this includes:
  - 1,100,000 disabled
  - 300,000 mutilated
  - 42,000 blinded
  - 15,000 with broken faces
- The deaths of soldiers created 700,000 widows and more than 1,000,000 orphans.
- Between 81,000 and 97,000 men from the French colonies were killed, including 26,000 Algerians.
- Of France's total population 1 out of 20 were killed.

As a result of the First World War, France's entire north-east was devastated. More than one thousand miles of canals, seven million acres of land, half the roads in the region, three thousand miles of railroads, and an estimated 220,000 houses were destroyed. The estimated cost of the destruction was 34 billion francs; this was later revised to 55 billion francs.

ACTIVITY P2.5

Write a paragraph describing four key tasks that the French government would need to do once the war ended.

Why was Britain less affected than France by the impact of the First World War?

What do you think French people would want most from the peace conference now that the fighting had stopped?

17

Chapter 1

Key Question 1: Were the peace treaties of 1919–1923 fair?

Focus points

■ What were the motives and aims of the Big Three at Versailles?

■ Why did all the victors not get everything they wanted?

■ What was the impact of the peace treaty on Germany up to 1923?

■ What were the terms of the other peace treaties?

■ Could the treaties be justified at the time?

What is this enquiry about?

As historians, your challenge is to study the treaties and weigh up how fair they were. You will need to think about issues of justice. What does 'fair' mean? When you consider the question about the treaties, make sure you discuss how you are using the word 'fair'. For example:

- Are you judging all the peace treaties to be fair or just one?
- Were the peace treaties fair to the winners or the losers or both?
- Is your assessment of the 'fairness' of the peace treaties affected by your views on the causes of the First World War? If so, where does the blame lie?
- Is your assessment based more on how badly a country was affected by the war?

You will also need to think about what the treaties were for, what they were intended to achieve:

- Punish the losers?
- Prevent another similar war breaking out?
- Compensate the winners?

Even though the Allied Powers had won the war, they did not have an entirely free hand. These factors shaped their thinking and decisions:

- The loss of human life and destruction caused intense bitterness and an unwillingness to compromise.

- The war had cost huge sums of money and some countries went bankrupt. To pay for the war, countries like France and Great Britain borrowed from the US. At the war's end, they were heavily in debt.

Allied Powers	Cost in Dollars in 1914–1918
United States	$22,625,253,000
Great Britain	$35,334,012,000
France	$24,265,583,000
Russia	$22,293,950,000
Italy	$12,413,998,000

Central Powers	Cost in Dollars in 1914–1918
Germany	$37,775,000,000
Austria-Hungary	$20,622,960,000
Turkey	$1,430,000,000
Bulgaria	$815,200,000

The peacemakers had to work quickly:

- The First World War had created conditions in which revolution could break out at any time just as it had done in Russia.

Source 1A: Shows the map of European countries before the First World War and after all the treaties had been signed.

- Millions were dying from an **epidemic** of Spanish flu that swept across Europe, killing as many as the First World War had.
- There wasn't just one peace treaty to agree on, there were five – one for each of the Central Powers. It took until 1923 for the last one to be put in place.

CHECK YOUR UNDERSTANDING 1.1

'Winning the peace' is an expression that means 'succeeding in the post-war period'. What circumstances in 1919 made this success so hard for the victors to achieve?

ACTIVITY 1.1

Look at Source 1A. Identify those nationalities that would judge the peace treaties to be 'fair' and those who would say it was 'unfair'.

This enquiry is a challenge: think about what you mean by 'fair'. You will reach your own conclusions about:

- the motives and aims of the Big Three (Great Britain, France and the US) when they met to discuss the treaty for Germany.
- why the Big Three did not get everything they wanted in the Treaty of Versailles.
- the impact of the treaty on Germany, from 1918 to 1923.
- whether people at the time thought the treaties were fair; consider different countries in turn.

TOP TIP

Don't be afraid of stating your own opinion. However, you must show how you reached that opinion and that means showing what the evidence is and how you've interpreted that evidence.

1.1 What were the motives and aims of the Big Three at Versailles?

'You hold in your hands the future of the world.' With these words the president of France opened the Paris Peace Conference on 18 January 1919.

National leaders and their delegations from 32 countries had to decide what should happen now that the First World War was over. Added together, they represented three-quarters of the world's population. Making the peace was difficult because of the nature of the problems to be solved

and the different viewpoints and aims of those taking part. Added to this, Germany and Russia were not invited.

The delegations worked for six months to produce the Treaty of Versailles, but this treaty only related to Germany, the lead country of the **Central Powers**. Of all the countries that were represented at Paris, the leaders of the US, Britain and France were the most important decision makers. You can see a photo of the three leaders in Source 1B. Known as 'the Big Three', each of these leaders had different motives and different aims when they arrived in Paris, but they were also under all sorts of pressure.

CHECK YOUR UNDERSTANDING 1.2

Why do you think that Russia and Germany were not invited to negotiate the Treaty of Versailles?

Why did Russia end up as a loser, even though it had been one of the Allied Powers in 1914?

Which of the Big Three was not a member of the Allied Powers in 1914 when the war began?

Source 1B: Georges Clemenceau, Prime Minister of France (middle in the photo), David Lloyd George, Prime Minister of Britain (left in the photo) and Woodrow Wilson, the president of the United States of America (right in the photo) in 1919.

Each of the Big Three had to take account of public opinion in their own country because Clemenceau, Wilson and Lloyd George were democratically elected leaders.

- The popular press in the Allied countries was a major influence on public opinion. Newspapers played a key role in stirring emotions and increasing expectations as they had done during the war itself. Hundreds of journalists went to Paris to report on the negotiations.
- During the war a number of secret treaties and agreements had been made. When these were revealed at the conference, they led to a lot of bitterness and argument.
- New lines had to be drawn on the maps of Europe and Asia, including the Middle East.

ACTIVITY 1.2

Use your knowledge and understanding about the First World War from Chapter 02 to respond to these questions:

- Which one of the Big Three was under the most pressure to meet the expectations of the public? Why was this?
- Which one of the Big Three was under the least pressure to meet the expectations of the public? Why was this?
- 'You hold in your hands the future of the world.' When the president of France spoke these words, how far was this an accurate assessment of the importance of the Paris Peace Conference?

The Big Three – what were their motives and aims?

Georges Clemenceau, Prime Minister of France

Clemenceau was nicknamed 'The Tiger' for his aggressive style in political debates (see Source 1C). He took a tough, hard-line approach to peace-making with Germany. As a Frenchman, his motives were shaped by recent history. He remembered the German invasions of France in 1870 and 1914 and demanded a harsh treaty to ensure that France was made secure and safe in the future. This was his most important aim. Clemenceau once said that his 'life hatred has been for Germany because of what she has done to France'. Germany was France's neighbour with no mountains or rivers to mark the border between the two countries. From Clemenceau's point of view, Germany had to be weakened so that there would never be a 'third invasion' of France. Not only should Germany

be weakened, but its people must pay heavily for the reconstruction that now needed to take place. Reparations must be paid, and on time. This was his second aim.

FACT FILE

'Third invasion': Clemenceau was referring to the two most recent attacks on France by Germany: during the Franco-Prussian War in 1870 and the start of the First World War in 1914, both of which were within living memory. Alsace and Lorraine had been lost to Germany following the Franco-Prussian War of 1870–1871; demanding their return had been a prominent feature in French politics ever since. Every schoolchild had been taught about their loss. Anyone succeeding in regaining them would be a national hero. It is impossible to overestimate the importance of Alsace and Lorraine to French politics from the end of the Franco-Prussian War to the end of the First World War.

KEY TERMS

Epidemic: an infectious disease that has spread over a wide area affecting thousands of people.

Disarmament: the process of destroying some or all weapons and armed forces that could be used in fighting a war.

Knowing that the French public was behind him, Clemenceau demanded tough measures to hurt Germany. His aims included:

- the **disarmament** of Germany's army, navy and air force
- high reparations to pay for all the damage done to France
- the return of the provinces of Alsace and Lorraine
- the Saarland (an area around the river Saar) to be handed to France
- the Rhineland (an area around the river Rhine) to be made an independent state so that there was a 'buffer' between France and Germany
- some German colonies to be handed to France.

However, Lloyd George and Wilson shared neither Clemenceau's motives nor his aims.

ACTIVITY 1.3

Explain how Sources 1C and 1D convey the aims of Clemenceau at the Paris Peace Conference. What tells you that C was published in a French newspaper and D is drawn by a German artist?

LA BAÏONNETTE

LE TIGRE

Source 1C: A cartoon from a French newspaper published in 1919.

Source 1D: A cartoon of Georges Clemenceau published in a German newspaper in 1919. Clemenceau is depicted as a vampire and Germany is the female figure in the bed.

David Lloyd George, Prime Minister of Great Britain

In Britain and France a majority of 'ordinary people' wanted the peacemakers to put the blame for the war on Germany. Punishment would go together with the blame. Newspapers called for the Kaiser to be tried and executed. 'Squeeze the German lemon until the pips squeak', wrote the First Lord of the Admiralty, Eric Geddes. These emotional responses to the bloody four-year war are quite understandable. After all, many of those who perished were from Britain and the British Empire; and those who survived often had the terrible scars of war. In addition, the war had cost the Great Powers the huge sum of £45,000 million and Europe's economies had been forced to switch from making goods to serving military needs. In doing so they lost overseas markets to their non-European competitors like Japan and the US. In 1918 the result of the general election in Britain returned the wartime government to power and indicated that the voters were in no mood for a moderate peace. Lloyd George could not ignore these voters.

Alongside this opinion, another developed. Some wanted something other than a punishing peace for Germany: never again should people have to endure another war. They believed that the Paris Peace Conference must try to prevent conflict by forming a new international organisation to keep the peace in Europe and the world.

During the election campaign of late 1918, Lloyd George promised that he would make sure Germany paid the full cost of the war. However, when he got to Paris in January 1919 he simply aimed for a moderate peace treaty – one that was in Britain's interests. The British Prime Minister was motivated not by revenge but by national self-interest.

He wanted to see the continuing growth and success of the British Empire. This meant that Lloyd George aimed to:

- re-establish a balance of power in Europe so that no single Great Power could dominate the continent
- return to trading patterns with Europe and the Empire that had made Britain so wealthy before the First World War
- preserve British **naval supremacy** so it could guard the British Empire and its shipping lanes.

These aims were based on one important principle: for Britain and Europe to recover economically, Germany must be allowed to recover some of its pre-war economic strength. If the reparations bill was too high, it would take money out of the Germany economy that was needed for rebuilding and recovery.

The First World War had transformed Britain's economic position in the world. Britain had lost its place as the world's financial centre to the US. It had huge debts from fighting the war, most of them to the US. Even so, Lloyd George went to Paris with some things in his favour: the German fleet was in British hands; some of the German colonies had been seized; and Germany, Britain's biggest trade competitor, had been crippled.

CHECK YOUR UNDERSTANDING 1.3

Why was Lloyd George in such a difficult position even after winning a general election in December 1918, which should have made his job as peacemaker easier in Paris?

Woodrow Wilson, President of the US

The US declared war on Germany in April 1917. Immediately, president Wilson announced that he was joining France, Britain and Russia as an 'Associated Power' and not as an ally. Wilson wanted to stress the fact that the US was different from the Allies: Britain and France were fighting for selfish motives, he argued, whereas the US was fighting for world peace.

Wilson arrived in Paris with wish to punish. He was an idealist and wanted the First World War really to have been the war to end all wars that propaganda had earlier declared it to be. He believed it was possible to achieve this if nations worked together to eliminate the causes of war. Published in January 1918, Wilson's aims were different from those of Clemenceau or Lloyd George. The American president presented the Versailles peace conference with his Fourteen Points on removing the causes of war. This is a shortened version of them:

1. No more secret treaties: these had become an issue when the Bolsheviks who had seized power in Russia in 1917 published the previous regime's secret treaties.
2. There should be no restrictions on ships sailing the seas during peace or wartime.
3. Barriers to free trade between nations (such as **quotas** and **tariffs**) reflect and create an economic power struggle between countries. They should be dismantled.
4. Armaments must be reduced in all countries to a level needed only for defence so that countries would have insufficient military force for aggression.
5. Disputes about colonies must be decided by taking account of the interests of the people in the colony and the governing country.
6. German troops must leave Russia.
7. Belgium's independence must be restored.
8. The provinces of Alsace and Lorraine must be returned to France.
9. The frontiers around Italy must be adjusted to match the people's nationality.
10. The different ethnic groups must be given **self-determination** in the Austro-Hungarian Empire.
11. Romania, Serbia and Montenegro should be restored; Serbia should have free and secure access to the sea.
12. The Turkish parts of the Ottoman Empire should form one country; other nationalities within the empire should be allowed to form their own country.
13. An independent Poland should be created with access to the sea.
14. A **League of Nations** should be formed in order to guarantee all countries independence and secure borders.

KEY TERMS

Naval supremacy: achieved when a country has when it owns more battleships than their competitors.

Quota: a strict quantity of goods that may be exported or imported under government control.

Tariff: a tax imposed by the government that has to be paid on imports or exports.

Self-determination: that an ethnic group should have the right to their own independent country instead of living as a **minority** inside a larger country dominated by a different ethnic group.

League of Nations: a membership organisation for nations (1920-1946), intended to promote international discussion, solve international disputes and so avoid war.

ACTIVITY 1.5

Study the causes of war identified by president Wilson.

1　Which ones seem to you most likely to cause major wars involving the Great Powers?

2　Which ones seem to you most likely to cause local wars involving minor powers?

3　Given your own knowledge of history and the world today – and remembering what you read in the introduction – what do you think are the key causes of war?

FACT FILE

Poland had not been an independent country for a century. With their country split in three by three powerful neighbours, Poles had lived in the empires of Germany, Russia and Austria-Hungary. Implementing Wilson's principle of national self-determination was greatly helped by the fact all three empires were defeated in the First World War, even though two had been on one side and one on the other.

ACTIVITY 1.6

1　Why were president Wilson's ideals so different from the aims of both Clemenceau and Lloyd George?

2　Look back at the table you created. Identify which of the Fourteen Points Clemenceau and Lloyd George would have agreed with. Which would they have disagreed with and why?

3　Complete the table you have on aims and motives. Which of the Big Three's aims do you think the German public would have thought would be most favourable towards them? Explain why.

FACT FILE

The League of Nations was the last of Wilson's proposals but potentially it was his most important – it was certainly the most radical. He wanted to establish an organisation that would include representatives from all countries in the world. The League would act to prevent disputes between countries developing into wars.

For the American president the principle of national **self-determination** was key to the long-term stability of Europe. Did Wilson mean the rights and liberties of all small nations? Did the president really want any people who called themselves a 'nation' to have their own state? The public announcement of this principle and its emphasis in points 9, 10, 12 and 13 inspired many different ethnic groups to seek representation in Paris.

Point 14 was the most important ideal that Wilson wanted to create out of the destruction of the First World War. His League of Nations would have representatives from all countries in the world – big and small – and they would meet together so that world peace could be achieved through negotiation not battle.

It was reported that when he first read the president's principles Georges Clemenceau exclaimed: 'Mr Wilson bores me with his Fourteen Points; why, God Almighty has only Ten [Commandments]!' Compared with Wilson's high ideals, Clemenceau was only interested in outcomes that would benefit France. Lloyd George was asked, after he returned to London, how well he had done at the peace conference. 'Not badly,' he replied, 'considering I was seated between Jesus Christ and Napoleon.' The Big Three did not always agree, as you can tell.

What did the Treaty of Versailles say about Germany?

If there was to be a treaty, Wilson, Lloyd George and Clemenceau would have to compromise on their demands. Eventually, after six months of negotiation and bargaining, the treaty was ready. Unrepresented at the negotiations, Germany was presented with a **diktat**, a dictated peace treaty.

What were the key points of the Treaty of Versailles?

Article 231 said that Germany and the other Central Powers had to accept full responsibility for causing the war in 1914. As a result, Germany would have to pay money and goods to France and Britain and the other Allied Powers. The sum was not agreed at the Peace Conference; instead, a Reparations **Commission** would make the decisions afterwards.

To ensure it could not cause another war, the treaty said that Germany:

- was limited to 100,000 soldiers
- was excluded from the arms trade
- was limited in the type and quantity of weapons it could hold

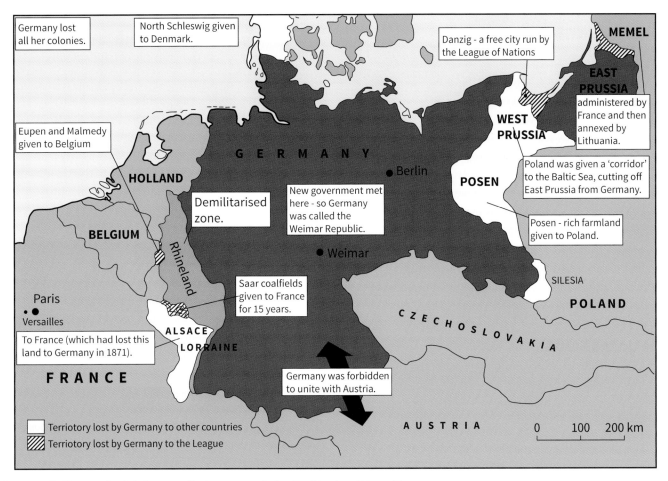

Source 1E: The territorial changes that were made by the Treaty of Versailles.

- could not make or stockpile chemical weapons, armoured cars and tanks
- lost its air force
- was limited to six battleships.

Germany kept the Rhineland, though the area was to be **demilitarised** (you can see the area in Source 1L). No German soldiers were to be stationed there; instead, Allied troops would occupy it for 15 years. However, Germany lost other territory (see Source 1E):

- All colonies went to other Great Powers.
- Alsace and Lorraine were given to France.
- Union with Austria (called Anschluss) was forbidden
- Under the 1918 Treaty of Brest-Litovsk Germany had taken territory from Russia: the treaty was cancelled and the area made into three newly independent states: Estonia, Latvia and Lithuania.
- Some territories were transferred following decisions reached at the Peace Conference. In others, the population voted in **plebiscites**.

> **KEY TERMS**
>
> **Diktat:** a treaty or other agreement which has not been negotiated but imposed, presented to the defeated without any discussions.
>
> **Commission:** a kind of committee, a small group of officials who together investigate an issue or dispute and then produces a report with conclusions.
>
> **Demilitarisation:** an area of land in which no soldiers and no weapons are permitted.
>
> **Plebiscite:** a popular vote on a specific question. These aren't usually held on the ordinary business of government (that's generally left up to a country's government and parliament to decide), but on major decisions such as rewriting the **constitution**. Some people use the words 'plebiscite' and 'referendum' as though they mean the same thing, others make a distinction, but both are a vote by the entire electorate of a country or region on a single important question.
>
> **Constitution:** the main set of laws by which a country is governed. It sets out the powers of the government and the rights and freedoms of the individual.

In addition, Germany was forbidden to join the League of Nations until it had proved itself to be a peaceful country.

CHECK YOUR UNDERSTANDING 1.4

What was the Treaty of Brest-Litovsk and why do you think that it was cancelled by the Treaty of Versailles? Explain why Article 231 was of crucial importance in shaping the rest of the Treaty of Versailles.

1.2 Why did the victors not get everything they wanted?

None of the Big Three left Paris entirely satisfied with the treaty that the Germans signed on 28 June 1919 in the Hall of Mirrors at the Palace of Versailles, just outside Paris. The final document was full of compromises that each of the Big Three had to make when negotiating with the others.

The United States

President Wilson left Paris immediately after the treaty had been signed and travelled back across the Atlantic to the US. What parts of the Paris Peace Settlement pleased president Wilson?

- The League of Nations. All parties agreed that the Covenant (Constitution) of the League should be included in all of the five peace treaties.
- Disarmament. All the defeated Central Powers had to disarm.

In line with Wilson's principle of national self-determination:

- The Rhineland was to be demilitarised but would remain part of Germany, not become a separate state. This also meant that, in time, Germany could become an important trading partner with the US.
- The collapse of the Austro-Hungarian, Russian and German empires in 1918 enabled **successor states** to be created in Europe: Poland was restored; Hungary was separated from Austria; Czechoslovakia and Yugoslavia were created.

Wilson could view these as successes.

In other ways, Wilson was disappointed that his aims remained unfulfilled:

- Point 2 of the Fourteen Points was never going to be acceptable to Great Britain because her navy was key to protecting the British Empire, so the principle of free navigation of the seas was rejected.
- The British and French empires had both increased in size as a result of the treaty. When Germany had her

colonies taken away, they were to be ruled on behalf of the League of Nations by Great Britain and France. This did not follow the principle of national self-determination.

Worse was to come for president Wilson. When he returned and presented the Treaty of Versailles to **Congress** for their approval, the number of votes in favour did not reach the necessary two-thirds majority needed. Wilson's dream of a new world order with the US leading the League of Nations was in tatters. He died a broken man in 1924.

ACTIVITY 1.7

Go back to your table and using three colours underline which of the Fourteen Points was fully met (green), partly met (orange) or not met at all (red). You can then use this for your revision.

CHECK YOUR UNDERSTANDING 1.5

Why was president Wilson unable to implement all of his Fourteen Points in the Paris Peace Settlement?

France

Clemenceau was reasonably satisfied with the outcomes of the Paris Peace Conference:

- Alsace-Lorraine, lost to Germany in 1871, was regained.
- The largest portion of reparations would go to France to enable her to rebuild the areas devastated in the First World War and to pay off debts owed to Great Britain and the US.
- With the Rhineland as a buffer between the two countries, guarded by Allied troops, French security was enhanced.
- The articles of the Versailles treaty would ensure that Germany would never be strong enough to start another war.
- An Anglo-American treaty committed the UK and US to support France if Germany invaded again. Unfortunately, this guarantee disappeared with the Congress vote against the Treaty of Versailles. Britain would not help France without US support.

On balance then, in spite of the all the changes made, France was still not secure. This was Clemenceau's biggest disappointment.

ACTIVITY 1.8

Go back to your table and use the same three-colour code as you have above.

CHECK YOUR UNDERSTANDING 1.6

In spite of being on the winning side, France lost the peace. Why wasn't Clemenceau able to obtain full satisfaction for France in the Treaty of Versailles?

Britain

Lloyd George had limited aims at the Peace Conference and he was pleased with the results. It was a difficult balancing act to ensure British interests were not damaged by a harsh peace. Too **punitive** a treaty would have meant years of slow economic recovery for Germany that would have hurt Britain as well as Europe. With the reparations total to be fixed at some point in the future, Lloyd George hoped that the fierce emotions he witnessed in Paris would cool to allow a calmer, more balanced approach to what Germany would be asked to pay.

Britain's empire grew. Germany's ex-colonies, including British Togoland (now part of Ghana), the northern Cameroons (now part of Cameroon), German South-West Africa (present-day Namibia) and German East Africa (now part of Tanzania) all became **mandates** for Britain to manage on behalf of the League of Nations.

Britain's naval supremacy was boosted when the Germans **scuttled** their fleet, sending it to the bottom of the sea at Scapa Flow in Scotland on 21 June 1919. The German Admiral did not want his ships to end up in British hands.

In 1918 the press had already given Lloyd George the unofficial title of the 'man who won the war'. Now, in 1919, he returned to London to an enthusiastic reception, particularly in the House of Commons where the treaty was approved by a huge majority of MPs.

ACTIVITY 1.9

Return to your table for the last time and use the three-colour code as you compare the results for Britain with Lloyd George's aims.

KEY TERMS

Successor states: new countries formed following the break-up of an older one, as in the case of Czechoslovakia, Austria and Hungary following the break up of Austria-Hungary

Congress: the US's elected law-making body, which helps to govern the country. It consists of two houses: the Senate and the House of Representatives.

Punitive: intended as a punishment.

Mandates: those countries that the Paris Peace Conference had asked the Great Powers to administer.

Scuttle: means deliberately sinking a ship. In wartime navies may do this so that the enemy cannot capture a vessel and begin to use it themselves.

TOP TIP

Lloyd George (Liberal), Clemenceau (Radical) and Wilson (Democrat) all came from the progressive wing of politics, and led reformist parties. You might have expected them to agree on the political principles of the treaties that ended the First World War. Of course, they did agree about some things. That they disagreed about others reflected their different characters, but also their different political circumstances at home.

CHECK YOUR UNDERSTANDING 1.7

1 Why did the Big Three have to take account of public opinion when negotiating the Treaty of Versailles? In which countries would public opinion welcome or oppose the treaty?

2 At the end of the Peace Conference, Clemenceau said: 'America is far away, protected by the ocean. Not even Napoleon himself could touch England. You are both sheltered; we are not.' What did he mean? How secure was France as a result of the Treaty of Versailles?

3 Why would the German government and public want to see the Allied Powers disarm? When Britain and France did *not* disarm, what effect did this have on Germans' view of the Treaty of Versailles?

1.3 What was the impact of the peace treaty on Germany up to 1923?

Germans responded to the Treaty of Versailles with demonstrations and hostile reports in the press. The main criticism was that the treaty was too harsh on Germany

Source 1F: A photo of one of many demonstrations by German citizens once the details of the treaty had been made public in May 1919. The placard reads: 'We Germans, living outside Germany, are protesting against the peace forced upon us and against the theft of our private property.'

and Germans. You can see some of the objections in Sources 1F and 1G.

ACTIVITY 1.10

Look at Source 1F:

1 Identify the age range of those who took part in the demonstrations. What does this tell you about the impact of the treaty?

2 Read the translation of the placard in Source 1F. In which areas of post-1919 Europe could this demonstration have taken place?

3 Read Source 1G. To what extent does it support the photograph in relation to the impact of the treaty on Germany? What does it add to your understanding of the impact of the treaty?

The immediate effect of the signing was a blaze of indignation in the German press and depression among the people. In Berlin an atmosphere of gloom settled on the city. Several newspapers appeared with black borders on their Versailles articles with headings like 'Peace with Annihilation'. The churches set aside 6 July as a day of mourning. On 24 June a number of German officers seized fifteen flags that had been captured from the French in 1870 and publicly burned them. There was mob violence in Berlin and Hamburg throughout the week of the signing of the peace.

Source 1G: Part of a report in *The New York Times*, July 1919.

KEY TERM

Annihilation: complete destruction.

In general terms, Germans disliked four features of the Treaty of Versailles:

- The peace treaty had been a diktat. There were no negotiations. German politicians had little choice but to sign it otherwise the naval blockade would have continued.

- Germans felt bitter at being held responsible for causing the war. For them, Article 231 was a moral criticism of the whole nation. Many were convinced by the intense wartime propaganda that the enemy caused the war. After all, wasn't Germany encircled by Russia and France in 1914?

- The Allies had demanded reparations from Germany. The exact sum was not fixed at Versailles. Germans read in their newspapers that they had to pay reparations, but if their resources, such as the Saarland coal mines, were going to be taken away from them, how could they pay the reparations?

- The tiny army of just 100,000 soldiers meant that Germany was not able to defend itself against its now much stronger neighbours, France and Poland.

ACTIVITY 1.11

1 Look back to the Treaty of Brest-Litovsk (March 1918) in chapter 2. Compare this treaty that the Germans imposed on the defeated Russia with the Treaty of Versailles. Which one was the more punitive? Explain your judgement.

2 In what ways could the Treaty of Versailles have been a lot worse for Germany?

3 Which parts of the Treaty of Versailles would have most upset:
    - a German now living in the newly created Poland.
    - a German mother whose son had died fighting in France.
    - a German politician who strongly supported Kaiser Wilhelm II and the old political system.
    - a German soldier who had to leave the army.

Source 1H: This is a photo of German soldiers marching back to Berlin from the front line in late 1918 following the Armistice on 11 November.

What impact did the treaty have on German politics?

The impact was deep and long-lasting. Look at Source 1H. A few months later, most of these soldiers would have been out of work because the Treaty of Versailles had reduced the army to 100,000. Many of them joined the Freikorps – bands of ex-servicemen. These unofficial groups hated the Weimar politicians for signing the treaty and wanted an opportunity to turn back the clock. In March 1920, under the command of Wolfgang Kapp, some of them staged a **coup** in the capital, Berlin. Their aim was to overthrow the Weimar **Republic** and install a **right-wing** government to overturn the treaty. The Berlin workers came out on strike and public services were stopped. The coup collapsed and the Weimar Republic survived. This was only one example of how the treaty affected politics in Germany. Other attempts to overthrow or undermine the democratic government included:

- a right-wing take-over in the Bavarian Republic in May 1919.
- the Munich or Beer Hall **Putsch** November 1923.
- Hundreds of murders of politicians and political activists.

Even high-ranking members of the Weimar government were not safe. In 1921 a right-wing gang called Organisation Consul murdered Matthias Erzberger (the Finance Minister; see Source 1I) while he was walking in the Black Forest. It was not just extremists who were delighted at his murder: one newspaper wrote that Erzberger 'had suffered the fate which the vast majority of patriotic Germans have long desired for him. Erzberger, the man who is alone responsible for the humiliating armistice; Erzberger, the man who is responsible for the Versailles Treaty of Shame. Erzberger … has at last secured the punishment suitable for a traitor.'

Source 1I: A photograph of Matthias Erzberger, finance minister, murdered in 1921.

In June 1922, the same group that killed Erzberger, assassinated Walter Rathenau, Foreign Minister (Source 1J). Why? Because he had been involved in arranging the Armistice and in trying to improve the Treaty of Versailles.

KEY TERMS

Right-wing: refers to a group or an individual that believes in an ordered society where discipline and tradition are valued. In general, right-wingers are nationalist and in favour of strong government. Right-wingers oppose socialism and **communism** because they think that social inequality is natural and desirable, and because both pose a threat to private property.

Republic: a state with no monarchy.

Coup or Putsch: an attempt by a group to take political power through force, including violence, not by winning an election. It puts political power into the hands of those with the power of armaments not arguments.

29

Source 1J: Walter Rathenau, foreign minister, assassinated in June 1922.

CHECK YOUR UNDERSTANDING 1.8

What do the murders of Erzberger and Rathenau tell you about the stability of the Weimar **democracy** and the level of public support it enjoyed?

The Treaty of Versailles had the unexpected consequence of pushing together the Weimar Republic and the USSR. Both countries had been excluded from the Paris peace negotiations. They had both lost in the First World War (also the USSR was the first communist state), and neither was allowed to join the new League of Nations. Since both countries were isolated it made sense to try and build a new friendship. The Treaty of Rapallo was an agreement signed on 16 April, 1922. Under its terms each gave up all territorial and financial claims against the other following the Treaty of Brest-Litovsk and the First World War. The two governments also agreed to restore diplomatic relations and to 'cooperate in a spirit of mutual goodwill in meeting the economic needs of both countries'.

ACTIVITY 1.12

What do you think was the impact of so much political violence in these early years of the Weimar Republic? To what extent was the Versailles Treaty to blame for the instability? Were there other factors?

The Weimar politicians who signed the Treaty had also signed the Armistice, seven months earlier in November 1918, following the abdication of Kaiser Wilhelm II. Mistakenly, the German public now began to believe a powerful myth – that the politicians and not the army generals were to blame for the country's humiliation and downfall at the end of the War. To many, the Weimar government was made up of cowards who had 'stabbed the Germany Army in the back' by signing the Armistice; and then the *same* cowards had let down the country by signing, instead of resisting, the treaty of Versailles. For these Germans, the men who signed the treaty seemed to be no different from the 'November Criminals' who signed the Armistice.

FACT FILE

The legend of the **Dolchstoss** was that the German army had not been defeated at all, it had been betrayed – 'stabbed in the back'. Large numbers of Germans, including many returning soldiers, came to believe this fiction. It was to prove enormously important in German politics, not least because it made it look as through the armed forces were honourable and trustworthy, while politicians were liars and unpatriotic.

FACT FILE

Elections in themselves were not new: Germany had had them for decades. But Germany had never voted to be a republic: the Kaiser had signed a document of abdication and left the country under pressure. Many mainstream politicians actively wanted the return of the royal family. Many citizens felt that the political structures had been imposed on the country by the very people who had betrayed it at the end of the war. This was not going to result in success.

Economic impact

At Versailles the Germans signed a treaty that did not include the total amount of reparations. This was because the Allied Powers did not have sufficient time to calculate the costs of four years of war and the bill for repairing war damage. Nevertheless, Germany started to make some payments immediately.

In May 1921 the Reparations Commission announced its decision: Germany would have to pay £6.6 billion. As a result of Versailles, Germany had lost all of her colonies, 13% of her land, 26% of her coal deposits and 75% of her iron ore deposits. Because of these losses the German government said it could not pay the reparations bill.

The German economy was in poor condition after the end of the First World War. Its government's expenditure was high but its income from taxes was low. There was a growing budget deficit that was resolved by borrowing and by printing money. This caused **inflation**. The announcement of the reparation bill in May 1921 made the situation worse, but it is important to remember that prices in Germany were already increasing. You can see this in Source 1K.

In December 1922 the Germans failed to deliver timber, part of the reparations, on schedule. Then in January 1923 they failed again – this time on a delivery of coal. The Prime Minister of France, Raymond Poincaré, sent the troops to make sure that the deliveries were made on time. He saw this as a test case for the enforcement of the whole of the Versailles Treaty.

CHECK YOUR UNDERSTANDING 1.9

Does Source 1K help you decide which factor worsened the **hyperinflation** in 1923: a) the French invasion of the Ruhr, or b) the German government's response to the invasion? What other evidence would help you justify your decision? In the opinion of the German middle class, who was to blame for their loss of savings?

KEY TERMS

Democracy: societies where the government has been elected by voters in free and fair elections. Liberal democracies feature freedom of speech, freedom of religion, freedom of the press and the right to a fair trial.

Dolchstoss: a German word meaning 'stab in the back'.

Inflation or Hyperinflation: inflation is when prices go up, hyperinflation is when prices go up a lot, quickly.

The crisis year when money died, 1923

The French and Belgians invaded the Ruhr (see Source 1L) in January 1923 to take for themselves what they were owed under the reparations agreement. A total of 60,000 French and Belgian troops took control of all industries and railways to seize resources instead of payments that were now overdue. The Weimar government called for non-violent opposition across the region and Germans united

behind this campaign. In places. In late March, French soldiers killed thirteen German workers – an event known as the 'Bloody Easter on the Ruhr'. Over 140 Germans were killed in clashes with French troops.

Date	German Marks needed to buy one ounce of gold
Jan 1919	170.00
Sept 1919	499.00
Jan 1920	1,340.00
Sept 1920	1,201.00
Jan 1921	1,349.00
Sept 1921	2,175.00
Jan 1922	3,976.00
Sept 1922	30.381.00
Jan 1923	372,477.00
Sept 1923	269,439,000.00
2 Oct. 1923	6,631,749,000.00
9 Oct, 1923	24,868,950,000.00
16 Oct, 1923	84,969,072,000.00
23 Oct, 1923	1,160,552,882,000.00
30 Oct, 1923	1,347,070,000,000.00
5 Nov, 1923	8,700,000,000,000.00
30 Nov, 1923	87,000,000,000,000.00

Source 1K: A table showing how inflation turned into hyperinflation during the period 1918 to 1923 in Germany.

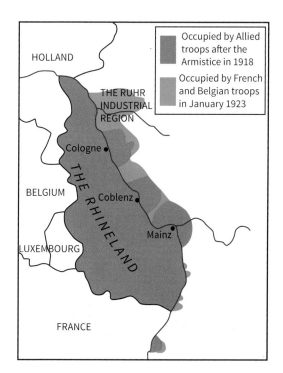

Source 1L: Occupation of the Ruhr Valley and the Rhineland. The map shows the different areas, large and small, which French and Belgian troops entered in force.

FACT FILE

The Ruhr is a river in Germany that flows into the Rhine. The region around it known in English just as 'the Ruhr') was rich in coal and iron, making it the heart of Germany's industrial strength. Source 1L shows the areas of the Ruhr and the Rhineland.

CHECK YOUR UNDERSTANDING 1.10

The boys playing in Source 1N have made a kite out of German paper money, which became increasingly worthless during 1923. How useful do you think this photograph is as evidence for historians? How does it compare to Source 1M?

Source 1M: A drawing of the moments before Schlageter was executed by a French firing squad in May 1923.

The government called for non-violent opposition: no one in the Ruhr should cooperate with the invaders. Government income fell as Germany's industry stopped in the Ruhr. During the occupation the government continued to print money. Civil servants, miners and others went on strike; all were paid by the government using paper money that was losing its value. Hyperinflation was taking hold and no one seemed able to stop it. People's savings were becoming worthless.

Source 1N: A photograph of boys playing in a park with a home-made kite using paper money.

Resistance to the occupation did not remain non-violent as the government had ordered. Saboteurs blew up bridges and railway lines. Albert Leo Schlageter (1894–1923) had been a decorated lieutenant in the First World War who joined the Freikorps, they took part in the Kapp Putsch (1920) and later (1933) became merged in with the Nazis. He led a group of nationalist saboteur operations against the French occupation. Schlageter was caught, tried and executed. The man accused of betraying him to the French authorities was soon murdered.

Not only did the occupation prevent coal, iron and steel from reaching the rest of Germany, it also reduced government income from valuable foreign exports to the world. To make matters worse, the German government's spending on the strikers increased rapidly, again funded by the increased printing of money.

By 1923, 300 paper mills and 2,000 printing businesses were working all day every day to keep up with demand for paper money. In the face of economic collapse, with high unemployment and hyperinflation, the strikes were eventually called off in September 1923 by the new **coalition government**, led by Gustav Stresemann. This was followed by a state of emergency. Despite this, civil unrest turned into riots and attempts to overthrow the Weimar Republic. Adolf Hitler attempted to take power in the Beer Hall Putsch of November 1923 and a separatist Rhenish Republic was proclaimed at Aachen in October 1923. Both coups were put down by forces loyal to Stresemann's government.

At this point, chancellor Stresemann and his Commissioner for National Currency, Dr Schacht, set about restoring confidence in a new currency. All the old currency was collected and destroyed; in its place the Rentenmark was issued in November. This dealt with the problem of hyperinflation.

KEY TERM

Coalition government: a government made up of several different parties. This was needed because no party had a majority in the Reichstag.

The effects of 1923

Although the French did succeed in their occupation of the Ruhr, the Germans through their non-violent opposition in the Ruhr and the hyperinflation that wrecked their economy, won the sympathy of many. This led to a major revision of the reparations that had been demanded by the Treaty of Versailles. Under heavy American financial pressure, the French were forced to agree to the Dawes Plan of April 1924, which substantially lowered German reparations payments. It also allowed American banks to make loans of 800 million marks to the German government.

ACTIVITY 1.13

1   Historian Gordon Craig wrote: 'Millions of Germans who had passively accepted the change from monarchy to the Weimar Republic suffered deprivations that shattered their faith in the democratic process and left them cynical and alienated.' Identify reasons why: a) many Germans did not like Weimar democracy, and b) why politicians were not trusted.

2   'The impact of the Treaty of Versailles until 1923 was exaggerated by the politicians but not by the German public.' To what extent do you agree with this view?

3   Was the economic impact of the Treaty of Versailles greater than the political impact?

4   The Weimar Republic survived the crisis year of 1923. This seems to suggest that the impact of the Treaty of Versailles was short term. What evidence do you need to assess the accuracy of this opinion?

1.4 What were the terms of the other peace treaties?

All the Central Powers that had been Germany's allies in the First World War had separate peace treaties. Historians use the phrase 'Versailles Settlement' or 'Paris Peace Conference' to describe not just the Treaty of Versailles, but **all** of the other treaties. These treaties had common features:

- a war guilt clause to support the claim for reparations
- reduction in military forces
- acceptance of the covenant (constitution) of the League of Nations.

Treaty of Saint-Germain with Austria, 10 September 1919

The pre-war empire of Austria-Hungary was dissolved. It lost 60% of its 1914 territory. You can see this in Source 10.

- The Allied Powers assumed that the minorities wished to leave the Austro-Hungarian Empire. However, the successor states (new countries created by the peace settlement) now included significant numbers of German speakers. For example, 3 million Germans now lived in the Sudetenland, part of Czechoslovakia.
- Article 88 of the Treaty forbade Austria to join with Germany. As a result the initial name of the new republic 'German-Austria' had to be changed.
- Conscription was abolished and the new Austrian Army was limited to 30,000 soldiers.
- Reparations were never set because Austria became bankrupt before the total could be formally agreed.

Treaty of Trianon with Hungary, 4 June 1920

Hungary was one of the successor states following the Paris Peace Conference. As you can see in Source 10, its territorial losses were dramatic. Not only was it landlocked, its population was now 7.6 million, some 36% of the pre-war kingdom's population. At the same time, 3.3 million ethnic Hungarians were now living outside the newly created Hungary.

- Hungary's army was limited to 35,000 and its navy no longer existed.
- Reparations had to be paid but the Hungarian economy was close to bankruptcy and, apart from some coal deliveries, this new successor state paid nothing to the Allies.
- Most Hungarians considered the Treaty of Trianon as an insult to their national honour.

ACTIVITY 1.14

Identify which areas of Austria-Hungary were given to which countries after the treaty was signed.

Source 1O: The territorial changes that were made by the Treaty of Saint-Germain and the Treaty of Trianon broke up Austria-Hungary.

Treaty of Neuilly with Bulgaria, 27 November 1919

Under the terms of this treaty:

- Bulgaria lost territory. Western Thrace was given to Greece. This meant that Bulgaria was now cut off from the Aegean Sea. Other areas were given to Yugoslavia and Romania.
- Its army was reduced to 20,000 men, it wasn't allowed to have an air force and it had to pay £100m in reparations.
- In Bulgaria, the results of the treaty are known as the 'Second National Catastrophe'.

Treaty of Sèvres with Turkey, 10 August 1920

This treaty marked the tearing apart of the Ottoman Empire.

- The terms of the Treaty of Sèvres were harsh.
- Huge swathes of Ottoman territory were awarded to Britain, France, Greece and Italy.
- The Ottoman army was reduced to 50,700 men and it wasn't allowed an air force.

- The Allies were to control Ottoman finances including supervising the national budget and total control over the Ottoman Bank.

The Treaty of Sèvres was rejected by Mustapha Kemal, the leader of the Turkish nationalist movement. He and his supporters fought a war against the terms and managed to reclaim some of the lost territory. A new treaty was negotiated.

Treaty of Lausanne with Turkey, 24 July 1923

You can see in Source 1P a different looking Turkey from the one that was agreed at Sèvres.

Other terms included the following points:

- The boundaries of Greece, Bulgaria and Turkey were settled.
- Turkey gave up its claims to Cyprus, Egypt, Sudan, Syria and Iraq.
- No reparation demands were made.
- No military restrictions were placed on Turkey's army.

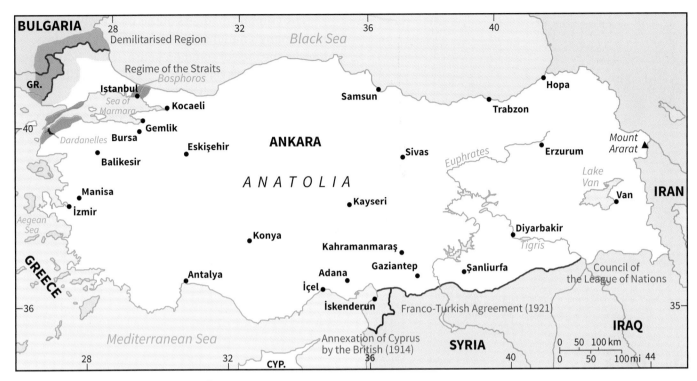

Source 1P: Turkey after the Treaty of Lausanne.

ACTIVITY 1.15

1 Which empires were broken up by the peace settlement?

2 Which of president Wilson's Fourteen Points were followed in the break-up of empires and the creation of the successor states?

3 Which of all the Central Powers suffered most from the peace settlement?

4 Which of president Wilson's Fourteen points can be identified in the treaties dealing with Germany's former allies?

5 What parts of the treaties (apart from Versailles) would have angered: a) Weimar politicians; and b) German ex-soldiers? Explain why.

ACTIVITY 1.16

Sources 1Q, 1R, 1S, 1T and 1U are about the Treaty of Versailles. You have to decide which category the sources belong to: Too harsh, Fair or Not harsh enough. To help you, draw a table like this one:

Which source?	Too harsh, Fair or Not harsh enough	Evidence for your decision	Is this source supported by your knowledge of the Versailles Treaty?
R			
S			

1.5 Could the treaties be justified at the time?

Once details of the Versailles Settlement became public, politicians, leaders, soldiers and ordinary citizens held different views. Most debate focused on the fairness or harshness of the different treaties, although the Versailles Treaty attracted most attention. The Versailles Settlement could be justified by the winners of the First World War; this was because it was the winners who wrote it, not the 'losers'.

Do not think of this treaty as merely a settlement with Germany. It is a very severe settlement with Germany, but there is nothing in it that she did not earn. Indeed, she earned more than she can ever be able to pay for, and the punishment exacted of her is not a punishment greater than she can bear, and it is absolutely necessary in order that no other nation may ever plot such a thing against humanity and civilization.

Source 1Q: Part of a speech by president Wilson delivered to the League of Nations in September 1919.

PEACE AND FUTURE CANNON FODDER

The Tiger: "Curious! I seem to hear a child weeping!"

Source 1R: This cartoon was published in the British newspaper, the *Daily Herald*, 13 May 1919. Has the child to the left just read the Treaty of Versailles?

This is not a peace treaty, it is an armistice for twenty years.

Source 1S: A comment by the French military leader, Marshall Foch, at the ceremony to sign the Treaty of Versailles

THE RECKONING.

Pan-German. "Monstrous, I call it. Why, it's fully a quarter of what we should have made *them* pay, if we'd won."

Source 1T: A British cartoon published in *Punch* magazine shortly after the Reparations Commission had announced the bill for Germany to pay: £6.6 billion.

The criminal madness of this peace will drain Germany's national life-blood. It is a shameless blow in the face of common-sense. It is inflicting the deepest wounds on us Germans as our world lies in wreckage about us.

Source 1U: Part of a speech made by a German Member of Parliament in the **Reichstag** in 1919.

CHECK YOUR UNDERSTANDING 1.12

1 How crucial was Article 231 (the war guilt clause) for the Allies to justify the peace treaties?

2 Why would French leaders be concerned that British attitudes were so mixed?

3 Why were both the French and the British concerned when the US Senate rejected the Treaty of Versailles?

4 Study Sources 1R and 1T: what contrasting views of the Treaty of Versailles do they present?

 KEY TERM

Reichstag: Germany's parliament during the imperial (Kaiser), republic (Weimar) and Nazi periods.

Review your learning

When the war ended, the Big Three came to Paris to write a treaty without discussing it with Germany. President Wilson's Fourteen Points were used as the basis for the treaty. Not one of the points mentioned reparations or blame for starting the war.

Lloyd George and Clemenceau did not agree with many of the Fourteen Points, so the Treaty of Versailles was a compromise. Other similar treaties were signed with Germany's partners, the other Central Powers. The Treaty of Versailles had serious political and economic effects on Germany between 1918 and 1923.

Historians disagree about the treaties which ended the First World War. Few think they were a triumph of diplomacy, but while many criticise their faults and failures, others think they were the best that could have been achieved by those people in those circumstances. What do you think? Before you answer, think about the evidence. You could do this by drawing up mind maps to assess the factors. Make sure you can answer the five questions listed at the beginning of this chapter as Focus points; then you will have enough evidence for you to attempt Key Question 1.

Summary points

One way to remember the different parts of the treaty is to use the mnemonic: **DRAWL**.

This stands for:

D	Diktat	The Treaty was not negotiated; there were no discussions. It was dictated to the Germans.
R	Reparations	Reparations imposed for all the damage that was caused during the First World War by Germany and the other Central Powers.
A	Armaments	No air force, army was restricted to 100,000, navy restricted to six ships, no submarines. Rhineland to be demilitarised and occupied by the Allies for fifteen years.
W	War guilt	Germany was held to be to blame for the war.
L	Loss of territory	Loss of territory reduced Germany's size, population and economic resources, including the loss of all her colonies.

The Big Challenge

When you think or write about this topic, these concepts/ideas will help:

- Armistice
- Big Three
- blame
- diktat
- dolchstoss
- fair
- harsh
- humiliation
- justice
- national self-determination
- negotiations
- November criminals
- plebiscites
- reparations
- revenge
- shame
- treaty
- War Guilt Clause.

Work with a partner. Using a large piece of plain paper, write out all the concepts listed, spacing them out equally. In a different colour, write underneath each one a brief definition.

Now draw lines to link any two concepts/ideas that are related to one another. You get one point for a correctly drawn line, but two points for writing on the line what the link is. There is no limit on the number of lines (links) you can draw and lines from one concepts could connect with several others.

Your next challenge is to decide if the treaties were fair or harsh. Before deciding, remember these points about the word 'fair':

- Are you judging **all** the peace treaties to be fair or just one?
- Were the peace treaties fair to the winners **or** the losers or both?
- Does your view of the causes of the First World War affect your assessment of the 'fairness' of the peace treaties?
- Does your view of 'fairness' relate to how badly a country was affected by the war?

Exam-style questions

1 What was the impact on Germany of the Versailles Treaty and how did Germany react to it?

2 To what extent did Clemenceau get everything he wanted from the Paris Peace Conference and the Versailles Treaty?

3 How far were Wilson's, Lloyd George's and Clemenceau's aims in the Paris Peace Conference compatible?

4 'The treaties at the end of the First World War were certainly not fair but then there was no possibility that they could have been fair.' To what extent do you agree with this judgement?

5 What were the aims of Woodrow Wilson, Lloyd George and Georges Clemenceau (the Big Three) at the Paris Peace Conference?

6 To what extent were the aims of the Big Three achieved at the Paris Peace Conference?

7 Describe the military restrictions imposed on Germany by the Treaty of Versailles.

8 What political and economic problems did the Treaty of Versailles cause for Germany?

9 Explain why Germans felt humiliated by the Treaty of Versailles.

10 Which was more important in causing German dissatisfaction with the Treaty: reparations or the war guilt clause?

11 To what extent was the Treaty of Versailles justifiable at the time?

12 Were all the Central Powers treated the same in the treaties that they had to sign?

Chapter 2
Key Question 2: To what extent was the League of Nations a success?

Focus points

- How successful was the League in the 1920s?
- How far did weaknesses in the League's organisation make failure inevitable?
- How far did the Depression make the work of the League more difficult?
- How successful was the League in the 1930s?

What is this enquiry about?

In all of the treaties that made up the Versailles Settlement after the end of the First World War (see Chapter 1), president Wilson had insisted on the inclusion of a reference to the League of Nations. This was to be the organisation that ensured the 1914–1918 conflict really had been 'war to end all wars'.

Your challenge in this section is to decide to what extent the League of Nations was a success. This means forming an opinion.

TOP TIP

When you have a question that begins with 'To what extent …? (or 'How far …?') you are being asked to offer an opinion. You will need to present the evidence that shows how you reached that opinion, of course. When you offer your opinion you will need to indicate the 'extent'. This diagram shows a range of options:

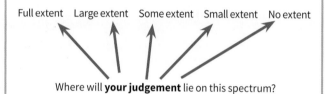

To what extent?

Full extent   Large extent   Some extent   Small extent   No extent

Where will **your judgement** lie on this spectrum?

Of course, making your judgement is only the final part of the enquiry. First you need to collect evidence by studying the investigations in this chapter so you can reach that judgement and justify it. Draw up a table like the following one and keep it handy for the different sections.

Focus question	Judgement: to what extent?	Evidence from the case studies to support the judgement
How successful was the League in the 1920s?		
How far did the League's organisation make failure inevitable?		

Focus question	Judgement: to what extent?	Evidence from the case studies to support the judgement
How far did the Depression make the work of the League more difficult?		
How successful was the League in the 1930s?		
Given all this, what is your overall judgement on the success of the League of Nations?		

ACTIVITY 2.1

Adapt the wording of the Top Tip diagram showing how to express a range of opinions so that it suits a question that begins 'How far …?'.

The Covenant of the League of Nations

What criteria should you use for judging the League's effectiveness? Well, one criterion you can use to judge the League is its Covenant that was agreed when it was set up. A Covenant is a set of rules setting out how members of an organisation should behave. When you look at each Case Study decide which of the Articles was triggered. If the League was successful then the Articles were followed and the action resolved the dispute.

 KEY TERMS

Arbitration: a method of resolving a dispute peacefully using an independent person or authority that is neutral who will listen to all the evidence like a judge and then issue a ruling.

Sanctions: are penalties or punishments imposed by an official body such as a court of law. A typical sanction in international relations is a ban on trade, which has an impact on the country targeted. The intention is to affect the country's decision-makers so that they change their policies, such as ending a war.

Section of the Covenant	The action League members should take
Articles 8 and 9	Members must promote **disarmament** so that countries will only have sufficient military strength to maintain national security.
Article 10	Any member who is attacked wll have the support of all League members.
Article 11	Any member can ask the League for help if it fears attack.
Articles 12 to 15	Disputes will be settled by a process: investigation of the issue, discussion in the League, then putting the issue before an international court, or going to **arbitration**. Members pledge not to go to war until three months have passed from the date at which the dispute was brought to the League's attention.
Articles 16	Members agree to take prompt action against anyone going to war. Such an attack will be seen as an act of war against all other Members. It could lead to economic **sanctions** such as the cutting of trade links and, possibly, military action of some kind.

CHECK YOUR UNDERSTANDING 2.1

Identify the difficulties that you would expect the League to face in trying to use these articles to stop conflict.

Here is a list of some crises and conflicts where the League of Nations intervened or attempted to intervene:

- Vilnius 1920
- Upper Silesia 1921
- Åland Islands 1921
- Corfu 1923
- Greece vs Bulgaria 1925
- Japanese invasion of Manchuria 1931
- Italian invasion of Abyssinia 1935
- Japanese invasion of China 1937

In this chapter, we will look at some of these examples of intervention. Each time, you will need to consider the extent of the League's success.

Collective security

This concept was essential for the League to maintain the peace: acting together, members could place economic and/or military pressure on aggressors. There were three processes by which the League could try to stop wars:

1   Moral disapproval: The Council would meet to condemn any act of aggression. The aggressor would cease its military actions knowing that the world was watching.

2   Economic sanctions: If moral disapproval failed, then the Council could exert pressure using economic sanctions against the aggressor. This could mean a trade boycott and refusing credit.

3   Military sanctions: If economic sanctions did not work, then the Council could use military sanctions. This might involve sending military help to the victim of the attack.

Collective security sounds like a sensible way to stop war, but remember the US was not a member of the League. Two other problems restricted the collective security approach:

- First, all decisions taken by the Council or the Assembly had to be **unanimous**. A majority of the members was not enough to take action.

KEY TERM

Unanimous: a decision has the support of every representative who is voting in a decision-making process, and so no one has opposed the proposal being voted on.

ACTIVITY 2.2

To meet the challenge of this enquiry you will need to keep a record of your judgements as you learn about what the League tried to do, its successes and its failures. You can use this table to help you organise your enquiry.

Where was the crisis?	When was the crisis?	What was the result: success/ failure/mixed?	Why was that the outcome?

- Second, the League did not have its own army so imposing military sanctions would prove difficult. Member states would have to send soldiers and resources; this would take time and there was no guarantee that members would do so.

2.1 How successful was the League in the 1920s?

In its first ten years the League dealt with thirty disputes between states. Now we need to look at some specific examples.

Case study A: The Åland Islands

The map in Figure 2.1 shows the Åland Islands. They are located between Sweden and Finland and both countries claimed them. Although 95% of the population was ethnic Swedes, the islands belonged to Finland. In June 1920, the dispute was referred to the Council of the League of Nations. The League ordered an investigation of the issue that scrutinised the claims and counter-claims. The conclusion was that the island should stay under Finland's rule. This was because to award the Åland Islands to Sweden would set a dangerous precedent – other Swedish communities living in Finland might make similar claims. Outside the area, other **minority** groups in Europe might want to do the same.

Alongside the decision to leave the Islands in Finnish hands, the League's report recommended that the Swedes should have more **autonomy** to preserve their traditions and customs; for example, the Swedish language should be taught in schools.

These decisions by the League meant that Finland maintained its borders but that the Swedes could pursue their lives keeping their Swedish customs. It was the first European international agreement concluded directly through the League.

KEY TERMS

Minority: a recognisable group of people whose religion, language, culture or ethnicity is different from that of most people (the majority) in a country or region.

Autonomy: the independence of an individual, or a group or a region to make decisions for itself without always asking permission, e.g. from a central government.

Results for the League of Nations:

Successes	Concerns
The development of autonomy was important and Swedish customs were preserved. It was only a formality that the people of the Åland Islands were Finnish citizens.	This dispute raised an important question in relation to president Wilson's principle of national self-determination. How far should the principle be applied?
Finland had preserved its borders so there was no precedent which might lead to countless other ethic claims thus destroying the Paris Peace Settlement.	

CHECK YOUR UNDERSTANDING 2.2

Why didn't the Åland Islands dispute turn into a war?

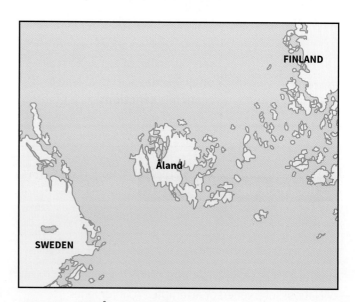

Figure 2.1: The Åland Islands.

Case Study B: The Corfu Incident, 1923

The map in Figure 2.2 shows Greece and its neighbours in the 1920s. An Italian, General Tellini, and four of his assistants, who had been marking out the new border between Albania and Greece for the

KEY TERM

Conference of Ambassadors: based in Paris, this group was a diplomatic body representing the Great Powers formed at the Paris Peace Conference in order to supervise the completion of issues not resolved by the treaties. It was this body that had sent Tellini to Greece to clarify the border between Greece and Albania.

CHECK YOUR UNDERSTANDING 2.3

Why didn't the Corfu Incident turn into a war?

Conference of Ambassadors, were murdered. The Greek authorities were unable to arrest anyone for the murder so in August 1923, Benito Mussolini, the Italian leader, ordered the occupation of the Greek island of Corfu to force the Greek government to compensate Italy for General Tellini's death.

Greece appealed to the Council of the League of Nations. Italy argued that their occupation was not an act of war. Robert Cecil (representing Britain on the Council) disputed this. He wanted to take a hard line against the Italians; he wanted sanctions to be imposed on Italy and a British naval presence off the coast of Corfu. However, the British government did not share Cecil's views; it did not want to damage trade relations with Italy. Instead, the Council decided to send a commission to the Albanian-Greek border to investigate Tellini's death. The commission reported that it could find no evidence that Greece had failed to investigate the murder properly. On 25 September, the Conference of Ambassadors met to consider the report. As a result of Italian pressure, Greece was made to pay 50 million lire as compensation. Two days later, the Italians began evacuating Corfu.

Results for the League of Nations:

Successes	Concerns
Greece was able to appeal to the Council when it felt it was not being fairly treated by the Conference of Ambassadors.	Italy committed an act of war, but this injustice was not punished by the other Great Powers.
Italy and Greece did not go to war and Italian forces did not stay in Greek territory for long.	The League of Nations had little involvement in the final settlement of the crisis. It appeared that the Conference of Ambassadors was more important.

Figure 2.2: Map of Greece showing Corfu and the border with Bulgaria in 1925.

Case Study C: Greco–Bulgarian confrontation, 1925

On 19 October, on the Greek border with Bulgaria (see Figure 2.2) some soldiers were playing a game of cards. What happened next resulted in the deaths of two Greek border guards and the retreat of others from their posts. News of this incident reached the Greek government, but the report was exaggerated and made it appear that the Bulgarians had launched an invasion. As a consequence, Greece ordered an attack on Bulgaria. The Bulgarian Foreign Minister informed the president of the Council of the League of Nations. He telegraphed both sides to end military action. When the Council met it instructed both sides to withdraw within their own borders. British, French and Italian officials went to the site to confirm that the Council's instructions had been obeyed. The confrontation was over.

A commission visited the area for three days. It found that Greek troops had taken crops and cattle as they retreated. In December 1925, the League's Council awarded compensation worth 30 million Bulgaria levas. Greece paid.

Results for the League of Nations

Successes
The Council's demand to end military action as a first step was obeyed.
The Council then investigated the reasons for the incident and reported them. In the past, small border incidents like this had started wars.

On this occasion, the 'successes' aren't really balanced by 'concerns'. However, the success does need to be put into context. It may have looked for a time as though Greece and Bulgaria were about to go to war, but in fact neither was in a position to conduct a serious military campaign. Both countries had domestic difficulties: Greece was struggling with one million refugees from Turkey; Bulgaria had been mostly demilitarised. This does not take away from the achievement of the League, but it does contextualise that success. Furthermore, neither Greece nor Bulgaria was allied to a Great Power who could have acted to support one of them. This alone was likely to have prevented the war from growing in importance and involving friends and neighbours, a prospect which was the great fear of any diplomat who remembered August 1914.

CHECK YOUR UNDERSTANDING 2.4

Why didn't the Greco-Bulgarian dispute turn into a war?

Case Study D: Vilnius

The population of the city of Vilnius included Poles, Jews and Lithuanians. After the First World War it was recognised as part of Lithuania. However, the Treaty of Versailles had left Lithuania's border with Poland unclear, so Poland brought the issue to the Council of the League (we explain the structure of the League in section 'How successful was the League in the 1920s?'). The League sent a commission to investigate. It drew up a **provisional** border and both states signed their agreement on 30 September 1920.

KEY TERM

Provisional: Temporary.

At this point, a Polish general marched into Vilnius with his soldiers. Was he secretly supported by the Polish government? We can't be sure. Lithuania was not a member of the League but it was still able to raise the matter with the Assembly of the League. Initially, there was a plan to send an international police force to the city; but neutral Switzerland forbade police units from crossing its territory.

The League's final effort to resolve the problem was a report by Belgian representative, Paul Hymans, on 21 September 1921. It recommended that both Lithuanian and Polish languages were granted official status; that all **minorities** in Lithuania should have equal rights to education, religion, language and association; and that steps be taken to align the two countries' foreign, economic and foreign policies.

The Hymans Plan was a delicate balancing act, but both sides rejected it. In January 1922, the League issued a public statement saying that it had exhausted all possibilities. So the occupation of Vilnius was allowed to continue. In March 1923, the Conference of Ambassadors recognised Vilnius as part of Poland.

Results for the League of Nations

Successes	Concerns
Left with a difficult issue by the Paris peacemakers, the League had responded with an innovative proposal – even if it was rejected.	Some contemporaries were outraged at the Polish takeover of Vilnius. The Polish government must have known about the general's actions and the League should have invoked Article 16.
The Vilnius issue made headlines around the world, but in the event there was no war.	Poland had a strong relationship with France, so a country was allowed to benefit from aggression.

CHECK YOUR UNDERSTANDING 2.5

Why didn't the dispute over Vilnius turn into a war?

ACTIVITY 2.3

Look back over the findings of your enquiry into case studies and the table you drew up (in section on 'collective security'). Compare the different disputes. What patterns to you see in terms of differences in the nature of the disputes? How far do you think these explain why they led to different results?

2.2 How far did weaknesses in the League's organisation make failure inevitable?

The new international organisation had three main parts: the Secretariat, Assembly and the Council (Source 2A). These are the functions of each one.

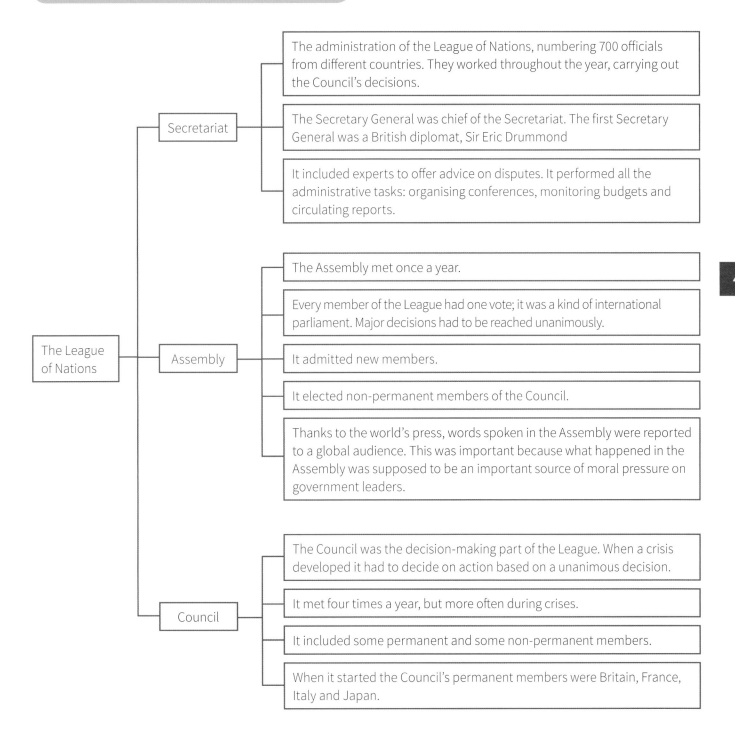

The League of Nations

Secretariat
- The administration of the League of Nations, numbering 700 officials from different countries. They worked throughout the year, carrying out the Council's decisions.
- The Secretary General was chief of the Secretariat. The first Secretary General was a British diplomat, Sir Eric Drummond
- It included experts to offer advice on disputes. It performed all the administrative tasks: organising conferences, monitoring budgets and circulating reports.

Assembly
- The Assembly met once a year.
- Every member of the League had one vote; it was a kind of international parliament. Major decisions had to be reached unanimously.
- It admitted new members.
- It elected non-permanent members of the Council.
- Thanks to the world's press, words spoken in the Assembly were reported to a global audience. This was important because what happened in the Assembly was supposed to be an important source of moral pressure on government leaders.

Council
- The Council was the decision-making part of the League. When a crisis developed it had to decide on action based on a unanimous decision.
- It met four times a year, but more often during crises.
- It included some permanent and some non-permanent members.
- When it started the Council's permanent members were Britain, France, Italy and Japan.

From the very beginning the organisation of the League had several weaknesses. First, it was established by the Treaty of Versailles; the treaty had many flaws but the League was supposed to enforce it. The Germans hated the treaty and the Italians and Japanese disliked parts of it, so the League was not fully supported. Second, the Assembly could only make a decision by a unanimous vote, and on the Council, all the permanent members had a veto. When there was a crisis, it was very hard to agree on what to do. Even when decisions were made the League had no army to enforce them. Its main 'weapons' were moral condemnation and economic sanctions – and these were not effective 'punishments' for aggression. Third, the League had no army of its own to ensure its decisions were followed through. This was of particular importance when the League faced serious challenges in the 1930s from Italy (in Abyssinia) and from Japan (in Manchuria). Fourth, the League's membership did not include all countries that had the economic and military potential to cause trouble. Details of this weakness are in the next section.

Despite these weaknesses, the League could have been made a force for peace if the Great Powers had wished. The articles of the covenant of the League provided for economic and military sanctions against the aggressors. The League failed because the leading powers never wanted a durable peace.

The League of Nations was always run on very little money. Between 1921 and 1927 it cost just $4 million per year. Britain was the biggest contributor ($550,000 per year), while others contributed what they could. Given so little funding, when crises arose the League had to issue calls for extra money. Sometimes it took a long time for governments to respond, so time and again the League turned to charities like the American Red Cross or Save the Children to react quickly to **humanitarian** disasters.

Source 2A: A photograph from 1936 of the Council of the League of Nations meeting.

 KEY TERM

Humanitarian: taking action to promote the welfare of people.

Who joined and who left the League?

Was the League seriously weakened as a peacekeeping organisation by its membership? Both the Assembly and the Council were weakened because not all of the Great Powers were members. Let's look at these in turn.

United States of America

Although president Wilson was a key supporter of the League, the American Congress voted three times between November 1919 and March 1920 not to join. Many Congressmen were worried that American involvement in the League would lead to American involvement in future wars. American soldiers had died fighting in the First World War and there was no enthusiasm to do that again. So, despite it having been an American president who wanted its creation, the US did not join the League at all.

Germany

The Allied Powers at the Paris Peace Conference refused to allow Germany to join the League when it started. The argument was that it had to show that it was a reformed Germany with a peaceful approach to international relations. In 1926 Germany did join and became a permanent member of the Council. However, Adolf Hitler saw the League as a club for 'winners' in the First World War and in 1933 he took the decision to take Germany out of the League.

CHECK YOUR UNDERSTANDING 2.6

In which part of the League were all the members represented?

Did 'small powers' have equal status with 'Great Powers'?

Why couldn't all members be part of the Council of the League?

Soviet Union

This great power was not invited to join the League because it was **communist**. Communists sought to overthrow **capitalism**. This frightened the other, capitalist, League members. The Soviet Union was not interested in joining what looked like a capitalist club run by the very powers – Britain, France, US and Japan – who had invaded the Soviet Union during its **Civil War** (1918–1920) in a failed attempt to determine the country's future. By 1934, it was clear that the Soviet Union was no longer an threat to capitalist countries and it was admitted to the League. It was expelled in 1939 for invading Finland at the start of the Second World War.

KEY TERMS

Capitalism: an economic and social system in which property is privately owned, the role of the state is small and people enjoy freedom of expression, of religion and have a choice of political party to elect as the government.

Communism: an economic and social system in which property and economic activity are controlled by the state. In communist countries, people have few rights and freedoms: religion is banned and the media is censored. Everyone works for the state.

Civil war: a war in *one* country between two or more sides from within that country.

Japan

Japan was one of the original members of the League and had a permanent seat on the Council. However, it left in 1933 following criticism over its invasion of Manchuria.

Italy

This great power was one of the original members. However, it left the League in 1937 following the economic sanctions that the League put in place because Italy had invaded Abyssinia.

Britain and France

These were the only two Great Powers who remained members during the League's existence. Reluctantly, these two had to carry most of the responsibility for making the League work. Britain was anxious about its empire, and France was most worried about the border with Germany. In the official circles of these Great Powers, the League of Nations, however, was an afterthought.

How successful was the work of the League agencies?

The League of Nations was established to try and keep peace in the world. To support this central aim, it undertook other activities that would help to make the world better and safer. The League's agencies and commissions tried to do something about the social and economic problems of disease, poverty, **exploitation**, prisoners of war and refugees – humanitarian issues. Through its actions, the League started to show the world how international cooperation could encourage peace through the successful management of these issues. How successful was the League in relation to these other activities?

As you read each investigation, with a partner decide whereabouts on the History Spectrum would you put each League activity and why. The Spectrum is a line on which you can record your judgements. You can see this in the introductory section to this chapter.

KEY TERM

Exploitation: a process in which a person or group is treated unfairly at work; it may be the result of, e.g. their age or ethnicity making them weak in negotiations, leading to overwork and underpayment.

The International Labour Organization

Source 2B: A photo of child labourers in a coal mine, United States, *c*.1912.

The International Labout Organization (ILO) was created in 1919. It fought for social justice. The working conditions that people experienced had to be safe, healthy and fair.

47

This included issues about hours of work, and the protection of women, children and the elderly. The ILO could make recommendations to national governments about labour matters. These would appear in the form of **conventions** that would be agreed by the ILO's annual conference. If accepted at that point, the conventions had to be presented to national parliaments within one year by League members. Little by little, an international network of labour laws and regulation had started to develop, and by 1939 the work of the ILO had agreed 67 conventions. For example, the ILO's efforts to regulate child labour resulted in children only working an 8-hour day in the Persian carpet industry and their rooms being properly ventilated. The ILO successfully restricted the addition of lead to paint and convinced several countries to adopt an 8-hour working day and 48-hour working week. It also campaigned to end child labour, increase the rights of women in the workplace, and make ship-owners liable for accidents involving seamen. After the death of the League, the ILO became an **agency** of the **United Nations** in 1946.

KEY TERMS

Convention: an agreement that does not have the force of law so its implementation depends on 'trust'.

Agency: an organisation which acts on behalf of others. Within the League different agencies focused on specific issues under the authority of the Council.

United Nations: an international membership organisation for states founded in 1946 to promote development, peace and human rights, it replaced the **League of Nations**

48

ACTIVITY 2.4

Study carefully the photo of child labour in Source 2B or 2C taken before the ILO was formed.

1 What issues can you see that the ILO would be concerned about?

2 The ILO's conventions did not have the force of law. Does this mean that the efforts of ILO staff were wasted?

3 Child labour still exists in the world today. What does this tell you about the difficulties of the ILO's work? And how will this affect your judgement about the effectiveness of the League's agencies?

Slavery Commission

The Slavery Commission aimed to **eradicate** slavery and slave trading across the world, and challenge forced

prostitution. Its main success was ending slavery in the mandates. The League secured a commitment from Abyssinia to end slavery as a condition of membership in 1923, and worked with Liberia to abolish forced labour and **intertribal** slavery. Records were kept to control slavery, prostitution and the **trafficking** of women and children. Partly as a result of pressure brought by the League of Nations, Afghanistan abolished slavery in 1923, Iraq in 1924, Nepal in 1926, Transjordan and Persia in 1929, Bahrain in 1937 and Abyssinia in 1942.

Source 2C: A photograph of child labour in Cameroon taken in 1919.

KEY TERMS

Eradicate: to abolish or get rid of.

Intertribal: an activity that is carried out between tribes of people rather than different countries.

Trafficking: the buying and selling of people or drugs.

Commission for Refugees

Led by Fridtjof Nansen (Source 2E), a Norwegian explorer, the Commission for Refugees was established on 27 June 1921 to look after the interests of refugees, including overseeing their return to their home country and, when necessary, resettlement. At the end of the First World War, there were between two to three million ex-prisoners of war from various nations dispersed throughout Russia. Within two years the Commission had helped 425,000 of them to return home. It established camps in Turkey in 1922 to support the country in dealing with a refugee crisis, helping to prevent disease and hunger. Working in very difficult circumstances and with a tiny budget, Nansen and his staff used imaginative methods to look after these people. They set up camps where they were needed; they taught new skills to refugees and provided them with identity papers, such as the Nansen passport, as a means of identification for stateless people. You can see a Nansen passport in the photograph in Source 2D. Nansen isn't forgotten. Each year, the United Nations gives the Nansen Refugee Award to men and women who have done outstanding work assisting refugees.

Source 2D: A sample Nansen passport.

Source 2E: Fridtjof Nansen with Greek refugees in Thrace, Greece, 1922.

The Health Organization

The First World War and its aftermath ensured that disease became an international matter. Four years of conflict had wrecked public health systems and marching armies had carried infections with them as well as their guns. The wartime shortages left populations short of the necessary nutrition needed to fight bacteria and viruses. Under the leadership of Ludwig Rajchman, the League's Health Organization became one of its most successful bodies. It established links with countries not belonging to the League, such as the US, Germany and the Soviet Union to provide an information service, technical assistance and advice on public health matters. For example, it supported Soviet Union in trying to prevent a typhus epidemic in the early 1920s by organising a public information campaign on health and sanitation. Eventually, by 1923, the worst was over.

The Health Committee reduced the incidence of **leprosy** and began an international campaign to eliminate mosquitoes, so in turn reducing the spread of malaria and yellow fever. Research institutes based in London, Copenhagen and Singapore developed internationally accepted vaccines for diphtheria, tetanus and tuberculosis. After the Second World War it became the World Health Organization – part of today's United Nations.

KEY TERM

Leprosy: a contagious disease that affects the skin and the nervous system.

ACTIVITY 2.5

Go back to your table and make a judgement about the extent of League success in dealing with humanitarian issues. Make sure you include evidence to support your view.

ACTIVITY 2.6

What does the word 'inevitable' in the title of this section mean? Some historians think the League was going to fail from the start, others disagree. Look at Sources 2B and 2C, and the table in the section 'How far did weaknesses in the League's organisation make failure inevitable?' that describes the functions of each part of the League. Can you decide if its failure was inevitable, given its starting point?

Given what you now know about membership of the League of Nations, identify the difficulties that the League faced in its role as peace-keeper.

Britain and France were members of the League, but how much commitment do you think they put into the organisation?

FACT FILE

Wall Street is the name given to the US market for stocks and shares of companies. People bought lots of shares in the 1920s because their investments always seemed to be making a good profit. This boom ended in October 1929 with the Crash; prices dropped suddenly and sharply. Many lost all their investments. The Wall Street Crash did not cause the Great Depression in the US but it did make it worse.

2.3 How far did the Depression make the work of the League more difficult?

What was the Great Depression?

During the 1920s, the US's economy grew very quickly; by 1928 the production of goods and food reached a point where the demand for both was satisfied completely. Suddenly, with overproduction and falling demand, the capitalist economies broke down. The Great Depression was a series of connected economic changes that hit the world's countries from 1929 and lasted well into the 1930s. Where order books for cars and household products had once been full, the 1930s saw a severe reduction in demand and cuts in production and trade soon followed. Factories closed, farmers went bankrupt and millions lost their jobs and joined long lines of the unemployed. To make matters worse the banking system failed and people lost their money.

Starting in the US, it spread to Europe and beyond. Across Europe, the numbers of unemployed rose dramatically. Many US banks had lent money to businesses in European countries; when the Wall Street Crash happened the lenders wanted their money back.

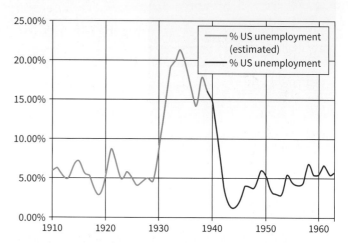

Figure 2.3: This graph shows the sudden and massive rise in unemployment in the US during the Great Depression.

ACTIVITY 2.7

What link is there between Figure 2.3 and what you can see in Source 2F?

The League of Nations was supposed to maintain the peace of the world by organising collective action on the part of its members to prevent war. Working collectively to keep the peace was hard enough in the 1920s: what difference did the Great Depression make to its peacekeeping function?

Whether League members or not, all governments were tested by the impact of the Great Depression on the people who elected them – and this applied to both Great Powers and small powers. Politicians now prioritised dealing with unemployment, suffering and poverty. Dealing with anything that was happening in another country came second.

KEY TERM

Dictatorship: one person governs a country without holding elections, and without being restrained by a parliament, keeping themself in power using the army and police.

Source 2F: A photograph of the Frank Tengle family at the time of the Great Depression in the state of Alabama in 1935.

ACTIVITY 2.8

The following list outlines the key consequences of the Great Depression on the League:

A Democratic governments came under pressure to cut spending and balance their budgets. Rearming was no longer important; democracies had to help their citizens before they paid for soldiers, guns and planes. As a result, League members lacked the military strength to confront aggressors.

B As world markets for goods and food shrank, the League's strategy of imposing economic sanctions on aggressors was not viewed favourably. Stopping trade with a small power would be bad enough, but with a Great Power sanctions would lead to deeper economic problems and make governments even more unpopular.

C Some democratic governments were replaced by dictatorships. These **dictatorships** were aggressive and very nationalistic. For example, in Germany, extremist parties became more popular, the Nazis came to power and democracy collapsed. Hitler promised German voters that he would rip up the Treaty of Versailles. In Japan, the military took over governing the country. To the generals, Japan's survival depended on its trade; finding new markets and raw materials was vital. In 1931 the Japanese army took the first steps in creating an empire that would benefit Japan economically.

1 Put **A**, **B** and **C** in order of importance for League members *given* the following problems:

I Two small powers dispute the ownership of a small section of their common border. Both are threatening to use force and they have significant trade links with the Great Powers in Europe.

II A Great Power run by a dictator starts to rearm and threatens to ignore important treaty obligations.

III A strong Great Power invades a weaker Great Power.

2 Peacekeeping in the 1920s had not been easy for the new League of Nations. What judgement will you make to answer the question 'how far'? Before you think about your own judgement, bear in mind these points.

- The phrase 'work of the League' does not mean just peacekeeping; it includes humanitarian activities too.
- In general, small and Great Powers behave in ways that benefit their own interests.
- The League's various agencies were only funded by its members, principally the Great Powers.

2.4 How successful was the League in the 1930s?

Much of the humanitarian work by the League's agencies continued to be effective in the 1930s. However, the impact of the Great Depression created new problems to solve in relation to peacekeeping. By the end of the 1930s the League could not prevent a second world war from starting. In this sense it failed in its primary purpose. After the 1939 German invasion of Poland, the League did not meet again until April 1946. Its existence came to an end when its assets were transferred to the newly formed United Nations organisation, based in New York City.

Three key events made it obvious to the world that the League was ineffective when faced with countries that pursued national rather than international interests.

- the failure of the Disarmament Conference
- the Japanese invasion of Manchuria
- the Italian invasion of Abyssinia.

Case Study A: the Disarmament Conference

In the years before the outbreak of the First World War, an arms race had taken place – for example, there had been a race between Germany and Britain to build warships called **Dreadnoughts**. Many thought that it was a cause of the 1914–1918 conflict. With the war over, disarmament was thought to be a key issue in maintaining world peace. president Wilson certainly thought so, it was one of his Fourteen Points (see chapter 3, section on Woodrow Wilson). In the Peace Settlement, disarmament was a feature of the treaties – but it was only the losers who were made to disarm.

The League arranged a conference to meet in Geneva between 1932–1934. High hopes of making progress on

KEY TERM

Dreadnought: named after HMS *Dreadnought* (a British battleship launched in 1906), was a type of battleship that was so fast, and so heavily armed and armoured, that no other type of battleship could match it.

this priority were disappointed very quickly because of the fears of individual countries and their reluctance to trust one another. France was willing to disarm, but only if guarantees were given by Britain and the US. Neither was willing to give them.

Hitler's plan was for **rearmament**, not disarmament. Arguing that France was not serious about disarmament, the Germans withdrew from the conference and shortly afterwards left the League.

If any progress was going to be made, all the major countries had to take part and by 1934, it was clear that this was not going to happen. In 1935, Hitler announced his **violation** of the disarmament clauses in the Treaty of Versailles. From now on, Germany rearmed very quickly, and soon after Italian and Japanese rearmament followed.

KEY TERMS

Rearmament: increasing the numbers of weapons and personnel in the navy, army and air force.

Violation: an action that has broken a rule or agreement made between countries or individuals.

Source 2G: This cartoon appeared in a British newspaper on 23rd May 1934, towards the end of the Disarmament Conference.

ACTIVITY 2.9

1   What is the cartoonist's view of the Disarmament Conference in Source 2G?

2   To what extent is there evidence in this section to support this view?

3   What other factors that are not illustrated in the cartoon caused the failure of the work of the conference?

Case Study B: Japanese aggression in Manchuria, 1931

The Great Depression meant that Japan's exports were finding fewer customers and so earning less income. Japan was not self-sufficient in food, so needed this income for vital imports.

Since 1905, the Japanese had controlled Korea and had further trading rights that extended over the border into the interior of Manchuria in north-east China (see the map in Source 2I). This is an area rich in minerals, farmland and forestry. Taking over Manchuria would help the Japanese economy because it would provide a source of food and raw materials and land for the surplus population to settle. To protect their trading rights, Japanese soldiers were allowed along the route of the South Manchurian Railway.

On 10 September 1931, Robert Cecil, the British representative on the League of Nations Council told the Assembly that he believed there was little prospect of a war over Manchuria. On 18 September, a bomb exploded on the South Manchurian Railway. The explosion was not that big because later a train passed the spot safely, but it had happened on a section of territory occupied by Japan's Kwantung Army. The Japanese had every right to be there because of the 1905 Treaty of Portsmouth. However, immediately after the explosion, part of the Kwantung Army moved quickly to take over the town of Mukden. The 'Mukden Railway Incident' was an artificial crisis designed to provide a reason to react with force (Source 2H).

China appealed to the League and the Council members (apart from Japan) demanded that Japanese troops promise to withdraw to the railway zone by 16 November.

Source 2H: A photograph showing a Japanese soldier in Manchuria, 1931.

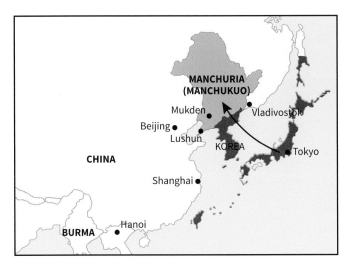

Source 2I: Japan invades Manchuria, 1931.

The Japanese representative at the League said that troops would be withdrawn when the time was right. This was a further deception. Chinchow was taken by the Japanese in December 1931 and Shanghai was threatened in January, the following year. This was taken very seriously by the western European countries because they had major business interests there. China now requested an investigation and asked for the Assembly to consider the situation. These complex circumstances were made worse by Britain's attitude towards Japan: Japan had genuine grievances against China that had to be addressed alongside the Mukden Railway Incident and Britain had a longstanding friendly relationship with Japan. However, doing nothing was not an option for the League.

FACT FILE

Chinese is written using a different script and the way of spelling Chinese names in the alphabet has changed over time. Chinchow is a town now spelled 'Shenyang', while Mukden is now spelled 'Jinzhou'. This can sometimes make looking places up confusing. We've used the spelling of names that was current at the time of the events we're discussing.

It was impossible for the League to ignore the fact that a large area of China had been occupied illegally (see the map in Source 2I). Members representing small states were particularly concerned and wanted the League to stop a great power acting as an aggressor.

The Lytton Commission

In December 1931, the Council decided to create a commission of enquiry to travel to the Far East and find out what was really happening in Manchuria. The commission led by Lord Lytton took until the end of February 1932 to journey east, by which time Japan had firmly established itself. In early March, the Japanese zone of occupation had turned into a **puppet state** called 'Manchukuo'.

KEY TERM

Puppet state: a state lacking all independence, being run by the government of another country. It pretends to be a real country, but does what it's told.

Lytton's investigation was thorough but his report was not completed until September 1932. The report concluded that the original position of Manchuria was not satisfactory and that a full discussion about the future of the region was needed after the crisis had been resolved. Lytton added that most people living in Manchuria did not support the Manchukuo regime and saw themselves as Chinese. Therefore, it would be necessary to establish Manchuria as an independent part of the Chinese state. All of these points

ACTIVITY 2.10

Below are seven ways to start a sentence about the League and the 1931 Manchuria crisis, plus one way to end that sentence. Put the beginnings with the end: how many of the resulting statements do you agree with?

The Great Depression seriously affected Japan …

The League did not have its own army …

The US and the Soviet Union were not members of the League …

The British were concerned about their friendship with Japan …

The Japanese military tried to solve its economic problems by extending its empire …

Japan left the League …

The Lytton Commission did not recommend tough action against Japan …

… so the League failed to stop the Japanese invasion of Manchuria.

The crisis was complicated. You might think all of the statements are at least a bit true. Now convert those sentences into short paragraphs – start with the same phrases as before, but this time add a bit of detail and in each case, this time end with the words 'and that is part of why the League failed to stop the Japanese invasion of Manchuria'.

53

were confirmed by a vote taken in the Assembly: 42 votes against 1. As a result of the vote, on 27 March 1933, Japan announced that it was leaving the League of Nations. Bad feeling between China and Japan continued until Japan launched further hostilities in the summer of 1937. Japan did not stop building its empire. Its aggression played a significant role in starting the war in the Pacific in December 1941. Is it possible this war could have been prevented if the League had been able to stop Japan in 1931?

Source 2J: A British cartoon from 19th January 1933 about the League of Nations' reaction to the invasion of Manchuria by Japan.

Source 2K: A British cartoon from 24th November 1932 about the League of Nations' reaction to the Lytton Report.

ACTIVITY 2.11

Sources 2J and 2K are both cartoons from a British newspaper of the time of the Manchuria Crisis.

1 Explain the criticism which Source 2J is making of the League of Nations.
2 Explain the criticism which Source 2K is making of the Lytton Commission and its report.

3 Which of points a) to f) would have been most significant for i) small powers facing aggression from other small powers; and ii) for political leaders thinking of expanding their borders and building an empire? Briefly explain your answer in each case.

   a The difficulties of applying collective security procedures were clearly on display for the world to see.

   b Japan was a Great Power; other Great Powers were very careful in the way that they handled the aggression in Manchuria.

   c It could be difficult to identify a clear aggressor.

   d League procedures could be long; it took nine months for the Lytton Commission to start its work and finish with its report.

   e Manchuria was different from other crises the League had faced. The scale of the aggression was greater and the consequences more serious.

   f The only result of the Manchuria crisis was a commission of inquiry; there were no sanctions and no threat of military action.

Case Study D: The Abyssinian Crisis, 1935–1936

Like Japan, Italy was a member of the League Council, and just like Japan, Italy had ambitions for territory. Benito Mussolini, the Italian dictator (called Il Duce), was a fascist (see Source 2L). His ambitions were rooted in Italy's history; he wanted to create a new Roman empire and make Italy 'great, respected and feared'.

Italy's interest in Abyssinia was long-standing. In 1896, Italy had attempted an invasion, but failed. Once Mussolini took power in the 1920s, the dream of conquering Abyssinia was back. You can see in the map in Source 2M how close the Italian colony of Somaliland is to Abyssinia. By 1932, invasion plans had been completed. The flashpoint came early in December 1934 at Wal-Wal, in a border region between the two countries. During the skirmish, about thirty Italians and three times as many Abyssinians died. Mussolini demanded compensation for the loss of life. With the tension increasing, other Great Powers started to get involved. They did so without reference to the League or its procedures. Selfish motives drove the great power leaders: they were anxious to build a strong buffer against Hitler's Germany. Britain and France wanted to build friendly relations with Mussolini because this would counter the threat from Hitler's Germany, which had by this point left the League and begun rearming.

Source 2L: A photo of Mussolini in April 1934 stirring the Italian crowds with dreams of a new Roman empire.

The Italian invasion was unprovoked aggression. The League promptly condemned it and imposed economic sanctions. Many emotional speeches were made during debates on the crisis. One delegate told the Assembly that 'great or small, strong or weak, near or far, white or coloured, let us never forget that one day we may be somebody's Abyssinia'. Sanctions included preventing the sale of armaments and other war materials and cutting credit to the Italian government and Italian firms.

The sanctions failed to hurt Italy's economy. Why? Because oil and coal, which were essential for running the war, were not on the list of prohibited trade. The Suez Canal, the main supply route for the Italian army, was kept open by its owner, Britain, who feared possible attacks on British colonies like Malta and Gibraltar by the Italian navy.

Britain and France now made a secret deal with Mussolini. The Hoare-Laval Plan stated that Italy would receive two-thirds of Abyssinia in return for stopping the war. This amounted to 60,000 square miles of Abyssinian territory. In exchange, some 3,000 square miles of Somaliland would be given to Abyssinia to provide an outlet to the sea. To begin with, the plan was secret, but the press found out and Hoare was forced to resign as British Foreign Secretary.

55

In January 1936, Mussolini appointed a new commander who launched a fresh attack. This time, Italian troops made greater progress, not least because they were using **mustard gas**. This time, the League was again considering imposing an **embargo** on oil, however France rejected the idea. By this time, Europe was becoming more and more concerned about Hitler's actions; in March 1936 he violated the Treaty of Versailles by remilitarising the Rhineland. The Italians were left alone and overran Abyssinia; the capital was taken on 5 May.

KEY TERMS

Mustard gas: a chemical weapon that was used during the First World War. It causes large blisters on exposed skin and lungs.

Embargo: a partial or complete end to trade with a country. It is an example of a trade sanction.

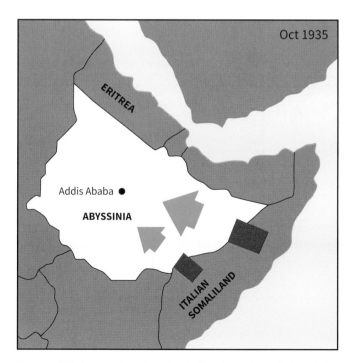

Source 2M: A map showing the Italian invasion of Abyssinia.

The Emperor of Abyssinia, Haile Selassie, travelled to Geneva to give an emotional speech to the Assembly on 30 June. With great dignity, his outrage at the use of chemical weapons against his people was communicated to the world. But with the war nearly over, League members had little wish for maintaining sanctions.

Sanctions were abandoned in July, and in December 1937 Mussolini's Italy withdrew from the League.

The consequences

This was the only occasion on which the League actually launched a full-scale security action. It went beyond investigation and negotiations to the imposition of economic sanctions. The problem for the Great Powers was that their increasing anxiety about Germany meant they had to keep a working relationship with Mussolini. The policy that France and Britain pursued was not consistent: they wavered between working within the League and independent action outside it. To Mussolini, France and Britain looked weak and confused. To other League members it was clear that the procedures had not saved a League member from complete destruction and so it was not to be trusted.

After Abyssinia, the League and collective security were sidelined more and more from the pursuit of international security by small and Great Powers.

CHECK YOUR UNDERSTANDING 2.8

1   Compare the two crises – Manchuria and Abyssinia – then consider what were the main differences and similarities between them. Did the League perform better in one crisis than the other?

2   'Great Powers always act in their own interests.' To what extent do Manchuria and Abyssinia illustrate this statement?

Review your learning

Historians disagree about the track record of the League of Nations, its strengths and weakness, successes and failures. You should assess the evidence, weigh it up and make up your own mind. Make sure you can answer the four questions listed at the beginning of this chapter as Focus points; then you will have enough evidence for you to attempt Key Question 2.

ACTIVITY 2.12

Source 2N: A British cartoon published in 1935. Mussolini, the Italian leader, is the larger figure and Low, the cartoonist, is commenting on the fact that Italy was a member of the League of Nations.

1   Study this British cartoon in Source 2N carefully. The figure in the middle is Italian dictator Benito Mussolini. The female figure to the right represents Western Civilisation. To what extent does the cartoon confirm the mnemonic in the Summary points, explaining the reasons for the League's failure?

2   'The League did not really fail in the 1930s, rather it was sidelined, as politicians chose increasingly to work beyond its corridors. The Covenant was not applied, its spirit was not honoured and the principles of universality were not taken seriously' (Martyn Housden, historian). To what extent does Martyn Housden agree with the cartoonist and the mnemonic?

Summary points

You have reached the end of this enquiry and should have completed the table at the start of this chapter. To help you remember the various causes why the League failed, here is a mnemonic. Work with a partner and see if you can develop each letter in WAS DUMB; ensure that you have some evidence to support each point. When you have done this, you could try and rank the different reasons in order of significance and justify the decisions.

WAS DUMB

- W – Weak
- A – Abyssinia
- S – Structure

- D – Depression
- U – Unsuccessful
- M – Manchuria
- B – Bullies

The Big Challenge

With a partner, review the structure and Covenant of the League of Nations:

- How could you make it more effective?
- If you were helping set up the League in the 1920s, how would you deal with the League's weaknesses?

You won't have to change everything: much of the work of the League's agencies was successful.

- Having completed your review, do you think that the League was doomed to fail from the start or was it undermined by later events?

Exam-style questions

1   'The organisation and structure of the League were very significant in causing its eventual failure.' Do you agree?

2   'If the League of Nations had been supported by the US and an army, then the League could have been very effective in preventing wars.' How far do you agree?

3   When it started, what did the League hope to achieve? What were the differing roles of the Council and Assembly of the League of Nations?

4   In 1939 the Second World War began. Does this mean that the League of Nations failed?

5   'Great power disagreement caused the failure of the League and nothing else'. To what extent do you agree with this judgement?

Chapter 3

Key Question 3: Why had international peace collapsed by 1939?

Focus points

- What were the long-term consequences of the peace treaties of 1919–1923?
- What were the consequences of the failures of the League in the 1930s?
- How far was Hitler's foreign policy to blame for the outbreak of war in 1939?
- Was the policy of appeasement justified?
- How important was the Nazi-Soviet Pact?
- Why did Britain and France declare war on Germany in September 1939?

What is this enquiry about?

In this chapter you will investigate the collapse of the international order in the 1930s. You will look at the militarism and nationalism of Japan, Italy and Germany, and the response of other countries.

You need to understand events from the perspective of the decision-makers at the time. If you succeed, then it will be an easier task to explain the outbreak of a second world war only twenty years after the first.

In contrast to the peaceful 1920s, the 1930s saw developments that eventually led to the outbreak of war in 1939. Although it is called the Second World War there were in fact two wars: one that broke out in Europe in September 1939 and one that started in 1931 with the Japanese invasion of Manchuria. Try to keep in mind this distinction. Here are two maps to help you.

59

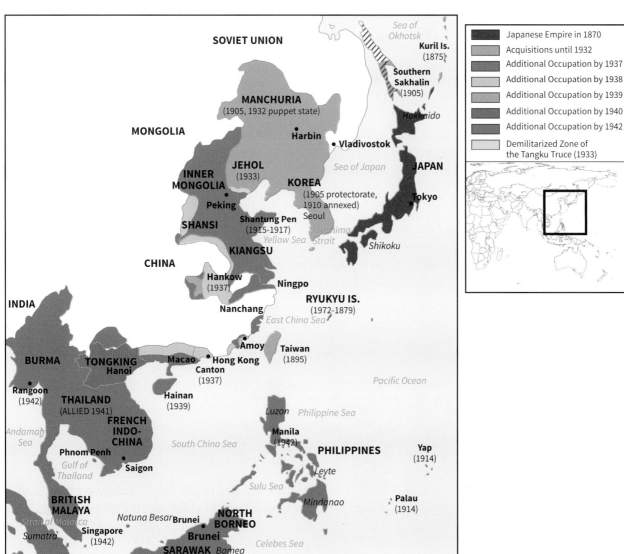

Figure 3.1: Japanese aggression in the Far East during the 1930s.

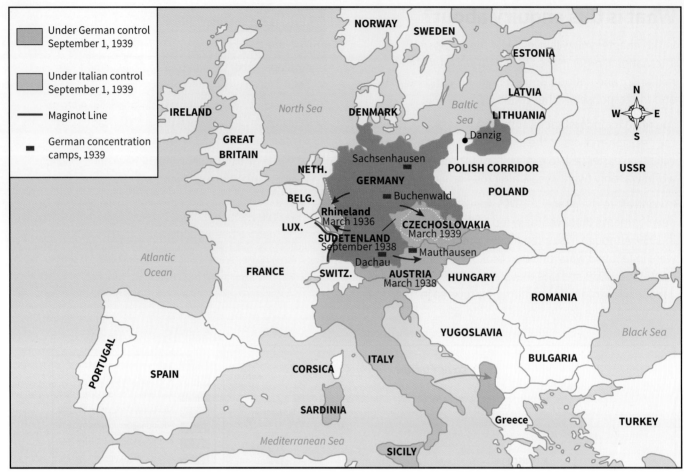

Figure 3.2: German and Italian aggression in the late 1930s. Note the purple arrows indicate German expansion and the green indicate Italian expansion.

ACTIVITY 3.2

Use the Fact File and the maps in Figures 3.1–3.3 to help you, as well as the Sources 3A–3F to answer the following questions:

1 What aspects of nationalism and militarism can you see portrayed in Sources 3A, 3B, 3C, 3D, 3E and 3F?

2 What evidence can you find on the maps and from your own knowledge that nationalism and militarism seem to have led to successes for Japan, Italy and Germany in the 1930s?

3 In Germany and Japan, governments became much more militaristic and nationalistic following the impact of the Great Depression. Why do you think this happened?

4 Why would the growth of nationalism and militarism endanger the international peace during the 1930s?

Figure 3.3: The map shows Italy in dark green; the Italian Empire in light green in 1939; and the dark grey areas are additional conquests made during the early part of the Second World War.

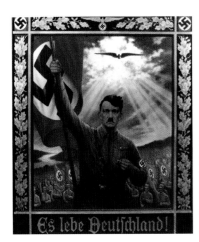

Source 3A: A propaganda poster from the Nazi Party, which governed Germany after 1933. The caption reads: 'Long Live Germany!'

Growing strength of Germany, Italy and Japan

During the 1930s Germany and Italy gradually drew closer together, in spite of Britain and France's efforts to keep them apart. The Rome-Berlin Axis was made official in 1936 and Japan joined a year later to form the Anti-Comintern Pact. As you have seen, all three governments were both nationalistic and militaristic and this gave

Source 3B: A photograph of the Italian leader, Benito Mussolini, surrounded by officers from the Italian army.

Source 3C: Unlike German cities during World War II, Madrid and other Spanish cities did not have well prepared bomb shelters. In this photo by Robert Capa taken during the Spanish Civil War in 1937 a mother scans the sky for German or Italian bombers. Her daughter is less concerned because her mother is holding her hand. Robert Capa wrote that 'Nowhere is there safety for anyone in this war. The women stay behind, but the death, the ingenious death from the skies finds them out.'

Source 3D: Propaganda poster from 1939, praising the virtues of 'Germans buy German Products; German Labour, German Products, and German Production.' Hitler wanted the German economy to become self-sufficient; this is called 'autarky'.

61

them common cause in reaching beyond their frontiers to create empires in Europe (Germany) in Africa and south-east Europe (Italy) and in the Far East (Japan). The key to their growing friendship was that their imperial ambitions did not clash so they were not in competition. Look back at the maps on pp. 59–60.

Successful invasions and empire building demand support from the general public, economies adapted for war, and strong armies, navies and air forces. Look at the Table 3.1. What similarities and differences are there between Germany, Italy and Japan in the 1930s bearing in mind what you know about nationalism and militarism?

TOP TIP

Three countries are key to understanding the collapse of peace in the 1930s: Japan, Germany and Italy. The governments of all three were committed to two policies:

Nationalism is a belief that encourages people to identify strongly with their country. Support for the nation becomes a duty and more important than any concern for the welfare of the individual. A nationalist government's main aim is the making the nation more powerful, and with that sometimes richer and bigger.

Militarism is the belief that a country should maintain a strong army, navy and air force and be prepared to use it aggressively to defend or promote national interests. It also suggests the glorification of military ideals such as duty, order, loyalty and obedience.

Table 3.1: The growing threat to peace during the 1930s.

Country	Military strength and spending during 1930s.	Alliances and policies.
Germany Dictatorship led by Hitler and the Nazis. Largely supported by the German public.	Hitler introduced conscription in March 1935. The German army grew from 100,000 to 300,000. By 1939 103 divisions were ready for war. In addition, there were 3,000 planes in the airforce. Hitler's government increased spending on armaments: in 1933 it was 5 billion RM*; this grew to 10 billion in 1936 and to 16 billion in 1938.	Wanted to scrap Versailles and find Lebensraum for growing German population. Left the League of Nations in September 1933. Supported the Nationalist rebels in the Spanish Civil War, 1936-9. Used this conflict to test new techniques in aerial bombing. **Signed treaty with Sources 3C and D. Italy in October 1936 to create the 'Rome-Berlin Axis'.** **In May 1939 Hitler signed the 'Pact of Steel', a military alliance with Italy.**
Italy Dictatorship led by Mussolini and the Fascists. Largely supported by the Italian public. Mussolini takes control of the army, navy and air force.	Tanks were of poor quality and the Italian artillery dated from the First World War. Army had 200,000 troops. Infantry were only lightly armed and lacked sufficient motor transport. Italy had the fourth largest navy in the world; it had several battleships but no aircraft carriers. Government spent a third of its entire budget on the military; by 1940 it reached 40%. However, a lot of this went to help General Franco, leader of the Nationalist rebels in Spain.	Wanted to rebuild the Roman Empire and find space for Italy's surplus population; wanted to break out of the Mediterranean 'prison' where France and Britain had several key military bases. Left the League of Nations in December 1937. Played a crucial role in supplying free weapons and materials as well as soldiers to the Nationalist rebels in the Spanish Civil War, 1936-9. **Signed treaty with Germany in October 1936 to create the 'Rome-Berlin Axis'.** Italy increasingly dependent on Germany for coal following the sanctions imposed on Italy by the League after Mussolini invaded Abyssinia. **In May 1939 signed the Pact of Steel, a military alliance with Germany.**
Japan Dictatorship led by the military. Largely supported by the Japanese public.	In 1931 the Japanese army had 198,880 troops; by 1937 this had grown to 300,000 and had reached 1.7 million by 1941. In 1941, the Imperial Japanese Navy had 10 battleships, 10 aircraft carriers, 38 cruisers (heavy and light), 112 destroyers, 65 submarines. By 1941, the Japanese air force had 1,500 combat aircraft.	Massive population increase but food and other raw materials had to be imported. Wanted to acquire an empire to ensure supply of raw materials that Japan needed and to challenge the British, French and Dutch empires in the Far East. 55% of Japanese oil is supplied by the US. Left the League of Nations in March 1933. Withdrew from the 1936 Second London Disarmament Conference because US and GB refused to treat Japan as their equal. **In September 1940 Japan signed the Tripartite Pact with Germany and Italy.** Called the Axis powers, the three become allies and promise to provide mutual assistance should any one of them suffer attack by any nation not already involved in the war. The Pact also formally recognized the two spheres of influence: 'the new order in Europe' will be led by Germany and Italy while Japan was 'overlord of Greater East Asia'.

*RM stands for Reichsmarks.

Source 3E: A photograph of a Japanese military parade during the 1930s.

Source 3F: A photograph of young Germans waiting to welcome Adolf Hitler.

3.1 What were the long-term consequences of the peace treaties of 1919–1923?

In Chapter 3 you learnt about the Paris Peace Conference. After the decisions had been made it was time to implement them. However, this is easier said than done. Italy and Germany were very dissatisfied with the settlement. Why was this?

Italy

Italy had joined the Allied Powers in April 1915 and had been promised territorial rewards for doing so. However, the Adriatic port of Fiume was not given to Italy, nor did Italy gain enough of Germany's colonies. The Italians felt they hadn't got what they deserved.

Germany

The Versailles Treaty had taken from Germany 25,000 square miles of territory and 7 million people. However, the terms did not leave Germany with nothing. The country still had considerable economic resources and no part of Germany had been destroyed in the same way that France had been on the Western Front. Germany might have been disarmed but it still had the resources to produce modern replacements at later. As early as 1925, just seven years after the end of the First World War, Germany's steel production was twice that of Britain. Furthermore, on its eastern border lay a collection of relatively weak successor states. To add a final humiliation, the principle of national self-determination seemed to apply to everyone except the Germans: the union with German-speaking Austria was forbidden.

During the 1920s, many political parties in Germany wanted to revise the Treaty of Versailles. However, one man in particular did not want it revised; he wanted it destroyed. His name was Adolf Hitler.

63

FACT FILE

Hitler was born in the multicultural Austro-Hungarian Empire. Austria's Germans had been a dominant political force there, but other people such as the Czechs had been campaigning for greater autonomy long before the Paris Peace Conference. Hitler (like many other Germans), did not take seriously the countries created by Wilson and the others who had imposed the Versailles Treaty: they were artificial and did not deserve to exist.

Hitler's foreign policy

Tearing up the treaties of Versailles and Saint-Germain was Hitler's foreign policy aim in the 1930s. His demands, his actions and his motives all came from the 'diktat' peace. Look at the map of Germany in the previous section. You can see the key actions between 1933 and 1939 were:

1936 – The start of German rearmament and the remilitarisation of the Rhineland.

1938 – The Anschluss (union) with Austria.

1938 – The transfer of Sudetenland from Czechoslovakia.

1939 – The invasion of Prague, the capital of Czechoslovakia.

1939 – The seizure of Memel.

1939 – The claims made over Danzig and the Polish Corridor.

ACTIVITY 3.3

1 What three elements of the peace treaties could be exploited by Hitler to build up fierce nationalism among the German people?

2 Why was militarism popular with many sections of the German population?

3 Why do you think Hitler started his programme of changes to the Treaty of Versailles with the remilitarisation of the Rhineland?

FACT FILE

If you look at the map of Czechoslovakia in Figure 3.4 you can see the Sudetenland on its western border. Most of the people living there were Germans (3.5 million), and it contained valuable raw materials. When the country had been created by the Paris Peace Conference, the border had been created with the natural defences of the mountains in mind. Accordingly, many of the country's military defences had been located there. Once the Sudetenland had been taken Germany, there was very little to protect Czechoslovakia from invasion.

Impact of the treaty on British and French opinion

In the years after 1919, the British government and public opinion were largely pleased with the punitive aspects of the Treaty of Versailles. As the 1920s closed and the

Depression took hold, this changed and many started to think that the Germans had been treated too harshly. The emergence of the Nazi Party led by Hitler was viewed in Britain as an understandable response to the punitive Versailles Treaty. If the treaty was unfair, many felt that it was the duty of the British government to help Germany in achieving the peaceful revision of the treaty. After all, the British were partly responsible for what was in it.

French politicians and public, however, believed that the Treaty of Versailles had not been tough enough on the Germans. To protect themselves they had wanted a treaty that would permanently weaken Germany. By the mid-1930s it was clear that Hitler was seeking to wreck the peace settlement. The French decided on two strategies: first, they built the very expensive Maginot Line, a row of forts on the border, to stop another German invasion; second, they worked with the British in achieving a peaceful revision of the treaty.

Source 3G: The Maginot Line circa 1940. You can see anti-tank rails protruding from the ground.

FACT FILE

The Maginot Line was built to avoid a surprise attack from Germany and to give the alarm if an attack happened. The government knew that it would take two to three weeks to mobilise the French Army and that the Line would give it valuable time in the event of an attack. It was made of fortifications, border guard posts and anti-tank rails. Not all parts of the Maginot Line were equally strong. You can see this in Sources 3G and 3H.

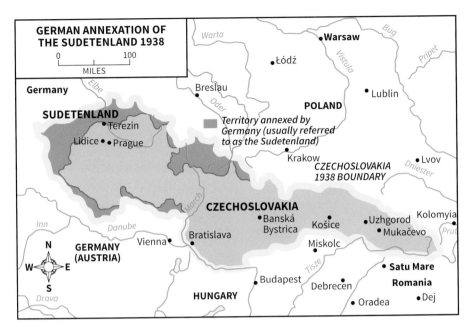

GERMAN ANNEXATION OF THE SUDETENLAND 1938

0 ____ 100 MILES

Territory annexed by Germany (usually referred to as the Sudetenland)

Figure 3.4: A map showing the territory of Czechoslovakia annexed by Germany in 1938.

Source 3H: A photo showing part of the Maginot Line in November 1939. It was a series of expensive fortifications that were built on the Franco-German border to keep the Germans out.

ACTIVITY 3.4

1 Why do you think the Maginot Line shown in Sources 3G and 3H appears to be in two sections, weak fortifications and strong fortifications?

2 What does this defence system tell you about French attitudes towards: a) Britain and b) the League of Nations?

3 What does the Maginot Line tell you about the long-term consequences of the peace treaties?

4 How did changing British attitudes towards the Versailles Treaty make it more likely that Hitler's demands would be met in the 1930s?

3.2 What were the consequences of the failures of the League in the 1930s?

You have already studied the impact of the new organisation called the League of Nations, set up after the end of the First World War. The League's failures in the 1930s had a significant impact on the actions of Japan, Italy and Germany – the three countries with governments that were both nationalistic and militaristic as well as being dictatorships.

Manchuria

In 1931, the Japanese invasion of Manchuria was the first time the League of Nations had faced a challenge from a great power. If the League had met the challenge and the Japanese had been stopped this would have been a **deterrent** to other Great Powers like Italy and Germany. However, with the world looking on, the League's failure to silence the Japanese guns showed not only Japan itself, but also Hitler and Mussolini that the League was incapable of stopping an aggressive country from making territorial gains.

KEY TERM

Deterrent: an action that puts off or deters a country from being aggressive towards others.

65

Abyssinia

Both Hitler and Mussolini were delighted at the outcome in the Far East. The League couldn't take effective action and it was proving impossible to put international interests ahead of national interests. This meant that further aggressive behaviour from Italy was extremely likely and that Hitler would soon be furthering his policy of destroying the Treaty of Versailles. The Italian conquest of Abyssinia in 1935 was humiliating for the League because the Great Powers – France and Britain – were shown to be playing a double game: they supported the application of sanctions while at the same time negotiating behind the back of the League with the aggressor, Italy, in the form of the Hoare-Laval **Pact**.

As time went on it was harder and harder for Britain and France to keep Italy on their side, detached from Hitler's Germany. Italy withdrew from the League in 1937. In September 1937, Mussolini visited Berlin. In November of the same year, Italy signed the Anti-**Comintern** Pact with Germany and Japan to present a united front against Soviet communism – an ideology all three countries hated.

The League's failure

Britain and France had never been entirely supportive of the League of Nations. It was now obvious to both governments that collective security through the League was finished – an alternative had to be found. Some sort of deterrent was needed to stop Germany and Italy from further aggression. Could Britain and France rearm?

During the Great Depression military spending had not been a government priority. Instead, France and Britain had hoped for the success of collective security. Public opinion in both countries was against rearmament, the ordinary citizen had more faith in the League than the politicians had.

Did the failure of the League result in appeasement?

By 1936 it seemed to the British and French governments that they had to start rearming. Both recognised that it would take several years for the plans to achieve full rearmament and readiness for a big war, if and when it came. In the meantime, Neville Chamberlain, the British Prime Minister, and French Prime Minister, Edouard Daladier pursued a new line with the dictators between 1935 and 1939, the policy of **appeasement**.

> ### KEY TERMS
>
> **Pact:** a treaty, a written agreement between two or more countries to act together in a particular way.
>
> **The Comintern:** a Soviet-led organisation that was designed to promote communist ideology in countries outside the Soviet Union.
>
> **Appeasement:** pacifying, seeking to calm down an angry opponent by giving in to some or all of their demands.

Source 3I: The appeasers at the Munich Conference in September 1938: from the left, British Prime Minister, Neville Chamberlain and French Prime Minister, Edouard Daladier, with Hitler and then Mussolini centre and right.

The British and French leaders met with Hitler and Mussolini in September 1938 to decide a response to Hitler's demand to take over the Sudetenland, part of Czechoslovakia. The Czech government was not invited to the meeting, but told afterwards that it should hand over the Sudetenland to Germany. Without allies, the Czech leaders agreed.

3.3 How far was Hitler's foreign policy to blame for the outbreak of war in 1939?

Most historians would agree that Hitler's foreign policy was largely to blame. This does not mean that other causes do not count; after all, Hitler acted, but other countries reacted. Historians are divided on whether Hitler had a long-standing plan to go to war, or whether he saw opportunities when they arose and used them shrewdly.

Between 1933 and the early part of 1936, Hitler had been chancellor of Germany without showing any military aggression. However, in the next three years he confused other European leaders: What did he want? What were his intentions?

Hitler had three foreign policy aims, but this still doesn't mean he was planning for war.

- To create a German Reich in which all German-speaking people lived.
- To destroy the treaty of Versailles and restore German pride and power.
- To seek *Lebensraum* in the east.

1935 – Saar Plebiscite

Hitler's three aims could not all be achieved at once. His first priority was to destroy the Treaty of Versailles and his strategy was to chip away at the terms of the treaty and see what the British and French reaction would be. The first step was in line with the terms of the treaty and not an attack on it. In 1919 in Paris the treaty had taken the Saar from Germany and put it under the control of the League of Nations for fifteen years (see 'What were the key points of the Treaty of Versailles?' section in Chapter 1). The year 1935 marked the end of League control and the timing of a plebiscite – a vote by Saarlanders to decide whether to become part of France, retain their separate status under the League or rejoin Germany.

The result of the plebiscite was very important because the Saar contained coalfields, factories and railway stations. A fierce campaign to rejoin Germany was fought by Nazi supporters living in the Saar. Opponents were intimidated and there was violence. However, League observers confirmed that the voting was fair and free; in January 1935 90.3% voted to return the Saar to Germany, 9% wanted to retain their status and 0.4% to become part of France. On 1 March the Saar officially rejoined Germany and stage 1 of unifying all Germans was complete.

Effects of the Saar plebiscite

1   The fact that the League had not complained about the violence during the campaign and invalidated the vote demonstrated weakness.

2   The huge majority in favour of rejoining Germany told the world how Germans felt about the treaty and that they were determined to tear it up.

3   The result was a boost for Hitler and his regime. It was the first step in bringing all Germans into one greater Germany, the Third Reich, and it set a precedent for

Hitler's future demands for the union with Austria and the taking of the Sudetenland in Czechoslovakia.

FACT FILE

Reich is the German word for 'empire'. In English, we tend to call Hitler's Germany the 'Third Reich', which is a curious half translation of *Dritte Reich* (Third Empire). The German expression was coined to show Nazi rule as following two earlier German empires. The German state under Nazi rule largely called itself the *Deutsches Reich* (German Empire), just as it had done both under an emperor and as a republic.

FACT FILE

Lebensraum is a German word for 'living space'. Hitler argued that Germany was justified in forcing the people to its east out of the way to allow the country to grow in size to fit its growing population. It may sound outrageous to declare you're going, for example, to push all the Poles out of Poland and give their land to your own people. But this was not very different from what had been agreed in the 1918 Treaty of Brest-Litovsk. Besides, the process might look to the Germans not very different from what other European countries had been doing in their colonies in places such as Africa and the Americas.

The Rhineland

In 1936, Hitler focused his attention on the Rhineland – see Source 3J. It was still part of Germany but it had been demilitarised by the Treaty of Versailles. German pride was further hurt because French, British and American troops were stationed there for fifteen years to ensure that no German invasion of France could happen again. Don't forget that French and Belgian troops had entered the Ruhr in 1923 and marched through the Rhineland to get there.

The remilitarisation of the Rhineland took place in 1936. Was this the first step to a planned war or was it an opportunity that Hitler took for himself and for Germany? In March 1936, two divisions of German troops marched into the Rhineland. Hitler predicted that neither France nor Britain would do anything. He was right. Why?

The French and British leaders recognised that the Rhineland was really part of Germany. Neither wanted to risk peace. Not only that, but once German troops were in place, Hitler followed up his surprise move with promises, even suggesting a non-aggression pact.

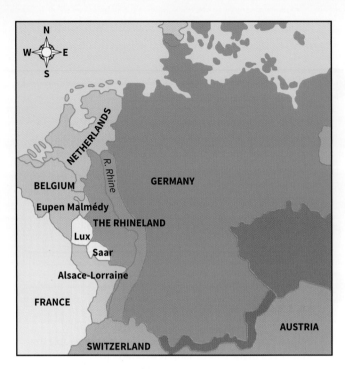

Source 3J: A map showing the position of the Rhineland. The area was demilitarised after the Treaty of Versailles.

> The 48 hours after the march were the most nerve-racking in my life. If the French troops had (challenged) us we would have had to withdraw with our tails between our legs ... the resources would have been wholly inadequate for even moderate resistance.

Source 3K: Hitler commented years later on the remilitarisation of the Rhineland.

> Hitler has got away with it! France is not marching. Instead, it is appealing to the League of Nations. Oh, the stupidity of the French. I learnt today that the German troops were under strict orders to beat a hasty retreat if the French army opposed them in any way.

Source 3L: William Shirer was an American journalist working in Berlin in 1936.

The Spanish Civil War, 1936–1939

The Spanish Civil War (1936-9) was a conflict that reflected the ideological divide that existed in Europe in the 1930s: fascism versus communism, liberal democracy versus dictatorship. It was a clash between left-wing and right-wing beliefs and values. Hitler and Mussolini saw the fighting in Spain as an ideal opportunity to test out military equipment that had only seen action on the training ground. Look at Sources 3N and 3O you can see the sort of support both Italy and Germany gave to the Nationalists, who had rebelled against the democratically elected left-leaning government. While the German and Italian governments helped the Nationalists, the Soviet Union (communist) helped the Republican side. Britain and France stayed out of the conflict, fearing that it might spread beyond Spain to the rest of Europe, although 'volunteers' crossed to Spain to join the Republican side.

Nearly three years of savage fighting followed; 270,000 people died. The Nationalists, led by General Franco, eventually won and he established a Fascist dictatorship that lasted until his death in 1975.

Although Franco kept Spain neutral during the Second World War and refused to become Hitler's ally, the Civil War was still important in Hitler's plans for the rest of Europe. The dive-bombing that the Luftwaffe inflicted on Spanish towns like Guernica was vital in providing practice for Hitler's air force (see Sources 3N and 3O); in time, dive-bombing would develop into the strategy called Blitzkreig (lightening attack) and be used in the Second World War. Not only this, but Mussolini and Hitler became closer in spite of British and French efforts to keep them apart. The success of the Nationalists in the Civil War boosted Hitler's confidence about the potential impact of his rearmament programme for the German army, navy and the Luftwaffe, in particular (see Source 3N). It was during the Civil War that Hitler was able to achieve success in Austria (1938) and Czechoslovakia (1938-9) – this time without starting a war.

ACTIVITY 3.5

1 What do Sources 3K and 3L suggest would have happened if the French had challenged the German divisions?

2 What lessons did Hitler take from this event?

3 Hitler knew that there was a serious financial crisis in France and that elections were taking place in six weeks' time. Does this provide evidence that Hitler was a 'planner' or an 'opportunist'?

Source 3O: May 1937: A photo of the Spanish city of Guernica after the German Luftwaffe had finished its attack using dive-bombing techniques.

Source 3M: A propaganda poster published by the Republican government in 1937. The text reads: 'Stand up against the Italian invasion of Spain'.

The Union with Austria (Anschluss), 1938

The Treaty of Versailles in 1919 prohibited the union of Germany and Austria because the Big Three wanted to make Germany weaker not stronger following the end of the First World War. As most Austrians spoke German, this decision ran counter to the principle of national self-determination, as outlined in president Wilson's Fourteen Points, and one of Hitler's aims was to include all German-speaking people in one Reich. By 1938 the Treaty of Versailles was being widely questioned and, with a population of 7 million, incorporating Austria into the Third Reich was key to Hitler's foreign policy. Britain and France pursued the policy of appeasement and considered Austria was too far away to care about, but Italy was next door to Austria. In 1934, Mussolini had put his army on alert to prevent an early attempt at Anschluss, but by 1938 Hitler was stronger and their relationship was closer than four years earlier.

The Anschluss was a striking example of Hitler's ability to combine 'consistency of aim and patience in preparation with opportunism and improvisation in execution'. To start with, Hitler was regularly speaking about his aim of creating a Third Reich and this had to include Austria; then, he was patient – he tried the Anschluss once in 1934 but was warned off by Mussolini – so he waited for four years. During this time the Austrian Nazis had undermined the government from within and Mussolini had decided to give Hitler whatever he wanted in Austria. The timing of Anschluss was not of Hitler's making, but when the opportunity presented itself he took it with both hands.

Source 3N: A photo of German Stukas from the Legion Condor.

chancellor Schuschnigg of Austria wanted to restrict the activities of the Nazis in his country. He asked Hitler for help. Hitler seized this opportunity. He demanded a series of conditions that would turn Austria into a German-controlled state. On 9 March Schuschnigg tried to regain the initiative from Hitler by calling a referendum that asked Austrians to vote for a 'free and German, independent and social, Christian and united Austria'. When news of the planned referendum reached Hitler he demanded Schuschnigg's resignation and changed his policy of 'gradual absorption' to 'immediate invasion' on 12 March. This shows Hitler's ability to improvise at short notice: his tactic changed from replacing Schuschnigg with Seyss-Inquart, a leading Austrian Nazi, to immediate incorporation of Austria into the Reich.

The Anschluss was over in days and was largely welcomed by Austrians themselves as you can see in Source 3Q. For Hitler this was another key part of the Versailles Treaty torn up, and without adverse reaction from Britain or France – both just protested because they thought there was little they could do without Italy's help.

Hitler had used his army beyond Germany's frontiers for the very first time. He was immensely popular in Germany because he had expanded German territory as well as increasing the population and resources of the Third Reich. The Fuhrer's confidence in his abilities and the perceived weakness of Germany's opponents reached new heights.

What next? In order to legitimise the takeover of Austria, Hitler organised a plebiscite in early April to prove to the world that the Anschluss was what people wanted. Austrians voted by a large majority to join the Third Reich; you can see one of the ballot papers in Source 3R.

CHECK YOUR UNDERSTANDING 3.1

Did Hitler plan the Anschluss or did it fall into his hands because he seized an opportunity to take it?

Source 3Q: A photo taken at the time of the Anschluss in March 1938. Here Austrian girls welcome some of the first German soldiers to reach Vienna.

Source 3R: This is a voting ballot slip from 10 April 1938. The text says "Do you agree with the reunification of Austria with the German Reich that was enacted on 13 March 1938, and do you vote for the party of our leader Adolf Hitler?" The large circle is labelled "Yes", the smaller "No".

Source 3P: A British cartoon by David Low, published in 1938 after the Anschluss. Britain is shown at the end carrying a basket representing the British Empire. The quote reads 'Why should we take a stand about someone pushing someone else when it's all so far away...' Is Low critical of the Anschluss or of Britain's response to it? Why does Low call his cartoon 'Increasing Pressure'?

70

1 What links together sources 3P, 3Q and 3R?

2 Why is the response to the Anschluss so different in sources 3P and 3Q?

3 What can you see in source 3R that suggests the plebiscite was not a fair process? Would a fairer process have changed the result of the plebiscite?

With Austria now incorporated into his Reich, Hitler still wanted to appear 'reasonable' in his new demands. Wasn't it reasonable to want the 3.5 million Germans living in the Sudetenland to join the Reich? After all, it was next to Germany (see Figure 3.5) and the Sudeten Germans were saying that they suffered discrimination at the hands of the Czech government in the capital, Prague. Hitler had other reasons to hate Czechoslovakia: the country was very new because it had been created in 1919 as part of the Paris Peace Settlement; to keep its frontiers secure, the Czech government had made alliances with both France and the Soviet Union; and Czechoslovakia was a democracy –something Hitler hated just as much as the Treaty of Versailles. So, how did Hitler approach the Sudentenland, given his aim to form a union of all Germans?

Figure 3.5: Map showing the position of the Sudetenland, part of Czechoslovakia in 1938.

Until late May 1938, Hitler had no immediate plan for attacking Czechoslovakia. On 28 March Konrad Henlein, the leader of the Sudeten Germans, was told by Hitler to make demands for 'home rule' for the Sudetens. This would, of course, be unacceptable to the Czech government because it would mean the break-up of their country. On 20-21 May Hitler was surprised to learn that the Czechs had partially mobilised its army in response to rumours of an imminent German attack. The rumours were untrue but instead of putting him off, Hitler now determined to 'smash Czechoslovakia' by 1 October, but he still was careful in case world opinion turned against him. So, throughout the summer of 1938, Hitler continued to encourage the Sudeten Germans to agitate for 'home rule'. By early September, he had secretly finalised his plans for small-scale military action against the Czechs. Then, Hitler made his move.

On 12 September, Hitler made a speech bitterly attacking Czechoslovakia and this sparked a Sudeten uprising. Believing a war was coming, the British Prime Minister, Neville Chamberlain, met Hitler at Berchtesgaden on 15 September. In their discussions, Hitler emphasized his desire for Anglo-German friendship and cooperation; but he also threatened war if the issue of Sudeten Germans was not resolved. It was at this point that Chamberlain said he was ready to agree to the peaceful cession of the Sudetenland to Germany, provided that the British, French and Czech governments agreed.

At their second meeting on 22 September at Bad Godesberg, Chamberlain reported that he had secured the approval of the three governments to the proposal. However, he now faced new demands from Hitler: the Sudetenland was to be occupied by German troops immediately. Chamberlain was horrified at Hitler's change of mind and he returned to London to prepare Britain for war. The British navy and the French army were instructed to mobilise.

What were the differences and similarities between this crisis and the Anschluss?

It was at this point that Hitler realized he was very close to a war with Britain and France that he did not want at this time. He therefore agreed to an international conference to be held at Munich, as suggested by Chamberlain and Mussolini. Neville Chamberlain (Britain), Edouard Daladier

(France), Mussolini (Italy) and Hitler (Germany) met on 29 September 1938 (Source 3I). All four agreed these points: the area called the Sudetenland would be given to Germany over a ten-day period; in any area where the population was mixed, plebiscites would be held to determine what would happen; the four leaders would guarantee the remaining part of Czechoslovakia once Polish and Hungarian claims had been satisfied.

When the Czech government were presented with the Munich Agreement it had little choice but to agree to it, even though it meant the break-up of their country. What else could they do? If they turned down the agreement it would mean the Czech army facing the much stronger German forces and the serious loss of Czech lives.

After the Munich Agreement had been signed, Prime Minister Chamberlain went to see Hitler and invited him to sign a document that pledged both men would do everything they could to promote the peace of Europe and to resolve any differences by peaceful means. With Hitler's signature and his own on this 'piece of paper', Chamberlain returned to London thinking he had saved Europe from war.

Arguments in favour of the Agreement	Arguments against the Agreement
Britain was not ready to fight a war in September 1938 and Chamberlain knew this.	If war had broken out against Germany, it is possible that Britain and France might have been supported by the USSR.
The Sudetenland was populated by Germans and therefore a war in 1938 would have been against the principle of national self-determination.	If war had started, Britain and France would have the backing of the 36 divisions of the Czech army fighting behind their strong defences on the frontier.
The British Empire was not united behind Britain in wanting to fight a war in 1938.	Munich came to be seen as the worst example of the policy of appeasement.
Britain's air defences were not ready and an attack by the Luftwaffe could mean defeat.	Britain and France, two Great Powers, had abandoned a small power, Czechoslovakia to its fate.

3.4 Was the policy of appeasement justified?

Source 3T is a photo of the England football team shortly before kick-off in the Berlin Olympic Stadium, taken while England was playing Germany on 14 May 1938. Hitler wasn't present. Every single player is giving the Nazi salute. Why?

Source 3S: A cartoon by David Low soon after the Munich Agreement was signed at the end of September 1938.

ACTIVITY 3.7

What would Neville Chamberlain say about the cartoon in Source 3S? What would Hitler say about the cartoon?

The Munich Agreement caused controversy in 1938 and it has done so ever since. What are the arguments on both sides of the debate?

Source 3T: The England football team in the Berlin Olympic Stadium, May 1938.

The answer is that British **Foreign Office** ordered the team to salute. Only two months earlier, Hitler had annexed Austria.

CHECK YOUR UNDERSTANDING 3.3

What messages did the salute shown in Source 3T send to:
a) the German public, b) Hitler and c) the British public?

KEY TERM

Foreign Office: the UK government department that manages relationships with other countries.

From 1936 onwards, the British and French governments pursued a policy of appeasement in relation to Hitler and his demands. Ever since the end of the Second World War, this policy and its supporters have been sharply criticised for not standing up to dictators such as Hitler and Mussolini. Appeasement has been seen as cowardly and weak. With every success against the appeasers, Hitler's confidence increased and he made new demands. The event that came to symbolise the awful cost of appeasement was the Munich Crisis of September 1938 that you have already studied. And yet, the policy of appeasement was developed by intelligent leaders and the policy made sense to them and many ordinary people during the late 1930s.

ACTIVITY 3.8

Look at these views of people at the time:
Neville Chamberlain called the Munich Agreement 'peace with honour'.

Winston Churchill said in the House of Commons that 'we have suffered a total and unmitigated defeat. You will find that in a period of time Czechoslovakia will be engulfed in the Nazi regime.'

1 Which of these views do you think would be supported by the Czech government?
2 Which of these views do you think would have looked right to most British people at the time?

At the time, Britain's air defences were incomplete. This made the country very vulnerable to an attack by the Luftwaffe. How does this fact alter your views on:

1 the Munich Agreement?
2 Hitler's planning for war?

ACTIVITY 3.9

Now your skills are needed to untangle the arguments about appeasement and weigh up the evidence. Then, you can make your own judgement about whether or not appeasement was justified.

Here are some arguments in favour of appeasement that people at the time might have made:

A 'Hitler is helping the western powers like Britain and France by standing up to Communism. We ought to be more concerned about the spread of communism from the Soviet Union than about Hitler. After all Hitler does believe in private property and Germany is a capitalism country. A strong Germany, led by Hitler, is a buffer against communism.'

B 'US mustn't be dragged into another European war. France and Britain needn't think they can rely on support from the US. If Britain and France want to stand up to Germany that's their business.'

C 'We could only stand up to Germany if the British Empire backs us and it is not certain that the British colonies would support another war against Germany.'

73

D 'The horrors of the First World War must not be repeated. That war was fought to end war, not to start another.'

E 'The Treaty of Versailles was unfair. If the wrongs are put right, Germany will be satisfied and become a peaceful nation again.'

F 'France is not ready for a war against Hitler. Britain must accept a compromise'.

B 'The policy puts too much trust in Hitler's promises. The agreements are based on the assumption that Hitler and Mussolini can be trusted and will act rationally: they can't and won't.'

C 'Appeasement is allowing Germany to grow too strong. Germany is much stronger than both France and Britain.'

D 'Appeasement frightens Stalin and the Soviet Union. Hitler is making no secret of his plans to expand eastwards. The policy of appeasement sends the message to the Soviet Union that Britain and France will not stand in his way.'

1 Which of these arguments do you think affected French and British public opinion the most?

2 Which of these arguments do you think affected French and British political leaders the most?

3 Which of these arguments do you think helped Hitler the most?

Now here are some different arguments, this time *against* appeasement, that people at the time might have made:

A 'The policy encourages Hitler to become aggressive. Each gamble he takes and gets away with is encouraging him to take a bigger gamble.'

E 'Chamberlain is a nice man but he doesn't understand Hitler. If the German leader hasn't let the Versailles Treaty stand in his way, why would he be held back by any new treaties and agreements?'

1 Which of these arguments do you think affected French and British public opinion the most?

2 Which of these arguments do you think affected French and British political leaders the most?

3 Which of these arguments do you think helped Hitler the most?

ACTIVITY 3.10

Here are three types of evidence to analyse: cartoons, contemporary comment and historians' verdicts.

1 Which of Sources 3U, 3V and 3W are in favour of appeasement and which are not? Explain with reference to the sources.

2 Is there anything you read in Sources 3X and 3Y that puzzles or surprises you?

3 Which cartoon seems to match Source 3X the closest?

4 Compare the historians' views in Sources 3Z and 3AA. To what extent do they disagree about appeasement?

the End

Source 3W: A British cartoon by David Low, published in March 1939.

Source 3U: A Soviet cartoon from 1939 showing Hitler's 'war machine' being pointed towards the USSR by two police officers, one French and one British. CCCP is Russian for the USSR.

Source 3V: This cartoon published in an American newspaper shortly after the Munich Agreement had been signed in September 1938.

The German visit was from my point of view a great success, because it achieved its objective, that of creating an atmosphere in which it is possible to discuss with Germany the practical questions involved in a European settlement. Both Hitler and Goering [Commander-in-Chief of the Luftwaffe] said separately, and emphatically, that they had no desire or intention of making war ... Of course, they want to dominate eastern Europe; they want as close a union as possible with Austria as they can get without incorporating her into the Reich.

Source 3X: This is part of a memorandum written by Neville Chamberlain, British Prime Minister, in November 1937.

The following special reasons make me confident. There is no actual rearmament in England, just propaganda. The construction programme for the navy for 1938 has not yet been fulfilled. Little has been done on land. England will only be able to send a maximum of three divisions to the continent. A little has been done for the Air Force, but it is only a beginning. France lacks men due to the decline in the birth rate. Little has been done for rearmament. The enemy had another hope, that Russia would become our enemy after the conquest of Poland. Our enemies are little worms, I saw them at Munich.

Source 3Y: Part of a speech made by Hitler to his military commanders, 27 August 1939.

Appeasement was far more than a weak ... policy of concession to potential aggressors. It was ... consistent with the main lines of British foreign policy going back to the nineteenth century.

75

'Appeasement' … meant a policy of adjustment and accommodation of conflicting interests broadly to conform with Britain's unique position in world affairs. It involved no preconceived plan of action, it rested upon a number of political and moral assumptions about the virtue of compromise and peace. It involved using the instruments of British power – trading and financial strength and a wealth of diplomatic experience – to their fullest advantage.

Source 3Z: British historian, R. J. Overy, wrote this in 1987.

Timidity was the main feature of French political leadership. At the critical moments – in March 1936 and September 1938 – leaders steered away from any suggestion of constraining Germany by force. This timidity had three main causes. Firstly, there was the caution of the military chiefs. Early in 1936 before Hitler walked into the Rhineland, Marshal Gamelin thought that France could not fight Germany with any certainty of victory. Secondly, French public opinion was deeply divided and the lack of national unity prevented a forceful response to Hitler's moves. Thirdly, from September 1935 onwards, military and political leaders were convinced that France could not fight Germany unless assured of British help. British help was considered vital for the protection of French shipping and supplies in the Mediterranean.

Source 3AA: British historian Anthony Adamthwaite, wrote this in 1977.

3.5 How important was the Nazi-Soviet pact?

Of all the consequences of the Munich Agreement, few were as important as the damage it caused the relationship between the Soviet Union and the British and French. For ten years or more there had been a feeling of distrust. Stalin suspected that the appeasers secretly preferred an accommodation with Germany than with the Soviet Union. In London and Paris, political leaders were suspicious that Stalin was secretly supporting communists in other countries and encouraging revolutions on the Russian model. They also wondered how strong the Soviet Union's military was: in the 1930s Stalin had been afraid of his own army and had many of its leaders imprisoned or executed.

The Munich Agreement was made without any reference to the Soviet Union. Was it intended to give Hitler permission to seek *Lebensraum* in eastern Europe? Stalin concluded that he could not trust the western powers and needed to make his own deal with Germany.

ACTIVITY 3.11

Study Sources 3S and 3W. Who and what is being portrayed? What is the cartoonist David Low saying about relations between Germany and Britain?

It should not therefore be surprising that in mid-August 1939, when peace was fragile, the British-French-Soviet military negotiations collapsed because of Poland's fear of allowing Soviet troops to cross its territory in the event of an attack on Germany.

From Hitler's point of view it was an urgent priority that his next move against Poland would not meet with Soviet opposition. Security for the Soviet frontier was Stalin's purpose. So, after just one day of negotiations, the Nazi-Soviet Pact was agreed. Viewed from the outside, the Pact took the form of a non-aggression treaty lasting ten years. Secretly, however, it divided the lands between Germany and the Soviet Union into 'spheres of influence': the western half of Poland was Germany's; the rest of Poland plus Latvia, Estonia and Lithuania fell into the Soviet sphere. Hitler received secret approval for his ambitions for Danzig and the 'Polish Corridor'. Stalin regained some territory lost at the end of the First World War, but also some time in which to build up for a future war. After all, British, French and Soviet leaders all suspected that war with Germany was inevitable and their efforts to avoid it were in part efforts to postpone it until they were ready.

ACTIVITY 3.12

Historian A.J.P. Taylor wrote that 'it is difficult to see what other course the Soviet Union could have followed'. Was it the fault of the western powers that Stalin decided a pact with Hitler was the only possible course of action?

Is it fair to say that French and British attitudes towards the USSR made war with Germany inevitable in 1939?

3.6 Why did Britain and France declare war on Germany in September 1939?

The last seven days in August 1939 were frantic. Could the French and British persuade Poland to give up Danzig as Hitler demanded? The Poles had seen the fate of Czechoslovakia and refused. No one in London or Paris wanted a repeat of Munich. Maybe Chamberlain and Daladier now, at this late hour, recognised the futility of appeasement. In September 1939, a general war started in the end because each side thought the other was bluffing. Hitler said to his generals: 'the men I met at Munich are not the kind to start another world war'. He was wrong. Daladier and Chamberlain had no wish to start a war. But Germany was working towards being the most powerful country in Europe, able to get its own way in everything. France and Britain couldn't accept this.

It had been possible to argue that the takeover of Austria and the Sudetenland was in line with the Wilsonian principle of self-determination. Hitler's actions over Czechoslovakia in March 1939 was a different matter and the 1 September 1939 invasion of Poland was clearly pure expansionism.

It took Britain and France two days to issue an ultimatum demanding German withdrawal from Poland. British Prime Minister Chamberlain, announced on the radio (Source 3BB): 'This morning the British ambassador in Berlin handed the German government a final note, that unless we heard by 11 o'clock that they were prepared to withdraw at once from Poland, then a state of war would exist between us. I have to tell you now that no such

undertaking has been received, and that, consequently, this country is at war with Germany.'

To Hitler's surprise, he was now at war with Britain and France. He had believed that the western powers would behave exactly as they had done after previous violations of the peace settlement.

Source 3BB: With appeasement in pieces, the British Prime Minister, Neville Chamberlain (seen here in a BBC studio), spoke to the nation from Downing Street on 3 September 1939.

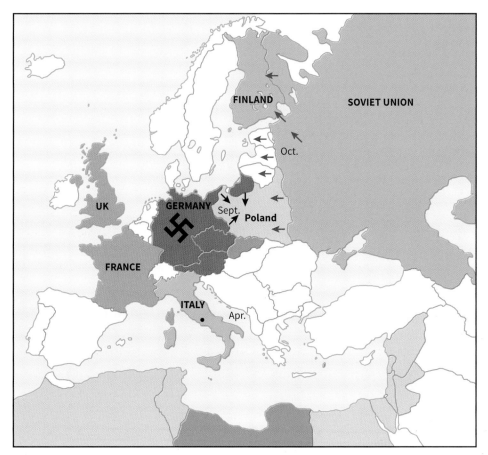

Figure 3.6: Europe at War: 1939. You can see the German expansion leading to the outbreak of war in September. Once the Germans attacked Poland from the west, the Soviet Union attacked it from the east.

ACTIVITY 3.13

If Britain and France had not declared war on 3 September 1939 what do you think might have been the consequences?

Suppose Hitler had only acted to bring all Germans together within one country in the 1930s – in line with the principle of national self-determination. Would that limited aim have been acceptable to France and Britain so that peace would have been secured?

Review your learning

The series of peace treaties following the First World War resulted in a range of problems. There was dissatisfaction in Italy, Germany and Japan. Germany was not disarmed properly so that it could not start another war. The new League of Nations could not provide collective security because it did not stop Italy or Japan invading Abyssinia and China. The Disarmament Conference the League sponsored did not succeed.

Hitler's demand that Germany throw aside the Treaty of Versailles made him popular. As Britain and France gave in to his demands, Hitler treated them both with contempt and did not believe they would go to war over Poland.

After the Germans occupied Prague, Britain and France promised to support Poland. Attempts to draw in the Soviet Union to oppose Hitler's aggression failed.

Historians disagree about the events in the 1930s and the 1939 outbreak of the Second World War. You need to assess the factors, weigh them up and decide yourself. Make sure you can answer the six questions listed at the beginning of this chapter as Focus points; then you will have enough evidence for you to attempt Key Question 3.

Summary points for revision

The 1930s is a complicated period. To help you learn, you need a structure like the one below. Copy out the table and, using the knowledge built up during this study, add examples.

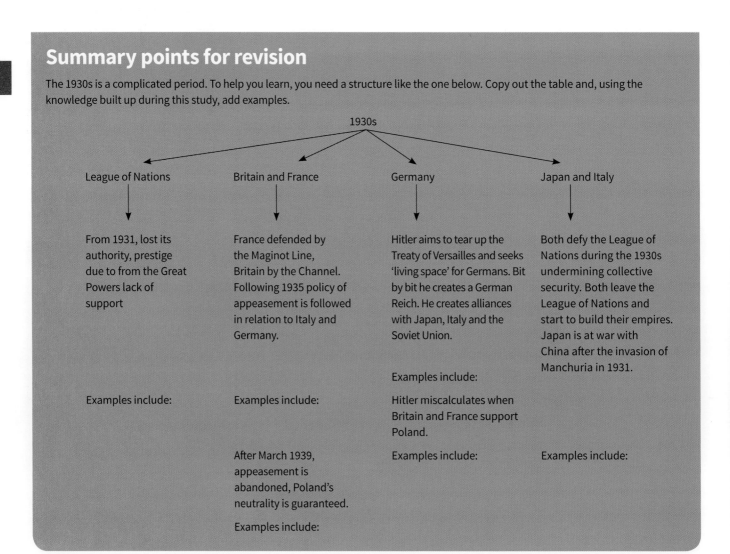

1930s

League of Nations

From 1931, lost its authority, prestige due to from the Great Powers lack of support

Examples include:

Britain and France

France defended by the Maginot Line, Britain by the Channel. Following 1935 policy of appeasement is followed in relation to Italy and Germany.

Examples include:

After March 1939, appeasement is abandoned, Poland's neutrality is guaranteed.

Examples include:

Germany

Hitler aims to tear up the Treaty of Versailles and seeks 'living space' for Germans. Bit by bit he creates a German Reich. He creates alliances with Japan, Italy and the Soviet Union.

Examples include:

Hitler miscalculates when Britain and France support Poland.

Examples include:

Japan and Italy

Both defy the League of Nations during the 1930s undermining collective security. Both leave the League of Nations and start to build their empires. Japan is at war with China after the invasion of Manchuria in 1931.

Examples include:

The Big Challenge

You need to be able to explain why war broke out in 1939. On a piece of plain A4 paper draw the diagram below. When you have drawn it, look at the centre box and then the other boxes around it. Your challenge is to draw arrows from one box to another box, with the final arrow pointing towards the middle box. The <u>only rule</u> is that when you draw an arrow the first box must explain the second box. So, in the picture below, what is written in Box A must explain what is written in Box B. You can draw as many arrows as you like. When you have drawn the arrows write on them what the link is.

The growth of nationalism and militarism in countries ruled by dictators

The impact of the Great Depression

Hitler's policy and actions during the 1930s

... so the British and French governments declared war on Germany

The failures of the League of Nations

The policy of appeasement

The Nazi-Soviet Pact

The long-term effects of the peace treaties, 1919–1923

Now write a short paragraph explaining and justifying whichever sentences you've just created.

Exam-style questions

1 How did Hitler go about revising the Treaty of Versailles between 1933 and 1936?

2 Was the Treaty of Versailles itself to blame for the outbreak of war in 1939 or was it the way it was implemented that was at fault?

3 *Lebensraum* (living space) was the crucial factor in causing the war in 1939.' How far do you agree?

4 'Instead of causing the war, appeasement kept the peace for longer in the 1930s.' How far do you agree?

5 'The Second World War was inevitable after: a) 1936, b) 1938, c) March 1939.' For each of the three dates, explain to what extent you agree with the statement.

Chapter 4

Key Question 4: Who was to blame for the Cold War?

Focus points

- Why did the USA-USSR alliance begin to break down in 1945?
- How had the USSR gained control of Eastern Europe by 1948?
- How did the USA react to Soviet expansionism?
- What were the consequences of the Berlin Blockade?
- Who was the more to blame for starting the Cold War: the USA or the USSR?

What is this enquiry about?

In this chapter you will investigate the deterioration of the wartime alliance between the USA and the USSR. You will discover that the problems in the alliance were visible during the war itself. As historians, you will need to evaluate the responsibilities of both countries for post-war hostility, see their actions in context (or indeed in a range of different contexts), and then reach a decision about 'blame'.

Ask yourself:

- Was the USA to blame?
- Was the USSR to blame?
- Were they both to blame?
- Was neither to blame?

Reaching a judgement is an important part of the enquiry, but it's only the last stage. First you need to collect evidence in order to reach that judgement, but also in order to show how you reached it.

> ### KEY TERM
>
> **Warsaw Pact:** was signed in 1955 as a response to NATO. It was a defensive military alliance of Eastern European states. Hungary, Czechoslovakia, East Germany and Poland were all members. However, the main decisions were made by the USSR.

4.1 Why did the USA-USSR alliance begin to break down in 1945?

What was the Cold War?

The Cold War was a military stand-off between the USSR and its allies and the USA and its allies. Beginning in the mid-1940s, it ran until the beginning of the 1990s. The reason for calling it 'cold' was that it was not directly fought. Instead, there was a competition to be the most powerfully armed and the most successful in space exploration: the 'arms race' and the 'space race'. However, a series of small wars were also fought between the superpowers' allies and client states. Despite a direct war never breaking out, the constant military threat experienced by both sides was as much of a continual influence on political decision-making, as an actual war.

The Cold War divided most of Europe into two hostile political and military alliances (Source 4A): NATO in Western Europe from 1949 and the **Warsaw Pact** in Eastern Europe from 1955. The old German capital Berlin was split in two by a wall.

> ### ACTIVITY 4.1
>
> Study Source 4A. Identify the countries on the map that are likely to cause tension between the two superpowers. Explain your choices.

81

Draw up a table like the one below and keep it handy for the different sections.

Focus question	How did it happen and whose fault was it?	Evidence from the case studies to support the judgement.
Why did the USA-USSR alliance begin to break down in 1945?		
How had the USSR gained control of Eastern Europe by 1948?		
How did the USA react to Soviet expansionism?		
What were the consequences of the Berlin Blockade?		
Who was the more to blame for starting the Cold War: the USA or the USSR?		

Source 4A: A map showing the two opposing military alliances NATO and the Warsaw Pact in Europe. Away from Europe, the USA and Canada were also NATO members, while in 1963 Mongolia asked to join the Warsaw Pact. Albania left the Warsaw Pact in 1968.

Source 4B: A Soviet poster produced in 1942 showing the Grand Alliance choking Hitler. At the very top of the poster it says: 'He (Hitler) won't get out of this noose'; the Soviet noose says: 'Alliance between the USSR, Britain and the USA'; the USA and British nooses say 'Agreement' and 'Partnership'.

ACTIVITY 4.2

Look at Source 4B. Which countries made up the Grand Alliance? What is the Alliance's key purpose? What message does Source 4B convey about the Grand Alliance? Use details in the poster to support your answer.

What was the 'Grand Alliance' and why did it begin to break down in 1945?

In June 1941 the Germans invaded the Soviet Union. This gave the USSR and Great Britain a common enemy. When the Japanese bombed the USA naval base of Pearl Harbor in December 1941, the USA entered the war. The Grand Alliance's objective was to defeat the Axis allies: Nazi Germany, Italy and Japan.

Ideological differences

The USA and the USSR were governed differently:

- the USA was a capitalist democracy with voting rights and multi-party elections
- the USSR was a communist one-party state with no opposition.

Leaders in the USA and in Britain believed that the Soviets wanted to spread communism beyond the USSR borders into central and eastern Europe and into Asia. Stalin suspected the West of wanting Hitler's army to weaken the Soviet Union. After all, in 1918 western countries had invaded the Soviet Union in an attempt to kill communism. In the 1930s, Britain and France made no attempt to work with the Soviet Union to stop Nazi aggression in Europe. Stalin thought that the capitalist countries would look for any opportunity to bring an end to Soviet communism.

Wartime disagreements

Winning the war against Hitler meant working together in partnership. To a large extent the Grand Alliance did so, but there were strains and stresses that eroded its effectiveness.

Lend–Lease

To help the Soviet Union, the USA government began sending it supplies. Under a system called Lend–Lease, the USA loaned military equipment for the duration of the war at no charge. By 1945, the USA had sent the Soviet Union supplies valued at nearly $11 billion. About 25% of this aid was in the form of munitions and 75% consisted of industrial equipment, raw materials and food. The USSR was highly dependent on rail transportation, but the war had nearly closed down rail equipment production; only 92 trains were produced. Under Lend-Lease, 2,000 locomotives and 11,000 wagons were supplied. Similarly, the Soviet air force received 18,700 aircraft from the USA – about 14% of Soviet aircraft production.

FACT FILE

Lend–Lease was intended to be what it sounds like: a loan. After the end of the Second World War, no one was certain how much the USSR would pay for the wartime supplies, nor how or when. A large amount of Soviet gold had already been shipped to the USA. Materials lost in fighting were written off as a shared wartime loss. Some further repayment was made, though the disagreement about how much was owing continued for several years.

THE WAY OF A STORK

Source 4C: A US cartoon published about Lend-Lease in January 1941.

ACTIVITY 4.3

Look at Source 4C. What is the impression of the Lend–Lease scheme given by the cartoonist? Make a list of the items that the bird is carrying. Why has the cartoonist drawn the Statue of Liberty in the background?

CHECK YOUR UNDERSTANDING 4.1

Think back to the 1930s and the Second World War. Why would the relationship between the USA and USSR be hesitant following events in the late 1930s and 1940?

Find out what kinds of goods the USA sent to the USSR and which other countries received them.

Tensions in the Grand Alliance: USA, USSR and Britain

As early as 1942, Stalin wanted the USA and Britain to invade western Europe to relieve pressure on the Red Army in the east. It didn't happen immediately. US President Franklin Delano Roosevelt (FDR) promised a second front but it was repeatedly postponed. Instead of an Anglo-American invasion of German-occupied France, Britain and the USA sent troops to North Africa and Italy, delaying the invasion of Europe itself until 6 June 1944.

The most important disagreement, however, was over the opening of a Second Front in the West. Although Stalin only grumbled when the invasion was postponed until 1943, he exploded the following year when the invasion was postponed again until June of 1944. In retaliation, Stalin recalled his ambassadors from London and Washington and fears soon arose that the Soviets might seek a separate peace with Germany.

Source 4D: From the website US Department of State.

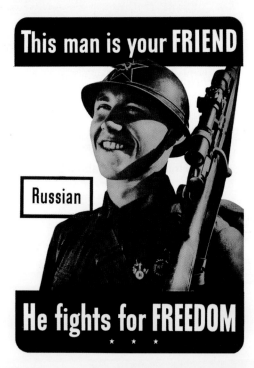

Source 4E: This poster was produced by the US government in 1942. It shows a uniformed Soviet soldier.

ACTIVITY 4.4

Why do Sources 4B, 4C and 4E suggest a different sort of relationship between the Grand Alliance partners from Source 4D? Do the different impressions mean that some of the sources B to E are more reliable than others for the historian trying to assess the strength of the Grand Alliance?

What does Source 4D tell you about: a) the USA and b) the USSR?

Wartime and post-war conferences

By late 1943 things were looking better for the Grand Alliance. With the end of the war closer, the leaders considered what kind of peace the Grand Alliance wanted.

The Tehran Conference 1943

The Big Three (Roosevelt, Churchill and Stalin) met in November 1943. At Tehran, Stalin got what he wanted – a date (June 1944) for the Anglo-American invasion of German-occupied France. In addition, there was agreement that, at the end of the war, the USSR could restore its 1918 border with Poland, while Poland would be compensated by its western border moving further west at the expense of Germany. You can see this in Source 4F.

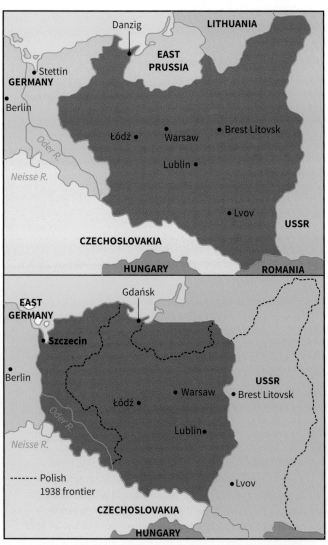

Source 4F: A map showing the borders of 1938 Poland and then, as a result of the Tehran agreement, the moving of its western border with Germany, so that it now runs along the Oder-Neisse rivers.

84

The Yalta Conference, February 1945

The war in Europe was in its final stages when Roosevelt, Stalin and Churchill met at Yalta. By this time the Red Army had occupied nearly all of central and Eastern Europe. The issues that had emerged at Tehran – especially those regarding Poland – now needed solutions. This table sets out what was achieved and what was left undone.

> **TOP TIP**
>
> The five steps that the Grand Alliance agreed should happen in Germany once peace came were:
>
> - demilitarisation (disbanding the armed forces)
> - de-Nazification (removing all former Nazis from positions of power)
> - democratisation (restoring free elections and a multiparty system)
> - de-industrialisation (reducing Germany's heavy industry)
> - decentralisation (taking power away from central government).

ACTIVITY 4.5

TROUBLE WITH SOME OF THE PIECES

Source 4G: Stalin, Roosevelt and Churchill depicted assembling a jigsaw puzzle of Europe at the Yalta Conference in February 1945.

85

Places and problems	Agreements	Remaining tension
Germany	1 Germany (and Berlin) to be temporarily divided into Soviet, American, British and French occupation zones. 2 Germany to pay $20 billion reparations, 50% to the USSR. 3 The implementation of the 5 steps (see Top Tips) in all four zones after its defeat; war crimes trials for captured Nazis.	The division of Germany was only temporary; a future conference would decide its future. Stalin wanted more reparations from Germany than was agreed, because of the destruction of so much of the USSR.
Poland	1 New Soviet–Polish borders give Poland German territory in the west as compensation for territory in the east surrendered to USSR. 2 Early elections.	1 The West rejected Soviet demands that Germans now in Poland should be repatriated to Germany. 2 Stalin wanted a Polish government that would be friendly to the Soviet Union. He supported the 'Lublin Poles' (mostly communist) while FDR and Churchill backed the 'London Poles' (non-communist).
Eastern Europe	Early elections in all east European countries liberated from Nazi Germany's control by the Soviet Red Army.	Stalin wanted governments friendly to the USSR, and was worried that free elections would not produce them.

Places and problems	Agreements	Remaining tension
Ending the war	Stalin agreed to join the war against Japan once Germany had been defeated. In return, the USSR would receive South Sakhalin and the Kurile Islands.	
United Nations Organisation (UN)	The creation of the United Nations – with a five-member **Security Council** – to replace the League of Nations at the end of the war.	Stalin wanted all Soviet republics to have seats in the proposed UN's General Assembly, but the USA and Britain only agreed to three.

It was not a question of what we would let the Russians do, but what we could get the Russians to do.

Source 4H: Future Secretary of State James Byrnes commented on the Yalta Conference that began on 4 February 1945.

To this day, many of Roosevelt's most vehement detractors accuse him of 'handing over' Eastern Europe and Northeast Asia to the Soviet Union at Yalta despite the fact that the Soviets did make many substantial concessions.

Source 4I: Office of the Historian. USA Department of State.

'spheres of influence' kept coming up in our discussions because the occupying forces had the power in the areas where their arms were present and each knew that the other could not force things to an issue ... the Russians had the power in Eastern Europe ... and that the only practicable course was to use what influence we had to improve the situation.

Source 4J: Taken from discussions held between US politicians and President Roosevelt before he left to attend the Yalta Conference in February 1945.

ACTIVITY 4.6

1 What is the message of the cartoon in Source 4G?

2 To what extent is the message supported by evidence from Sources 4H, 4I and 4J?

3 Source 4I suggests that some historians have been critical of President Roosevelt's actions at the Yalta Conference. What alternatives were left open to Roosevelt and Churchill in February 1945?

What changed between February and July 1945?

In the USA, Roosevelt died in April and was replaced by his vice-president, Harry S. Truman. Truman had little experience of foreign affairs, but took a more hard-line attitude towards the Soviet Union's security fears. In April, he met with the Soviet Foreign Minister, Molotov, and lectured him on the importance of sticking to agreements. Molotov complained that he had never been spoken to so rudely at an official meeting. Truman replied: 'Carry out your agreements and you won't get talked to like that.' In May 1945, after Germany's surrender, President Truman abruptly ended the Lend–Lease scheme to the USSR. This was a serious blow to the war-devastated Soviet Union. As a result, relations had deteriorated still further by the time the Allies met at Potsdam in July 1945.

In the UK, Clement Attlee, who had been deputy prime minister in a wartime coalition government, replaced Churchill as British prime minister after a general election in July.

FACT FILE

Harry S. Truman (1884–1972) was the 33rd President of the United States (1945–1953). Born in Missouri, he grew up on his family's farm. When President Roosevelt died in April 1945, the job of leadership passed to Vice-President Truman. Close to the end of the Second World War, Truman approved the use of atomic weapons against Japan, to force a surrender without the need for an invasion and massive loss of American lives; that decision remains controversial. After the war, Truman assisted in the founding of the United Nations, issued the Truman Doctrine to contain communism, and passed the $13 billion Marshall Plan to rebuild Europe.

The Potsdam Conference, July–August 1945

At the Potsdam Conference, the Allies were represented by Truman, Stalin and Attlee. It soon became clear that, with Germany beaten and Japan on the verge of defeat, under Truman's leadership the USA attitude hardened towards the USSR. Potsdam saw agreement on some plans for the future, but no relaxation of tension.

Places and problems	Agreements	Remaining tension
Germany	1 Division of the country and the capital, Berlin, into four zones. 2 Payment of reparations confirmed, but amount was reduced and industrial goods had to come from each power's own zone. The USSR had to provide agricultural goods from its zone in return for industrial goods from the three western zones. 3 Decision on the 'Five Ds' and war crimes trials was confirmed.	1 In the end the Soviets were only given limited reparations. 2 Disagreements about de-Nazification led to each zone implementing this separately; the Soviets were worried that former Nazis could return to power in the western zones. 3 The West wanted a quick economic recovery for Germany, but Stalin wanted to keep Germany weak. 4 Stalin was concerned about the impact of the capitalist western zones on the eastern zone.
Poland	Stalin agreed to let more 'London Poles' (non-communists) join the 'Lublin Poles' government (mostly communist) already in place.	Although Stalin agreed to allow more 'London Poles' to join the existing government, Truman's request for elections in Poland was turned down.
Eastern Europe	1 The USSR would take land from Germany, Romania and Czechoslovakia; the three Baltic republics (Latvia, Lithuania and Estonia) would become part of the USSR. 2 Germans living in Poland, Hungary and Czechoslovakia would be moved to Germany.	The USA was concerned about growing Soviet control in Eastern Europe – Poland, Hungary, Romania, Bulgaria and Czechoslovakia.
The war	Following Germany's surrender in May 1945, the USSR had been preparing to attack Japan, as agreed at Yalta. Truman informed Stalin that the USA had developed a new and powerful weapon, the atomic bomb.	1 Truman decided to use the new atomic bombs on Japan, partly to keep the USSR out of the Pacific War. 2 Truman refused to allow the USSR a role in the post-war occupation of Japan. 3 Truman refused to share atomic secrets with the USSR. Stalin immediately ordered the Soviet atomic weapon programme to be accelerated, so starting the nuclear arms race.
United Nations	1 UN was formally created. 2 The USA, the USSR, Britain, France and China would be the five permanent members of the Security Council, each with a **veto**.	As the Cold War developed, both East and West increasingly used their power of veto to block or delay UN actions that didn't suit them.

FACT FILE

Germany had used Poland as an invasion route into Russia/USSR in 1914 and 1941. Stalin believed it was vital that the USSR should be able to control Poland (and other Eastern European states) after the Second World War – or at least ensure that a friendly government ruled it.

KEY TERM

Veto: the right to stop a bill from becoming law.

At Yalta, Roosevelt and Churchill had agreed that the Soviet Union would receive back from Poland the land it had seized at the end of the Russo–Polish War in 1921. German territory would go to Poland in compensation.

There remained serious differences over how Poland should be governed. Stalin broke the promise of free elections, but FDR and Churchill could do little about it; the Red Army's occupation created political reality. Officials advising the president concluded that as it was not possible to change the situation in Eastern Europe, Soviet power had to be contained elsewhere.

At Potsdam, Truman argued that the USSR should take reparations from its zone of Germany. As this was mainly rural and poorer than the industrial western zones, Stalin objected. Eventually, it was agreed that the USSR could also have 25% of the machinery from the three western zones, but only if the USSR sent 60% of the value of these industrial goods to the West in the form of raw materials (especially coal). The Soviets demanded German coal from the western zones, but the Americans wanted it to help in the economic recovery of western Europe.

Further disagreement occurred because the Soviets were treating their eastern zone of Germany as if it was part of the USSR. German factories were dismantled and moved to the Soviet Union. Stalin wanted to punish the Germans and take their resources. Although some reparations had been delivered, the Soviets were not supplying food in return as agreed. The USA argued that no more reparations should leave their zone until the Soviets exported the food, clothing, timber and machinery that were needed. The Soviets refused. The difficulties in implementing and interpreting the Yalta and Potsdam agreements was a significant cause of the Cold War.

The leaders of the Grand Alliance decided to set up the Allied Control Council to run Germany, and to divide the capital, Berlin (which was deep within the Soviet zone) into four zones. Demilitarisation and the other steps were taken to ensure that, even when reunited, Germany would not be a threat, a point about which the USSR felt especially strongly.

What were the aims and attitudes of the Big Three as they gathered around the conference table? How much power and influence did each of the leaders have?

ACTIVITY 4.7

At the Yalta and Potsdam conferences, four main areas of disagreement began to emerge: Germany, Poland, economic reconstruction and nuclear weapons. Whose fault were these disagreements? Use your table to capture the evidence for either side.

What was the Soviet attitude to peace-making?

Stalin's foreign policy was shaped by the severe losses and devastation that the Soviet Union had twice suffered (see Sources 4K and 4L). He had to make sure that the Soviet Union would not be invaded again. As 11 million Soviet troops marched westwards pushing back the retreating German army, Stalin wanted to take advantage of the military situation in Europe to strengthen Soviet influence and prevent another invasion from the West. To do this, the Red Army held on to as much of Eastern Europe as possible. Stalin wanted a **buffer zone** between the Soviet Union and Germany. In addition, he believed that the USSR should receive reparations that matched its losses. On top of all this, Stalin was looking for financial assistance to repair his country.

About 30 million soldiers and civilians died
25 million homes destroyed
31,000 factories destroyed
84,000 schools destroyed
10.5 million made refugees
17 million cattle killed
100,000 state farms destroyed.

Source 4K: This table shows features of the devastation that the Second World War caused in the Soviet Union.

	1940	1942	1944	1945
Bread (in millions of tons)	24	12.1	10	11
Meat (in thousands of tons)	1,417	672	516	624
Butter (in thousands of tons)	228	111	106	117
Clothing items (in millions)	183	54	47	50
Shoes, pairs (in millions)	211	52.7	67.4	66.1

Source 4L: This table shows the comparison of output by the Soviet economy and the impact of the war.

KEY TERM

Buffer zone: a group of countries that surround a major state and act as a protective barrier. The countries of Eastern Europe that shared a border with the USSR were taken over by Stalin to create a buffer zone against the West.

1 Looking at Sources 4J, 4K and 4L – why was it so hard for the people and government of the USA to understand Stalin's point of view in the peace-making process?

2 Put some of the data in Sources 4K and 4L into words. What strikes you as particularly significant?

3 Which data in Source 4K helps to explain the output figures in Source L?

What was the USA attitude towards peace-making?

Roosevelt (FDR), Stalin and Churchill shared certain objectives. All wanted to limit the power of Germany and prevent another war. The Allies wanted cooperation to continue in peacetime. They wanted a world organisation for maintaining peace to replace the League of Nations; the United Nations was set up in New York towards the end of 1945.

However, FDR wanted to break up empires and spheres of influence. He believed that all states should have the right to self-determination. In addition, he hoped democracy would flourish so people could enjoy free elections and free speech. For Truman, the lesson of the 1930s' policy of appeasing Hitler was that democracies had to stand up to dictators. His approach was **containment**: Soviet influence and power must be contained by the USA and its allies.

> **KEY TERM**
>
> **Containment:** keeping the USSR within certain boundaries and borders, preventing them from advancing their power and influence.

Truman's thinking was influenced by economic considerations, too. The USA wanted to prevent any repeat of the Great Depression, and believed free trade was the means to do this. Individual countries should agree that imports could not be restricted by tariffs and quotas. At the 1944 Bretton Woods Conference, plans were laid for a World Bank so that countries who were committed to free trade policies could borrow money to invest (e.g. in infrastructure projects such as roads and bridges). These developments suited US interests well. Between 1940 and 1944 output from US industry increased by 90%. The US economy needed a revival in Europe to ensure a market for American goods. Policy-makers in Washington were concerned that when the war ended there would be a collapse in demand.

Both the spread of communism and the closing of markets to free trade had to be opposed.

The US government failed to understand the Soviet Union's concerns with security. The attack on Pearl Harbor was the only serious damage on USA territory; few bombs fell on American soil – nothing to compare with the Soviet experience. The USA saw every Soviet action not as defensive, but as part of an expansionist plan and believed that every communist word or deed anywhere in the world was part of Stalin's master plan.

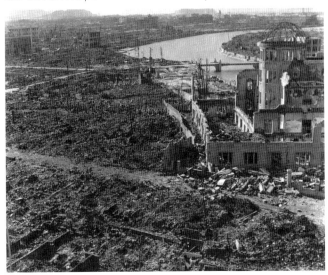

Source 4M: A photograph showing the destruction wrought by the atomic bomb the USA dropped on Hiroshima on 6 August 1945; a second nuclear bomb was dropped on Nagasaki on 9 August.

"WHY CAN'T WE WORK TOGETHER IN MUTUAL TRUST & CONFIDENCE?"

Source 4N: A British cartoon published in November 1945 shows President Truman asking the question of Attlee and Stalin.

Truman and the atomic bomb

Although the Allies reached agreement on several difficult issues, this progress was undermined in August 1945

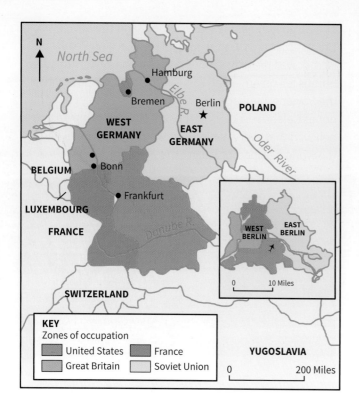

Source 4O: A map showing the division of Germany into four zones of occupation after the Second World War.

KEY
Zones of occupation
- United States
- Great Britain
- France
- Soviet Union

when the USA exploded the world's first atomic bombs on Hiroshima and Nagasaki in Japan. This weapon was a new threat to the Soviets. The US Secretary of War, Henry Stimson, argued that the Soviet Union should be offered an atomic partnership if some concessions on Eastern Europe were made. However, Truman and his Secretary of State, James Byrne, saw the atomic bomb as a way of ending the war against Japan without Soviet assistance. This would prevent any Soviet demands for influence in Asia, a region seen as vital to USA interests.

ACTIVITY 4.9

What is the message of the cartoon in Source 4N? How does the photograph in Source 4M inform your understanding of the cartoon?

What do you think explains Stalin's attitude towards Germany in Source 4P?

Even after the defeat of Germany, the danger of war/ invasion will continue to exist. Germany is a great state with large industry ... it shall never accept its defeat and will continue to be dangerous.

Source 4P: Part of a speech made on the eve of the Yalta Conference, 28 January 1945, by Stalin.

CHECK YOUR UNDERSTANDING 4.2

1   Identify the issues that kept the Grand Alliance together and the issues that caused tension between them.

2   Which issue was more important in causing the break-up of the Grand Alliance: Germany or Poland? Explain your answer.

4.2 How had the USSR gained control of Eastern Europe by 1948?

When Germany surrendered in 1945, there were 11 million Red Army soldiers in Eastern Europe. These soldiers had pushed the Germans out of Poland, Romania, Hungary, Czechoslovakia and Bulgaria. When the war ended, many of the soldiers stayed in place.

Stalin did not achieve control over Eastern Europe immediately. In different countries he took different actions and moved at different paces. In general, there were two phases:

1   1944–1947: Stalin and his advisers worked with the local politicians to set up coalition governments in which communists served alongside people from other parties.

2   1948–1949: 'people's republics' emerged, one-party communist dictatorships under the rule of Moscow.

Czechoslovakia

The Czechoslovaks were positive towards the Soviet Union; many still felt betrayed by Britain and France when they gave in to Hitler's demands at the Munich Conference in 1938.

Dr Edvard Benes had been president of the **exile** Czech government in London. He flew to Moscow and signed a treaty of friendship. When he returned to Prague it was with a Moscow-approved coalition government. Members of the Czech Communist Party ran the ministries of the interior and information.

The communists emerged from a relatively free and fair election in May 1946 as the largest party with 31% of the vote. Communists took control of key departments such as law and order; this enabled them to arrest political opponents. The Czechoslovak Communists became popular partly because they drove the remaining German population (many had already fled) out of Czechoslovakia and allowed Czechs to move into these areas.

To force new elections in February 1948, all of the non-communist ministers resigned. New elections were blocked and the vacancies in government were filled with communists. Foreign Minister Jan Masaryk, a popular non-communist politician and son of the country's founding president, was murdered in March 1948.

Hungary

Hungary had been a wartime German ally. Most Hungarians were strongly anti-communist. In the election of November 1945, communists won only 17% of the vote. They were given one government post – Ministry of the Interior. Communists used the secret police to persecute non-communists. In 1947, falsified elections gave communists control of a coalition government. In 1948 the Communist Party merged with the Social Democratic Party and took power.

Poland

Poles and Russians had a history of conflict. In London there was a Polish government in exile. In Poland itself the Soviet Union created a government in the city of Lublin. A compromise government was formed in June 1945, but it was mainly the same as Lublin government.

Elections were held in January 1947. The election was stage-managed to give the impression that the government had the backing of the people; an alliance of left-wing parties, including the communists, were said to have won 80% of the vote, but there is evidence that the real figure (even after the intimidation of rival parties) was more likely 50% or less. A coalition government made up of several parties ruled Poland; the Communist Party had five positions in a cabinet of 24. However, these included the important roles in charge of security, economy and education. Opposition politicians were arrested, locked up or even murdered.

Romania

Romania was another wartime German ally. Soviet troops remained in place once the Germans had been pushed back. A coalition government was formed in 1945; important posts were reserved for communists. There was a gradual takeover of the police and security services. In 1946 falsified elections produced an overwhelming victory for the communists and their allies. Show trials were used to eliminate political opponents. In December 1947, King Michael was forced to **abdicate**.

Bulgaria

In Bulgaria (Germany's former ally), a coalition containing communists was formed called the Fatherland Front. Gradually, this government was purged of anti-communist rivals. In 1946 the monarchy was abolished. In 1947 a new constitution was implemented that destroyed any opposition to the communists.

Yugoslavia

Yugoslavia was not part of the Soviet Empire. Josip Broz (known as Tito) was a communist but he led the liberation of his country from the Nazis. Stalin was tempted to invade Yugoslavia once Tito showed he was not going to be controlled from Moscow, but decided against it because of Tito's immense popularity. Yugoslavia remained an independent, communist country throughout the Cold War.

Iran

Although Stalin established a secure sphere of influence in the **Soviet Bloc** by the end of 1948, he was not successful everywhere. In 1946, he broke an agreement with the British to leave oil-rich Iran six months after the end of the war. It was only after pressure from the USA and the United Nations Security Council that Soviet troops left.

Turkey

In Turkey, Stalin demanded a naval base for the Soviet Union on the Dardanelles, a narrow strait linking the Black Sea and the Mediterranean. The Soviets sent ships to the area to increase pressure on the Turkish government. However, when Stalin found out that the USA and the British were supporting Turkey, he reconsidered.

> **KEY TERMS**
>
> **Exile:** a person who has been forced out of or escaped their own country; also the process of driving out or fleeing; also the state of being in a foreign country against your will.
>
> **Soviet Bloc:** the group of east-European states that were aligned with the Soviet Union, taking their political direction from Moscow. It is also sometimes called the Communist Bloc or the Eastern Bloc.

Source 4Q: A British cartoon from March 1946 showing Winston Churchill, the British wartime Prime Minister, taking a look at developments in Eastern Europe.

CHECK YOUR UNDERSTANDING 4.3

1 What were Stalin's motives in building the Soviet bloc in Eastern Europe?

2 On the evidence you have seen so far, which of the countries that made up Eastern Europe was: a) easiest to control and b) hardest to control in the period 1945–1948?

3 Which of these words describe the way that Stalin gained control of Eastern Europe by 1948? Which countries do they apply to?

- violence
- threats
- democratic elections
- popular support
- illegal and undemocratic methods
- propaganda
- cautious and careful.

4 Why wasn't it possible for the United States President Harry Truman to influence or intervene in events behind the Iron Curtain?

ACTIVITY 4.10

1 What is being shown in Source 4Q and what does it mean?

2 Look back at Source 4A. What was it about Yugoslavia's geographical position that may have helped it stay outside the Soviet empire?

4.3 How did the USA react to Soviet expansionism?

Some historians argue that Truman played a significant role in worsening USA–Soviet relations, particularly in the way he reacted to Soviet expansionism in Eastern Europe.

Truman's policy towards the USSR

The president's policy towards the USSR was very different to that of his predecessor, FDR. Where FDR had been flexible, Truman was hard-line; where FDR got on well with Stalin, Truman was more cautious.

Truman appointed Averell Harriman as the US Ambassador to the Soviet Union; Harriman did not trust the Soviet leadership. Lend–Lease aid to the Soviet Union was suddenly ended on 11 May 1945. All of this set the tone for the final conference of the war at Potsdam, outside Berlin.

The Potsdam conference started late because Truman wanted to learn the results of the test explosion of the world's first atomic bomb. While the Americans had shared this secret development with Britain, they had kept it from Stalin. Now Truman told Stalin that the USA had a new, powerful weapon. Stalin nodded: 'Use it well.' He knew about the bomb already, because Soviet spies inside the Manhattan Project were passing back information to scientists working on a Russian version. The atomic bomb did not make Stalin more flexible over Eastern Europe; the gradual Soviet takeover went on.

Some historians argue that one of the reasons Truman took the controversial decision to drop the atomic bomb on Japan was because he wanted to show Stalin the immense destructive power that the USA possessed. First Hiroshima and then Nagasaki were completely destroyed in August 1945 (see Source R). The war in the Pacific was over, but the Cold War had just begun.

"All the News That's Fit to Print"

The New York Times.

LATE CITY EDITION
Partly cloudy, less humid today.
Cloudy and warm tomorrow.

VOL. XCIV..No. 31.972. NEW YORK, TUESDAY, AUGUST 7, 1945. THREE CENTS NEW YORK CITY

FIRST ATOMIC BOMB DROPPED ON JAPAN; MISSILE IS EQUAL TO 20,000 TONS OF TNT; TRUMAN WARNS FOE OF A 'RAIN OF RUIN'

HIRAM W. JOHNSON, REPUBLICAN DEAN IN THE SENATE, DIES

Isolationist Helped Prevent U. S. Entry Into League—Opposed World Charter

CALIFORNIA EX-GOVERNOR

Ran for Vice President With Theodore Roosevelt in '12 —In Washington Since '17

Jet Plane Explosion Kills Major Bong, Top U.S. Ace

Flier Who Downed 40 Japanese Craft, Sent Home to Be 'Safe,' Was Flying New 'Shooting Star' as a Test Pilot

KYUSHU CITY RAZED

Kenney's Planes Blast Tarumizu in Record Blow From Okinawa

ROCKET SITE IS SEEN

125 B-29's Hit Japan's Toyokawa Naval Arsenal in Demolition Strike

REPORT BY BRITAIN

'By God's Mercy' We Beat Nazis to Bomb, Churchill Says

ROOSEVELT AID CITED

Raiders Wrecked Norse Laboratory in Race for Key to Victory

Steel Tower 'Vaporized' In Trial of Mighty Bomb

Scientists Awe-Struck as Blinding Flash Lighted New Mexico Desert and Great Cloud Bore 40,000 Feet Into Sky

NEW AGE USHERED

Day of Atomic Energy Hailed by President, Revealing Weapon

HIROSHIMA IS TARGET

'Impenetrable' Cloud of Dust Hides City After Single Bomb Strikes

Source 4R: The front page of *The New York Times*, 2 August 1945.

93

The Grand Alliance leaders never met again after Potsdam. To discuss the details of the four zones of occupation and reparations, the Foreign Ministers met later on in the year. The Grand Alliance had not yet broken up but agreements about the future of Europe, were proving increasingly difficult to make.

ACTIVITY 4.11

Study Sources 4R and 4S:

What do they tell you about US attitudes towards the Soviet Union?

Think back to Stalin's takeover of Eastern Europe. Does the poster in Source 4T exaggerate what happens when communists rule a country?

There isn't a doubt in my mind that Russia intends an invasion of Turkey and the seizure of the Black Sea Straits to the Mediterranean. Unless Russia is faced with an iron fist and strong language another war is in the making. Only one language do they understand – how many divisions (soldiers) have you? I'm tired of babying the Soviets.

Source 4S: President Truman criticises his Secretary of State Byrnes for being too trusting of Stalin, December 1945.

Source 4T: An American poster published in 1947.

Stalin presented his views to me. He said that whoever occupies a territory also imposes on it his own system. Someone expressed doubt that the Germans would be able to recuperate within fifty years. Stalin disagreed. No, they will recover very quickly. It is a highly industrialised country with a very skilled workforce. Give them twelve to fifteen years and they'll be on their feet again ...

Source 4U: A record of a discussion held with Stalin by a Yugoslavian communist in 1944.

Truman's advisers wondered what Stalin intentions were in Eastern Europe. In February 1946, some commentators interpreted a speech by Stalin as a threat of war. George Kennan worked in the American embassy in Moscow. Kennan sent a now-famous 'Long Telegram' to Washington later that month, describing his worries. He explained that Russia's hostility towards the outside world was centuries old. The Soviet rulers assumed that one day, capitalism and communism would fight. Stalin would constantly seek to extend Russian power. The USA should resist with a policy of containment.

Just a few weeks later, in March 1946, Churchill was invited by Truman to make a speech. This was called the Iron Curtain speech.

Source 4V: A photo of Soviet and American soldiers meeting at the River Elbe, in May 1945 as the two countries' armies, advancing from west and east, meet in the middle of Europe.

A shadow has fallen upon the scenes so lately lighted by the allied victory. Nobody knows what Soviet Russia and its communist international organisation intends to do in the immediate future.

From Stettin in the Baltic to Trieste in the Adriatic, an iron curtain has descended across the continent. Behind that line lie all the capitals of the ancient states of Central and Eastern Europe – Warsaw, Berlin, Prague,

---

ACTIVITY 4.12

1   Read Source 4U. Given what you know about the First World War and the Second World War, how accurate was Stalin's judgement about Germany?

2   Why would the British and Americans think that the recovery of Germany was a good development and not a negative one?

3   Look at Source 4T. Why is the image of USA–Soviet relations so different from Sources 3E and 3V?

Vienna, Budapest, Belgrade, Bucharest and Sofia ... all are subject in one form or another, not only to Soviet influence but to a high measure of control from Moscow.

The Communist parties, which were very small in all these Eastern European countries, have been raised to pre-eminence and power far beyond their numbers and are seeking everywhere to obtain totalitarian control. Police governments are prevailing in nearly every case, and so far, except in Czechoslovakia, there is no true democracy.

Source 4W: Part of Churchill's speech made at Fulton, Missouri in March 1946.

After the Soviet Union refused to withdraw from Iran six months after the end of the Second World War, it was Truman's pressure and disguised military threat to the Soviets that made Stalin withdraw the Red Army soldiers. American magazine *Newsweek* warned that 'the Soviet government has made up its mind that capitalism must be destroyed if communism is to live'. Truman's 'iron fist' approach seemed to be supported by an analysis of intelligence data – the Clifford Report concluded that the Soviet Union was expansionist and was targeting Greece and Turkey to gain access to the Mediterranean Sea.

ACTIVITY 4.13

Study Source 4W. Both Churchill's speech and Kennan's Long Telegram became famous and they were certainly read in Moscow. Put together, what do you think was the reaction of the Soviet leadership? Which of statements would have upset them the most? Why?

What finally ended the Grand Alliance?

In 1946, it seemed to Britain and the USA that communism was on the march everywhere. In France and Italy, the communist parties were popular and likely to do well in elections. In Greece, a civil war was raging with the British supporting one side and Yugoslav leader Tito the other. Stalin kept the Soviet Union away from the Greek conflict. For one thing, he had agreed that Greece would be part of the western allies' sphere of influence; for another, he wanted the fighting in Europe to be over.

In February 1947, an urgent telegram arrived at the White House: the British government could no longer afford to intervene in Greece and Turkey. It would withdraw its soldiers soon. The White House panicked. Truman and his advisers could see Greece turning communist unless something was done, and done quickly.

Truman Doctrine

At the present moment in world history, nearly every nation must choose between alternative ways of life. The choice is too often not a free one. One way of life is based on the will of the majority and is distinguished by free institutions, guarantees of individual liberty, freedom of speech and religion and freedom from political oppression. The second way of life is based upon the will of the minority forcibly imposed on the majority. It relies upon terror and oppression, a controlled press and radio, fixed elections and the suppression of personal freedoms. I believe it must be the policy of the United States to support free peoples who are resisting subjugation by armed minorities or by outside pressures. The seeds of totalitarian regimes are nurtured by misery and want. They grow in the evil soil of poverty and strife. The free peoples of the world look to us for support in maintaining their freedoms.

Source 4X: On 12 March 1947, President Truman addressed Congress. His speech signalled a turning point in American foreign policy and set the scene for the next four decades of Cold War conflict. This became known as the Truman Doctrine.

ACTIVITY 4.14

1 Look back at Source 4A: what does it add to your understanding of Congress accepting the Truman Doctrine and voting for financial aid to Greece and Turkey?

2 Look at Source 4X. Why didn't President Truman name the Soviet Union in his speech?

3 Source 4Y suggests that Stalin did not like President Truman's Doctrine. Why has the cartoonist put Truman's statement in a pipe? What reasons would Stalin have for disliking the Doctrine?

Source 4Y: A US cartoon showing Stalin's reaction to news of the Truman Doctrine.

THE MARSHALL TREE

Source 4Z: A cartoon illustrating attitudes towards the Marshall Plan in 1948.

Congress voted for an immediate $400m in aid to be sent to Greece and Turkey without delay. Under the Truman Doctrine, the USA reversed the attitude it had adopted when Congress refused to back Wilson and join the League of

THE RIVAL BUSES

Source 4AA: A British cartoon published in *Punch* magazine on 18 June 1947.

Nations. Now the country had an open-ended commitment to fight communism anywhere in the world. Historian Daniel Yergin argues that after the crisis in Greece, 'American leaders saw a Russian mastermind at work in every local crisis'.

ACTIVITY 4.15

Study Source 4Z. Using details from the image, describe what the cartoon is depicting and what its message is. Does it seem to you to offer a fair and balanced comment?

Study Source 4AA. To what developments is the cartoon referring? Is the cartoon an accurate representation of those developments?

FACT FILE

The purpose of Cominform was to coordinate actions between the various communist parties under Soviet direction. It was a Soviet-dominated organisation of communist parties founded in September 1947 at a conference in Poland. Soviet leader, Josef Stalin, called the conference in response to signs that some East European governments were thinking of joining the Marshall Plan. After realising Stalin's opposition to this move, none of them did.

Marshall Plan

The Truman Doctrine was closely followed by the necessary economic aid. It was not possible for the US President to introduce a new policy without the necessary resources to back it up.

The new resources were announced by Secretary of State George Marshall in June 1947. The European Recovery Programme, or 'Marshall Plan' as it is almost always called, was intended to help Europe recover economically and so prevent the growth of communism. A total of $13.3 billion was invested in Europe between 1948 and 1953. The Plan was offered to all European countries – capitalist and communist alike. The USSR rejected the idea of offering help to Germany, as it broke the Potsdam agreement of July 1945. Suspicious of America's motives, they refused to take part and instructed their allies in the Soviet Bloc to refuse also. All complied obediently.

How did the Soviet Union react?

Stalin was not upset by the Truman Doctrine, but was concerned by the Marshall Plan. The plan was against Soviet interests. If any east European country accepted the invitation, their economy would be tied to that of the USA. In turn, this would undermine Soviet control. Stalin could not allow this to happen.

In response to the Marshall Plan, Stalin convened a meeting of Communist Party leaders in September 1947. At that conference, the leaders were left in no doubt about the threat to communism created by the Plan. The Soviet response was the creation of Cominform (Communist Information Bureau).

CHECK YOUR UNDERSTANDING 4.4

1 Why do you think some countries did not receive any Marshall Aid?
2 The Soviets called Marshall Aid 'dollar imperialism'. What do you think they meant?
3 The list below gives factors that resulted in the Truman Doctrine and the Marshall Plan. Rank them in order of significance and explain your decisions.
   a ideological differences
   b fear of another Great Depression
   c the British decision to withdraw from Turkey and Greece
   d the post-war economic problems in Europe
   e Kennan's Long Telegram
   f Churchill's Iron Curtain speech.

4.4 What were the consequences of the Berlin Blockade?

The Grand Alliance was finally broken by the developments in 1947. A Cold War had broken out in full public view.

What to do with Germany?

After the First World War, German delegates had to sign the Treaty of Versailles. After the Second World War no such treaty was drafted and no one from Germany was required to sign it. Why was this?

The question of what to do with Germany split the Grand Alliance. There was broad agreement that:

- The country would be divided into four zones, each administered by an ally – France, UK, USA, USSR. A conference would then agree Germany's future shape and nature.
- Berlin, the capital, would also be divided into four zones.
- The Soviet Union could take reparations from Germany.
- Poland's border would be moved to the west to the Oder-Neisse River.
- The Grand Alliance agreed to de-Nazify, demilitarise and democratise Germany.
- Governing Germany would be the job of the Allied Control Council. This would decide matters that affected the whole country.

Meetings did take place to discuss in greater detail the future of Germany; for example, the London Conference between September and October in 1945. However, each time the Foreign Ministers met there were more disagreements – there were very few joint decisions. This was because each side took a different approach to Germany.

The contrasting views and aims of the western allies and the USSR

Aims of Britain, France and the USA	Aims of the Soviet Union
The western governments remembered the lessons from the end of the First World War: a humiliating and punitive peace treaty would only create resentment and lead to the wish for revenge.	The Soviet Union remembered the invasions in 1914 and 1941. Germany was defeated but it would soon recover and pose a future threat to Soviet security. It had to be punished and weakened economically so that it would not have the resources to start another war.
The German economy was vital for the whole of Europe and the USA saw it as a good market for American goods. Therefore, it was important that it recovered and the USA could help by giving it Marshall Aid.	Germany had to be stripped of its industrial resources and the equipment taken back to the Soviet Union to help its economy rebuild itself. Reparations amounting to $20 billion were to be taken by, or given to, the Soviet Union.

The Grand Alliance splits apart, 1947–1948

In 1945, the USA had turned down a Soviet request for a loan to cover the cost of occupying the eastern zone in Germany. The London conference had resulted in deadlock about the future of Germany.

In January 1947, Britain and the USA created a single economic unit called the Bizone (or 'Bizonia') out of their respective German zones. The French added their zone a year later: Trizone. Stalin was worried that the western powers were no longer interested in agreeing on the future for the whole of Germany.

The Moscow Conference of Foreign Ministers met forty-three times in March 1947; once again no agreements were made. In March 1947, the three western powers agreed to unite their zones politically, that is, into one government for all three zones.

The USA decided to make Marshall Aid available to the western zones of Germany. Stalin reacted by stopping and searching all freight shipments into West Berlin.

In June 1948, the western powers introduced a brand new currency for use in all four German zones. The Soviets refused to allow this in their eastern zone.

The Berlin Blockade and the Berlin airlift

Stalin reacted to the new currency by cutting off West Berlin by water, road and rail; then, he turned off the gas and electricity. He hoped to force the western powers out of the city so he could bring the entire city under Soviet rule. His advisers told Stalin that they thought the West Berliners and the western powers would surrender after four to six weeks because they could not survive without essentials like fuel and food.

The western response had to be carefully thought out. The wrong move could spark a war. Only a year earlier, President Truman had publicly stated his Doctrine: doing nothing would mean the American policy was meaningless. However, if he tried to use force to open the roads and railways, this might provoke a military response.

Britain, the USA and France jointly agreed not to give in and promised to supply the West Berliners with supplies from the air. Over the next eleven months, the three airports in West Berlin had regular landings by aircraft full of coal, food and fuel for the isolated citizens. Children who fell ill were flown out of the city so they could have medical help in the West. By 1949, planes were landing every 90 seconds in a constant queue of airlifted supplies; in all, 277,000 flights over eleven months fed the city. Although the airlift appeared to be an entirely unselfish act, you should note that West Berlin was a nest of espionage and intelligence gathering. Losing such a wonderful base in East Germany would harm opportunities for spying and reduce the impact of western propaganda broadcasts by radio.

What could Stalin do? His advisers had misjudged the West. The six weeks projected deadline came and went. He dared not shoot down any plane for fear of sparking a military response. Instead, the Soviets tried to block radio signals. This had little effect. In the end, Stalin lifted the blockade in May 1949.

The Berlin Blockade transformed the West's public perception of Berlin from being a supporter of Nazism to being the symbolic island of freedom and democracy. The city from now on had to be protected whatever the cost.

THE BIRD WATCHER

Source 4BB: A British cartoon from 1948 showing the Berlin Airlift and Stalin.

ACTIVITY 4.16

Look at Sources 4BB and 4CC. Why didn't Stalin issue orders to shoot down the planes before they reached West Berliners?

Is Source 4BB a pro-western cartoon or a pro-Soviet one? Use details to explain your answer.

The blockade was over, but it had signalled the end of the Grand Alliance. The division of Europe was now complete and lasted for over forty years. The Iron Curtain was in place. Truman wrote this:

> **The Berlin Blockade was a move to test our capacity and will to resist. This action and the previous attempts to take over Greece and Turkey were part of a Russian plan to probe for soft spots in the Western Allies' positions all around their own perimeter.**

Formation of NATO

Politicians in western Europe were worried that Stalin would continue to look for weaknesses to exploit and to follow his expansionist policies. The fear remained that

Source 4CC: A photo of supplies arriving by plane for the West Berliners during the Berlin Blockade.

he might launch an invasion of western Europe. So, in April 1949, west European governments asked the USA for a military commitment to Europe. Truman agreed to join and lead the North Atlantic Treaty Organization or NATO. This was a significant change American foreign policy and underlined the genuine fear of the USSR and of communism that existed in the USA and in western Europe. Along with the USA, eleven other countries became members: Britain, France, Canada, Italy, Denmark, Iceland, Norway, Portugal, Belgium, Holland and Luxembourg. This new organisation had one central purpose: an armed attack against one or more of them would be considered an attack on all. This was collective security.

Once NATO was in place, the western powers stopped waiting for the Soviets to agree on the future of Germany. Instead, in May 1949, the formal unification of the western zones took place: the Trizone was now the **Federal Republic of Germany (West Germany)**. A new constitution was agreed and national elections were held in August 1949. Konrad Adenauer, leader of the right-wing Christian Democrats, became the first Chancellor (Prime Minister) of West Germany. Although responsibility for the internal development of FRG was now in Adenauer's hands, the country's foreign policy was still controlled by the western powers until 1951.

West Berlin was not part of West Germany so British, French and American soldiers remained there to defend the city from an attack.

The Soviets reacted quickly to the creation of West Germany. In October 1949, the new German Democratic Republic (East Germany) was announced. East Berlin was part of East Germany and became the country's capital. All government responsibilities were in the hands of the communist Socialist Unity Party created in 1946 by the forced merger of the Social Democratic Party and the German Communist Party in the Soviet Zone.

Although the USSR did not immediately create a military alliance to oppose NATO, it did tighten its control over its satellite states. In January 1949, the Council for Mutual Economic Assistance (COMECON) was created to coordinate the development of the national economies of each of the Soviet Bloc countries. Each of the east European economies would develop along similar lines to that of the Soviet Union.

In August 1949, the Soviet Union successfully tested its first atomic bomb. Now, the USA no longer had a monopoly on atomic weapons. The nuclear arms race had begun and would continue throughout the Cold War.

The Berlin Blockade was the first Cold War crisis. Both sides had survived without any military force being used. Now that each side possessed nuclear weapons, great care had to be taken not to provoke the enemy into firing them. In this sense, although the blockade was a crisis, it actually stabilised the superpower relationship. The situation in Berlin now settled down.

In May 1955, West Germany joined NATO with the condition that it could have no biological, chemical or atomic weapons. Britain and the USA promised to base troops in West Germany.

Formation of the Warsaw Pact

The response from the Soviet Bloc to these developments in western Europe was to create a central command for their armed forces. On 14 May 1955, eight communist countries agreed to unify their armed forces. The principle

of collective security behind NATO was now in place for Eastern Europe.

The Warsaw Pact central command was dominated by the Soviet Union. The commander-in-chief was always a Soviet army officer. The same can be said of the deputy and the three branches of the armed forces: army, navy and air force. These military developments tightened further the Soviet Union's control of Eastern Europe.

CHECK YOUR UNDERSTANDING 4.5

1   'No one wanted Germany to be divided after 1945, but it still happened.' What were the key factors that resulted in a divided Germany by 1949?

2   'Fear' is the key to understanding the Berlin Blockade and its failure. Do you agree with this explanation of the Blockade?

3   Historian Mary Fulbrook wrote: 'It is conceivable that Germany could have remained united, as a neutral power (as was the case with Austria), with the Iron Curtain running along a different frontier.' What would need to have been different for this outcome to have happened?

4.5 Who was the more to blame for starting the Cold War: the USA or the USSR?

If you look back to the section 'What was the Cold War?' you will remember that two different views of the Cold War were given: one blamed the Cold War on the USSR, the other on the USA. In this section you will have the opportunity to make a final judgement. Perhaps you think that both superpowers were to blame or that one was more to blame than the other. Whatever your judgement you will need to back it up with evidence.

This section will sum up the arguments and evidence on both sides and leave you to decide.

In what ways was the USSR to blame for the Cold War?

Communism was an ideology that was naturally expansionist. The USSR view of the future was that communism could not coexist with capitalism, one or the other had to die. From the West's point of view, Stalin intended to impose communism on as many countries as possible.

Evidence

Stalin did not stick to the Yalta agreement. Between February 1945 and July when the Potsdam conference took place, communist governments were installed in Poland and Romania. By the end of 1948, communists controlled all of Eastern Europe.

Stalin did not appreciate the importance that Truman and Churchill placed on free elections for the liberated countries. Democracy was not important in Stalin's peace-making; he wanted friendly governments bordering the USSR.

The creation of COMECON made sure that each part of the Soviet Bloc followed the same economic model as the Soviet Union. The establishment of COMINFORM is evidence that he intended to undermine capitalist countries through national communist parties.

Stalin's personality

The personality of the Soviet leader was a significant factor in bringing about the Cold War. He was obsessed with his country's security and defence and was paranoid about his own safety. He could not allow liberated countries to be anti-Soviet.

Although Stalin had advisers and listened to their advice he made the final decisions about Soviet foreign policy. He was also the one leader who was a constant; in other countries, leaders came and went. He was in power during the Second World War, he attended the wartime conferences and he saw the division of Europe by an Iron Curtain.

CHECK YOUR UNDERSTANDING 4.6

Now you have read the evidence, put it in rank order of importance to show that the USSR was to blame for starting the Cold War.

How can Stalin's role in the Cold War be defended?

The role of the USSR and of Stalin in particular can be defended using the following evidence.

Some historians argue that the West did not fully appreciate the Soviet Union's security concerns at the end of the war. Russia had been invaded three times in fifty years (1914, 1918 and 1941). Furthermore, Stalin believed that the West's policy of appeasement in the 1930s was a deliberate plan to allow Nazi Germany to expand eastwards rather than westwards.

Stalin's suspicions of the West were confirmed by examples of wartime secrecy. The USA had not shared the atomic bomb with its Grand Alliance partner. In addition, Britain and the USA had refused to open a second front to relieve the pressure on the Red Army fighting the Germans in the east.

In April 1945, President Roosevelt died. His successor, Harry Truman, took a harder line with the Soviets in discussions and stopped the Lend–Lease loans to the USSR.

Taken together, Sources 4U and 4DD explain why Stalin was so concerned about security for the USSR. A revived Germany was a nightmare for Stalin; Germany had to be crushed and kept neutral.

ACTIVITY 4.17

What evidence can you see in Source 4EE that could be used to *defend* Stalin from the charge that he was to blame for starting the Cold War?

In what ways was the USA to blame for the Cold War?

Argument 1: 'Dollar Imperialism' was the motive for USA involvement in Europe.

The economy in the USA had recovered from the Great Depression during the Second World War. In fact, it did more than recover, it doubled in size. President Truman and his advisers were worried that, once peace arrived and the US military forces came home, there would be another economic slump. To stop another depression, it is argued that the USA needed to have a European market for the goods it was producing.

Evidence

The USA ended its Lend–Lease arrangements with the USSR in 1945; ships that were on their way to the Soviet Union were turned around back to the USA. Stalin had no warning of this. Marshall Aid was really designed to ensure the recovery of a capitalist, free-market Europe so that Europeans could buy American goods.

The creation of Bizonia and then Trizonia was a clear breach of the Potsdam agreement and was an attempt to introduce capitalism across the whole of Germany.

World War II Deaths

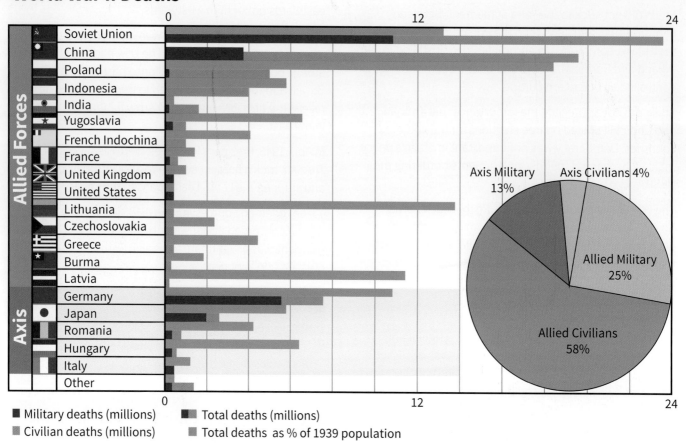

- ■ Military deaths (millions)
- ■ Civilian deaths (millions)
- ■ Total deaths (millions)
- ■ Total deaths as % of 1939 population

Source 4DD: A table showing the comparisons of deaths by country during the Second World War.

Argument 2: President Truman did not trust the Soviets' words or deeds.

Truman had been confrontational with the USSR after Roosevelt died in April 1945 and this soured Soviet–US relations. He believed having and using the atomic bomb would make it easier to impose his will on the Soviet Union. This is one of the reasons he ordered the bombs to be dropped. The Truman Doctrine and Marshall Plan were seen by the USSR as provocative and designed to isolate the USSR. Why wasn't their enormous wartime sacrifice being properly rewarded?

The foreign policy of the USA is characterized by a striving for world supremacy.
The real meaning of the many statements by President Truman and others is that the United States has the right to lead the world. All the forces of American diplomacy – the army, the air force, the navy, industry, and science – are enlisted in the service of this policy. [They have established] a system of naval and air bases stretching far beyond the boundaries of the United States, through the arms race, and through the creation of ever newer types of weapons.

Source 4EE: Part of the 'Novikov Telegram' sent by the Soviet Ambassador to the USA, Nikolai Novikov on 27 September 1946.

How can the role of the USA be defended?

The role of the USA and of President Truman in particular can be defended using the following evidence.

Stalin's dismissive attitude towards the 'London Poles' illustrated his wish to break the wartime agreements. The Truman Doctrine was a defensive and not an offensive reaction to the developments in Greece and Turkey. West European governments invited and welcomed the Marshall Plan. They had a choice and made it freely to join the European Recovery Programme. This is in contrast to Stalin's forcible takeover of Eastern Europe by 1948.

ACTIVITY 4.18

Now you have read the evidence, put it in rank order of importance to show that Truman was to blame for starting the Cold War.

What evidence can you see in Sources 4FF and 4GG that could be used to defend Truman from the charge that he was to blame for starting the Cold War?

Source 4GG: A USA cartoon from March 1948 showing the Soviet 'bear' approaching a desperate Western Europe.

Source 4FF: A pro-western poster to celebrate the Marshall Plan and its impact.

CHECK YOUR UNDERSTANDING 4.7

1   President Truman was under pressure at the start of the Cold War. Congress and public opinion after the war swung against the Soviet Union. Why did Truman have to take account of other views, but Stalin did not?

2   Why was the Soviet Union affected more badly by the war than the USA?

3   'Truman and not Stalin was more to blame for starting the Cold War.' How far do you agree with this view?

Review your learning

The Cold War lasted approximately 45 years. It came after the Second World War ended when the two superpowers were the only Great Powers left after the most deadly war in history, with the UK and France, Japan and Germany all severely weakened. From 1941 to 1945 the USA and USSR were partners with Great Britain in the Grand Alliance. Although all three partners agreed on some broad aspects of the peace, they disagreed about the detail. In spite of conference after conference, the Cold War broke out because of their conflicting objectives and priorities. Trust no longer existed; the Grand Alliance shattered. Instead of partnership there was hostility; instead of cooperation there was mistrust; instead of open discussion there was espionage.

Historians disagree about the causes of the Cold War so you need to assess the factors, weigh them up and make up your own mind about the key question. Make sure you support your argument with evidence. Make sure you can answer the five questions listed at the beginning of this chapter as Focus points; then you will have enough evidence for you to attempt Key Question 4.

Summary points

- The USSR and the USA were allies in the Second World War, with Nazi Germany, Fascist Italy and militarist Japan as common enemies.

- Being in the Grand Alliance didn't mean the members agreed about more than the importance of defeating the enemy.

- Even during the war there were disputes.

- Once the enemy was defeated, the motive for cooperating disappeared, and soon cooperation did too.

- Each side misunderstood the views and needs of the other, both felt threatened.

- The USSR succeeded in holding on to the territories taken during the defeat of Germany.

- The USA was determined to contain the USSR, preventing it from pushing its power and influence any further.

- East Europe would be regarded as a Soviet victory, but the Berlin Blockade and airlift were a USA victory.

The Big Challenge

You need to be able to explain why a Cold War broke out.

First, with a partner, discuss what you think the year was in which you think the Cold War began. Write a short paragraph explaining your choice. If your partner disagrees with you, summarise both their opinion and why you disagree with it.

| 1943 | 1944 | 1945 | 1946 | 1947 | 1948 |

Second, discuss with your partner why the Cold War broke out. Below is a list of possible causes. Put them in order of importance.

- Ideological differences
- Security needs
- Economic opportunities
- Disagreements over German and Poland
- Personalities of Stalin and Truman
- Truman Doctrine and Marshall Plan.

Write a paragraph explaining why you chose that order, particularly drawing attention to the cause you think is the most important. If you and your partner reached different conclusions and put the items in different orders, summarise their opinion and explain why you disagree with it.

Third, discuss why it was a 'cold' not a 'hot' war: how did the crises not lead to a Third World War? Write a paragraph explaining what you think and why you think it. As before, discuss your partner's opinions and how far you agree or disagree with them. Remember, this is a speculative activity, but you still need to put forward evidence. The point is that what happens in history should not be regarded as inevitable. Thinking about what didn't happen (and why) can support our understanding of what did (and why).

Exam-style questions

1   What was agreed and what was left undecided at the Yalta Conference in February 1945?

2   What role did ideological differences play in starting the Cold War?

3   How significant was George Kennan's Long Telegram in shaping Truman's decision to contain communism?

4   Following the Potsdam Conference, what caused an increase in tension between the Soviet Union and the West?

5   What methods did Stalin use to take over Eastern Europe between 1945 and 1948?

6   What was the Truman Doctrine and why was it important in ending the Grand Alliance?

7   What was the Marshall Plan and why was it important in ending the Grand Alliance?

8   'It was Stalin's fear of what the western powers were doing in their German zones that made him Blockade Berlin.' How far do you agree with this statement? Explain your answer.

9   Why was NATO formed in 1949?

10   'The start of the Cold War can be blamed on the Soviet Union in general and on Stalin in particular'. To what extent do you agree with this view?

Chapter 5

Key Question 5: How effectively did the USA contain the spread of communism?

Focus points

- Case study 1: USA and events in Korea, 1950–1953
- Case study 2: USA and events in Cuba, 1959–1962
- Case study 3: American involvement in Vietnam

What is this enquiry about?

When Lenin's Bolshevik party came to power in Russia in 1917 it was not well received internationally. The USA was one of several powers who sent troops to fight in the Russian Civil War (1918–1921) hoping to destroy the new communist regime. This failed, and no American president would recognise the communist government in Moscow until Franklin Delano Roosevelt in 1933. The need to unite to fight fascism during the Second World War meant the two powers then became allies in 1941. This was a temporary alliance: events after 1945 showed that the relationship between the world's two remaining superpowers could not remain friendly.

From 1950 to 1973 there were many tests of the policy of containment, but three major examples stand out: the Korean War, the Cuban Missile Crisis and the war in Vietnam. This chapter assesses the results of these interventions and asks you to reach a judgement about the success of the policy of containment. After studying these three examples you will need to return to this question. To reach a judgement you will need to:

- Understand the cause and consequence of each event.
- Evaluate American policy and strategy – what were they trying to achieve and how close did they come to success?
- Assess whether the threat of communism had increased or decreased after a quarter of a century of containment.

5.1 Case study 1: USA and events in Korea, 1950–1953

Background to a crisis

In January 1950, President Truman ordered a review of the USA's foreign policy. This was in response to the increasing level of threat that developed in 1948 and 1949. Several incidents had raised concerns about the global spread of communism:

- 1948: Czechoslovakia was taken over by a communist government.
- 1948–1949: the Berlin Blockade brought the two superpowers close to conflict.
- 1949: the communists finally won the Chinese civil war under Mao.
- 1949: the USSR produced a nuclear weapon, at least three years in advance of American estimates.

FACT FILE

Chairman Mao

In the Chinese Revolution of 1949, the communists under Mao Zedong defeated the US-backed Nationalists led by Chiang Kai-Shek. This came at the end of an intense civil war from 1945 to 1949 in which Chiang received significant amounts of support from President Truman. However, his forces were poorly led and corrupt commanders even sold their new weapons to Mao's men. The victory raised fears in Washington as China was a member of the **UN Security Council**. It increased the possibility of communism spreading in Asia. Communist forces were also fighting for control of Indochina and the Philippines.

KEY TERM

UN Security Council: the main decision-making body of the UN for military and security matters. It has 15 members in total, 5 permanent and 10 temporary. The 5 permanent members are the USA, Britain, China, France and Russia (previously the USSR). At Stalin's insistence, each permanent member had the power of veto, which meant they could block any measure.

The result of Truman's investigation was National Security Council report 68 (or 'NSC 68'), which outlined four options:

1. Continue with the USA's existing policies.
2. Fight a preventative war to block Soviet expansion.
3. Withdraw behind the shield of 'fortress USA' and do nothing about the expansion of communism around the world.
4. Start a programme of massive rearmament to surpass the forces available to communism.

Truman chose the fourth option. USA armed forces had been run down since 1945, but now they were to be expanded. Containment was to be put forcefully into practice. This remained American policy until the end of the Vietnam War.

What caused the Korean War?

From 1910 to 1945 Korea had been ruled as a colony by Japan. Young Koreans were taught at school in the Japanese language and all political opposition was banned. Koreans were used as conscripts as the Japanese waged war from 1937 to 1945. When the war ended Korea was liberated by Soviet troops in the North and American troops in the South. As in Germany, the country was divided and ruled by occupying forces. The dividing line was the 38th parallel.

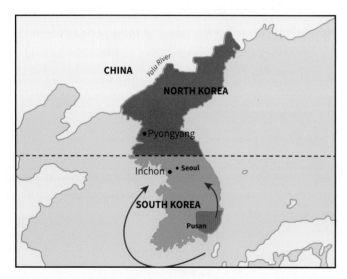

Figure 5.1: A map of the Korean peninsular, showing the 38th parallel, which divided North Korea from South Korea. Note how close both capitals, Pyongyang and Seoul, are to the border. Note also how small is the area of Pusan, to which the South retreated, and how bold MacArthur's counter-attack on Inchon was.

Korean communists in the North were led by Kim Il-sung. During the Second World War he was in Moscow and was trained for leadership by Stalin. In the South, anti-communists led by Syngman Rhee were installed as the new government by the Americans. All foreign troops withdrew in 1949 after agreement was reached in the UN. However, fighting soon broke out between northern and southern forces along the border.

Source 5A: A huge statue of Kim Il-sung in Pyongyang, North Korea. He was succeeded by his son and grandson, who continued to develop his cult of personality.

Kim Il-sung was keen to reunite Korea under his leadership but knew that conquering the South would require outside assistance. He approached Stalin in early 1949 but his proposal for an invasion was rejected as the Berlin Blockade was still going on. A year later and Stalin's mood was different. The development of nuclear weapons and the Chinese revolution made an invasion of the South much easier. He gave Kim Il-sung his support; on 25 June 1950 the North launched a full-scale invasion of the South. Source 5D shows a western view of Stalin's role and how the USSR presented it.

It was a formidable force numbering 200,000 troops – 10,000 of whom had been specially trained in the USSR. Another 40,000 had gained experience fighting in the Chinese Civil War 1945–1949. These soldiers were also supplied with Soviet equipment such as T-34 tanks. Southern forces were ill-equipped, poorly trained and numbered no more than 100,000. They were soon retreating as the North Koreans poured over the 38th parallel. The capital city, Seoul, was taken swiftly, and all Korea was occupied, except for Pusan in the far south (see Figure 5.1).

American reactions to the invasion of South Korea

Although the invasion came as a surprise, the USA had been watching events closely in the Korean peninsula. Experience of directly running South Korean affairs from 1945 to 1948 had not been easy. Rhee was elected president in 1948, however, the South was deeply divided politically and Rhee ruled as a dictator. In April 1950 he performed poorly in elections due to corruption in his government. While the USA had been quite happy to withdraw their forces from 1948 to 1949, the changing events in Asia made them reconsider giving strong support to Rhee as the best hope for containment.

A second reason for US interest in Asia concerned the reaction to the Chinese revolution of October 1949. Mao was now in power in China but the USA refused to accept this; they continued to recognise Chiang Kai-shek as the rightful leader. He had lost the civil war and escaped to Taiwan in 1949. Events at the United Nations took a surprising turn in January 1950 when the USSR refused to attend the Security Council over the failure to accept Mao's government. They were still refusing to attend Security Council meetings in June when South Korea was invaded. This gave the Americans a unique opportunity to use the UN to establish a coalition of powers against the spread of communism.

CHECK YOUR UNDERSTANDING 5.2

Consider the motives for US involvement in Korea. Which of the two reasons for the USA entering the war was more significant and why?

President Truman appealed to the UN to come to the aid of Rhee. The response was remarkably quick (see Source 5C). On 27 June it ordered member nations to support the South. Truman sent American forces from Japan led by General Douglas MacArthur, a US general from the Second World War Pacific campaign with a formidable reputation. Another fourteen nations contributed to the UN army and five sent medical support. This was the first time that the UN had gathered an international army and it was determined to show that it was stronger and more capable than its predecessor, the League of Nations.

Korea is a small country, thousands of miles away, but what is happening there is important to every American.

On Sunday, June 25th, Communist forces attacked the Republic of Korea.

This attack has made it clear, beyond all doubt, that the international Communist movement is willing to use armed invasion to conquer independent nations. An act of aggression such as this creates a very real danger to the security of all free nations.

The attack upon Korea was an outright breach of the peace and a violation of the Charter of the United Nations. By their actions in Korea, Communist leaders have demonstrated their contempt for the basic moral principles on which the United Nations is founded. This is a direct challenge to the efforts of the free nations to build the kind of world in which men can live in freedom and peace.

This challenge has been presented squarely. We must meet it squarely …

Source 5B: Truman's televised speech on 19 July 1950.

CHECK YOUR UNDERSTANDING 5.3

Look at Source 5B. Was Truman right in claiming that events in Korea were 'important to every American'? In what ways does this source add support to the policy of containment?

The course of the war, 1950–1953

The events of any war can often seem confusing so it helps to break them down into clear phases.

Phase 1: liberating the South

The early success of the northern forces saw Rhee's army surrounded in Pusan. Even the American forces who had landed early had been unable to do much to prevent this. They were told they would be back in Japan within six weeks and not to pack much equipment. Instead, they found themselves in a heavy battle. MacArthur's response was to launch a bold amphibious landing further north that would allow him to cut off the northern army. In September, he landed his forces at Inchon in the west of the peninsula (see Figure 5.1). This was a very difficult task as there was a sea wall and dangerous conditions for landing the boats. Despite this he managed to get his forces on land and defeated the communist troops. By early October they had retaken Seoul and reached the 38th parallel.

CHECK YOUR UNDERSTANDING 5.4

Look at Figure 5.1. What were the intentions of MacArthur's strategy?

Phase 2: 'rollback' – the UN invasion of the North

The original mission had been completed. The South had been freed from communist forces, which meant that containment had been achieved. Yet MacArthur was keen to move beyond the 38th parallel and roll back communism – and not just in North Korea but perhaps also in China. He saw this as a great opportunity not only to prevent communism from spreading but also to make it disappear in Asia.

Truman was less enthusiastic, but when he arrived in Korea to meet MacArthur it was clear which man was in control. MacArthur accepted a medal from Truman but declined to meet the President for lunch to discuss strategy. Instead, he got back to work to prepare his invasion of the North. Despite the Chinese warning that they would get involved, MacArthur sent his forces across the border and pushed onwards throughout late October. In November, the Chinese responded by sending 500,000 troops, whom they called 'volunteers' across the Yalu River, which marks the border with North Korea.

ACTIVITY 5.3

Assessing change and continuity: Did this mark a continuation of containment (as MacArthur thought) or was it a significant change to the policy (as Truman thought)?

Phase 3: the Chinese counter-attack

It was at this point that UN forces began to struggle. The Chinese were less well armed but had superior numbers. The cold conditions caused guns to jam, which removed any advantage the UN soldiers had in terms of equipment. China also had aerial support from Russian MiG-15s which were faster than American planes, could fly higher and had superior firepower. It was undoubtedly the most feared

combat jet of the period and caused considerable panic in Washington. By the end of November it was obvious that MacArthur's men were suffering heavy casualties and were in retreat. In January 1951 Chinese forces recaptured Seoul.

As this offensive continued, Truman was asked repeatedly at press conferences whether he would agree to the use of nuclear weapons. He had authorised their use on Japan so would he do so again? He refused to rule it out categorically, which caused considerable alarm with his UN allies. British Prime Minister Attlee flew to Washington in December 1950 to tell Truman of his opposition. Accepting international concerns, Truman clearly stated that he would not use nuclear weapons.

Phase 4: stalemate and peace talks

A UN counter-attack in early spring managed to halt the Chinese forces at the 38th parallel. As the original plan had been to liberate South Korea up to this line Truman considered peace talks. It was clear that MacArthur disagreed and he publicly criticised the president. Truman took the significant decision to sack MacArthur. This was deeply unpopular with the American public and Truman decided not to run for the presidency again in 1952. Under the new commander, General Ridgeway, American strategy switched to defence and a Chinese offensive was successfully fought back, with heavy casualties being inflicted.

Source 5C: A cartoon from June 1950. President Truman and the United Nations are rushing to take part in the Korean War in support of South Korea. Both are flying over the grave of the League of Nations.

ACTIVITY 5.4

Why has the cartoonist in Source 5C drawn President Truman in such a hurry? How does this cartoon convey the differences between the League of Nations and the United Nations in respect of peacekeeping?

In July 1951 the two sides sat down to discuss peace terms. The main disagreement was the issue of prisoners of war (POWs). As there had been so much movement of troops up and down the Korean peninsula large numbers had been captured on both sides. Approximately 130,000 communist soldiers were held in the South and they had been given the option to remain there. Half of them accepted. In the North conditions were appalling as half of US POWs died in the winter of 1950/1951.

CHECK YOUR UNDERSTANDING 5.5

The Korean War is often called the 'forgotten war'. How can we explain this? What evidence in this section would support this view? Study Source 5E. Describe how it represents the soldiers. What does this tell you about the way in which the American public viewed the war after it was over?

BELIEVE IT OR KNOUT

Source 5D: A *Punch* cartoon published in June 1950.

The Chinese took over the running of these camps to improve conditions but also to provide indoctrination of UN soldiers. Eventually, in September 1953 there was an exchange of 77,000 communist fighters for 12,700 UN troops in Operation Big Switch.

The end of the war

As peace talks dragged on in 1952 and 1953 there seemed no likely end to the war. Truman's replacement as president in January 1953 was Dwight 'Ike' Eisenhower, a Second World War general. He promised to end the Korean War. Two months later Joseph Stalin died, and after a power struggle Nikita Khrushchev took his place in the USSR. With new leaders in place it was more possible to bring about a peace. The UN helped arrange a ceasefire on 27 July 1953, which was accepted by all sides – except Syngman Rhee. The international involvement in the fighting was brought to a close but there has never been a peace treaty between North and South, so technically the war is not yet over.

The most tragic consequence was the horrific loss of life. Seoul and Pyongyang were both extensively damaged and the civilian casualties were 3 million – around 10% of the total population. Other losses by country were:

- North Korea: 406,000 combat deaths
- South Korea: 217,000 combat deaths
- China: 500,000 combat deaths
- USA: 36,914 combat deaths and illness, with another 7,800 still unaccounted for
- UN: 3,000–4,000 deaths, including 686 British losses, with 1,102 missing in action. the highest number out of coalition forces after the USA.

Weapons such as **napalm** were used, which had catastrophic human and ecological results. Chinese casualties were high, but arguably Mao was the main victor. The war helped him to consolidate power in China and ended a period of more than a century of Chinese defeats at the hands of western powers.

KEY TERM

Napalm: a petrol-based chemical weapon. It sticks to its target and burns at a very high temperature. It is often used to clear forests (preventing the enemy from having a place to hide) but when it comes into contact with skin it causes horrific burns.

Source 5E: The Korean War memorial in Washington DC.

ACTIVITY 5.5

The USA spent $67 billion on the war and in addition to combat deaths over 100,000 soldiers were injured. Were these costs justified to contain communism?

5.2 Case study 2: The Cuban Missile Crisis, 1959–1962

Khrushchev and Eisenhower got on better than Stalin and Truman when they met in 1955, the first meeting between Soviet and American leaders since 1945. Yet the arms race and spy networks developed to such a point that neither side could trust the other. Major incidents made relations worse. The U2 incident (see 'Causes of the Missile Crisis') showed the extent of spying, while the Berlin Wall became an icon of the Cold War (see Key Question 6).

Technology played an important role in raising tension. In 1957, the Soviets put the first satellite (called Sputnik) into space and they also developed long-range nuclear missiles called ICBMs. In 1959 the USA developed Polaris missiles which could be launched from submarines. The underlying theory of the arms and technology race was **Mutually Assured Destruction** (MAD). Neither side would start a nuclear war because launching weapons would ensure that both sides would be destroyed. This gave little comfort to civilians around the world.

The USA's reaction to the Cuban Revolution, 1959–1961

In 1898, the USA defeated the Spanish in a short war that gave them effective control over Cuba. After this, American businesses had taken over trade on the island and owned much of the land and natural wealth – particularly the

valuable sugar and oil industries. From 1933 they supported the corrupt dictator Batista, but he was overthrown in 1959 by Fidel Castro. Castro came to power along with colleagues such as his brother Raul and the famous revolutionary Ernesto 'Che' Guevara. Castro's followers were a mixture of communists and Cuban nationalists, but they were all hostile to American influence on their island.

FACT FILE

Fidel Castro (pictured in Source 5F) led the 1959 Cuban Revolution. He adored legendary Cuban nationalist Jose Marti but had also read Karl Marx. He was the son of a wealthy farmer and studied law before becoming a full-time revolutionary. His rise to power involved one of the great **guerrilla** campaigns of the 20th century: his 300 men defeated 10,000 regular soldiers in the Sierra Maestra mountains. He ruled Cuba for almost half a century.

KEY TERM

Mutually Assured Destruction: concept put forward by the Secretary of Defence Robert McNamara in a speech in 1962. At this point the USA had 25,000 nuclear weapons and the USSR had about half as many. His logic was that neither side would risk war due to inevitable death and destruction for all.

Source 5F: Fidel Castro (centre) with his guerrilla fighters in the Sierra Maestra in 1958.

This revolution was troubling for Washington, given Cuba's strategic and economic significance. Castro let the USA keep its base at Guantanamo Bay and guaranteed the safety of Americans in Cuba. However, he wanted to show Cuba's new freedom from American control so in 1960 he signed a trade agreement with Moscow and received weapons as well. This led to a series of 'tit-for-tat' measures:

- Castro nationalised $1 billion of American investments in Cuba, including oil refineries.
- Eisenhower started a trade embargo, which included sugar, Cuba's most valuable export. The USSR agreed to buy sugar from Cuba to save its economy.
- The USA announced it would not buy oil from Cuba. Again, the USSR bought the oil instead, even though it was very inconvenient to send Soviet ships to Havana.

Castro had never been a member of the Cuban Communist Party, however, when he met Khrushchev at the UN in 1960 they embraced like old friends and he now called himself a 'good Marxist-Leninist'.

The **CIA**'s response was to train a group of 1,400 Cuban exiles to invade the island and overthrow Castro. The USA mistakenly believed that Castro was unpopular and poorly armed. In April 1961, the Cuban exiles landed at the Bay of Pigs but were easily defeated (see Source 5G). Castro had 20,000 soldiers supported by Soviet tanks. By this time Eisenhower had been replaced by John F. Kennedy so the defeat was hugely embarrassing for the new president. When he met Khrushchev at the Vienna Summit in June 1961 the relationship between the two superpowers was at an all-time low.

Source 5G: Castro's soldiers celebrate their victory at the Bay of Pigs in April 1961. They are sitting in a boat captured from the CIA-trained invaders. Notice the weapons they are carrying.

ACTIVITY 5.6

Select facts from this section to create a flow-diagram showing the main developments in Cuba from 1959 to 1961.

Causes of the Missile Crisis

The introduction of nuclear weapons to Cuba was decided by Khrushchev in the summer of 1962. As part of NATO, the USA had put strategic nuclear weapons in Italy and Turkey. These were so close to the USSR that little response time would be possible if a missile was launched. Khrushchev wanted to counter this threat by placing nuclear missiles on Cuba – only 90 miles from the USA's eastern coast. Over the summer, Che Guevara and Raul Castro met with Soviet leaders to arrange for the shipment and installation of the missiles.

In September 1962, Kennedy warned the USSR that he would prevent 'by whatever means necessary' the placement of nuclear weapons on Cuba. Khrushchev gave his word that this would not happen. On 14 October, a U2 spy plane flew over Cuba and took pictures of missile silos. Two days later Kennedy was shown the conclusive proof that Khrushchev had broken his word. After the Bay of Pigs embarrassment, Kennedy was reluctant to rely on his military chiefs alone so he formed a special team called **Ex-Comm** to provide him with advice. He knew that 20 Soviet ships carrying nuclear missiles were on the way to Cuba.

113

KEY TERMS

CIA: Central Intelligence Agency. It was founded in 1947 by the National Security Act. Its mission statement was to collect, evaluate and share intelligence relating to national security.

Ex-Comm: 'the Executive Committee of the National Security Council'. It included the usual NSC people but Kennedy also invited significant non-military figures: his brother Robert Kennedy (the Attorney-General); Theodore Sorensen (White House Counsel); Truman's Secretary of State Dean Acheson; and former ambassador to the USSR Tommy Thompson, who knew Khrushchev personally.

CHECK YOUR UNDERSTANDING 5.6

What were Kennedy's motives for turning to Ex-Comm with its extra advisers? What different perspectives did the latter bring?

ACTIVITY 5.7

Look at Figure 5.2 and the cities that were within range of Soviet missiles. What effect would this have on Kennedy during the crisis? Now consider Khrushchev's position. What could he have asked for in return for removing the nuclear threat?

The week of crisis

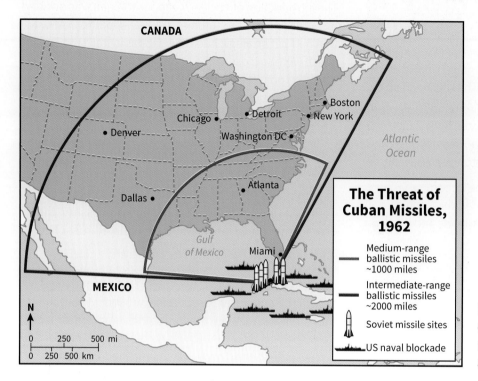

Figure 5.2: A map showing the range of medium- and intermediate-range nuclear missiles if launched from Cuba at the United States.

Here are the key events of the crucial week:

- **21 October:** USA informed Britain about the discovery of missile silos. Kennedy broke the news in a TV address to the nation.
- **22 October:** Kennedy ordered a naval blockade of Cuba. Khrushchev publicly denied that there were missiles on Cuba.
- **23 October:** Khrushchev sent a letter stating that Soviet ships would attempt to sail through the USA blockade.
- **24 October:** Soviet ships carrying warheads turned back before the USA blockade. However, some missiles and warheads made it to Cuba before the blockade was in place. The USA threatened an invasion; Castro called for a nuclear strike from the USSR.
- **25 October:** there was a clash in the UN between Adlai Stevenson and Valerian Zorin. The USA provided photographic evidence of the missile sites (see Source 5H).
- **26 October:** Khrushchev's first offer was made in a letter to Kennedy: the missiles would be withdrawn if the USA promised not to invade Cuba. This was the first Soviet admission that missiles actually existed on Cuba.

- **27 October:** a U2 spy plane was shot down over Cuba and the pilot killed. Kennedy was urged to start an invasion but he delayed. Khrushchev made a second offer in another letter to Kennedy: he demanded that the USA remove missiles from Turkey in exchange for removal of the Cuban missiles. Kennedy responded to Khrushchev's first offer, ignoring the second. Robert Kennedy met with USSR ambassador Anatoly Dobrynin. No official deal would be done, but the USA would guarantee not to invade Cuba again and remove Turkish missiles in the 'near future'. The USSR couldn't reveal that this was done in exchange for the removal of Cuban missiles.
- **28 October:** Khrushchev accepted these terms, ending the crisis.

ACTIVITY 5.8

Look at the time-line of events and identify the moment you think was the key turning point. Then compare your choice with your partner. Justify to each other what you think the most vital moment was.

Source 5H: The famous battle at the UN between ambassadors Adlai Stevenson and Valerian Zorin on 25th October 1962. Stevenson humiliated Zorin by producing aerial reconnaissance pictures of the missile sites proving that the Soviets had been lying. What effect did this revelation have on the development of the crisis?

Analysis

Kennedy had five realistic options:

1   Don't react: the USA had more nuclear weapons and the Turkish site gave them the same advantage. MAD meant that nothing essentially had changed. However, this would be a sign of weakness after the Bay of Pigs.

2   Surgical air attack: the aerial destruction of all the missile silos. However, Soviet engineers would be killed and if one silo remained it could still be used to counter-attack.

3   Invasion by the US army: this would remove the missiles, and communism, altogether. However, a similar Soviet response (for example in Berlin) might be expected.

4   Use diplomacy: the UN could provide a forum for discussions but Khrushchev still denied that the missiles existed. Again, it might look like weakness.

5   Blockade: it could prevent warheads arriving, and avoid hot war. However, it might trigger a similar Soviet response (a repeat of the Berlin Blockade?). Also, some missiles were already in Cuba and could be working within a week.

Kennedy chose a blockade (publicly called a 'quarantine' to make it sound healthy and less like an act of aggression) as this struck a balance between appearing to be weak and using violence. This option was still not guaranteed to work.

ACTIVITY 5.9

Kennedy chose a blockade but what would have happened if any of the other four options were pursued? Debate in groups whether the best option was taken.

Ultimately Khrushchev backed down, even though he later claimed it was a triumph for him personally, and for Cuba. Others in Moscow did not share this view – he was deposed by Leonid Brezhnev in 1964. Kennedy managed to resist his military advisers, who called for air strikes and invasion, but took a huge risk in doing so. The final settlement terms looked much better for him, though in reality the USA had a less powerful position than before the crisis: Castro was still in power and they lost their Turkish missile sites. Yet to US and world opinion, he successfully stood up to Khrushchev and saved everyone from a nuclear war.

HERBLOCK'S CARTOON

"Let's Get A Lock For This Thing"

Source 5I: An American cartoon showing Kennedy and Khrushchev during the Cuban Missile Crisis, 1962.

The crisis began over Cuba but Castro wasn't involved in negotiations to end it. On 24 October he told Khrushchev to launch a nuclear attack so it is perhaps unsurprising that he was kept out of decision-making afterwards. When he found out about the deal to end the crisis it came as a complete surprise. His outrage was quite extreme – as was his language about Khrushchev. It took some time to repair relations between Havana and Moscow.

CHECK YOUR UNDERSTANDING 5.7

What role did Castro play in the outbreak of the crisis? Study Source 5I. What view is the cartoonist taking of the Cuban Missile Crisis and what message are they communicating to the American reader?

The aftermath of the crisis

The Cuban Missile Crisis was the closest that the two superpowers came to a nuclear war. A hotline was set up between the White House and the Kremlin to improve communications in the event of a future crisis. In August 1963 they signed the Nuclear Test Ban Treaty where both promised not to test any more nuclear weapons. This didn't reduce their stockpiles but it did stop the arms race. Khrushchev didn't survive much longer in power but Fidel Castro did – he only stepped down as Cuba's leader in 2008 and was succeeded by Raul Castro. Kennedy was assassinated in November 1963 and his successor was the Vice-President Lyndon Baines Johnson (or 'LBJ').

ACTIVITY 5.10

Had the USA contained communism? Or had it avoided a nuclear catastrophe at the cost of preventing the spread of communism? Write a paragraph debating these issues and come to a conclusion about the success of containment in 1962. Remember to give a clear justification for your answer.

TOP TIP

The film *13 Days* is a film about the American government during the period of the missile crisis. It was based not on the account of events given by Robert Kennedy, from whose book the film takes its name, but in fact from an entirely different book. It does use information not available to a previous film, *The Missiles of October*, but its choice of a political adviser as the film's hero was controversial, as participants in the crisis denied he had been involved in the decision-making. It is worth watching but bear in mind the issues with historical accuracy.

5.3 Case study 3: The war in Vietnam, 1961–1975

Background: the French war in Vietnam

Source 5J: The Vietnam War Memorial in Washington DC. It lists the names of all the US soldiers killed in action.

ACTIVITY 5.11

Look at Source 5J. If Korea is the forgotten war, then Vietnam is one of the most well-known conflicts – but a painful one for Americans to recall. Compare and contrast this memorial to Source 5E. Which do you think is more effective and why?

From the 1860s, France controlled the colony of Indo-China, which comprised Vietnam, Cambodia and Laos. After the French defeat by the Nazis in 1940 they lost control of Indo-China to Japan. At the end of the war the communist leader **Ho Chi Minh** (see Source 5K) announced that Vietnam was independent. However, the French regained control, which soon led to war. From 1946 to 1954 French losses reached 72,000 men, which was actually more than the USA later. The Chinese revolution of 1949 made matters worse as Mao supplied arms to the North Vietnamese forces, the **Viet Minh**.

FACT FILE

Born Nguyen That Thanh in 1890, Ho Chi Minh travelled widely and helped to found the French Communist Party. He also trained in Moscow and China and founded the Viet Minh in 1941 to fight the Japanese. It was at this point that he changed his name to Ho Chi Minh which means 'bringer of light'. He fought the French from 1946 and was made President of North Vietnam in 1954. He supported the **Viet Cong** in their fight against the Americans until he died in 1969. When the Viet Cong captured Saigon they renamed it Ho Chi Minh City. His body was embalmed and is on public display there (Source 5K).

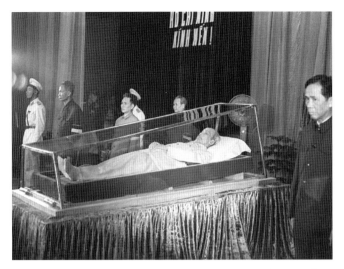

Source 5K: Ho Chi Minh's body was publicly displayed after his death in 1969, adding to his cult of personality.

Despite being given $2.6 billion by the USA in aid from 1950 to 1954 the French were unsuccessful in Vietnam. They withdrew after a heavy defeat at Dien Bien Phu in March 1954. They had controlled the towns but Ho Chi Minh's guerrilla forces controlled the north and the countryside. Peace was signed through the 1954 **Geneva Agreements**. The main points set out in the peace treaty were:

- Indo-China would be divided into four: North and South Vietnam, Laos and Cambodia.
- North Vietnam was divided from the South at the 17°N line of latitude. Northern forces were to withdraw from the South.
- All foreign troops would withdraw from Indo-China.
- Elections would be held in 1956.
- An international commission would ensure that the settlement was respected.

Several nations (including the USSR, China and Britain) signed the agreements, but the USA refused. In 1956 Eisenhower persuaded President Diem not to hold elections because evidence suggested the communists would win.

ACTIVITY 5.12

Why did Eisenhower refuse to sign the Geneva Agreements? Try to work out which points would have been problematic for containment.

Reasons for American involvement

Civil war soon broke out and in 1960 the National Liberation Front was created in South Vietnam, thereafter known as the Viet Cong. They were a mixture of anti-government forces, including Buddhists, patriots and communists. They used **guerrilla tactics**, operating from a complex network of tunnels and underground bases that even included whole hospitals. Even if the Americans could find an entrance they struggled to get through as many were booby-trapped. The Viet Cong successfully waged war against President Diem's government and were supplied through the Ho Chi Minh Trail. This ran through neighbouring Laos and Cambodia and allowed for weapons and supplies to be secretly brought south from North Vietnam and China.

ACTIVITY 5.13

Look at Figure 5.3 and use the internet to learn more about the Ho Chi Minh Trail. Select five key facts that demonstrate its significance in the Viet Cong's success in the war.

CHECK YOUR UNDERSTANDING 5.8

Look at Source 5L. What similarities do you find between the personalities or careers of Diem and Syngman Rhee? Why did the USA back these two men?

Kennedy's first foreign policy action on becoming president in 1961 was in Laos because the communist group Pathet Lao were trying to overthrow the monarchy. The Viet Minh and the Pathet Lao had worked together to fight the French. Eisenhower told Kennedy the country was like 'a cork in a bottle'; once it popped, the whole

 KEY TERMS

Viet Minh and **Viet Cong:** names were given by western politicians and journalists to Vietnamese communist forces. The former is a contraction of 'Vietnamese' and 'Ho Chi Minh', while the latter is a contraction of a Vietnamese expression for 'Vietnamese communists'.

Geneva Agreements 1954: the main points set out in the peace treaty on Indo-China.

Tactics: manoeuvring troops and weapons in battle in order to achieve a short-term military aim.

Guerrilla: 'little war' in Spanish. A guerrilla war is one in which small groups use raids, assassinations and sabotage against larger armies. Guerrilla fighters are hard for their enemies to identify; the Viet Cong would use children and old people to pass messages and hide weapons. Fidel Castro and Che Guevara were also expert guerrilla fighters.

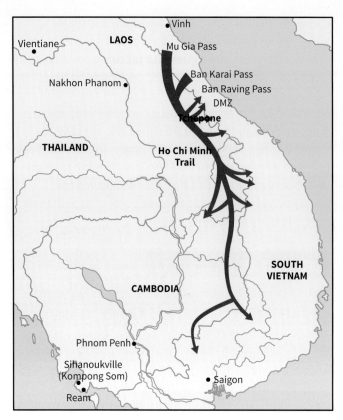

Figure 5.3: The Ho Chi Minh Trail which the North used to send Viet Cong fighters and supplies to support them into the South.

region could fall to communism. The CIA therefore trained an anti-communist force and supplies were flown in from Thailand (by 'Air America'). Aerial bombing began and continued heavily until 1975.

Source 5L: President Ngo Dinh Diem at a parade in New York in 1957. He was from a noble family and served as a minister to the Emperor Bao Dai. He removed the emperor in 1954 and worked with the USA. However he was a strict autocrat and gave powerful positions to his family. He was notoriously corrupt and often rejected American advice.

In South Vietnam 16,000 military advisers were sent to help Diem, including the specially formed Green Berets, a unit of special forces similar to the marines or the British SAS. Yet in 1963, Buddhist protests against the government began. Kennedy had tired of Diem especially after an embarrassing defeat at Ap Bac. In November 1963 the CIA helped stage an internal coup which ended in the bloody execution of Diem and his advisers. Coincidentally, Kennedy was also assassinated later that month.

Source 5M: A Buddhist monk self-immolating in protest at Diem's religious policies in 1963. He was sitting in the lotus position in the central square in Saigon as he burned to death. Diem was a strict Catholic and refused to let anyone celebrate Buddha's birthday.

CHECK YOUR UNDERSTANDING 5.9

Look at Source 5M. What do you think the monk's motives were for doing this and what were the intended consequences?

Johnson and increasing US involvement

Lyndon B. Johnson (president 1963–1969) succeeded Kennedy. He was a firm believer in the **Domino Theory**.

KEY TERM

Domino Theory: if one country fell to communism, so would its neighbours and their neighbours in turn – falling like a line of dominoes. The theory was first outlined by Eisenhower in 1954 at a press briefing on Vietnam. The exact phrase he used was the 'falling domino principle'.

The next presidential election was due in November 1964, so he was also under political pressure to be seen being tough on communism. In August, before the election, he was given the opportunity to expand American involvement in the war through the Gulf of Tonkin incident, when a USA warship was alleged to have come under North Vietnamese fire. Congress gave the president authority to send more military power to Vietnam.

U.S. Imperialism, Get Out of South Viet Nam!
L'impérialisme américain hors du Sud-Vietnam!
¡Fuera el imperialismo norteamericano del Sur de Vietnam!

Source 5N: This poster was published in 1963.
What does this poster suggest about the war that the Americans were involved in and the people they were fighting against?

American tactics

In 1965 the Viet Cong attacked the US base at Pleiku. American bombing intensified through Operation Rolling Thunder. The Viet Cong were still being supplied by the USSR and China through the port of Haiphong as the USA were afraid to bomb it for fear of hitting Soviet ships. These supplies were taken via the Ho Chi Minh Trail. Johnson was advised to send ground troops by General Westmoreland. Despite his reluctance, he agreed.

The USA was now involved in a total war. Their tactics for victory were:

- Heavy use of aerial bombing to destroy Viet Cong strongholds. Chemical weapons such as napalm and Agent Orange were used to destroy trees and jungle, useful hiding places for the enemy.
- 'Search and destroy' missions. Combat units would go out into the countryside to locate Viet Cong weapons stores, bases and fighters. They would punish any villages helping the enemy.

119

Source 5O: Children fleeing the village of Trang Bang after a napalm bombing in 1972.

CHECK YOUR UNDERSTANDING 5.10

Vietnam is often called the 'first media war' as reporters and TV crews followed troops and reported without restriction. Look at Sources 5M and 5O. What impact would these have on public opinion and why?

ACTIVITY 5.14

Discuss in groups the legacy of war reporting since Vietnam. It what ways did it change the way war is fought as a consequence? Keep this in mind when you study the Gulf War.

FACT FILE
The little girl running naked at the front centre of the photograph in Source 5O was called Phan Thị Kim Phúc; she was nine years old. She later converted to Christianity and went to live in Canada.

This photograph came to symbolise the horror of war in Vietnam. It shows the effects of napalm; the children are running away from a bombed village and the young girl's clothes have been burned off. Such images shocked world opinion and caused massive anti-war protests in the USA.

The year 1968 was a vital one in the war. Despite the US government claiming that victory was close, the North Vietnamese Army became more heavily involved. The Tet Offensive (launched on 'Tet', the Vietnamese New Year) saw Viet Cong troops almost capture the US embassy in Saigon. Although it failed, the offensive showed Westmoreland's claim that the Viet Cong were close to defeat was innacurate. Anti-war protests in the USA increased after this, especially when the My Lai massacre was revealed in 1969. The consequence of this dramatic year was that Johnson announced to the American people that he would not seek re-election as president.

FACT FILE

My Lai massacre

In March 1968, Charlie Company was sent on a 'search and destroy' mission to the small village of My Lai. They slaughtered 374 men, women and children (plus their livestock) and burned the village down. No Viet Cong were found. It only ended when a USA helicopter pilot called Hugh Thompson landed and threatened to shoot the American soldiers unless they stopped. The incident was kept secret for a year but when it became public knowledge an investigation was launched. Of the 14 men charged only the commanding officer Lt William Calley was found guilty. He was sentenced to life in prison for this war crime but was pardoned by President Nixon in 1974.

The new president, Richard Nixon, promised to end the war but didn't want to withdraw in a humiliating fashion. His policy of **Vietnamisation** reduced USA troop numbers significantly. In 1970 he extended the aerial bombing into Cambodia. He did this without telling Congress, which increased public criticism when it was discovered. During nationwide protests (which escalated after My Lai became public knowledge), four students were killed at Kent State University by the Ohio National Guard. By 1972 even some war veterans were protesting against Nixon, throwing away their medals. Nixon also

replaced the Cambodian ruler with Lon Nol, who became a corrupt leader and was deeply unpopular.

Source 5P: The aftermath of the Kent State University protests in May 1970.

ACTIVITY 5.15

In May 1970, a protest against Nixon's expansion of the war into Cambodia took place at Kent State University. The governor of Ohio sent in the National Guard and they opened fire on the crowd. Four students died. A later investigation called the use of arms 'unnecessary, unwarranted, and inexcusable'. Over 500 universities were shut down afterwards as protests escalated. What impact do you think (a) the events at Kent State University and (b) Source 5P had on public opinion in the USA in 1970? Take into account issues around age, ethnicity, social class and education.

Source 5Q: Boxer Muhammad Ali (born Cassius Clay) in 1966 pointing to a newspaper headline about anti-war protests.

Look at Source 5Q. Research the actions of Muhammad Ali in this period. He was a fierce critic of the war in Vietnam. What did he do and how significant was his opposition in shaping public opinion?

Peace talks did make progress in 1972 as they were led by Nixon's National Security Adviser, Henry Kissinger. To force the hand of the North, Nixon launched the heaviest aerial bombardments yet, Operation Linebacker I and II. He also made a secret promise to the South that the USA would support them if they were invaded again by the North. Again, Congress was not told this.

In January 1973, a peace treaty was signed, with US troops withdrawing from Vietnam. The South would have to fend for itself – especially as Nixon was forced to resign in 1974 over the **Watergate scandal**. The North invaded the South in March 1974 and won a decisive victory in April 1975. When they seized the capital, Saigon, they entered the US embassy, forcing helicopters to evacuate staff. It was a profoundly humiliating moment for the USA and marked their total defeat in Vietnam. Cambodia and Laos also fell to communism the same month.

Source 5R: An American official punches a Vietnamese man to prevent overcrowding on the helicopter airlifting staff out of the country in April 1975, after the fall of the US embassy.

CHECK YOUR UNDERSTANDING 5.11

Why did the USA lose the war in Vietnam? Which factors were most significant?

What does Source 5R tell you about the end of American involvement in the Vietnam War?

KEY TERM

Vietnamisation: the reduction of US troop levels and getting the South Vietnamese Army (ARVN) to do more of the fighting.

The **Watergate scandal** erupted after a group of men were arrested breaking into the Watergate hotel in Washington DC to steal documents from the Democrats' offices during the USA presidential campaign. They were caught and when it was revealed that Nixon was involved he had to resign in disgrace.

Effects of the Vietnam War

These were just some of the consequences of the war:

- South Vietnam lost 2.5 million civilians.
- 300,000 citizens of South Vietnam were tortured in 're-education camps' after the war.
- North Vietnam lost 650,000 men and the Viet Cong lost 1 million.
- The USA lost 58,220 men.
- 1.5m people escaped Vietnam in boats in 1975–1990, heading for Hong Kong and Australia.
- Vietnam's economy was destroyed by bombing. Use of chemical weapons massively increased cancer rates and led to babies being deformed at birth.
- Many US soldiers became drug addicts. By 1971 four times more men were treated for drug addiction than combat wounds.
- Congress passed the War Powers Act to restrict the president's ability to send troops abroad.
- Communism in Cambodia under Pol Pot led to mass murder during 1975–1979 in which more than 2 million people were killed, almost one-third of the population.

Why did the Americans lose the war?

There are two broad reasons for the American defeat in Vietnam. They both contributed significantly to the withdrawal of troops in 1973 though historians disagree which cause was more significant:

1   Military factors: the Viet Cong were too well organised and difficult to identify. The Ho Chi Minh Trail kept them supplied and they dressed like villagers and farmers so they blended in with civilians. They had also been fighting the Japanese and the French with the same guerrilla tactics so they were very experienced, unlike American soldiers who fought for one year then returned home. This meant that

ordinary soldiers didn't build up much experience. Modern technology was of little use in Vietnam and was probably counter-productive as it cost the USA political support.

2   Domestic factors: the public was increasingly against the war and as propaganda was so important in the Cold War the USA could not afford to be seen to be killing innocent civilians. Protests like Kent State University divided the nation and Johnson and Nixon became figures of hate, leaving office with their reputations in pieces. As early as 1966 more than the half the US public disapproved of the conflict. No president could keep on fighting when the media was showing the horrific nature of the war through TV, photographs and articles.

What of containment? A third factor in the American withdrawal was that Vietnam became less strategically important as the domino theory was proved to be incorrect. Cambodia and Laos fell to communism but Thailand and the Philippines did not. In the late 1960s the USSR and China argued and there was even the possibility of war between them. Nixon's policy of détente (meaning 'relaxation') improved relations with the USSR and China so whatever happened in Vietnam seemed to have less disastrous consequences than might have been imagined in the 1960s.

ACTIVITY 5.17

What had once been French Indo-China eventually fell to communism but does this mean that containment failed? After all, the dominoes didn't fall beyond this region as the Americans had feared. It could be argued that the severity of the war did at least prevent the Cold War spreading any further. Compare the war in Vietnam to the one in Korea. Which one was more effective in terms of containment and why? Make a list of reasons for each war then come to a judgement.

ACTIVITY 5.18

Use the bullet points here to make a spider diagram with these states: USA, North Vietnam, South Vietnam, Cambodia and Laos. As well as the consequences add in the key leaders and events which caused them. This will be useful for revision.

Review your learning

How effectively did the USA contain the spread of Communism: this is the key question that links the three examples you have studied.

Summary points

- The USA reacted to the development of the Cold War by establishing a new policy of limiting Soviet expansion called containment.

- The first test of this policy was in the Korean War of 1950–1953. The North Koreans were pushed back but the UN forces led by the USA failed to make any further gains.

- The Cuban Missile Crisis was the closest threat to the USA. President Kennedy had to use skilful diplomacy to ensure a peaceful end to the conflict, but he had to allow Fidel Castro to remain in power.

- The war in Vietnam was a disaster for USA, and for containment. After US troops withdrew all of Vietnam came under communist control.

The Big Challenge

For each example of Korea, Cuba and Vietnam, develop a set of revision notes. Use the heading 'Key features'. Make sure that you know the order of events, the main individuals and the key concepts in each example. Try to keep these notes short; there is a lot of information to learn so we're trying to focus on the most important basics to begin with. Concentrate on things which you think everyone should know. For example, 'domino theory' is a vital concept, but knowing that 300,000 South Vietnamese suffered in camps after the war is more expert level knowledge. Keep to the core information for just now.

When you feel confident that you know the main features of the three examples, link them together. The overall question is about containment. Can you answer these?

- What were the USA's aims in each conflict? In what ways were they trying to contain communism?
- Which president was most successful in containing communism: Truman, Eisenhower, Kennedy, Johnson or Nixon?
- What specific examples can you give which show that containment was successful?
- What were the main failures of the policy?

Exam-style questions

1   What was the domino theory?

2   Describe the causes of the Korean War.

3   What were the main features of the agreement reached after the Cuban Missile Crisis?

4   Why were the Viet Cong so difficult for the Americans to fight against?

5   Why did Truman get involved in the Korean War?

6   Why did Khrushchev decide to put nuclear missiles in Cuba?

7   The 'USA lost the war in Vietnam because of poor military strategy.' How far do you agree with this statement?

8   To what extent was the Cuban Missile Crisis a success for Kennedy?

9   'The Korean War was a success for Truman's policy of containment.' How far do you agree with this statement?

YOU ARE LEAVING
THE AMERICAN SECTOR

ВЫ ВЫЕЗЖАЕТЕ ИЗ
АМЕРИКАНСКОГО СЕКТОРА

VOUS SORTEZ
DU SECTEUR AMÉRICAIN

Chapter 6

Key Question 6: How secure was the USSR's control over Eastern Europe, 1948–c.1989?

Focus points

- Why was there opposition to Soviet control in Hungary in 1956 and Czechoslovakia in 1968, and how did the USSR react to this opposition?
- How similar were events in Hungary in 1956 and in Czechoslovakia in 1968?
- Why was the Berlin Wall built in 1961?
- What was the significance of 'Solidarity' in Poland for the decline of Soviet influence in Eastern Europe?
- How far was Gorbachev personally responsible for the collapse of Soviet control over Eastern Europe?

ANFANG
DES DEMOKRATISCHEN SEKTORS
VON GROSS-BERLIN

Achtung!
Baustelle

10 km

What is this enquiry about?

This enquiry looks at what happened in Eastern Europe after Stalin had established a buffer zone up to 1949. It is important to remember that all the states within this buffer zone had suffered greatly under Nazi occupation. Some communist leaders had escaped because they knew they would be executed if found by the Nazis. They spent the war in Moscow and knew Stalin personally. He therefore wanted them to be in power when the Red Army defeated the Nazis in 1945.

Hitler's forces were defeated by two key groups:

1   Local partisans, which were resistance movements that often included communists, like Tito's group in Yugoslavia.

2   The Red Army of the USSR, which played a decisive role.

To understand the events covered in this enquiry we need to keep in mind differing perspectives:

- Many communists believed Moscow offered the best source of protection after the atrocities of the Nazi occupation. There was also widespread gratitude to the Soviets.
- Others on the left believed that their country should be fully independent without taking orders from the USSR, and found inspiration in Yugoslavia's leader, Josef Tito.
- A third group wanted to ally with the US and the West.

What happened between 1949 and 1989 was a complex interplay between these three perspectives.

Soviet power seemed too strong to be challenged successfully, a viewpoint reinforced by events in Budapest and Prague. Why was this? Another vital question surrounds Berlin. Why was this one city so politically and strategically important? Finally, if Soviet power was indeed so strong then why did it collapse in the 1980s? Was Poland the main cause of this collapse? Was one man – Mikhail Gorbachev – primarily responsible for the end of communist rule in Eastern Europe?

FACT FILE

Josef Tito was born Josef Broz in what is now Croatia; he led partisan resistance to the Nazis. Tito was a communist but he believed in being independent. He resisted Stalin's demands and formed the non-aligned movement in the Cold War with Nehru of India and Nasser of Egypt. This group of nations refused to side with either the US or the Soviet Union. Tito ruled Yugoslavia until his death in 1980.

Source 6A: Josef Tito, leader of Yugoslavia in May 1970. What impression do you get from this photo? How did his public image differ from Stalin's?

Figure 6.1: A map of Eastern Europe in 1949.

ACTIVITY 6.1

The term 'geopolitics' refers to the impact that geography has on international politics. With a partner discuss the map of the buffer zone in Figure 6.1. Why was it so vital to the Soviets? Which sections of the buffer zone were most important to overall security? Think about such issues as the position of the countries and the length of their borders.

6.1 Why was there opposition to Soviet control in Hungary in 1956 and Czechoslovakia in 1968, and how did the USSR react to this opposition?

The situation in Hungary

There were several reasons why Hungary was resistant to Soviet control in 1945. It was a strongly religious nation and the Catholic church was a very powerful institution. Hungary was also a joint partner in the Austro-Hungarian Empire from 1867 to 1918. Hungarians were nationalistic and preferred to be the rulers not the ruled.

The Red Army occupied Hungary in the Second World War but the Communist Party lost the election of 1945. Stalin rigged elections in 1947 to ensure that he controlled the government. His main ally in Hungary was Mátyás Rákosi. He was a firm communist who spent the Second World War in the USSR. He now led the government and persecuted all opposition ruthlessly. For example, in 1949 he imprisoned Cardinal Mindszenty who was head of the Hungarian Catholic Church. He also executed the foreign minister László Rajk in 1949. Rajk was a communist but was critical of Stalin's attempts to control Hungary. In Rákosi's show trials, modelled on those of Stalin in the 1930s, around 100,000 Hungarians were sent to labour camps.

Rákosi's position was weakened when Stalin died in 1953. That year there were anti-communist demonstrations in East Berlin that were crushed by the police and the army. The USSR also withdrew troops from Austria, stationed there since the end of the Second World War. Consequently, many saw this as a sign that communism was being relaxed in Europe.

Rákosi lost his position as Prime Minister to fellow communist Imry Nagy. Nagy had participated in the 1917 Bolshevik Revolution and also spent the Second World War in Moscow. However, unlike Rákosi he was not a Stalinist and wanted reforms. A power struggle began because

Rákosi remained General Secretary of the Hungarian Communist Party while Nagy was Prime Minister. It seemed that Rákosi had won when he managed to remove Nagy from office in 1955.

TOP TIP

Organising information is a key skill. Keep an electronic document with the names of the key people. For each one add a single sentence saying who they are and refer back to this as you read through the chapter. It will help you recall information on the leading individuals.

Causes of opposition in 1956

While this power struggle was going on in Budapest a similar one was going on in Moscow. After Stalin died in 1953, Nikita Khrushchev competed with other powerful figures for control of the government. In early 1956 it was clear that Khrushchev had won. He made a famous **secret speech** against Stalin in February 1956 in which he criticised the dictator's rule and admitted that mistakes had been made. This created a problem for all the Stalinist governments in Eastern Europe: would they be able to continue as they had before?

FACT FILE

Nikita Khrushchev

Khrushchev joined the Bolsheviks in 1918 and was a Stalin loyalist in the 1930s. He joined the Politburo in 1939 and was a key figure during the war. He managed to win control of the Communist Party after a long power struggle following Stalin's death. He led the USSR during a critical period in the Cold War before being removed from power in 1964. He was the only Soviet leader to die during the Cold War and not be buried at the Kremlin.

KEY TERM

Secret speech: Khrushchev stunned his audience by launching a fierce attack on Stalin. Some people fainted. It would have been punishable by death in Stalin's era; now Stalin was dead Khrushchev was announcing a change in direction. Although initially secret, Khrushchev allowed news of it deliberately to leak out. Rioting soon broke out in Poznan, Poland, which left 100 people dead. Khrushchev considered using force to restore order but eventually decided to reach a deal with the Poles. As long as they stayed in the **Warsaw Pact** he would allow more moderate communists to run the government. This brought the reformer Władysław Gomułka to power and calmed the situation in Poland.

Hungarian students had demonstrated in sympathy with the protestors in Poland. As events gathered momentum Rákosi was removed in July 1956 but his replacement was another Stalinist called Ernő Gerő. However, Gerö was unable to control a campaign within the Hungarian Communist Party to correct the errors of the purges in 1949. There was a state funeral for Rajk on 6 October, which became a public demonstration. Up to 200,000 people took to the streets of Budapest to protest against almost a decade of Stalinist control by Moscow. Three weeks later students rioted and tore down a statue of Stalin (see Source 6C). The police tried to restore order but Hungarian soldiers took the side of the protestors. The situation was critical.

Sources 6B and 6C: A 15-year-old Hungarian girl armed with a machine gun, and rebels dismantling the statue of Stalin in October 1956.

ACTIVITY 6.2

Compare Sources 6B and 6C. Which of these images would have been more concerning for the USSR? Debate this as a class and come to a conclusion based on what you have read about the events of 1956.

Khrushchev surrounded Budapest with Soviet soldiers but seemed to prefer a peaceful solution. He allowed Nagy to become prime minister and reforms were passed. Nagy promised free speech, democratic elections and the release of political prisoners such as Cardinal Mindszenty. However, unlike the situation in Poland, Hungarians could not be pacified by these gains. They were encouraged by broadcasts coming from **Radio Free Europe** based in Munich. They were being told to carry on the fight and were given the impression that western powers (especially the US) would come to help.

KEY TERMS

Radio Free Europe: founded in 1950 to provide radio broadcasts for people living in communist countries in Eastern Europe. It was funded by the US Congress and assisted by the CIA. It reached tens of millions of people and broadcast in 15 different languages.

127

Nagy had to decide whether to stay loyal to Moscow or back calls for more reform. On 1 November he took a fateful step. He announced that Hungary would leave the Warsaw Pact and asked the United Nations for help.

> The Government of the Hungarian People's Republic has received trustworthy reports of the entrance of new Soviet military units into Hungary. The president of the Council of Ministers ... objected to the entrance of new military units into Hungary. He demanded the immediate and fast withdrawal of the Soviet units. He announced to the Soviet ambassador that the Hungarian government was withdrawing from the Warsaw Pact, simultaneously declaring Hungary's neutrality, and that it was turning to the United Nations and asking the four Great Powers to help protect its neutrality.

Source 6D: From a telegram issued by Imre Nagy to all foreign embassies in Hungary on 1 November 1956.

Soviet response

This went too far for Khrushchev. At dawn on 4 November he sent in 200,000 men and 4,000 tanks. Fighting in Budapest lasted for a week. It is impossible to know the death total for certain. The Soviets lost around 700 soldiers and estimates on Hungarian deaths range from 3,000 to 30,000. Although the world was shocked it was distracted by events in Egypt where the UK and France were involved in the **Suez Crisis**. The promise of aid on Radio Free Europe proved false and Nagy was removed from power. He was replaced by Janos Kadar who went on to rule the country for the next three decades. In 1958 Nagy and his colleagues were executed in secret. Like Rajk he was eventually given a full public funeral, but not until 1989 when communism was collapsing in Hungary.

KEY TERM

Suez Crisis: The Suez was designed by the French and built using Egyptian labour in the nineteenth century. The British bought a 44% controlling stake in it but lost control of it to Nasser in 1956. Britain and France colluded with Israel to attack Egypt and regain control of the canal, so the ensuing crisis distracted the world from events in Hungary as they happened at the same time.

The situation in Czechoslovakia

Czechoslovakia was a new nation, created out of the Austro-Hungarian Empire in 1919. It was economically the strongest of the Eastern European countries as it had well-developed industries and had prospered between the First and Second World Wars. However, it was weakened by the Munich Treaty of 1938; in which Hitler gained the Sudetenland. He then broke this agreement in 1939 when he invaded and captured Prague. The Czechs were very unhappy that they had been abandoned by the western powers so this helped to create a strong communist underground movement. After the war they won nearly a majority in the elections of 1946. Though not in power, communists were given control of the police and army after pressure on the new government from Moscow.

However, communists struggled to maintain popularity. Czechoslovakia was hit by the harsh economic conditions of the winter of 1946/1947. When new elections were due to be held in 1948 it was clear that communists would struggle. Stalin ordered a complete takeover of government by force. Two weeks later the foreign minister **Jan Masaryk** died in mysterious circumstances. Prime Minister Klement Gottwald – a strong ally of Moscow – blamed the West for his alleged suicide. He then introduced a Soviet-style constitution and banned all forms of political opposition.

FACT FILE

Jan Masaryk was the son of Czechoslovakia's founder, Tomas Masaryk. He was a popular liberal and the only non-communist left in the government. He was definitely under huge pressure at the time of his death but there were many unusual aspects of his apparent suicide. For example, the doctor who examined him died two weeks later – again as the result of an apparent suicide.

Masaryk's death encouraged the United States Congress to support the Marshall Plan. Washington realised that if Czechoslovakia could fall under communist control then so might all other major European states. The Prague government was denied Marshall Aid by Stalin, which caused resentment over the loss of independence.

Causes of opposition to Soviet Rule

Despite these issues there was little disturbance in Czechoslovakia. Poland, Hungary and East Germany had all shown their discontent from 1953 to 1956 in the period after Stalin died but Czechoslovak protests were more restrained. The poet and playwright Václav Havel wrote anti-totalitarian plays in the 1960s and was twice imprisoned for his outspoken political views. Attitudes hardened in the mid-1960s because the economy was clearly failing. Housing was poor, wages were low and attempts at reform by the government all failed.

Complaints against the government became more prominent in 1966. Reformist groups wanted change but they were careful to learn the lessons of the Hungarian uprising of 1956. Their aim was not to end communism, but relax it. Throughout 1967, student protests were held, which demanded the removal from power of communist party leader Antonín Novotný (leader since Gottwald's death in 1953). In January 1968, Novotný was replaced as First Secretary of the Communist Party by the reformer Alexander Dubček.

Prague Spring 1968

In April 1968, Dubček introduced a number of reforms starting a period known as the Prague Spring. He described his policies as '**socialism with a human face**'. The leader of the USSR since Khrushchev was removed in 1964 was Leonid Brezhnev. Dubček tried to make it clear that he did not intend to end communism or leave the Warsaw Pact. However, his reforms were extensive and included the following:

- Freedom of speech – newspapers could criticise the government.
- Czechoslovaks were allowed to travel abroad to visit countries beyond the Iron Curtain.
- Businesses could run themselves, rather than being told what to produce by the government.
- Workers' councils could be formed, similar to **trade unions**.
- A new parliament was to be freely elected.

Brezhnev's reaction was predictably negative. In July 1968 senior Soviet leaders visited Prague and warned Dubček about the possible consequences of his reforms. Military preparations were being made, just as they had been in 1956 over Hungary.

Soviet invasion and its consequences

Much like Imry Nagy, Dubček was emboldened by domestic support for his reforms. He turned to Romania (led by Nicolai Ceauşescu) and Yugoslavia (led by Joseph Tito). Both men were willing to stand up to Moscow and Dubček hoped that they could unite against Brezhnev. This was a clear miscalculation. In August Brezhnev carried out his threat and sent in 200,000 troops and 2,000 tanks to capture Prague. There was far less violence than in Budapest in 1956 – 72 protestors were killed – but the government was toppled. Dubček was arrested but wasn't executed. He

returned to politics in 1989 when communist rule collapsed in Czechoslovakia.

CHECK YOUR UNDERSTANDING 6.3

Compare and contrast the events of 1956 and 1968. Why was there less violence in Prague than there had been in Budapest?

ACTIVITY 6.4

In pairs look up Ceausescu and Tito online. What role did they play in Eastern European politics? Tito in particular was a problem for Stalin. Why was this?

There were two main domestic consequences:

1. An estimated 150,000 people managed to escape the country into Austria and Germany during the Soviet invasion as security temporarily collapsed on the border.

2. A lone protest was made by a student called Jan Palach. He died after setting fire to himself in Wenceslas Square.

Externally there two main consequences:

1. The Chinese were furious with Brezhnev. They had disapproved of the Hungarian invasion of 1956 and this made the relationship with Beijing even worse. Shots were exchanged along the Chinese-Soviet border and the following years saw tension increase almost to the point of war.

2. The crushing of the Prague Spring gave rise to the **Brezhnev Doctrine**. When this doctrine was eventually abandoned by Mikhail Gorbachev it was a critical factor in the end of the Cold War.

KEY TERMS

'**Socialism with a human face**': was meant to show that socialist (in this context communist) policies could and should be more about human needs than power politics.

Trade unions: organisations campaigning for increased wages and improved working conditions for members

Brezhnev Doctrine: stated that Moscow had the right to interfere with military force if any country in Eastern Europe attempted to abandon communism.

Source 6E: A cartoon from September 1968 by Herblock of the *Washington Post* showing Brezhnev (right) crushing the Prague Spring.

6.2 How similar were events in Hungary in 1956 and in Czechoslovakia in 1968?

Historians often take two different examples and study them side by side to identify similarities and differences. This is called a comparative analysis. In this section we'll do a comparative analysis of events in Hungary and Czechoslovakia. Before reading on, look Activity 6.5.

Similarities in causes

In both cases there was a battle to control the government between leaders who were close to Moscow and leaders who were sympathetic to public opinion. In Hungary this was between Rákosi and Nagy. In Czechoslovakia it was

between Gottwald and Masaryk in 1948, and then in 1967/1968 between Novotný and Dubček.

Both countries had reason to resent direct control by Moscow. Hungary was very religious and nationalistic. Czechoslovakia had a strong economy and a developed sense of capitalism.

Differences in causes

Hungary was a reaction to events in the USSR (the death of Stalin) and in Poland. What began as a sympathy protest for the Poles developed into demands for their own freedom. In Prague the causes were economic weakness and poor standard of living, not events elsewhere.

The two events were separated by 12 years – the Hungarians still thought that they could leave the Warsaw Pact (and communism) once Stalin had died. The Czechoslovaks knew in 1968 that this wasn't possible so their aims were less radical. They also knew there would be no outside support given American involvement in Vietnam.

Similarities in events

In both cases there was an alliance of reform-minded communists and those who were more nationalistic. Both groups agreed that their country should have more freedom from Moscow. Also, students were central to the protests in both Budapest and Prague.

The USSR allowed the situation to develop up to a point, then used lethal force to crush opposition. Khrushchev and Brezhnev were alike in that they couldn't allow a breach in the buffer zone so used violent methods to assert Moscow's authority.

Differences in events

The Prague Spring was perhaps less of a threat than Nagy's reforms. Dubček never threatened to leave the Warsaw Pact. Nagy, on the other hand, would have and appealed to the United Nations.

The Hungarians believed that they would get outside support because of Radio Free Europe. This meant that there was far more violence and consequently deaths in Hungary than in Czechoslovakia.

ACTIVITY 6.6

Evaluate the role of the US in Hungary and Czechoslovakia. Could more have been done? What would the consequences have been in each case?

Similarities in consequences

In each case the events led to a strengthening of Moscow's control over the buffer zone while the authority of the West was weakened. The US failed to support the Hungarians in 1956 in part because of the Suez Crisis and they failed to support the Czechoslovaks in 1968 due to Vietnam. (Fear of starting a third world war was also an issue, of course.) The consequence of this was that opponents of communism knew they would have to do things for themselves in the future.

Both countries had to wait until the late 1980s before they could again show opposition to communism.

Differences in consequences

The number of deaths in Budapest was far higher than in Prague. This applies also to the leaders: Nagy was executed, Dubček was not.

Interestingly, Brezhnev used Warsaw Pact forces in Prague whereas Khrushchev used USSR forces in Budapest. Moscow was aware in the late 1960s that they had to show a united eastern European stance against opposition.

ACTIVITY 6.7

Now look back on your table from the last activity.

1   Were your similarities and differences the same as in the text?

2   Given what you now know of the two events, which do you think is stronger: the similarities or the differences? Write a paragraph explaining your answer.

TOP TIP

The comparative analysis method works very well for other aspects of the Cold War. Try using it for learning about the wars in Korea and Vietnam in Key Question 5.

I must say, I am convinced that you must share some of the blame for your present situation.

Source 6F: An extract from an open letter written by Václav Havel to Alexander Dubček, dated August 1969.

CHECK YOUR UNDERSTANDING 6.5

Is Havel's analysis in Source 6F fair? Could the same be said for Nagy in Hungary?

6.3 Why was the Berlin Wall built in 1961?

When Eisenhower was inaugurated as president in 1953 he took a more relaxed attitude to Berlin than Truman. On a visit to Britain in 1956, Khrushchev told the media: 'You do not like Communism. We do not like capitalism. There is only one way out – peaceful co-existence.'

Eisenhower was hopeful of working with Khrushchev to decrease Cold War rivalry if they could find a solution over Berlin. However, events in the late 1950s meant that tension actually increased.

Inter-Continental Ballistic Missiles

Hungary in 1956 showed Khrushchev's brutal side. The West had no idea how to handle him as he was volatile and unpredictable. At the UN in 1960 he famously interrupted British Prime Minister Harold Macmillan several times during a speech by slamming his fists on the table, and a week later he interrupted and insulted the Philippine delegate by taking off his shoe and hammering the desk with it. This behaviour was worrying with the development of Inter-Continental Ballistic Missiles **(ICBMs)** in the arms race. Any political crisis could have more serious military effects than perhaps was the case in the late 1940s.

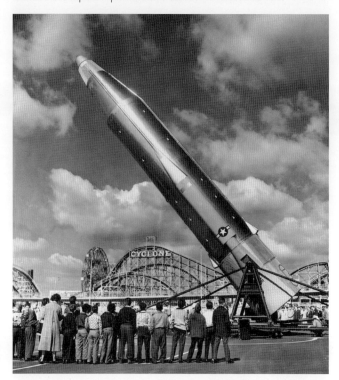

Source 6G: A photo from May 1959 of one of the US ICBMs surrounded by American school children.

The situation in East Germany

East Germany's population had fallen to 17 million by 1961, which meant it was the only Eastern European country to have a decreasing population. Approximately 2.8 million people had escaped from the communist world by going to West Berlin up to 1961, as there was no physical separation of the zones. This included many skilled workers and intellectuals so this was harming the East German economy (so costing the USSR money). Khrushchev therefore made finding a solution a priority.

Eisenhower didn't want to be put in the same situation as Truman, where a crisis over Berlin could escalate into a major war. In November 1958 Khrushchev demanded that Berlin be evacuated by foreign military powers within six months. Eisenhower responded with a different proposal; Berlin should be controlled by the United Nations and both sides should withdraw.

While this would reduce the possibility of conflict, it didn't solve the Soviet problem of emigration to the West through Berlin. Yet Khrushchev was still keen to discuss

Eisenhower's idea. He became the first Soviet leader to visit the US when he arrived for a tour in September 1959. The trip was a great success so the two men agreed to meet again for talks in Paris in 1960.

U2 Incident

The KGB (a secret police force and Soviet government spy agency) was aware of **U2** flights over Soviet territory but the planes flew too high to be shot down. In May 1960, new Soviet S-75 anti-aircraft defences damaged a U2 plane. The American pilot, Gary Powers, parachuted to the ground and was captured. At first Eisenhower denied that the plane was spying. The official line was that it was a weather plane that had gone off-track. Khrushchev then had Gary Powers paraded on Soviet TV, exposing the lie. Eisenhower admitted the truth but refused to apologise.

CHECK YOUR UNDERSTANDING 6.6

Look at Sources 6H and 6I. How would you have handled the incident if you were in Eisenhower's position?

The Paris summit was cancelled by Khrushchev. Eisenhower had served his second term as president and the election of 1960 was won by John F. Kennedy. He had promised to take a tougher line with Moscow.

CHECK YOUR UNDERSTANDING 6.7

Who was more to blame for the breakdown of relations from 1958 to 1961, the US or USSR?

 KEY TERMS

Inter-continental Ballistic Missiles (ICBMs): rockets first developed by the USSR in 1958 to carry explosives, including nuclear explosives. The US followed in 1959 (pictured in Source 6G) and in 1962 developed the sophisticated Minuteman missile. They have a range of over 3,500 miles so they can cross continents. Previously nuclear bombs (like the ones used on Japan in 1945) had to be dropped from planes.

U2: developed by Lockheed for the CIA and missions began in 1956. They could reach heights of 70,000 feet (twice the height flown by passenger aircraft) and their cameras could get a clear image of a piece of ground that was only 76 cm in width. The USSR could detect the planes on radar but couldn't shoot them down as they were too high up. They therefore developed S-75 missiles that could reach a higher altitude, as the US found out in 1960.

Sources 6H and 6I: A U2 spy plane, and the wreckage of the U2 shot down over the USSR in May 1960. The US government claimed it was a weather plane.

Kennedy and Khrushchev: the Vienna summit 1961

The relationship between Kennedy and Khrushchev was more like the early days of the Cold War. They were due to meet for the first time at the Vienna summit in June 1961. Just before this meeting, the CIA failed in an attempted invasion of Cuba to overthrow Fidel Castro's government (see Chapter 5, Case Study 2). The same month, the Soviets had another major propaganda victory when Yuri Gagarin became the first man in space.

Vienna marked one of the lowest points in the US–Soviet relationship. Khrushchev attacked Kennedy over Berlin. He banged his fist on the table and shouted: 'I want peace but if you want war that is your problem!' Kennedy responded: 'If that's true, it's going to be a cold winter.' Straight after the meeting Kennedy increased US military spending by $3.25 billion.

On 25 July, Kennedy addressed the American nation in a televised speech. He warned: 'We seek peace but we shall not surrender.' With so much tension and fear over Berlin, the movement of people to the west of the city became

KEY TERM

Defect: when a person changes allegiance and physically moves across a political divide from one state to the other, they are said to have defected.

a stampede. Over 1,000 people per day were **defecting** through West Berlin.

Building the Berlin Wall

Khrushchev chaired a meeting of Warsaw Pact leaders in Moscow, including East Germany's communist leader Walter Ulbricht. Ulbricht was instructed to build a wall around West Berlin (keeping its citizens penned in), but not to cut off western access to the city. Overnight on Sunday 13 August workers began putting up barbed wire and concrete pillars as Soviet tanks stood close by. By the time the news reached Washington, the city was already physically separated.

Many West Berliners had been out in the East that night, in nightclubs or visiting family. They were forbidden to return home so were stranded. Many tried to swim across the river or even jump from buildings to get back to West Berlin. Three days later the barbed wire was replaced with a concrete wall about 6 feet high. West Berliners could visit the East if they had a special visa. There were seven checkpoints at which they could cross. East Berliners could visit the West with special permission too, but they could only pass at the point where the US and Soviet zones met – Checkpoint Charlie (Source 6J).

Source 6J: The famous sign at Checkpoint Charlie in 1956.

133

ACTIVITY 6.8

Consider the impact that the Wall had on the daily lives of Berliners.

The Wall ran for 103 miles around the perimeter of West Berlin. It separated families, and even the underground rail network was shut down. The sewers were blocked and booby-trapped to stop people from escaping through them. Over time the Wall became more heavily fortified. There were electric fences, guard towers with snipers, landmines and many other features. The Soviets called it the 'Anti-Fascist Defence Wall' because it was supposedly protecting them from future German or western aggression.

TOP TIP

German news outlet *Die Welt* produced an excellent animation of the Wall, which can be found on YouTube. The video is called 'Walled In!'

US response and the crisis of October

Despite pressure from the Mayor of West Berlin, Willy Brandt, Kennedy didn't act. The Soviets hadn't completely cut off the city (as they had in 1948) and no clear act of aggression had taken place. He did reappoint the main figure of the airlift, General Clay, and 1,500 US troops were sent along the Autobahn from West Germany to increase the garrison. They weren't stopped by the Soviets. In public Kennedy spoke in support of West Berliners but in private he wasn't willing to risk war.

Source 6K: Tanks from the two superpowers face each other across the street during the crisis of October 1961.

Source 6L: Peter Fechter's body in no man's land, 17 August 1962.

However, a crisis erupted in October after a trivial incident. An American official and his wife were denied entry to East Berlin where they were due to see a play. General Clay was outraged and sent tanks to Checkpoint Charlie. Soon Soviet tanks appeared as well. A short distance separated them, with gun barrels pointed at one another for 16 hours. At the height of the crisis Kennedy managed to send word to Khrushchev that he would withdraw if the Soviets did. They agreed, so the crisis passed, but the world had come close to war over Berlin – again.

ACTIVITY 6.9

Look at Source 6K and compare it to the Berlin Blockade of 1948/9. Was this a more serious incident? Give reasons for your answer.

Peter Fechter, an 18-year-old, was the first casualty as he was shot trying to jump over the barbed wire (Source 6L). As he was in **no man's land**, East German soldiers waited for orders as to what to do. In full view of observers on both sides, he bled to death.

By 1989, 171 people had been killed trying to escape across the Wall. However, the most famous photograph was of the first ever defector over the barbed wire in Source 6M.

KEY TERM

No man's land: the area of contested ground between two enemy trench systems or two countries' border controls'.

Source 6M: East German border guard Hans Conrad Schumann spontaneously jumped the fence on 15 August 1961 – the day before construction began on the Wall.

ACTIVITY 6.10

Study Sources 6L and 6M. How might the Soviet Union explain these incidents? Relate your answer to the Soviet name for the Berlin Wall: the 'Anti-Fascist Defence Wall'.

6.4 What was the significance of 'Solidarity' in Poland for the decline of Soviet influence in Eastern Europe?

Poland was problematic for the USSR. It was the largest country in the buffer zone with a population of 26 million when Stalin died. The population was 95% Catholic so resisted the communist idea that religion was a myth. Protests in 1956 brought Wladyslaw Gomulka to power and he ruled until 1970. However, the economy wasn't

growing. In 1970 Gomulka was replaced by Edvard Gierek after protests about rising bread prices. The population had grown to 35 million by 1979 so huge financial assistance was needed; $3bn per year was given by the USSR to keep the economy working.

In summer 1980 there was a large strike in Gdansk, again over food prices, which led to 45 people being killed by soldiers. Gierek was removed and replaced by Stanisław Kania. However, wages remained low, food was in short supply and unrest was growing. As Brezhnev entered his final years the Soviet state was becoming increasingly corrupt. Its main focus for foreign policy was Afghanistan, where Soviet troops entered in 1979 and stayed there for a decade.

Stalin, Khrushchev and Brezhnev are travelling in a train. The train breaks down.

'Fix it!' orders Stalin.

They repair it but still the train doesn't move.

'Shoot everyone!' orders Stalin. They shoot everyone but still the train doesn't budge.

Stalin dies.

'Rehabilitate everyone!' orders Krushchev.

They are rehabilitated, but still the train won't go. Khrushchev is removed.

'Close the curtains,' orders Brezhnev, 'and pretend we're moving!'

Source 6N: A Russian joke about the different Soviet leaders.

CHECK YOUR UNDERSTANDING 6.8

What can we infer from Source 6N about the leadership style of Stalin, Khrushchev and Brezhnev?

Solidarity ('Solidarnosc'), 1980–1989
The situation was more complicated for Moscow to control than it had been for Hungary or Czechoslovakia. This was for four major reasons:

1   The solution in 1956 and 1968 was to change the leaders; Gomulka and Gierek had been replaced yet problems continued.

2   The Soviet economy was also struggling in the 1980s, a problem made much worse by the cost of their war in Afghanistan.

135

3   In 1978, Archbishop of Krakow Karol Wojtyłła was elected Pope John Paul II, the first Polish Pope. He visited Poland in 1979 to emotional scenes; around 2 million people lined the streets of Warsaw to welcome him.

4   In 1980 Ronald Reagan was elected president of the US. He was far more aggressive towards communism and raised hopes in Eastern Europe that he might do more than previous presidents.

Source 6O: Pope John Paul II visits Poland in 1979 for an 8-day tour.

ACTIVITY 6.11

Look at Source 6O. What does this tell us about communist control in Poland in 1979? Research Pope John Paul II's role in the Cold War online. Write a paragraph summarising his importance in undermining Soviet authority in Eastern Europe.

Following the strikes in the summer a new trade union called Solidarity was formed in Gdansk by a local electrician called Lech Wałęsa (Source 6P); it soon had 9 million members. The government banned Solidarity but the Polish Supreme Court declared in November that it was a legal organisation. The government had to come to an agreement with Solidarity; trade unions and the right to strike were allowed, as well as increases in pay and pensions. This was an amazing victory for Polish workers. Over the winter, Brezhnev considered sending in troops as he had done in Prague in 1968. Instead, he decided to remove Kania and appoint a military ruler who could break Solidarity's power, General Jaruzelski.

In 1981 Jaruzelski declared martial law and took serious action against strikes. In one incident a mine in Upper Silesia was flooded by riot police. The miners on strike were below ground so they all drowned. He also imprisoned Wałęsa and the other leaders of Solidarity. All of these measures failed to break the movement. Wałęsa was released following public pressure and in 1983 he was awarded the Nobel Peace Prize. In 1984 the government faced a significant crisis over a priest called Jerzy Popiełuszko who had links to Solidarity. He had been beaten to death in jail by police; 250,000 people attended his funeral.

Source 6P: Lech Wałęsa is thrown in the air in celebration after the first Solidarity congress in 1981.

In 1988 a nationwide campaign of strikes paralysed Poland's economy. Jaruzelski had failed to get popular support for his economic reforms and now the mood across Europe was changing. Free elections were finally held in Poland in June 1989. Solidarity won 99 out of 100 seats in the Senate. Jaruzelski was forced to bring them into his government. One year later, with communist regimes collapsing across Eastern Europe, Lech Wałęsa was elected as president of Poland.

ACTIVITY 6.12

Selecting evidence: Choose three facts from this section which you feel best illustrate the problems in Poland up to 1980. Why did you choose these? Compare your selection with a partner and justify your choices.

Why did Solidarity succeed?

To analyse the reasons for Solidarity's success we can organise the information into two categories:

1   Internal factors

    a   The cost of living was too high – especially food prices – and aid from the USSR actually prevented the economy from growing as there was no incentive to try new methods.

b   Lech Wałęsa proved to be a formidable opponent for Jaruzelski, and Pope John Paul II was a hero in Poland. Many Poles attribute the collapse of communism to the power of Catholicism.

c   The extent of support for Solidarity and its organisation were vital. Events in 1956 and 1968 were quite uncoordinated in comparison, and with 9 million members – a quarter of the population – the government couldn't arrest everyone involved.

2   External factors

a   Poles also received strong backing from Ronald Reagan and British Prime Minister Margaret Thatcher. She visited a shipyard in Gdansk in 1988 during the strike campaign.

b   Solidarity was seen in a similar light to other great freedom movements of the period. The main one was the ANC in South Africa, so Nelson Mandela and Wałęsa were often mentioned in the same context by the media.

c   The USSR had a crisis of leadership in the early 1980s. Brezhnev died in 1982 and was followed by two leaders in quick succession. Yuri Andropov died in 1984 and Konstantin Chernenko died in 1985. There was no question of Moscow sending in the military to impose order, especially with soldiers committed in Afghanistan from 1979 to 1989.

ACTIVITY 6.13

1   Using the factors above, make a mind map showing the interrelationship of the reasons for Solidarity's success.

2   Which do you think was more important: the internal or external factors?

3   Finally, research Lech Wałęsa online and write a brief biography of him. Was he more influential in Poland than Pope John Paul II? Give reasons for your answer.

CHECK YOUR UNDERSTANDING 6.9

Why did Solidarity prove more difficult to contain for the USSR than events in 1956 or 1968?

6.5 How far was Gorbachev personally responsible for the collapse of Soviet control over Eastern Europe?

Source 6Q: Mikhail Gorbachev meeting workers in Moscow in 1985.

ACTIVITY 6.14

What does Source 6Q suggest about Gorbachev's leadership style compared to previous Soviet leaders like Stalin and Brezhnev?

As was the case with Poland, the Soviet Union was experiencing economic problems in the 1970s and 1980s. Corruption became a serious issue under Brezhnev and the old system of planning economic growth under **five-year plans** was heavily criticised. It prevented new methods and innovation at a time when the wider world was seeing huge change as microchip technology was introduced. These pressures had to be dealt with by new leader Mikhail Gorbachev, who came to power in 1985; a period of significant change began. His reforms were designed to modernise and improve communism but instead it collapsed by 1991. Was it his fault? Or was the situation already past the point of saving?

KEY TERM

Five-year plans: the basis for communist economies. These involved the government deciding what was needed by the population and then setting targets for production. There was no private business and little incentive to create new products.

Gorbachev's reforms

Two major reforms were introduced by Gorbachev:

1   Perestroika – this means 'restructuring'. The aim was to breathe life into the economy and encourage new ideas. Workers could set up their own businesses from 1986 as central planning was abolished.

2   Glasnost – this means 'openness'. This allowed greater freedom of speech and an end to punishing critics of the government. In 1986 the prominent critic Andrei Sakharov, a famous physicist, was released from prison. An elected parliament called the Congress of People's Deputies was also introduced.

This had a huge impact on Soviet life. Criticism poured out and party leaders at all levels were challenged for their corruption and incompetence.

Gorbachev also changed the USSR's foreign policy. He met president Reagan at summits in Geneva in 1985 and Reykjavik in 1986. These meetings, which included Margaret Thatcher, focused on reducing weapons stockpiles and ending the war in Afghanistan. In 1987 the Intermediate Nuclear Forces (INF) Treaty was signed, which led to 2,692 missiles being destroyed by 1991. However, the most crucial step for Eastern Europe was Gorbachev's speech to the United Nations in December 1998 (Source 6R). He announced massive cuts in Soviet weapons and forces stationed in Eastern Europe. This signalled the end of the Brezhnev Doctrine.

The relations between the Soviet Union and the United States of America have a history of five and a half decades. As the world changed, so did the nature, role and place of those relations in world politics. For too long a time they developed along the lines of confrontation and sometimes animosity – either overt or covert. But in the last few years the entire world could breathe a sigh of relief thanks to the changes for the better in the substance and the atmosphere of the relationship between Moscow and Washington.

Source 6R: From Gorbachev's speech to the United Nations on 7 December 1988.

CHECK YOUR UNDERSTANDING 6.10

Why did relations improve between Moscow and Washington in the 1980s? Make a list of reasons and put them in order of importance.

Consequences in Eastern Europe

At a meeting with Eastern European leaders in March 1989 Gorbachev confirmed that he was abandoning the Brezhnev Doctrine. This meant that these states would have to find their own solutions for dealing with domestic opposition. As with Khrushchev's 'secret speech' in 1956, expectations had been raised and soon there were challenges. Hungary opened its borders to allow free movement into Austria, breaching the Iron Curtain, and Solidarity won the Polish elections. The most striking protest was the 'Baltic Chain', formed on 'Black Ribbon Day' on 23 August 1989, an international day of protest against human rights violations in the USSR. The cities of Tallinn, Riga and Vilnius were linked together by a 675 kilometre human chain of 2 million people. It was a clear challenge to Soviet authority.

Source 6S: The Baltic Chain in August 1989 was an example of non-violent protest.

ACTIVITY 6.15

Compare the Baltic Chain protest shown in Source 6S to those in Hungary in 1956 (Sources 6B and 6C). Why was the non-violent protest more effective as a means of criticising the USSR?

The moment which symbolised the end of the Cold War took place in Berlin. The hard-line East German communist leader Erich Honecker was removed in October 1989. Reforms were being considered by the new leader Egon Krenz such as allowing East Germans to emigrate permanently. In a day of confusion on 9 November a press conference was held where an official suddenly announced that Berliners could move

138

across the checkpoints without a passport or permit. He had misread the document he had been given, and the consequence was enormous. That night 2 million Berliners flooded the checkpoints and crossed the divide. Bemused soldiers watched as they started to pull the wall down. Twenty-eight years of separation ended overnight.

Demonstrations in Czechoslovakia that month brought about a peaceful change known as the 'Velvet Revolution' (or the 'Gentle Revolution'). Václav Havel was elected president in 1990. In Hungary, Kadar had resigned in 1988 and with the border opened to Austria in 1989 the collapse of communism soon followed. A centre-right government was formed in 1990.

TOP TIP

There are some excellent films about life in Germany before and after the fall of the Berlin Wall. In particular, *Goodbye Lenin* and *The Lives of Others* have been critically acclaimed. They are recommended viewing if you want to understand the beliefs and feelings of ordinary people in East Germany.

Role of Ronald Reagan

Events seemed to accelerate after 1985 when Gorbachev came to power. However, there were longer-term causes that can be attributed to US president Reagan. He was elected in 1980 and took a totally different stance against communism.

Reagan ended the period of relaxed relations with Moscow (known as détente). The US boycotted the Moscow Olympics in 1980, so the Soviets boycotted the Los Angeles Olympics in 1984. Reagan called the Soviet Union the 'evil empire' in a speech in 1983.

He believed the Cold War could be won by massively increasing weapons spending beyond the limits that the Soviets could afford. From 1981 to 1986 he increased the US's defence spending from $179 billion to $370 billion. Part of this was the ambitious Strategic Defence Initiative (SDI). SDI would have created satellites to shoot down ICBMs in flight. The media called it 'the Star Wars' programme because it sounded like science fiction and many have doubted whether it was even possible. If it was it would have made all Soviet ICBMs obsolete. The USSR did not have the money to keep pace with this.

ACTIVITY 6.16

Reagan's supporters claim he ended the Cold War by defeating the USSR in the arms race. His critics say he risked a 'Second Cold War'. Which interpretation do you agree with and why?

Reagan's stance has been described by some historians as a 'Second Cold War' as the relationship with the Soviets deteriorated so suddenly and sharply. At the end of 1983 a Korean passenger jet was shot down by Soviet planes when it accidentally entered their air space. American criticism was so hostile that some in Moscow thought they might launch a nuclear attack. Relations had not been this tense since 1962.

When Gorbachev came to power Reagan maintained his attitude but was persuaded to talk to the new leader by UK Prime Minister Margaret Thatcher.

I am cautiously optimistic. I like Mr. Gorbachev. We can do business together. We both believe in our own political systems. He firmly believes in his; I firmly believe in mine. We are never going to change one another. So that is not in doubt, but we have two great interests in common: that we should both do everything we can to see that war never starts again … And secondly, I think we both believe that they are the more likely to succeed if we can build up confidence in one another and trust in one another.

Source 6T: Margaret Thatcher in a TV interview in 1984. She met Gorbachev just before he came to power.

Although they met in summits, Reagan opened up the issue of Berlin by visiting the city in June 1987. He gave a speech in which he issued a dramatic challenge to Gorbachev (see Source 6U).

There is one sign the Soviets can make that would be unmistakable, that would advance dramatically the cause of freedom and peace. General Secretary Gorbachev, if you seek peace, if you seek prosperity for the Soviet Union and Eastern Europe, if you seek liberalisation: Come here to this gate! Mr Gorbachev, open this gate! Mr Gorbachev, tear down this wall!

Source 6U: Reagan's speech in Berlin, 12 June 1987.

139

ACTIVITY 6.17

Read Source 6T and then research Margaret Thatcher's role in the Cold War online. Compare and contrast her views with those of Reagan and Gorbachev. How significant was she in ending the Cold War?

CHECK YOUR UNDERSTANDING 6.11

Did the thaw in relations start from the Soviet side or from the West?

Communism collapsed across Eastern Europe in 1990. The effects spread inside Russia too, where communism ended in December 1991 as the USSR disintegrated into the separate republics that made up the union. Gorbachev's reputation inside and outside Russia could scarcely be different. He won the Nobel Peace Prize in 1990 and was hailed as a great statesman around the world. Yet when he stood for election to be president of Russia in 1996 he won only 0.5% of the vote, coming 7th.

ACTIVITY 6.18

Who do you think had a greater impact on ending communism in Eastern Europe, Gorbachev or Reagan? Write a paragraph on each leader giving evidence as to why they were responsible, then reach a decision on who had the more significant impact and why.

Review your learning

Go back to the focus points listed at the beginning of this chapter. You should have a good understanding of the three main countries covered in this chapter: Hungary, Czechoslovakia and Poland. You should also have a good idea of the different Soviet rulers: Khrushchev, Brezhnev and Gorbachev. Use your knowledge of these to answer the questions.

CHECK YOUR UNDERSTANDING 6.12

This chapter contains a large number of names of political leaders. Make a list of all the important people for each country covered. Write one sentence for each one stating who they were, like this example:

Country	Name	Who they were
Czechoslovakia	Alexander Dubček	Communist reformer and Prime Minister who led the Prague Spring.

When you've finished your list, make a flashcard for each one and test yourself on these regularly so that you can recall them more easily.

The Big Challenge

Selecting and deploying information

Make a list of reasons why each of the three countries might be a problem for Moscow:

- Hungary
- Czechoslovakia
- Poland.

Think about political reasons, economic reasons and other factors like size of population.

Now complete this table for the three Soviet leaders:

Leader	Leadership style and aims	Major events when they were in power	US presidents they had to deal with
Khrushchev			
Brezhnev			
Gorbachev			

This summary should help you understand the importance of context. What challenges did they face? What limits were there when taking actions?

Summary points

- Protests against Soviet dominance in Hungary in 1956 and Czechoslovakia in 1968 were both ruthlessly crushed by Moscow.

- Hungarian demands were more radical and were motivated by the belief that foreign help was coming. Czechoslovak demands, despite being more modest, were also too dangerous to be considered.

- The Berlin Wall was built as a reaction to growing tensions in the 1950s and early 1960s; it remained until 1989.

- The Solidarity movement in Poland was different to the events of 1956 and 1968 because it was more widespread and had greater international support.

- By the end of this period, Mikhail Gorbachev's changes had not resulted in a reformed, more humane and responsive communism, taking over the government of the Warsaw Pact countries. When not enforced by military power, Soviet control of East Germany, Hungary, Czechoslovakia and Poland collapsed, and without that control the communist governments quickly fell from power.

Exam-style questions

1 Describe the main events in Hungary in 1956.

2 What were the main features of the Prague Spring?

3 What reforms did Gorbachev introduce in the Soviet Union?

4 Why was there opposition to communist control in Hungary?

5 Why was Solidarity so popular in Poland?

6 Why did Reagan's policies cause problems for Soviet leaders?

7 'Opposition to Soviet rule in Hungary was not a serious threat to Moscow.' How far do you agree with this statement?

8 How far was Gorbachev responsible for the end of communist control over Eastern Europe?

9 'Events in Poland were the main reason why Soviet authority collapsed in Eastern Europe.' How far do you agree with this statement?

Chapter 7

Key Question 7: Why did events in the Gulf matter, c.1970–2000?

Focus points

- Why was Saddam Hussein able to come to power in Iraq?
- What was the nature of Saddam Hussein's rule in Iraq?
- Why was there a revolution in Iran in 1979?
- What were the causes and consequences of the Iran–Iraq War, 1980–1988?
- Why did the First Gulf War take place?

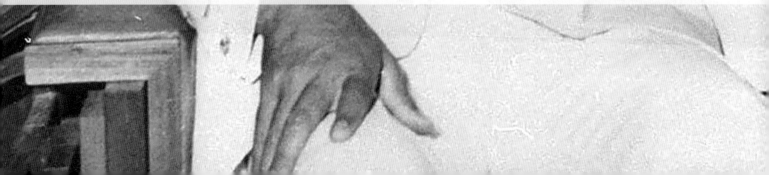

What is this enquiry about?

Just as the map of Europe was redrawn in the aftermath of the First World War, so the map of the Middle East also changed dramatically. The Ottoman Empire was partitioned and one of new the states created was Iraq. The state of Persia survived a period of partial occupation and the overthrow of the ruling monarch and the establishment of a new royal family, which would remain in power until the 1970s. These neighbouring countries would develop a rivalry with profound consequences for the region and the world. The rise of Saddam Hussein and **Ayatollah** Khomeini in the late 1970s led to regional warfare and political change whose effects are still being felt today. It was also an important component of the Cold War as these conflicts drew in the superpowers of USA and the USSR. In this chapter you will explore these questions:

- Why did the regimes of Iraq and Iran change in the late 1970s?
- Evaluate the role played by oil in the development of these states.

- Analyse the causes of war and identify the consequences.
- Assess the impact wars in the Gulf had on the rest of the region and the wider world.

ACTIVITY 7.1

Study Figure 7.1 and contrast the situation in the Middle East before and after the First World War. What are the main differences? What effects would these have on people who lived in the Middle East? What consequences can you foresee?

7.1 Why was Saddam Hussein able to come to power in Iraq?
The development of Iraq from 1920 to 1958

In 1920, the British took three provinces of the eastern Ottoman Empire – Mosul, Baghdad and Basra – and created a new country called Iraq. A monarch, King Faisal I, was put on the throne in 1921 and expected to run this

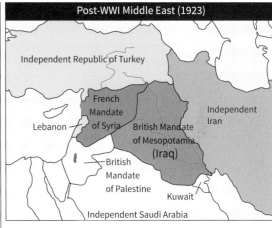

Figure 7.1: The map left shows the extent of the Ottoman Empire in 1914. The map on the right shows how this had changed by 1923 with new states being created in the Middle East.

new state. This was easier said than done. There were several reasons why Iraq was difficult to rule:

- The population was 80% Arabian and spoke Arabic, but 20% were **Kurdish** and spoke a different language.
- **Shia** Muslims were slightly in the majority but the government was dominated by **Sunnis**. This often led to tensions, especially as neighbouring Iran was approximately 95% Shia.

KEY TERMS

Ayatollahs: the most senior religious leaders in Iran. They are experts on philosophy and law and became the leaders of Iran after the revolution.

Kurds: an ethnic group, not a religious one; most Kurds are Sunni, but they also include Shias, as well as Christians and other faiths and traditions. The Kurds are the largest ethnic group in the world who do not have their own state. As well as Iraq, there are large populations in Iran, Syria and Turkey.

Sunni and Shia: the two main branches of Islam. This division followed back to a disagreement about the leadership (caliphate) in the 7th century CE. The majority of Muslims across the world are Sunni but Iran is 95% Shia. Iraq has a slight majority of Shia but the Ba'ath Party leadership was largely Sunni.

- Oil had been discovered but was controlled by the Iraq Petroleum Company (IPC). This was a foreign firm and the British had the majority share. Some 95% of Iraq's oil revenue went to the British, French and Americans.
- Iraq's borders were established by the British but were unsatisfactory for two reasons. First, there was continual conflict with Iran over their common frontier. Second, in the south the Iraqis had little access to the Gulf. Their coastline was only 36 miles long. The single port, Basra, was 50 miles inland and was accessed via the Shatt-al-Arab strait. Kuwait had greater access to the sea and also had joint control of the Rumaila oil field. Many in Iraq felt that Kuwait should have been included in their country. They blamed the British for deliberately limiting their influence in the Gulf.

Although Britain granted independence to Iraq in 1932, the London government kept control of oil, Iraq's defence and foreign policy. In 1941 a rebellion was launched by Rashed Ali but was soon crushed. Britain occupied the country during the war from 1941–1945 and kept the monarchy in power afterwards. This British support for the king only made his government unpopular and it was overthrown in a military coup in 1958. The young King Faisal II, Crown Prince Abdullah and the Prime Minister Nuri al-Sa'id were among many who were killed in the violence.

TOP TIP
When researching online you may find different spellings of names. This is because Arabic script and the alphabets you are familiar with are different. For example, you might see Hussein spelt as Husayn. Either is fine, as long as you are consistent and stick to the one spelling when writing an answer.

CHECK YOUR UNDERSTANDING 7.1

Why were the British unpopular in Iraq? Make a list of reasons into a mind map. Think about the ways in which these reasons were inter-connected.

The rise of the Ba'ath Party 1958 to 1968

The new government was led by Brigadier Abd al-Karim Qasim. The army had been inspired by pan-Arabism, a doctrine that aimed to unite all Arabs and end interference by western powers in the Middle East. This was fuelled by the rise of Gamal Abdel Nasser who became president of Egypt in 1954. In 1956 he stood up to Britain, France and Israel during the Suez Crisis, which made him a hero in the Arab world. Arab nationalism became a powerful force in the Middle East in the 1960s and appealed to many Iraqis.

CHECK YOUR UNDERSTANDING 7.2

What would be the benefits and problems posed by the military regime in Iraq?

The **Ba'ath Party** had been founded in Syria in 1947 by Michel Aflaq and truly represented pan-Arabism. It wanted to establish a united, **secular** Arab state. Their slogan was 'unity, freedom, socialism'. The Ba'ath Party in Iraq pushed for greater Arab nationalism in the 1960s and soon came to oppose the new government, whose military leaders were believed to rule in their own interests and not that of all Arabs.

KEY TERMS

Ba'ath Party: founded in 1947 in Syria. It aimed to unite Arabs in one single state and remove western influence.

Secular: 'non-religious'. A secular government is one not founded on religious principles, isn't committed to a religious programme and doesn't promote religion.

In 1963 the Ba'athists overthrew and executed Qasim, but they lost power to Colonel Abd al-Salam Arif. He died in a plane crash in 1966 and power passed to his brother, Abd al-Rahman Arif. The Ba'ath Party was banned, but was secretly reorganised by Ahmad Hasan al-Bakr. Al-Bakr came from Tikrit and he promoted his young relative Saddam Hussein, who came from the same town (see Source 7A). In 1968 they rose up against the government and this time were successful in holding on to power. They secured their position by removing potential enemies in the army and putting trusted Ba'athists in positions of political power. The most important body was the **Revolutionary Command Council** (RCC), which made all the key decisions and could also make laws. Al-Bakr was the chairman and Saddam was made deputy in 1969.

KEY TERM

Revolutionary Command Council (RCC): the main decision-making and law-making body of the Iraqi government after 1968.

Source 7A: Al-Bakr (right) pictured with Saddam Hussein in 1978. Saddam called him 'the father leader'.

CHECK YOUR UNDERSTANDING 7.3

What were the main beliefs of the Ba'ath Party?

Saddam Hussein's rise to power

Although Saddam Hussein did not become president of Iraq until 1979, it was clear that he was the most powerful figure in the new government from as early as 1970. Born in 1937, Saddam was from a poor background in Tikrit. His father was a shepherd and appears to have died before his son was born, so Saddam was raised by an uncle who hated

the British and had taken part in the failed 1941 rebellion. This seems to have had a strong effect on Saddam's development. In 1957 he joined the Ba'ath Party but had to escape to Cairo in 1959 after being part of an attempt to assassinate Qasim. He was jailed after the Ba'athist coup of 1963 failed but managed to escape from prison. When al-Bakr reorganised the party, Saddam was made Deputy Secretary General, and soon took control of the militia and the security network of the government in 1968.

Saddam was an admirer of Stalin and had a reputation for being ruthless. He trusted few people and those that he did were usually from Tikrit. He worked well with al-Bakr in the early 1970s but by the time he became President in 1979 their relationship was more difficult. Al-Bakr resigned on health grounds but it has been speculated that Saddam threatened to remove him by force if he didn't quit. Saddam consolidated his power by purging his enemies in the armed forces and the party. He was now President, Secretary General of the Ba'ath Party, Chairman of the RCC, and head of the armed forces. It had taken over a decade but he was now the undisputed ruler of Iraq.

CHECK YOUR UNDERSTANDING 7.4

What characteristics did Saddam Hussein possess that enabled him to take control of Iraq?

ACTIVITY 7.2

Make a timeline of Saddam's rise to power. In pairs choose the five most important events. Why did you select these events over others? Make sure you can justify your answer.

7.2 What was the nature of Saddam Hussein's rule in Iraq?

Government and propaganda under Saddam

The main institutions of government in Iraq were:

- the Revolutionary Command Council (RCC)
- the Ba'ath Party
- the **Republican Guard**
- the army
- the National Assembly.

KEY TERM

Republican Guard: formed in 1969, they were the elite troops of the Iraqi state. They were separate from the army.

The Ba'athists were not the only political party as the communists also had a reasonable following. Elections to the National Assembly were first held in 1980 and the Ba'athists won three-quarters of the seats, but Kurd and Shia parties were also represented. However, the National Assembly possessed no real power. Its only purpose was to provide Saddam with a place to make speeches. The communists were allowed to exist just to keep the USSR happy as Iraq's main international ally. Saddam alone made the major decisions and often purged the government and army of those he believed disloyal. After becoming president in 1979 he had 66 leading figures tried, with 22 sentenced to death. The video footage of their executions was circulated around the party as a warning.

On the model of Stalin, Saddam developed a cult of personality. State propaganda called him al-batal (the hero) and al-mufakir (the thinker). Iraqis joked that the real population of the country was 28 million – 14 million Iraqis and 14 million statues of Saddam. Propaganda was promoted in the main newspaper *al-Thawra* and all TV stations were owned by the Ministry of Culture and Information. Posters were made showing leaders from the region's ancient past, such as Nebuchadnezzar, shaking hands with Saddam and looking up to him. Ancient cities such as Babylon and Nineveh were the subjects of archaeological digs to link the new regime to the glorious past.

ACTIVITY 7.3

Draw a diagram showing the structure of Iraq's government and society. Cover all the key institutions and try to show the order of importance. Try to remember all the key terms so that you can use them in an answer.

Source 7B: A propaganda image of Saddam Hussein on display in 2002.

CHECK YOUR UNDERSTANDING 7.5

Look at Source 7B. What message is the poster trying to convey and what techniques does the artist use to do so?

The economy and oil

The 35 years that Saddam was in power from 1968 to 2003 can be divided into three clear phases. The first period up to 1980 was a time of great prosperity and economic and social progress. The wars with Iran and Kuwait during 1980–1991 destroyed the economy and plunged the nation into debt. The final phase, 1991–2003, was marked by stagnation made harder by international sanctions imposed by the United Nations over weapons production.

The government **nationalised** the oil industry in 1972 to end foreign control of it. The timing of this was incredibly fortunate as a war in 1973 between Egypt and Israel led to **OPEC** blocking sales of oil to Europe and USA. Consequently, oil prices rose sharply. When the Ba'ath Party came to power, Iraq's annual oil revenue was less than $500 million. By 1979 it reached $26 billion. This had a significant impact on the average income of each person. It rose from $382 per year when oil was nationalised to $2,726 by the end of the decade. Car ownership also went up by over 150%. Some Gulf states, including Kuwait, were producing more than OPEC allowed, which lowered the cost of oil worldwide. Iraq argued that for every $1 drop in the price of a barrel of oil they lost $1 billion per year.

KEY TERMS

Nationalise: the state takes possession of an industry, so that it is no longer owned by private individuals but by the state.

OPEC: The Organization of the Petroleum Exporting Countries was founded in 1960 and is dominated by Middle Eastern countries. Its aim is to regulate the production and supply of oil among its members to keep the price of oil stable.

This massive increase in finance was used to develop public services and help ordinary people. Taxes were reduced and pensions improved. However, war in the 1980s was a disaster, leaving Iraq $100 billion in debt. The Gulf War in 1990–1991 made the situation worse through restrictions on Iraq's trade. After the Gulf War, Iraq's gross domestic product (GDP) stood at $28bn per year. By 1999 it had only increased slightly to $31bn. The boom of the 1970s was now just a memory.

> The complete emancipation of women from the ties which held them back in the past, during the ages of despotism and ignorance, is a basic aim of the Party and the Revolution. Women make up one half of society. Our society will remain backward and in chains unless its women are liberated, enlightened and educated.

Source 7C: Extract from a speech delivered by Saddam Hussein at the Third Conference of the General Federation of Iraq Women, 17 April 1971.

Social change: women, farmers and education

The 1970s was a positive time for many. The Ba'ath Party was **secular** and believed women should be educated and have important jobs in society (see Source 7C). By 1980 half of all teachers and dentists were female, as were one-third of university students and doctors. The law was changed to end forced marriage and make divorce easier. However, this progress didn't last. As Saddam's ideology changed in the 1990s he relied more on tribal support to maintain his regime. This meant that old-fashioned customs became more important than progressive ideas. A law was passed allowing families to kill women they believed to be guilty of adultery. This was based on the ancient tribal principle of 'erasing dishonour with blood'. Women were forbidden to travel abroad unless accompanied by a male relative on their father's side of the family.

CHECK YOUR UNDERSTANDING 7.6

How far did Saddam live up to his promise to improve the position of women in Iraq, which he made in Source 7C?

The poorest members of Iraqi society were usually farmers and agricultural workers, including many Shia in the south. In 1958 as much as 55% of Iraq's farmland was owned by the richest 1%. In 1970, the government set limits on property ownership with surplus land taken away and given to poorer farmers. Over 250,000 benefited from this reform. Money made from oil was used to build roads, hospitals and electric power stations. These changes were important in building support for Saddam in the early years of his rule.

Education was a major priority. In 1978, a campaign was launched to end illiteracy within three years. All

children and adults were forced to attend special schools for at least two years. Although the campaign didn't meet its targets, it taught 2 million people basic reading and writing. **UNESCO** commended Iraq for this success. Secondary school attendance increased by two-thirds and university places nearly doubled. All this was seriously disrupted by the wars of the 1980s and there was little money for education after 1991.

CHECK YOUR UNDERSTANDING 7.7

How successful were the reforms of the 1970s?

KEY TERM

UNESCO: the United Nations Educational, Scientific and Cultural Organization.

TOP TIP

There are a lot of facts and numbers to recall, especially when looking at economic history. Don't try to remember them all at once. Build up a list with two or three facts that you can memorise, then add to this list gradually. It might help to organise the numbers, for example put them in order of smallest to largest or separate into facts like percentages or money.

Relations with the Shi'ites and Kurds

Saddam was a Sunni Arab who worried constantly about the loyalty of ordinary Iraqis. Although he didn't persecute the Kurds and the Shia immediately, they suffered increasingly as time passed. The Kurds had been allowed a great deal of cultural and administrative freedom after Saddam made a deal with them in 1970, but when he failed to keep these promises they rebelled in 1974. They were helped by the Shah of Iran but when a treaty was agreed with the Iranians in 1975 at Algiers it left the Kurds in a difficult situation. They agreed a ceasefire but it was clear that Saddam didn't trust them. In 1988 at the end of the war with Iran he used chemical weapons on the Kurdish town of Halabja killing 5,000. When he was defeated in the Gulf War the Kurds rose in rebellion but received no international support. Again, they were bombed and as many as 2 million escaped over the border to Iran and Turkey. They were only made safe to return by the enforcement of a 'no fly zone' above the 36th parallel, by the Americans and the British.

ACTIVITY 7.4

Draw a table showing the positive and negative elements of change in Iraq.

Positive	Negative

In groups, discuss whether or not Iraqi society made progress overall under Saddam Hussein. In the debate give evidence to support your arguments.

Shia protests against Saddam began in 1977 and increased in 1979. A group called al-Da'wa ('Islamic Call') were active in protests, so Saddam ordered the execution of the leading Shi'ite cleric Mohammad Baqir al-Sadr and had his sister killed. This was a significant cause of the war with Iran as Ayatollah Khomeini accused Saddam's government of being un-Islamic and called on Iraqis to remove him from power. Shi'ites remained loyal during the war with Iran yet after the Gulf War they had tired of Saddam's rule and rose in rebellion. As with the Kurds there was no international support so Saddam sent his loyal Republican Guard to deal with the rebels. Some 30,000 were killed and another 70,000 fled across the border to Iran. A 'no-fly zone' was imposed below the 33rd parallel which restored some safety, but the damage was done.

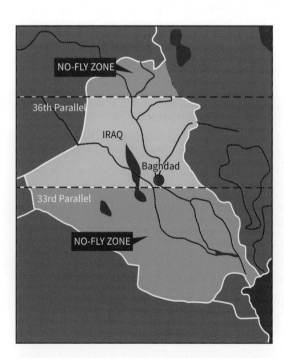

Figure 7.2: The no-fly zones established to protect the Kurds in the north and the Shia in the south. The northern line is the 36th Parallel and the southern line is the 33rd Parallel.

ACTIVITY 7.5

Saddam faced opposition from various groups throughout his period in power. What were the main reasons for this?

7.3 Why was there a revolution in Iran in 1979?

Iran under the Pahlavis 1926–1953

The final dynasty to rule Iran was the Pahlavis. After the First World War an army officer called Reza Khan seized power in Tehran and was crowned as Reza Shah in 1926. He began to modernise a country that was still mainly peasant-based and had little industry or education. Reza Shah was secular and restricted religious influence. He removed Arabic words from the Persian language (Farsi), ended the wearing of veils by women and established Tehran University. In 1935 he ordered that the country was to be known as Iran and not Persia.

Oil had been discovered by the British in 1908 and they had a contract that entitled them to keep 84% of all profits. Reza Shah struggled to renegotiate this deal and during the Second World War it was feared that Nazi Germany might occupy Iran's oil fields. Britain feared a repeat of the events in Iraq in 1941. With the Soviets they deposed Reza Shah and installed his young son Muhammad Reza Shah as king. Iran was militarily occupied from 1941 to 1945, with American troops arriving in 1942.

Oil made Iran a crucial territory in the Cold War. Growing American influence provoked a reaction in 1950 from the National Front led by Mohammad Mossadeq. He became

Source 7D: The Shah (centre) pictured in 1950. He was known as the 'suitcase ruler' because he packed his bags and fled in 1953, only to return a few days later. In his early years he struggled for authority.

Prime Minister in 1951 and nationalised the oil industry. However, Britain and USA led a boycott of Iranian oil and the CIA helped to depose Mossadeq in 1953. The Shah temporarily fled to Italy but was restored to power (see Source 7D).

Government and reform under the Shah 1953–1971

The Shah was backed by the Americans but there was a strong communist party, called the Tudeh, which was supported by the USSR. The National Front was outlawed and restrictions were placed on free speech. Finally, the **ulama** hadn't supported the coup of 1953 as they disliked Mossadeq and the Tudeh's secular views, but in the 1960s they became the most serious opposition group.

The Shah took personal control of the country, aided by increased oil revenues. A new deal was made with Britain and the USA that gave Iran 50% of oil proceeds. This was used to expand the military and fund reforms. Politically, there were elections to the Majlis (parliament) where two official parties were allowed to debate issues. However, they were puppet organisations and Iranians knew them as the 'Yes' and 'Yes sir' parties. The Tudeh were banned and political opponents were ruthlessly pursued by the secret police, **SAVAK**.

President Kennedy pressurised the Shah in the early 1960s to relax political control, so in 1963 he started the 'White Revolution' (so-called because it was meant to transform the country without bloodshed). The three aims were land reform, education and women's rights. There was some success as 2 million peasants became landowners for the first time. A literacy **corps** was created of 100,000 students who went to villages to teach peasants to read and write. Women gained some additional rights under a reform of family law, for example, their husbands needed to ask their consent to take another wife. Average annual income per person increased from $200 in 1963 to around $2,000 by the end of the Shah's reign.

KEY TERMS

Ulama: Muslim clerics are known collectively as the ulama. In Iran they are highly influential.

SAVAK: the Iranian government's Organisation for Intelligence and Security. They used torture to obtain information and were greatly feared. The exact number of agents is not known but could have been as many as 60,000.

However, the White Revolution's benefits were unevenly spread. The increase in wealth came mainly from oil, especially after 1973. Improved health care caused a population boom:

Tehran became a city of 4.5 million people and half of the Iranian population was under the age of 16. Furthermore, the Shah was a figure of ridicule. He was out of touch with ordinary Iranians as he travelled everywhere by helicopter. He staged an elaborate propaganda celebration in 1971 at Persepolis to mark 2,500 years of Iranian monarchy (see Sources 7E and 7F). It cost at least $100 million. Images were broadcast on television of the Shah and his foreign guests sipping champagne in huge marquees in the desert while many ordinary Iranians lived below the poverty line. Instead of increasing his authority it did a great deal of damage.

ACTIVITY 7.6

What similarities do you notice in the development of Iraq and Iran? Make a list of common features. Which state made more progress up to 1979?

Source 7E: The tented city built at Persepolis in 1971 to hold the Shah's celebrations.

CHECK YOUR UNDERSTANDING 7.8

What did the Shah hope to achieve with the 1971 Persepolis celebrations?

Religious opposition

The Shah's major critic was Ruhollah Khomeini. Born in 1902 into a respected family, he trained as a religious scholar. He rose to the level of ayatollah in 1961 and suddenly gained fame in 1963 by preaching against the government. He was arrested by SAVAK after a raid in which several of his supporters were killed. Demonstrations broke out in Tehran so he was released, but his continued criticism of American influence and the Shah's corruption led to another period in prison. He was exiled in 1964 to Turkey but then went to Iraq where he

FACT FILE

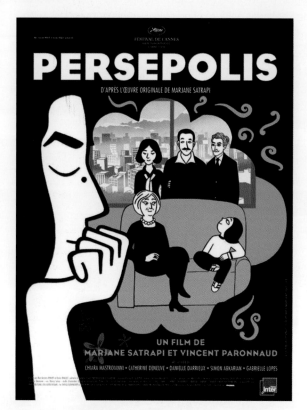

Source 7F: Poster of the 2007 film adaptation of Marjane Satrapi's book, *Persepolis*.

Graphic novel *Persepolis* by Marjane Satrapi covers the causes and consequences of the revolution against the Shah. It is an excellent book to read to understand the context of this period and was made into a film.

continued to preach against the Iranian government from the holy Shia city of Najaf.

Ayatollah Khomeini found agreement with many Iranians because of the great inequality of wealth. He told government to aid the poor before the White Revolution began so it looked as if the Shah was only responding to his critics. Khomeini also attacked American influence, which increased dramatically in the 1960s and 1970s. Nearly one million Americans are estimated to have visited Iran in this period and 50,000 became permanent residents. They mainly worked in defence because the American government sold so many weapons to the Shah. However, they rarely mixed with Iranians and lived in their own compounds. Iran was covered in advertising for American products and cinemas showed Hollywood films. Many of these were highly offensive to Khomeini because of their content. He wanted Iran to be free of western

interference. In 1971 he published *The Government of the Islamic Jurist* in which he argued that religious scholars should run the country. He continued to promote this idea in the 1970s as an alternative to the Shah.

> **The British imperialists penetrated the countries of the East more than 300 years ago. Being knowledgeable about all aspects of these countries, they drew up elaborate plans for assuming control of them. Then came the new imperialists, the Americans and others. They allied themselves with the British and took part in the execution of their plans.**

Source 7G: An extract from the writings of Ayatollah Khomeini.

CHECK YOUR UNDERSTANDING 7.9

What role did foreign influence play in the revolution? Was it the most important cause?

What role in Iranian history is Khomeini attributing to western countries in Source 7G?

From protest to revolution

In the 1970s the Shah spent his enormous oil revenue on weapons. Between 1972 and 1976 he spent $10 billion on US-made equipment and Iran had the fifth largest army in the world. However, this spending led to increasing costs of living as prices rose rapidly. In 1977 Jimmy Carter became US president. He urged the Shah to end political oppression, so activists were released from jail and some freedom of speech was allowed. This led to an outpouring of criticism, especially when Ali Shari'ati died in London. He was an immensely popular figure and was believed to have been murdered by SAVAK.

FACT FILE

Ali Shari'ati was a popular teacher and author. He studied at the Sorbonne in Paris but was frequently imprisoned after he returned to teach in Iran. He left for London in 1975 but was assassinated there in 1977. Only Khomeini could rival his political influence.

In January 1978, the government attacked Khomeini in a newspaper article. This led to mass protests in his home city of Qom, which the military crushed, killing many. The customary 40-day mourning period ended with further protests, and the same thing happened. Approximately 100 protestors were killed in Tabriz.

Incredibly, this happened twice more despite the government realising that it created a cycle of protests that were highly emotive.

At this point a decision was made to deal with the inflation problem. The timing was poor. Over the summer of 1978 government spending cuts caused high unemployment, which only added to the sense of crisis. On 8 September a mass demonstration in Tehran ended in the worst violence so far. The military killed several hundred people on 'Black Friday'. Khomeini was still in Iraq but it had become unsafe for him there. Saddam Hussein apparently offered to assassinate him but the Shah declined. Instead, Khomeini left for France staying just outside Paris where he was interviewed by the world's media.

In December 1978 the ten days of **Muharram** offered another chance to protest. The government didn't dare attack demonstrators during this holy period. Around 2 million people filled the streets of Tehran carrying pictures of Khomeini. The Shah, who was ill with cancer, was powerless to stop these events. His illness wasn't publicly known but he refused to launch any more attacks on his own people. He left Iran with his family in January 1979.

KEY TERM

Muharram: the first month of the Islamic calendar is Muharram. During this period Shia Muslims remember the death of the Imam Ali at the Battle of Kerbala. It is an emotional religious period of mourning that lasts for ten days.

The following month Khomeini returned from France. His press officer commented later that they didn't know if they would be killed on the tarmac when they landed or welcomed as heroes. In fact, millions came out to celebrate. This revolution marked the end of foreign influence over Iran and the beginning of a period of government by radical religious leaders. It sent shockwaves throughout the Middle East and the wider world.

ACTIVITY 7.7

How can we explain the Iranian revolution of 1979? Draw a table showing the mistakes made by the Shah and the reasons why Khomeini was popular. Which side was more important in causing the revolution?

SPIRITUAL LEADER

"...There is no reason why a criminal should be tried in the first place... Once his identity is established, he should be killed right away." –Khomeini

©1979 HERBLOCK

Source 7H: An American cartoon from 1979. Why was the reaction in the USA to Khomeini so negative?

CHECK YOUR UNDERSTANDING 7.10

What can we infer from Source 7H about Iran In 1979?

7.4 What were the causes and consequences of the Iran–Iraq War, 1980–1988?

The causes of the war

There were three principal causes of the war:

- the dispute over the Shatt al-Arab waterway
- the issue of Kurdish resistance in the north of Iraq
- the rise to power of Ayatollah Khomeini.

Iran and Iraq agreed a deal in 1937 about the Shatt al-Arab waterway. This channel of water is vital as it provides Iraq's only access to the Gulf. After the Ba'ath Party came to power the Shah ended this agreement in 1969 and started providing support to Kurdish rebels in the north of Iraq. In 1975 the two sides met at Algiers and agreed a new deal that was favourable to Iran. They ended support for the Kurds and in return gained greater rights over the Shatt al-Arab.

When Ayatollah Khomeini came to power Saddam Hussein was initially friendly towards the new government. He hoped they could maintain the Algiers Agreement and not interfere in each other's affairs. However, Khomeini attacked Saddam for being 'un-Islamic' and resumed support for the Kurds. He called on Iraq's Shia population to overthrow the Ba'athist government. Saddam responded by expelling 100,000 Shi'ites and dumping them over the border into Iran.

Diplomatic relations were ended and in the summer of 1980 both sides started shelling each other across the border. In September both rejected the Algiers Agreement. Iraq made the first move by bombing Iranian airfields and sending thousands of troops across 400 miles of border in what they hoped would be a quick victory. Saddam had gambled that the Iranian revolution had caused chaos in their military and thought this was the perfect time to strike.

> **CHECK YOUR UNDERSTANDING 7.11**
>
> Which of the three main causes of the war was most important and why?

The war on the ground

Saddam had limited objectives so he used only half of his armed forces. He had to maintain the western border with Syria as war had nearly broken out there in the mid-1970s.

The resistance shown by the **Iranian Revolutionary Guard** was impressive and the brutal battle over Khorramshahr in the south gave an indication of what was to come. As winter began both sides settled down to a war of **attrition**.

Iran made the most of this period to reorganise and launch devastating attacks in 1981, lifting the siege of the key oil town of Abadan. Saddam withdrew his forces behind the border in 1982 and asked for peace talks. This was ignored as Khomeini's main aim was to topple Saddam's government; he hoped Shi'ites in Iraq would welcome Iranian forces. However, Iraq's Shia population was Arabic and didn't speak Farsi so they stayed loyal to Saddam.

Iranian offensives continued from 1983 to 1985 but failed to break Iraqi lines. Their main objective was to capture Basra but Saddam used chemical weapons such as **sarin gas** to defend against assaults. Both sides launched attacks in 1985. For Iraq this was the first time they had gone on the offensive since the early months of the war. In 1986 the Iranians finally made a breakthrough in the south, capturing the Fao Peninsula, as well as attacking in the north. This almost cut off Iraq from the

Gulf, but desperate defence saw them hold on to the Shatt al-Arab.

> **KEY TERMS**
>
> **Attrition:** a strategy where both evenly balanced sides try to wear each other down gradually, hoping that the toll on the enemy, especially in terms of casualties, will be heavier than the cost to themselves. Victory comes from exhausting the opponent rather than capturing their territory.
>
> **Iranian Revolutionary Guard:** ('Pasdaran' in Farsi), founded in 1979 to protect the Islamic revolution. It is separate from the regular army so there is often tension between the two, not least because the IRGC are usually paid more and receive preferential treatment. They are considered to be Iran's elite troops.
>
> **Sarin gas:** a nerve agent which, in sufficient quantities, leads to a painful death. Victims lose control of their body and suffer convulsions, then paralysis.

For Iran, 1986 was the high point of the war. Economic costs and mounting casualties restricted their capability to attack, whereas Saddam received support from abroad (see the section on 'foreign involvement'). He also allowed his generals more freedom to make decisions after they threatened to rebel against him. The war ended with successful Iraqi operations to relieve Fao and a brief invasion of Iranian territory.

Source 7I: Iranian soldiers in a trench with machine guns and gas masks in January 1987.

> **ACTIVITY 7.8**
>
> Many historians have made comparisons with the First World War (See Source 7I). Using the information in this section, consider which aspects of the war were similar to 1914–1918 and which were different. What does this suggest about the nature of the fighting in the Iran–Iraq War?

The war at sea

As the ground war stalemate continued, Saddam switched the focus to the Gulf in 1984 to attack Iranian shipping. This expanded the regional importance of the war as Iran threatened to close the Straits of Hormuz to all international shipping if they were prevented from exporting oil. One-fifth of the world's oil travels through this channel. Saddam therefore increased attacks on ships going to and from Kharg Island, Iran's major oil refinery. Iran responded by attacking ships from Kuwait and Saudi Arabia as they were Saddam's biggest financial backers. This became known as 'the Tanker War'.

In 1987 the Kuwaitis and Saudis appealed to the USA for help. Their ships were allowed to fly USA flags as a convoy system evolved which was reminiscent of the Second World War. The American navy was drawn into conflict and shot down an Iranian passenger plane heading to Dubai, killing 290 civilians. It had been mistaken for an Iranian fighter plane. The Iranians could not match US naval power in the Gulf and this made the war unwinnable by 1988.

Figure 7.3: A map of the Gulf showing neighbouring states and the Shatt al-Arab straits.

CHECK YOUR UNDERSTANDING 7.12

The Strait of Hormuz separating Iran and Oman is one of the most economically important waterways in the world. Why would closing the strait help Iran and hurt Iraq?

The war in the air

Iran had planes supplied by the USA to the Shah. However, the withdrawal of American advisers and mechanics meant many of these were unserviceable. The Iraqi air force was functional but less sophisticated. As foreign intervention increased it benefited Iraq more than Iran through the supply of spare parts.

In 1984 'the War of the Cities' began. Each side bombed the other's key cities hoping to weaken civilian morale. Iraq used Soviet-made Scud missiles and they also attacked sites of economic value such as oil fields at Kirkuk and the Sirri Islands.

By 1988 Iraq had aerial superiority and attacked Tehran, causing the city to be evacuated. Saddam also ordered three chemical attacks on the Kurds in the north, causing horrific scenes in Halabja where 5,000 died and another 10,000 were wounded inhaling poison gas. Aerial warfare caused enormous civilian and economic damage but was insufficient to win the war overall.

KEY TERM

War of the Cities: five major attacks on urban areas during the Iran-Iraq War. The aim of destroying civilian morale failed to do its job, much as in the Second World War. Instead, it only intensified hatred for the enemy on both sides and may even have prolonged the war.

153

CHECK YOUR UNDERSTANDING 7.13

Consider the impact of the war on civilian lives. How would it have changed their opinions of their leaders?

Foreign involvement

Both sides had problematic relations with the outside world when the war began. However, by 1984 it was clear that most world powers preferred an Iraqi victory. The USSR provided substantial aid to Saddam. In 1983 they sent $2 billion of equipment including the latest T-72 tanks and MiG-29 planes. The French also sold him $5.6 billion of weapons. Iraq's most important financial backers were the Gulf monarchies of Kuwait and Saudi Arabia, who provided tens of billions of dollars in loans.

In 1979, an attack on the American embassy in Tehran led to hostages being held for over a year. Supporting Saddam was the lesser of two evils for President Ronald Reagan. Diplomatic ties with Baghdad had been cut in 1967 but now the USA embassy was restored so they provided Iraq with intelligence and financial aid. This support sustained Iraq through a war in which they were mostly on the defensive.

Iran's religious radicalism worried most Gulf states but they weren't completely isolated. Turkey sold supplies to both sides. Countries backed Iran if they either resented Saddam (such as Libya and Syria) or the Americans (such as North Korea). Others (such as South Africa and Taiwan) were happy to sell weapons to anyone that could afford to buy. The most incredible example of arms sales actually came from the Americans. In return for the release of US hostages in Lebanon they sold Iran weapons, despite supporting Saddam. The 'Iran-Contra Scandal' caused a great controversy when it was exposed (see Source 7J).

CHECK YOUR UNDERSTANDING 7.14

How influential was foreign involvement in the outcome of the war?

Source 7J: An American cartoon drawn in 1987 showing President Reagan making up excuses for the 'Iran-Contra' weapons deal.

The extent of foreign involvement shows how crucial the war was for the Middle East and the wider world. Yet the international opportunism of selling weapons meant that the conflict lasted much longer than it might otherwise have done.

Peace and the consequences of the war

Saddam offered peace talks in 1982 but Khomeini was resolute in calling for an end to the Ba'athist regime. A UN peace proposal known as Resolution 598 was put forward in July 1987. Khomeini initially rejected it but a year later the Iranian leadership finally accepted the terms of a ceasefire. Khomeini stunned Iranians when his message was read out on radio accepting an end to the fighting. It was a humiliating climb-down but there was no alternative. Even so, it took until 1990 to achieve a final peace deal and prisoners of war were not fully exchanged until 2003.

Accepting the resolution was truly bitter and tragic issue for everyone, particularly me … Death and martyrdom would have been more bearable to me …. How unhappy I am because I have survived and have drunk the poisoned chalice of accepting the resolution.

Source 7K: Khomeini's radio address to the Iranian people announcing the end of the war.

CHECK YOUR UNDERSTANDING 7.15

Read Source 7K. Why do you think Khomeini rejected peace in 1982 but accepted the ceasefire in 1988?

Casualties were extensive. This was in part due to Iranian tactics of using 'human waves' which were often unsupported by air or artillery support. From 1982 Khomeini even allowed boys aged 12–18 to join a militia called the Basij (see Source 7L). The admission forms were called 'passports to paradise'. Huge numbers were slaughtered as they went into battle with little training or weapons and in some cases were even used to clear minefields by walking into them. Reliable figures are hard to find but the Iraqi government claimed they lost 250,000 lives and the Iranian official toll now stands at 190,000. Other estimates claim the joint total was over 1 million, and it is possible that a quarter of Iraqi losses were civilians killed by their own government.

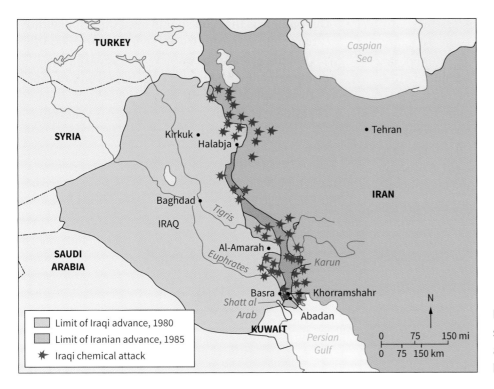

Figure 7.4: A map of the conflict showing the main areas of advances and the sites of chemical attacks by Iraq.

CHECK YOUR UNDERSTANDING 7.16

Look at the map in Figure 7.4 and think about why Saddam resorted to using chemical weapons. What were the long-term consequences of this?

Source 7L: A young Iranian member of the Basij in January 1986. Iraqi officers reported that they had to force their men to carry on firing when they were shooting at young boys. Later interviews showed that these young boys were encouraged by TV adverts to fight and many thought it was a game.

7.5 Why did the First Gulf War take place?

Causes of the Gulf War

There were two principal causes for the First Gulf War: economic and political. The Iran–Iraq War had left Saddam with significant financial problems:

- Iraq owed $100 billion in loans.
- The country's infrastructure had been heavily damaged with rebuilding costs estimated to be even higher than its debt.
- The army had one million men. There would be no jobs for these men if they were demobilised.

Saddam argued that Iraq had been defending all Arab states from Iran so they should cancel his debts. This was refused by the **Gulf Cooperation Council**. Saddam was particularly hostile to Kuwait, the United Arab Emirates and Saudi Arabia. There was also a dispute about oil production. The price had dropped from its peak of $41 per barrel in 1982 to just $18 due to overproduction by the Gulf monarchies. OPEC set a maximum production limit to try to keep the price at $22 per barrel but Kuwait and others were ignoring this. Adding to the tension, Saddam claimed that Kuwait was stealing oil from the shared Rumaila oil field so it owed him $10 billion. To pressure them he surrounded Kuwait's borders with his armed forces.

KEY TERM

Gulf Cooperation Council (GCC): founded in 1981, and consists of six Arab states that surround the Gulf. These states had loaned substantial sums to Saddam to fight Iran.

This was all linked to longer-term political issues between the two states. When Iraq became a country in 1920 they refused to recognise Kuwait. They felt that the border was unfair as Kuwait had much better access to the Gulf and only accepted the situation in 1963. After making their financial demands in 1990, a meeting was arranged between the two in Jeddah, Saudi Arabia. Kuwait offered $9 billion in compensation. This might seem like a fair compromise but in Arabian politics it was a calculated snub; Saddam could not get everything he wanted. Although he promised Egyptian president Hosni Mubarak and US ambassador April Glasnie that he wouldn't attack, Saddam wouldn't accept any loss of face and ordered his forces to invade on 2 August 1990.

ACTIVITY 7.9

An Egyptian diplomat said, 'The invasion is a black and white situation. But the reasons for the invasion are not so black and white.' What do you think he meant? In pairs look at the causes of the war and try to decide which was more important, the long term or the short term.

Operation Desert Shield

Initially, USA President Bush didn't condemn the attack but British Prime Minister Margaret Thatcher was more outspoken. The alarm was also raised by Iraq's troops now being positioned on the Saudi Arabian border. Having taken over Kuwait Saddam was in control of 20% of the world's oil production. If he invaded Saudi Arabia too it would jump to 40%. This was unacceptable to the western powers and when King Fahd of Saudi Arabia was shown pictures of the Iraqi build-up of forces he agreed to allow foreign troops to be deployed in his country. A **UN resolution** condemned the invasion and a coalition of 32 nations agreed to take action if Iraq refused to withdraw.

KEY TERM

UN Resolution: a decision taken by the United Nations that is meant to be binding on its members. Twelve resolutions were passed during the Gulf War, starting with Resolution 660, which condemned the attack.

Our opinion is that you should have the opportunity to rebuild your country. But we have no opinion on the Arab-Arab conflicts, like your border disagreement with Kuwait ... We hope you can solve this problem using any suitable methods ... via President Mubarak. All that we hope is that these issues are solved quickly.

Source 7M: Quote from US Ambassador April Glasnie, taken from the transcript of her discussion with Saddam Hussein on July 25, 1990, before the invasion of Kuwait.

The defence of Saudi Arabia was called 'Operation Desert Shield'. Saddam's army in Kuwait numbered 500,000 men, so vastly outnumbered Saudi Arabia's forces. The UN Security Council set a deadline for Iraq to withdraw by 15 January. In the meantime 250,000 US troops were sent to the Arabian peninsula. By November they numbered 400,000. Saddam refused to negotiate with the Kuwaiti royal family who had fled to Saudi Arabia and he didn't take the UN warnings seriously. When the deadline expired on 15 January he was fully prepared for war. He believed that America's experience in Vietnam would make them reluctant to engage in warfare. Just as in 1980 over Iran, he miscalculated.

ACTIVITY 7.10

Consider the build-up to the war from Iraq's perspective. Was Saddam justified in thinking there would be little reaction to his invasion of Kuwait?

Operation Desert Storm

At 3 a.m. local time on 17 January, Operation Desert Storm began. The first stage involved aerial bombing under 'Operation Instant Thunder' as 1,000 **sorties** were launched on the first night. The aim was to

 KEY TERM

Sortie: an aeroplane, ship or unit of troops going out on a specific mission.

disrupt communications, attack strategic sites and hit the Iraqi ground forces. The effect was devastating. American technology was far in advance of the Iraqis, particularly the F-117A stealth bomber, which was undetectable by radar.

The coalition forces were two-thirds American but many Arab states such as Egypt and Syria were involved in small but symbolically important numbers. Saddam knew the best way to undermine the coalition was to broaden the war to include Israel. He therefore launched Scud missiles, which many feared had chemical warheads at Tel Aviv and Haifa. While citizens of those cities were issued with gas masks the Americans persuaded Prime Minister Yitzhak Shamir not to respond. This held the coalition together.

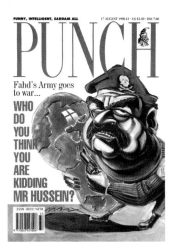

Source 7N: The cover of a British magazine in 1990. Why had international opinion of Saddam Hussein changed so much from 1988 to 1990?

Source 7O: General 'Stormin' Norman Schwarzkopf posing for a picture for a profile of him in Life magazine, 1991. The media were captivated by his charisma and success during the war, which earned him the nickname 'Storming' or 'Stormin' Norman.

ACTIVITY 7.12

The war was played out through the media. CNN became famous through their coverage of it. Look at Source 7O, and research General Schwarzkopf and consider his role as leader of the coalition forces. Evaluate the relative importance of:

- his knowledge of the Middle East
- his relationship with the media
- his military strategy.

ACTIVITY 7.11

Look at Source 7N. Write one sentence showing British reaction to Saddam Hussein at these moments in time:

- 1979 – on becoming president
- 1980 – on starting war with Iran
- 1990 – on invading Kuwait
- 1991 – on defeating him in the First Gulf War
- 2000 – after the imposition of sanctions and arguments over weapons development

How can you explain the changing British attitude towards Iraq in this period?

The war wasn't entirely one-sided. Iraqi forces caught the coalition by surprise when they attacked Saudi Arabia on 29 January. The Battle of Al Khafji was short and ended in defeat, but a huge mistake was made on 13 February when two stealth bombers hit a civilian shelter. Before this the media had been shown video footage of incredibly accurate air attacks. Now 400 civilians were dead.

The Iraqi air force had been neutralised and six USA aircraft carriers patrolled the Gulf. This left the war on the ground. This was much more difficult as Saddam had half a million experienced soldiers in Kuwait and the conditions were difficult. The coalition leader, General 'Stormin' Norman Schwarzkopf sent 300,000 men and 1,500 tanks to Iraq's western border under cover while making it look as if his main assault would come in the south of Kuwait. Iraqi forces were hit from both sides. As they fell back in retreat they tried to escape on the main road north. The 'highway of death' was heavily bombed from the air with 2,000 vehicles destroyed. A British journalist said it was 'one of the most terrible harassments of a retreating army from the air in the history of warfare'.

Source 7P: The Highway of Death in the aftermath of the attacks in February 1991.

ACTIVITY 7.13

What types of vehicles can you see in Source 7P? What does this tell us about the flight of Iraqi soldiers?

The end of the war

The ground war lasted only 100 hours. A ceasefire was accepted on 3 March. However, the tragedy was not over. Retreating Iraqi soldiers in the south started a rebellion as they felt abandoned by their government. Saddam's Republican Guard crushed this uprising with some severity. A Kurdish rebellion in the north was also brutally suppressed. As planes dropped bombs around 2 million people fled for the borders. An estimated 20,000 died from exposure in the harsh mountain conditions.

If Iraq's financial positon was weak after the war with Iran, it was now catastrophic. As part of the UN ceasefire, chemical and biological weapons had to be destroyed before economic sanctions were lifted. Saddam made life difficult for the weapons inspectors so the sanctions were maintained. This hurt ordinary people; infant mortality increased five-fold. Iraq wasn't allowed to import chlorine because it could be made into poison gas, but this meant water couldn't be treated. Raw sewage was dumped into the Tigris and Euphrates rivers. Throughout the 1990s rationing was imposed on essential items.

For Kuwait the financial losses were enormous. The Iraqi forces set fire to 85% of Kuwait's oil wells (see Source 7Q) as they retreated, which meant no oil

could be produced for two years. The environmental impact was appalling. Two of the largest oil spills ever seen seeped into the Gulf. The government had to pay $20 billion for Operation Desert Storm and another $65 billion to rebuild the country. Saudi Arabia's costs amounted to $55 billion.

Given that the war lasted only 42 days the death total for the Iraqis was dreadful. Best estimates suggest that 82,000 soldiers and 7,000 civilians lost their lives. In comparison the coalition lost 139 soldiers, of whom 79 were Americans.

Source 7Q: Kuwait's oil fields burning after being set alight by retreating Iraqi forces.

CHECK YOUR UNDERSTANDING 7.17

Look at Source 7Q. What were the human and environmental consequences of the war? Draw a diagram showing how these two effects were interlinked.

Review your learning

You should be able to identify the changes in both Iran and Iraq up to 1979. Was war unavoidable? Could Khomeini and Saddam have lived as neighbours? The war of 1980–1988 was so destructive that it had significant impact on the wider region, especially the economy. Oil was instrumental in this as it tied the wider world to the Middle East. The invasion of Kuwait threatened Saudi Arabia and raised the unwelcome possibility of Saddam controlling up to 40% of the world's oil supply. This was also a post-Cold War order in which the USA believed it could reshape the politics of the region. The full consequences of this realignment have yet to be seen.

The Big Challenge

Think first about the two revolutions. Compare and contrast the rise to power of Saddam Hussein and Ayatollah Khomeini. Are there any similarities? What was different about the two events? Think about causes as being economic, political and cultural in nature. An important element to consider is ideology: what did each leader believe and why were their beliefs popular? How did these beliefs differ from the regimes that they replaced?

Now think about the two wars. What were the main causes? Try to identify two or three factors that caused each war. Again, think about similarities and differences. Did Saddam need to go to war in 1980 and 1990? What was the impact of each war on the civilian population?

What were the consequences? It helps to draw up a table like this for your revision:

Cause	Event	Consequence

In each column put down the key events. For causes, try to think of two or three factors. Could you write a paragraph on each one? For the event simply write down four or five of the most important things that happened so you cover the core information. A brief timeline would do. For consequences, do the same as you did for causes; identify two or three main things that happened as a result of the wars. Could you write a paragraph for each one?

Summary points

- Saddam Hussein rose to power as a consequence of pan-Arab nationalism spreading; the Ba'ath Party went through a series of changes in the 1960s and by 1979 he became the undisputed leader of the country.

- Saddam's state was progressive in the 1970s, at war in the 1980s and regressive in the 1990s. Throughout this period it was a strict dictatorship.

- Iran underwent a revolution in 1979 as a result of rising religious opposition to western culture and the unpopularity of the Shah's government.

- As Ayatollah Khomeini believed that Iraq was 'un-Islamic' under Saddam, the two states went to war over a border dispute. This lasted for eight years and was devastating for both countries.

- The First Gulf War was a consequence of the Iran–Iraq War. Heavily indebted, Saddam sought to ease his financial problems by invading Kuwait, stoking decades-old rivalries between the two states.

Exam-style questions

Discuss these questions with a partner, make notes and then ask another pair to mark them for you. Then choose one for a full exam-style answer.

1   Describe the main events that led to the Iranian Revolution.

2   Why did Saddam Hussein come to power in Iraq?

3   'Neither side can claim victory in the Iran–Iraq War.' How far do you agree with this statement? Explain your answer.

4   What was Operation Desert Storm?

5   Why did Saddam Hussein invade Kuwait?

6   'Modern technology was the main reason for the coalition victory in the Gulf War.' How far do you agree with this statement? Explain your answer.

Chapter 8
Depth Study A: The First World War, 1914–1918

What is this depth study about?

Archduke Franz Ferdinand, the heir to the throne of the Austro-Hungarian Empire, was assassinated in Sarajevo on 28 June 1914, sparking an international crisis. By August 1914, all Europe's major countries were at war. Most people seem to have thought it would 'be over by Christmas', and men volunteered to fight worldwide. In fact, the war was not won until 1918. Your challenge is to understand why winning the war took so long.

In August 1914, there were two alliances:

Triple Entente, The Allies	Triple Alliance, The Central Powers
Britain and Empire	Germany and Empire
France and Empire	Austria-Hungary and Empire
Russian Empire	
Serbia	
Montenegro	
Belgium	
Japan	

Later, other powers joined the war:

Italy (from April 1915)	The Ottoman Empire (from Nov 1914)
Portugal (1916)	Bulgaria (from October 1915)
Romania (1916)	
Greece (1917)	
United States (from April 1917)	

! TOP TIP

The official name of Austria-Hungary from 1868 was the Austrian-Hungarian Monarchy/Empire, but was often called the 'Dual Monarchy' in English. Historians tend to call it 'Austria-Hungary', but you may encounter other names.

The key questions we will be examining are:

1   Why was the war not over by December 1914?

2   Why was there stalemate on the Western Front?

3   How important were other fronts?

4   Why did Germany ask for an armistice in 1918?

8.1 Why was the war not over by December 1914?

Focus points

- How was the Schlieffen Plan intended to work?
- How important was Belgium's reaction to the Schlieffen Plan?
- How successful was the British Expeditionary Force (BEF)?
- Why did both sides introduce trenches?

How was the Schlieffen Plan intended to work?

Germany's Schlieffen Plan was important in shaping the war. The German Chief of Staff, Count Alfred von Schlieffen, designed the plan in 1905. Germany was worried about fighting France and Russia at the same time, after they became allies in 1894, and Schlieffen's plan was Germany's response to the threat of a war on two fronts.

- Schlieffen assumed that Russia was dangerous but would take six weeks to mobilise.
- Germany had to defeat France before Russia's army mobilised.
- Ten per cent of the German army was kept to defend against a Russian advance in the east.
- An army of 1.5 million men (90% of the German army) would move by rail through Belgium, Luxembourg and the Netherlands, to invade France. Germany's northern forces would be eight times stronger than its southern ones, since they had further to travel.
- The army would swing around the French army, encircle Paris and France would collapse.

CHECK YOUR UNDERSTANDING 8.1

The Schlieffen Plan looked good on paper.

1   What were the key assumptions on which it was based?

2   What could potentially go wrong?

Timeline

28 June	Gavrilo Princip assassinated Archduke Franz Ferdinand.
14 July	Germany promised unlimited support to Austria.

23 July	Austria gave Serbia an ultimatum, demanding to be allowed to deal with the assassination.
25 July	Serbia, with Russian support, rejected almost all of the ultimatum. Austria mobilised against Serbia.
30 July	Russia mobilised against Germany and Austria.
1 August	Germany declared war on Russia.
2 August	Germany invaded Luxembourg and demanded free passage through Belgium.
3 August	Germany declared war on France and invaded Belgium. Since 1839, Belgium's neutrality had been guaranteed by Britain.
4 August	Britain declared war on Germany.
6 August	Austria declared war on Russia.
12 August	Britain and France both declared war on Austria.

ACTIVITY 8.1

1   Study the timeline. Of the countries that became involved in the crisis in July 1914, which was most to blame for the outbreak of the war? Explain your answer.

2   Study the table comparing the alliances on the previous page and answer the following questions. Explain your answers fully.

   a   Select and explain the strengths and weaknesses of both alliances in 1914.

   b   Compare the similarities and differences between the two alliances in 1914. Which side was stronger?

   c   Why did Britain feel threatened by Germany in the years before 1914?

   d   Why did Germany believe she was threatened by the Triple Entente?

When Russia mobilised in support of Serbia on 30 July, the German war plan was already starting to go wrong. There are various reasons why the plan failed, but two of them occurred before the Germans invaded Belgium.

Modifications to the plan

Schlieffen died in 1906, and the plan was changed by the new Chief of Staff, von Moltke. Two divisions were withdrawn to defend against the French. He also altered the invasion plan to take a more direct route through Belgium.

Russian mobilisation

The Russian army mobilised first, and it attacked Germany within two weeks. The Germans were caught by surprise. Two German army corps were sent to fight the Russians.

How important was Belgium's reaction to the Schlieffen Plan?

The German army met much stronger opposition in Belgium than expected. The Belgian army was outnumbered, but German forces took thirteen days to capture the key fortress town of Liege. Brussels was occupied on 20 August, but the Belgians destroyed bridges, flooded the land, put up barricades and blocked roads. The German invasion was slowed down because of exhaustion, supply problems and casualties. The Belgian defence also delayed the Germans so much that the BEF arrived in time to fight the Battle of Mons.

How successful was the British Expeditionary Force (BEF)?

The Schlieffen Plan assumed that Britain would not protect Belgium. The Belgian government appealed to Britain for help when Germany declared war, and Britain sent its army – the BEF – immediately.

> **FACT FILE**
>
> The BEF was designed to defend the Empire. It was only 120,000 soldiers, but they were highly trained, experienced professionals, led by General French. Kaiser Wilhelm reportedly called them 'General French's contemptible little army', and the BEF nicknamed themselves 'The Old Contemptibles'.

The BEF fought the Germans at Mons on 23 August: 70,000 British with 300 heavy guns faced 160,000 Germans with 600 guns. Despite the BEF performing well, the Germans pushed forward and the British retreated south of the River Marne, outside Paris.

However, the BEF and the Belgians slowed the German army advance, making the Schlieffen Plan impossible to achieve. Nevertheless, by the end of August, Moltke believed that the war was almost won. The Belgians were defeated. The British were in retreat. France had put its own Plan 17 into effect and it had failed. However, after Moltke found his forces were no longer strong enough to encircle Paris, he swung them south-east to pursue the BEF.

At the Battle of the Marne, 5–12 September 1914, the BEF and 150,000 French soldiers counter-attacked as the Germans prepared to attack Paris. The Germans were close to victory, and were only defeated when 6,000 French reserve troops were brought to the front line from Paris in 600 taxis.

Source 8A: French reserve soldiers being brought to the front line in taxis in September 1914.

ACTIVITY 8.2

Study and interpret Source 8A. Pictures of crowds of civilians watching taxis transporting soldiers to the front line were published in France during the war. Why do you think images like this were published?

The failure of the Schlieffen Plan

Beginning on 8 September, another French attack forced the Germans to retreat 40 miles, and the Germans dug in to the north of the River Aisne. The Battle of the Marne was a strategic victory for the Allies, who pushed back the Germans and captured lost ground amid heavy losses on both sides. The Schlieffen Plan had failed.

Why did both sides introduce trenches?

After the Germans retreated to the River Aisne, they dug a system of defensive trenches. In late September 1914, the Allied armies tried unsuccessfully to force the Germans back. Three months of mobile warfare followed as the two sides fought as they moved north. The Germans wanted to capture the Channel ports and cut off supplies from Britain. This became known as the 'race to the sea'. During this period of intense fighting and worsening weather, exhausted soldiers began to dig defensive trenches. Over time these stretched 470 km from the English Channel to Switzerland.

The First Battle of Ypres

At the First Battle of Ypres (19 October–22 November 1914), the BEF held a 35-mile-long salient (bulge) along a ridge

outside the town of Ypres. The Allies aimed to retake Lille in France and Brussels in Belgium. The Germans wanted to capture the ports of Dunkirk, Calais and Boulogne. The Germans attacked the BEF, the French and Belgians. **Cavalry** and machine guns failed to break through. Heavy losses on both sides at Mons, and now Ypres, meant that the BEF had been almost wiped out. Now the British had to rely on volunteers.

KEY TERM

Cavalry: Soldiers who fought mounted on horses.

8.2 Why was there stalemate on the Western Front?

Focus points

- Why did the war become bogged down in the trenches?
- What was living and fighting in the trenches like?
- How important were new developments such as tanks, machine guns, aircraft and gas?
- What was the significance of the battles of Verdun and the Somme?

Why did the war become bogged down in the trenches?

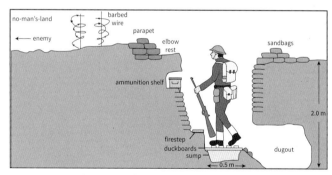

Figure 8.1: A diagram of a typical trench from the Western Front.

What began as a war of movement now became a war of attrition. Trench warfare developed, as both sides dug trenches to shelter from enemy fire.

By 1915 it was clear that defence was easier than attack. The trenches were easily defended with machine guns. The Germans dug in especially deep and made their trenches strong because they had already captured lots of enemy territory and did not need to move forward, unlike the Allies, who needed to push the Germans back. The two front lines could be as little as 15 metres apart, as at

Hooge, near Ypres. Elsewhere, they could be a kilometre apart. Here there was relative safety, or even boredom.

On neither side did the generals understand the new nature of warfare. Many British commanders believed that cavalry breakthroughs would win the war. Until 1918 the major battles on the Western Front involved vast numbers of men climbing out of the trenches and walking straight towards the enemy guns. These rarely achieved significant breakthroughs.

Generals also ignored or misused new weapons, such as gas and tanks, which were often unreliable. Even in August 1918, when the British army used tanks, 75% broke down within four days.

What was living and fighting in the trenches like?

Soldiers did not spend all their time fighting in the trenches. They were organised into platoons of 60 men and each platoon was supposed to spend 4 days in the front line, before being relieved by replacements. They then spent 4 days in a reserve trench, and finally 4 days resting, behind the front line. In practice, some soldiers stayed in the front line for longer than 2 weeks before being relieved.

Source 8B: Men of the Lancashire Fusiliers in a flooded British trench near Messines in Belgium, January 1917.

Source 8C: German soldiers in 1916 in a trench with a machine gun.

Conditions in Western Front trenches varied a great deal. Trenches in northern France were dug in chalky ground. In Belgium, especially at Ypres where lots of fighting took place, the ground was wet. Generally, German trenches were dug on higher ground and so could be deeper than Allied trenches. The big dangers of living in the trenches were:

- Rats: they thrived in the poor conditions of dead bodies, discarded food and other waste.
- Lice: these tiny insects lived in soldiers' clothing and sucked their blood.
- Disease: not washing for days or weeks, limited toilet facilities and little fresh water meant that disease was very common. There were 6,000 British dysentery cases, and over 15,000 cases of kidney infection on the Western Front in 1917.
- The weather: In Flanders, after heavy rain, trenches flooded. At Passchendaele in 1917, thousands of men disappeared in the mud. Wet weather also brought trench foot, a condition that led to **gangrene**. There were 70,000 cases of trench foot in British trenches in 1917. In winter, frostbite affected thousands. In summer, heat made the smell caused by decaying bodies, horse manure and soldiers' **latrines** unbearable.
- Shell shock: this term was later used for those who suffered mental breakdowns.
- Boredom: during the long wait between major battles, trench life was tedious.

CHECK YOUR UNDERSTANDING 8.2

Compare the diagram in Figure 8.1 with the photographs in Sources 8B and 8C of trenches on the Western Front. What differences do you notice? Contrast Sources 8B and 8C: what do the differences suggest about (a) British and German trenches or (b) the different circumstances in which the photographs were taken?

 KEY TERMS

Gangrene: a medical condition caused by loss of blood supply, especially to parts of the body farthest from the heart (e.g. toes), which leads the flesh there to die.

Latrines: field toilets.

The first air raid of the war was on Paris on 30 August 1914. From September, British planes raided German airfields and in December 1914 German planes bombed Dover. German Zeppelins also bombed London in May 1915, killing seven people and causing huge damage. Zeppelins were large and filled with inflammable hydrogen, however, so the British soon developed planes that could shoot them down easily. The British also found ways of limiting the effects of the raids – with blackouts, searchlights and night fighter planes – so they were not crucial to the war overall. In late 1916 Gotha bombers began bombing Britain. There were 103 air raids, killing about 1,400 people, during the war. Britain also bombed German cities.

Even by 1918, the potential of aircraft was still not fully understood. Aircraft were too small and lightly armed to damage major targets. Larger planes, which were expensive, could not carry enough bombs. Overall, fighting in the air had no significant impact on the war.

Gas

Poison gas was first used at Ypres in April 1915 and proved a deadly weapon. It was used until the end of the war. Adolf Hitler was blinded by gas in October in 1918 and spent the last weeks of the war recovering in hospital. Gas could be released from canisters and allowed to drift towards the enemy, if the wind blew in the right direction. Gas shells, which broke open when they hit the ground, could also be used. Early gas masks offered little protection, but later designs proved more effective.

Source 8J: French soldiers wearing early gas masks at the Second Battle of Ypres, spring 1915.

Source 8K: American soldiers wearing gas masks in 1918.

There were three types of poison gas:

- Chlorine gas: within seconds of inhaling its vapour it destroyed the victim's respiratory organs, bringing on choking attacks. Killed 1,976 and injured 164,457.
- Phosgene gas: phosgene caused less coughing so more of it was inhaled; phosgene often had its impact up to 48 hours after inhalation.
- Mustard gas: the most lethal – almost odourless, it burned on contact and caused serious internal and external blisters several hours after exposure. Killed 4,086 and injured 16,526 during the war.

Gas was terrifying, but it was not a decisive weapon. It could blow the wrong way and attackers had to wear gas masks, which reduced visibility and movement. British figures recorded that only 3% of gas casualties were fatal, 2% were permanently invalided and 70% were fit for duty again within six weeks. Despite the horrors that it caused, gas only accounted for 4% of war deaths.

What was the significance of the battles of Verdun and the Somme?

In 1916, the Germans and the British each launched major new offensives designed to break the deadlock and win the war on the Western Front. The Germans aimed to win the war by attrition, while the British hoped for a major breakthrough. Both attacks were catastrophic failures that killed over one million men.

Battle of Verdun, February–December 1916

The longest battle of the war was fought at Verdun. Germany believed that the French were close to breaking point in early 1916, so the German Commander, General von Falkenhayn chose to attack France at the major fortress town of Verdun. The fortress was a symbol of French military strength, and Falkenhayn calculated that

ACTIVITY 8.5

Source 8L: British soldiers awaiting treatment after a gas attack in 1918.

Source 8M: *Gassed* by J.S. Sargent, 1919. The artist spent several months on the Western Front in 1918.

Study Sources 8J and 8K. What do they tell you about the development of military technology during the Great War? What does this tell you about the changing nature of the war itself?

Study Sources 8L and 8M. Which of these two images is more useful as historical evidence?

In 1919, Source 8M was criticised for glorifying the suffering of gas victims. In what ways do you think the painting might make war seem heroic? Explain your answer, with reference to the painting.

French pride would never allow them to surrender it. His aim was simply to force France to keep reinforcing Verdun, kill as many French soldiers as possible, break the morale of the French army and 'bleed France white'. He expected that France would surrender and Britain would withdraw.

Beginning on 21 February 1916, German guns shelled the French front line. A gas attack was launched, and then 140,000 German soldiers with flamethrowers attacked. Fort Douaumont was captured early in the battle, but

168

despite outnumbering the French, the Germans could not make a significant breakthrough. Both sides suffered appalling casualties.

On 25 February, General Pétain was put in charge of defending Verdun. He ordered, 'They shall not pass', and French resistance was strengthened. The only French route into the city – 'the sacred way' – was widened and constantly repaired after German bombardments, so that the city received 4,000 tons of supplies each week and was reinforced by 20,000 men per day. Harsh discipline was used to put down developing **mutiny** and 1 in 10 mutineers was shot.

KEY TERM

Mutiny: a group openly rebels against or overthrows a military authority.

To relieve pressure on the French, the British launched the Battle of the Somme. On 11 July Falkenhayn ended the Verdun offensive and transferred men to the Somme. Fighting continued until December 1916, but nothing was gained by either side.

Casualties at Verdun, February–December 1916	
French	362,000
German	337,000

Verdun showed that as long as the defending side could sustain casualties, trench warfare made attacking virtually impossible. It was the most significant use of attrition during the war, and Verdun saw some of the most savage fighting. The Germans did not launch another major offensive on the Western Front until 1918.

Battle of the Somme, July–November 1916

There was a widespread belief in Britain that a major victory on the Western Front could bring a decisive breakthrough in the war. To support this, conscription had been introduced in January 1916, and 100,000 reinforcements were arriving every month. The British army numbered almost 1.3 million men by spring 1916.

On 1 July 1916, a new British commander, Sir Douglas Haig, launched a massive attack on German trenches at the River Somme. This was supposed to be a limited offensive: fifteen divisions would attack for fourteen days, open up a gap in the German lines through which cavalry would pour. The German front lines, cut off from their supplies, would be forced to surrender.

Source 8N: 'Britons: Lord Kitchener Wants You': The famous British Army recruiting poster from 1914.

The leadership and tactics of Haig at the Somme

Source 8O: Sir Douglas Haig, at his desk in the railway carriage used as a mobile office.

FACT FILE
Field Marshal Sir Douglas Haig was Commander-in-Chief of the British army on the Western Front from December 1915 until the end of the war. He was convinced that a large-scale attack or 'Big Push' was the way to win on the Western Front.

The plan consisted of three parts:

1   Heavy shelling for 7 days, which was designed to destroy German defences, inflict heavy casualties and clear barbed wire. Five large mines beneath the German trenches were to be detonated.

2   Infantry advance at 7.30 a.m. on 1 July. Soldiers had to walk slowly and clear remaining Germans from front line trenches.

3   A second wave of attack, including cavalry, would sweep through.

The attack failed, and 1 July 1916 became the worst day in British military history. The campaign was a serious failure for various reasons:

- The bombardment failed to destroy German barbed wire. German soldiers survived the attack because they sheltered in deep, reinforced and well-supplied concrete bunkers. Once the shelling stopped, the Germans knew an attack was coming.
- The British suffered 57,470 casualties on the first day: 19,240 killed and almost 40,000 wounded. Most of these casualties were suffered in the first 20 minutes of the battle.
- When Haig ended the attack in November, only seven miles had been gained.
- The Somme became a battle of attrition that claimed over a million casualties in total.
- German forces on the Western Front retreated to a strengthened defensive position (the Hindenburg Line) after the battle.

169

FACT FILE
The Hindenburg Line was a 145 km line of fortifications from Arras to the River Aisne. Its deep and well-built trenches were up to 5.5 km from front to rear, protected by extensive areas of barbed wire, underground bunkers and tunnels, heavy artillery positions and concrete machine-gun posts. Following damage from the Somme offensive, in February 1917 the Germans retreated to the Hindenburg Line. They remained there until March 1918.

Haig has been severely criticised for his leadership and tactics. Some evidence suggests that he deserves his nickname, the 'Butcher of the Somme':

- His planning was poor.
- Allowing the attack to continue long after it was clearly failing led to hundreds of thousands of additional casualties.
- Haig was inflexible, unimaginative and did not learn from his mistakes. In 1917 he ordered another major attack at Passchendaele, near Ypres. In three months of muddy fighting in rainy conditions, the British captured just four miles. He remained dedicated to his

belief that cavalry would win the war, when he should have understood that this was impossible. He failed to appreciate the potential of the tank.

- Haig refused Lloyd George's suggestions for a unified Allied Command in 1917, failed to cooperate with French generals in 1917 and 1918, and only reluctantly accepted Foch as his superior in 1918.

- The war was won on the Western Front, not through Haig's 'Big Push' tactics but with surprise attacks without massive bombardments – tactics learned from the Germans.

Other evidence shows Haig does not deserve this reputation:

- The Battle of the Somme was planned at short notice. Haig originally planned a major battle near Ypres in 1916, but was forced to rethink after the German attack on Verdun.

- He was only given about half the forces that be believed he needed to win at the Somme.

- Haig was not alone in failing to understand how war had changed. Most other First World War commanders used the same tactics as Haig.

- Haig's tactics changed at Vimy Ridge, in April 1917. Tunnels were dug to allow attackers to get closer to enemy lines and soldiers were issued with maps so that attacks could continue even if officers were killed.

- Haig's tactics were costly, but they did wear down the German forces and contribute to their defeat in 1918.

- Haig was a caring man and his private papers show that he felt deeply sorry about the loss of his men.

ACTIVITY 8.7

Try to recall what you have studied in the last section. Organise a list of all the reasons why the Battle of the Somme was a significant battle in the history of the First World War.

8.3 How important were other fronts?

Focus points

- Who won the war at sea?
- Why did the Gallipoli campaign of 1915 fail?

- Why did Russia leave the war in 1918?
- What was the impact of war on civilian populations?

In addition to the Western Front, there was fighting on various other fronts around the world. Many people believed that a breakthrough on one of the other fronts had the potential to end the war.

Who won the war at sea?
Royal Navy

Britain's navy was seen as the most important of the armed forces before 1914. It was the strongest navy in the world, and it was vital to the creation and strength of the British Empire. The British government was determined to protect it.

Source 8P: HMS *Dreadnought*, 1907.

In the years before 1914, the major powers had devoted resources to developing large, powerful navies. Germany's naval construction programme sparked an arms race with Great Britain that significantly increased tension. Both sides built as many Dreadnoughts as possible (see Source 8P).

There were few major naval engagements during the First World War. Neither side really won the only major battle. Even so, Britain's ability to control the English Channel and the North Sea played a significant part in its eventual victory. A British priority was to keep open the supply lines between Britain and its trading partners, and between Britain and France. Another was to blockade Germany.

When war broke out in 1914 the Royal Navy expected that there would be a major battle with the German High Seas Fleet.

The German Navy's Dreadnought-class battleships were too valuable to lose, so they were mainly used as a deterrent, to carry out small attacks on the Royal Navy, to bombard English seaside towns, or to lay mines. The German Navy used submarines more than surface ships.

There were a series of minor naval battles in 1914–1915:

1   28 August 1914: Battle of Heligoland Bight. The British attacked Germany's Heligoland naval base, killing over 700 sailors and destroying 6 ships. They lost only 35 British sailors.

2   1 November 1914: Battle of Coronel. German cruisers under Admiral von Spee sank two British cruisers (killing 1,600 British sailors) near Chile.

3   8 December 1914: Battle of the Falkland Islands. British cruisers sank four German ships and killed 1871 sailors. Only 10 British men died.

4   16 December 1914. The German fleet bombarded Scarborough, Whitby and Hartlepool on the Yorkshire coast, killing 137.

5   24 January 1915: Battle of Dogger Bank. Royal Navy battlecruisers sank a German armoured cruiser, and the Germans lost 954 men.

Battle of Jutland and its consequences

The only major sea battle during the First World War was at Jutland on 31 May 1916. It involved 250 ships and 100,000 men and lasted three days.

German Admiral von Scheer's plan was to tempt the British Grand Fleet from its base at Rosyth, trap them and

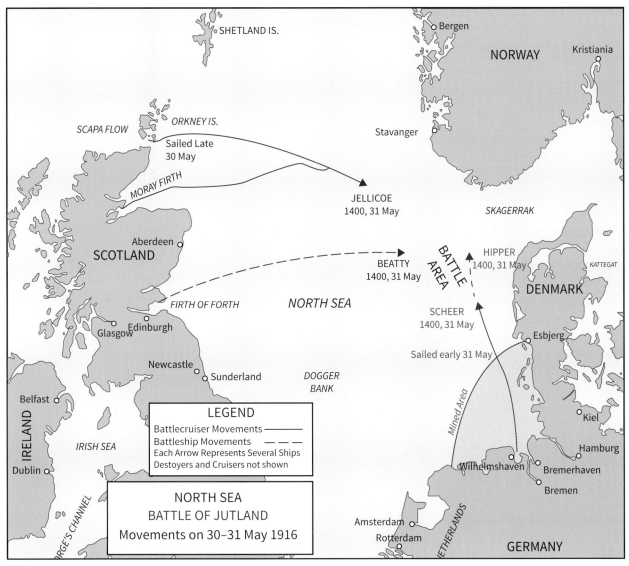

Figure 8.2: The Battle of Jutland, 31st May 1916.

destroy as many ships as possible. The aim was to reduce the British numerical advantage and end the Royal Navy's blockade of German ports.

Commander of the Grand Fleet, Admiral Jellicoe, was aware of the plan. He sailed out of port earlier than Scheer expected and lay in wait. Jellicoe's fleet outnumbered Scheer's, with faster and better armed ships, though with some weaknesses in their armour. Fighting was intense and, realising that he was sailing into a trap, Scheer sailed home as night fell, using his submarines for cover.

The result was indecisive and both sides claimed victory. An American journalist wrote at the time: 'The German fleet has assaulted its jailer, but it is still in jail.'

The results of the Battle of Jutland

	Scheer's German High Seas Fleet	Jellicoe's Royal Navy
Ships lost at Jutland	11 ships, including 1 battle cruiser	14 ships, including 3 battle cruisers
Casualties	3,058	6,784
Serviceable ships after the battle	10	24
Immediate consequences of the battle	Broke off the action and returned to port. Never risked a major sea battle again	Maintained its control of the North Sea. Sustained its blockade of German ports

ACTIVITY 8.8

Who do you think won the Battle of Jutland and why?

Submarines, the U-boat campaign and the convoy system

After 1916, the Royal Navy blockaded Germany, causing severe food and supplies shortages. At the same time the German fleet was attempting to blockade Britain. Britain was vulnerable to a possible German blockade in 1914, since 60% of Britain's food was imported. Germany was outnumbered in surface ships, so the Germans used more submarines. They were effective. Just one U-boat sank three British warships in September 1914.

Unrestricted submarine warfare

Initially, Germany avoided targeting non-military ships, especially those from neutral nations. However, failing in its attempt to starve Britain, in 1915 Germany turned to a campaign of unrestricted submarine warfare. German ships now targeted both military and merchant ships around Britain.

The effects of the campaign on Britain were devastating. In early 1917 the Germans had 120 submarines at sea, and Germany believed that losses of 600,000 tons of shipping per month would be enough to cause a British collapse. During spring and summer 1917 Britain and her allies lost 1,505 merchant sailors and 2.78m tons of shipping, forcing Britain to introduce food rationing, but it did not lead to surrender. To counter the threat posed by the U-boats, Britain deployed a range of strategies:

- Q ships: disguised as merchant vessels, but with guns hidden under fake lifeboats and funnels, Q ships were deployed to lure submarines to the surface where they could be attacked. Twenty-three Q ships were sunk by U-boats in 1917, but Q ships only sank 6 U-boats.
- Mines: thousands were laid across the North Sea.
- Convoy system: from summer 1916, David Lloyd George, the British Prime Minister, ordered the Navy to sail battleships in convoys with merchant ships across the Atlantic. Between May 1917 and November 1918 only 168 merchant ships (out of a total of 16,539) were sunk by U-boats in the Atlantic.

By October 1917 the Germans had lost more than 50 submarines and the danger was over.

The failed tactic had provoked international outrage when a German U-boat sank the British passenger liner *Lusitania* on 7 May 1915, as among the 1,198 lives lost were 128 Americans. Pressure on the US government to declare war increased when an American liner, the *Arabic*, was sunk in August 1915. Germany temporarily abandoned the policy, but Germany's unrestricted use of submarines drew the USA into the war.

CHECK YOUR UNDERSTANDING 8.3

1 What motivated the Germans to use unrestricted submarine warfare?
2 Consider the consequences of Germany's policy of unrestricted submarine warfare. How successful was it?

All vessels, irrespective of cargo and flag, have been sent to the bottom, without help and without mercy. Even hospital and relief ships were sunk with the same reckless lack of compassion. Germany's submarine

warfare is directed against the whole world. I will not choose the path of submission, and allow the most sacred rights of the nation and of the people to be ignored and violated. With a profound sense of the tragic character of the step I am taking, but I advise Congress to declare that the recent actions of the German Government is nothing less than war against the United States.

Source 8Q: American president, Woodrow Wilson's speech to Congress on 3 April 1917.

ACTIVITY 8.9

Study and interpret Source 8Q. What does it tell us about the consequences of unrestricted submarine warfare?

Why did the Gallipoli campaign of 1915 fail?

There were disagreements in the British government between those who thought the war must be won on the Western Front (the 'Westerners') and those who believed a breakthrough would come in the east. The 'Easterners' were led by Winston Churchill.

Churchill persuaded the British government that a naval attack on the Turkish capital, then called Constantinople, would force the Ottoman Empire to surrender. The British government wanted to send military aid to Russia through the Dardanelles Straits.

CHECK YOUR UNDERSTANDING 8.4

What motivated the British government to launch the Gallipoli campaign?

The campaign was planned as a naval offensive. The Royal Navy bombarded Turkish forts along the Dardanelles Straits in March 1915. Obsolete British and French battleships, accompanied by fishing trawlers converted into minesweepers and manned by civilians, were expected to clear the straits of mines and destroy the Turkish defences easily. The minesweepers failed and the Turkish guns were not all destroyed. On 18 March 1915 alone, the Allies lost six ships. This naval attack warned the Ottoman forces that the Allies were preparing a major offensive; 70,000 new Turkish troops were sent to defend the peninsula.

The Allies now began planning a land invasion of the Gallipoli peninsula. The officer appointed to lead the

campaign was Sir Ian Hamilton. The land campaign was badly planned. The British did not know how many Turkish troops were in the area, their maps were inaccurate and they relied on old tourist guidebooks for intelligence. Hamilton had been advised by Greek military leaders that he would need 150,000 men to take Gallipoli, but Lord Kitchener, who disapproved of the plan, was unwilling to take troops from the Western Front, so Hamilton received five divisions totaling 78,000 men. They were inexperienced troops from Australia and New Zealand (the Anzac Army Corps), two British divisions and a French colonial division. It took the Allies five weeks to prepare, and the Ottoman forces used this time to strengthen themselves.

FACT FILE

The Anzacs
Australia and New Zealand both declared war on Germany and her allies when Britain did in 1914. Around 100,000 New Zealanders served overseas, of whom over half became casualties, including around 18,000 killed. From an Australian force of over 400,000 men, almost half were killed, wounded or captured. The Gallipoli campaign was the first time Anzac troops saw action, but they also served in most of the other theatres of war.

The British invading force of 70,000 suffered 20,000 casualties at Cape Helles. Many casualties were suffered on V Beach, where an old coal haulier, the *SS River Clyde,* was used to land the troops. Turkish machine gunners had a direct line of fire on the troops as they landed, and of the first 200 men out of the ship, only 21 survived.

The landing of the Anzacs, at Anzac Cove, as Kabatepe became known, also failed. Strong currents carried the boats around a mile from the drop-off point. They were faced by a narrow beach, high cliffs and Turkish defenders, who were well dug in and who had been trained by a German general. Over 2,000 Australians became casualties on the first day of the landing.

Hamilton commanded the invasion from a ship, so he was out of touch with the beaches, and poor communications meant he could not change the plans anyway. Junior officers were too inexperienced and several opportunities to advance inland before the Ottoman defenders reorganised were missed. The Allies underestimated the Turkish soldiers, but especially after Mustafa Kemal (later called 'Ataturk') was appointed to lead the defence, the Ottoman Army proved itself brave and effective. Between April and July, Allied troops dug in and waited for orders, while the Ottomans reinforced their positions. There was deadlock at Gallipoli.

In August 1915, the Allies landed 20,000 more men at Suvla Bay, but this was also a failure. Facing little opposition, they again failed to break through Turkish defences. The fighting was as difficult as on the Western Front. Shortages of fresh water and poor food supplies caused malnutrition; and flies, rotting unburied corpses and poor sanitation led to disease. In summer the men faced intense heat, in autumn torrential rain and in winter snow and frostbite.

Hamilton was replaced in October, and the new commander decided to withdraw the entire force. The evacuation was completed without loss of life by January 1916.

Results of the Gallipoli campaign
In total, over one million men fought in the Gallipoli campaign:

- Over one-third became casualties. The Allies lost over 250,000 men. The Easterners' plan had failed.
- The Ottoman Empire lost a similar number, and they fought on.
- The expedition's failure also led to a number of political consequences.
  - The head of the Royal Navy resigned in May.
  - In November 1916, Winston Churchill resigned from the government.
  - In December 1916, Asquith resigned as Prime Minister and was replaced by David Lloyd George.

The Turks in the trenches facing the landing had run, but those on the ridges kept firing upon the boats coming ashore, and that portion of the covering force which landed last came under a heavy fire before it reached the beach. The Turks had a machine gun in the valley on our left, and this seems to have been turned on to the boats containing part of the Twelfth Battalion. Three of these boats were still lying on the beach some way before they could be rescued. Two stretcher-bearers who went along the beach during the day to effect a rescue were both shot by the Turks. Finally, a party waited for dark, and crept along the beach, rescuing nine men who had been in the boats two days, afraid to move for fear of attracting fire.

Source 8R: An account of the Gallipoli campaign by Charles Bean, the official war correspondent with the Australian army.

ACTIVITY 8.10
1 Whom do you blame for the failure of the Gallipoli campaign? Why?
2 Construct a list of all the reasons why the Gallipoli campaign failed. Organise them in order of importance.
3 Study and interpret Source 8R. How useful is this source for an historian studying the Gallipoli campaign?

Why did Russia leave the war in 1918?
It is important to remember that, as well as the fighting on the Western Front, the First World War also saw a different but vitally important series of battles in the east, between Russia, Austria-Hungary and Germany.

Events on the Eastern Front and the defeat of Russia
A patriotic upsurge, and a speedy mobilisation that surprised Austria and Germany, meant that the war started well for Russia.

Despite early successes against the Germans in the north and the Austrians in the south, it became clear that the Russian army had some significant weaknesses.

- Russian commanders Samsonov and Rennenkampf failed to cooperate.
- The Russian army was short of rifles, ammunition and boots.
- Russian solders were brave, but many officers had little training in modern tactics or weapons.
- Russian wireless messages were not encoded and the Germans could read them.

The Russians suffered two huge defeats at German hands before the end of 1914:

- At the Battle of Tannenberg (23–30 August 1914), the Russian losses were 170,000 killed, wounded or captured and the loss of 350 big guns. The Germans suffered 20,000 casualties.
- At the First Battle of Masurian Lakes (7–14 September 1914), the Russians lost another 125,000, while the Germans lost 10,000. The Russian commander, Samsonov, shot himself.

The Russian army fared better against Austria-Hungary, but by 1915 the war was going badly.

- One million men had been killed and the Russians had retreated 600 miles.

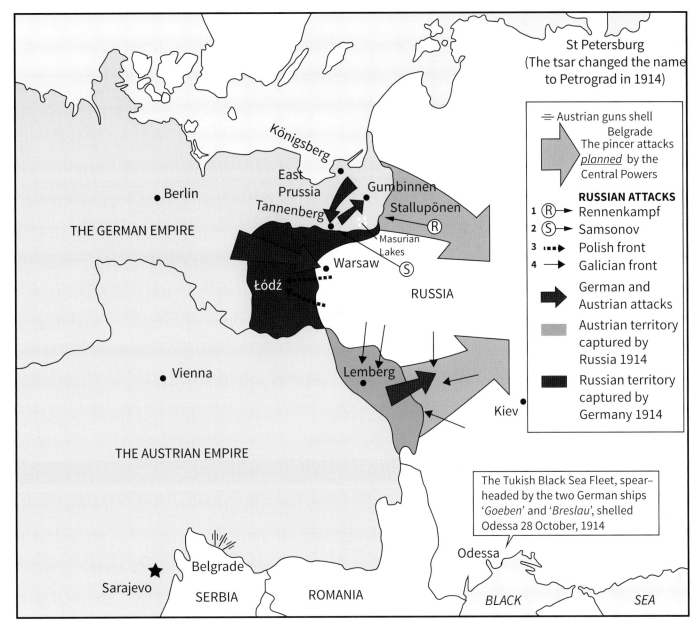

Figure 8.3: The war of movement, the Eastern Front 1914.

- There were shortages of shells and poor coordination on the front line.
- The government was unable to organise the war effort effectively.
- When the army's commander resigned, Tsar Nicholas decided to appoint himself as Commander-in-Chief. Now every military problem reflected badly on the tsar himself.

In 1916, General Alexei Brusilov planned a major attack designed to knock Austria out of the war and divert German forces before the Somme offensive in July 1916. The offensive lasted three months, and it was initially a great success. The Russians advanced around 30 km along a 400 km front, and took 400,000 prisoners. The Austrian army never recovered, but the Russians lost over 1 million men and could not launch another offensive. The offensive relieved pressure on the Allies on the Western Front as Germany had to rush in troops to prop up Austria's army.

The war had a serious impact on all aspects of life in Russia:

- Russia's military campaign was disastrous. By January 1915, 25% of the Russian army had been killed, wounded or captured.
- The First World War had a huge impact on Russia's economy and inflation rose by up to 900% for some foods.

- Millions were directly affected by the fighting or by the casualties, and the conscription of 13 million peasants into the army created labour shortages in the countryside, causing food shortages.
- The conduct of the war reflected badly on the government and the Russian royal family, as the Emperor was commanding the army.

In February 1917, a revolution forced Nicholas II to abdicate and a Provisional Government was established to rule Russia. The Provisional Government tried to maintain the war effort and was itself overthrown in a revolution led by the Bolsheviks in October 1917. The Bolsheviks signed an armistice with Germany and Russia withdrew.

The Eastern Front had been important because:

- The Russian attack in 1914 helped to defeat the Schlieffen Plan because it forced the Germans to withdraw troops from the west before they had defeated France.
- It meant that the Germans had to fight a war on two fronts for most of the war.

Having won, the Germans now transferred troops to the Western Front for their 1918 Spring Offensive.

'Pals battalions' of war on civilian populations

The British government decided to allow the hundreds of thousands of volunteers to serve alongside friends and neighbours. These were known as the 'Pals battalions'. Units like the Manchester Pals were in the first wave at the Somme. This meant that if a unit suffered heavy losses, all the young men from a town were killed at the same time, with devastating effects on the areas they came from.

ACTIVITY 8.11

Why do you think that the British government was motivated to send men to fight in 'Pals' battalions'?

KEY TERM

Pacifism: opposition to violence and war.

	Britain	Germany	Rest of the world
Restrictions on everyday life	Within four days of the outbreak of war, the government introduced the Defence of the Realm Act (DORA), which gave the government extensive powers intended to secure public safety and order. These powers included the introduction of press censorship, imprisonment without trial, reduced opening times for public houses (pubs) and the introduction of daylight savings.	The government's War Raw Materials Department organised the response to the British blockade. It set prices and regulated the distribution of materials to key war industries.	On entering the war, the USA passed legislation to restrict any action that might threaten the war effort. The 1917 Espionage Act made it illegal to interfere with the recruitment of troops or to pass on classified information. Conscientious objection became an offence. The 1918 Sedition Act made it an offence to use abusive language about the US Constitution, the armed forces or the government.
Recruitment	Britain relied on a volunteer army for the first two years of the war, managing to recruit over 3 million men between 1914 and 1916. Conscription was introduced for all single men aged 18–41 in January 1916. The measure was extended to married men within that age range in May 1916.	All men served in the regular army from age 17, then the reserves until they were 45. The system of reserves meant that in August 1914, the army expanded from 800,000 to 3.5 million soldiers.	In 1914, all Frenchmen over 20 served in the army for three years, and in the reserves for a further 25. The French army numbered almost 3 million at the outbreak of war.

	Britain	Germany	Rest of the world
Conscientious objectors	Approximately 16,000 men refused to be conscripted, and these were known as conscientious objectors. While approximately half of these accepted a non-combatant role in the armed forces, a significant minority did not and were either imprisoned or forced to join a military unit in France.		In Canada, the USA and New Zealand, men could refuse to fight, but only if they were members of groups with a history of **pacifism**.
Food shortages and supplies	German unrestricted submarine warfare and naval blockade had a devastating effect on the economy. Britain increased the area of farmland in order to produce more food, increased imports from USA and introduced rationing of sugar and meat in January 1918, extending it to other goods later.	Severely affected by food shortages during the war, and took several measures, including developing ersatz (substitute) goods such as acorns to replace coffee beans. Clocks were brought forward an hour to give people the opportunity to tend their vegetable gardens after work. Millions of pigs were slaughtered in order to save grain. After the disastrous potato harvest in 1916, turnips were issued as a replacement. Rationing was introduced in 1916.	Food shortages in Russia were had two main causes: the poor quality of the country's railway network and the lack of incentive for peasants to produce more food as the war dragged on. The amount of food in the cities declined and inflation rose: during 1914–1916, the cost of meat rose by 232%.
The impact on women	Women in Britain made up 37% of the workforce by 1918. Women in low-paid domestic jobs took the opportunity to move into better paid jobs in munitions factories and public transport.		In Russia, by 1917, 43% of the industrial workforce was female. Russia recruited an all-women battalion in 1917 to fight. In France, by 1918 one-third of the labour force in arms production was female. Women in France benefited from the allowances paid by the government to soldiers' wives.
Civilians	A long-running process had been gradually increasing the number of people who could vote in elections in many countries. The war encouraged this to go further. In 1918 Britain granted the vote to women who passed some property-owning and age qualifications at 30 and to those men over 21 who did not have the vote. In Britain a 1928 change to the law meant that all men and women over 21 could vote. Canada and Austria extended the suffrage to women in 1918, Germany in 1919, and the USA in 1920.		
	The home front was dangerous for civilians. Approximately 940,000 civilians died as result of military action, and another 5.9 million died of disease, malnutrition and accidents. Twenty million people died in the 1918 Spanish Flu epidemic.		

8.4 Why did Germany ask for an armistice in 1918?

Focus points

- What was the importance of America's entry into the war?
- Why was the German offensive of 1918 unsuccessful?
- Why did revolution break out in Germany in October 1918?
- Why was the Armistice signed?

The end of the war on the Eastern Front enabled the Germans to move 1 million men to France. Germany was unable to capitalise on this advantage because by 1918:

1. The British naval blockade caused starvation. The war was increasingly unpopular at home.

2. The USA had joined the war and thousands of fresh American troops were arriving.

What was the importance of America's entry into the war?

Many Americans wanted the USA to stay neutral in the First World War. Until 1916, president Woodrow Wilson won much support by promising to keep the USA out of the conflict. Wilson attempted to broker peace deals during 1915–1916. By April 1917, however, there was growing support for the idea of entering the war on the allied side:

- By 1917, the USA had lent £850m to Britain and almost as much to France. This would be lost if Germany won.
- The USA had no wish to see Europe dominated by a single power, especially an autocratic one.
- Unrestricted submarine warfare created popular anger: four US ships were sunk by U-boats in March 1917.
- The British intercepted a telegram from German Foreign Minister Arthur Zimmermann to Germany's ambassador in Mexico. The Zimmermann telegram said that if Mexico joined the war on Germany's side and attacked the USA, Germany would give Mexico some American territory at the end of the war. The British showed the telegram to the USA government in February 1917. US public opinion was outraged.
- There was sympathy in the USA for Britain and France, as democratic countries fighting **autocratic** empires.

After the autocratic Russian tsar abdicated in March 1917 it was no longer contradictory to fight alongside the Russians.

On 6 April 1917, Wilson declared war on Germany.

KEY TERM

Autocratic state: one ruled by an autocrat, someone who cannot be challenged and whose power is not limited. Germany was a democracy, but its parliament had little control over large areas of government activity. Britain and France represented Germany as an autocratic empire; however, that's how Germany saw Russia.

How did the USA affect the war?

Initially, the USA sent only 300,000 soldiers to France, who had little impact. Eventually, about 1,250,000 US soldiers served in Europe. They were not prepared for trench warfare and their casualty rates were high. The arrival of large numbers of American soldiers provided a huge psychological boost to the Allies.

The commander of USA forces, General Pershing, allowed Marshal Foch, the Allied commander, to use American soldiers as reinforcements during 1918.

The USA's entry led the German High Command to launch the Ludendorff Offensive.

Why was the German offensive of 1918 unsuccessful?

FACT FILE

General Erich von Ludendorff
Ludendorff made his reputation when he was a commander on the Eastern Front in 1914–1915. Together, Hindenburg and Ludendorff dominated the German government after 1916. Ludendorff was mainly responsible for persuading Wilhelm II to agree to an armistice in November 1918.

In 1918, General Ludendorff planned a massive offensive.

German Spring Offensive

At 4.40 am on 21 March 1918 the Germans launched a massive surprise attack. The Germans bombarded a 60 km line of British trenches with 3.5 million shells in just five hours. They used specially trained 'storm troopers' armed with light machine guns, light trench mortars, grenades and flamethrowers. They employed **creeping barrages** and poison gas in devastating highly coordinated surprise attacks.

KEY TERM

Creeping barrages: a line of artillery fire advancing ahead of attacking infantry, usually at a rate of 50 metres per minute. The creeping barrage was first used by the British at the Battle of the Somme in 1916. The method was successful, especially against localised targets, although it required a high degree of coordination. A 'fire waltz' was a creeping barrage that hit enemy trenches and moved on, only to reverse and catch the defenders as they emerged from shelter.

The Germans launched four major attacks between March and July.

1   21–30 March

- The Germans attacked at the Somme, advancing 65km in three weeks, inflicting 250,000 casualties, capturing 1000 big guns and destroying 200 tanks. They lost almost 240,000 men. Haig and Pétain were unable to co-operate, so Marshall Foch was appointed supreme commander of all Allied forces in France.

2   9–30 April

- The German attack in Belgium cost the Allies over 100,000 men (for similar losses on the German side). Although the Allies were under pressure, they survived with the help of 300,000 American soldiers who arrived just in time. The Germans, who were tiring, failed to break through.

3   26–30 May

- The German attack advanced 18km in one day on the road to Paris, and both sides suffered over 100,000 casualties.

4   9–12 June

- German attacks pushed the Allies back to within 50km of Paris. The Allies lost over 200,000 men.

By August, German casualties during the 1918 offensives had reached 1 million. These men were highly trained, and their replacements were not as good. The Germans failed to split the French and British forces, which had been their main intention.

The Ludendorff Offensive failed because:

- By leaving their defensive positions along the Hindenburg Line, the Germans abandoned their biggest advantage.
- Operation Michael transformed the war into one of movement. Although German troops were better trained for this kind of fighting, the Allies had more men, tanks and aircraft, and this proved to be decisive.
- As German attacks pushed further into enemy territory, it became harder to keep men supplied, and the salient on the new front line was hard to defend against counter-attacks.
- Troops from the Eastern Front were unprepared for fighting on the Western Front. After fighting on the Eastern Front they were given no rest before being sent to the west, arriving exhausted and with low morale. Alcoholism, avoiding duties and desertion became common. Half a million German soldiers had flu by August 1918, making 11 out of 13 divisions unfit for offensive action.

The allied counter-attack

The Allies began to counter-attack, with huge success. On 18 July, the French stopped the German advance outside Paris.

Foch's major counter-offensive began near Amiens on 8 August 1918. British, French, Canadian and Anzac troops launched surprise attacks, with creeping barrages, tanks and aircraft supporting infantry advances. Allies' intelligence was precise and their attacks were devastatingly effective. The German army collapsed and lost 75,000 men, including 50,000 taken prisoner. The Allies advanced 11 km in one day and the Germans retreated to the Hindenburg Line. The German retreat continued until October.

Foch launched a final assault on 29 September. The Hindenburg Line was broken for the first time, as Australian, American and British troops, supported by 150 tanks, attacked at the St Quentin Canal (see Source 8S). Ludendorff's confidence was gone: he asked the new German chancellor, Prince Max of Baden, to request an armistice.

By the end of October the Hindenburg Line had been breached in numerous places and German troops were in full retreat. By the time the Armistice was signed on 11 November, all German troops had left French territory.

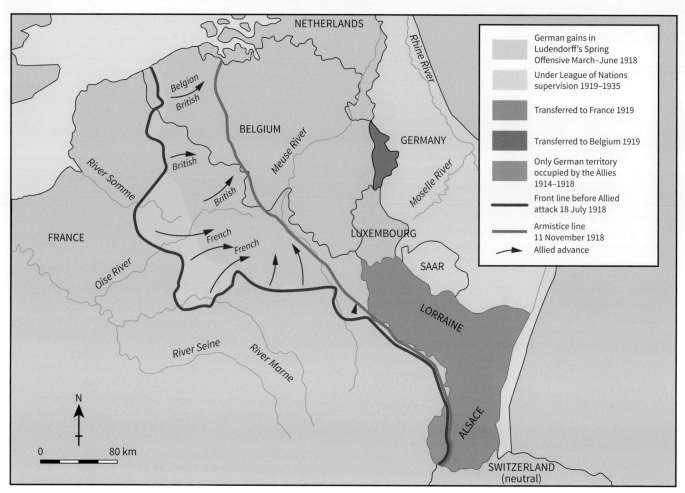

Figure 8.4: Operation Michael and the Allied counter-attacks.

ACTIVITY 8.12

Look back at the previous section and study Figure 8.4. Why was the German Spring Offensive unsuccessful?

CHECK YOUR UNDERSTANDING 8.5

Why was the Allied counter-attack so successful?

Why did revolution break out in Germany in October 1918?

Official statistics show that the blockade caused over 750,000 civilian deaths. Rationing and food shortages hit urban workers hardest. Working conditions had worsened, hours had increased, wages had fallen, prices had risen, and strikers were conscripted and sent to the front. In October

Souce 8S: Victorious Allied troops resting, having captured the Riqueval Bridge over the St Quentin Canal in October 1918.

1916, 30,000 people attended peace demonstrations, and socialist groups passed a Peace Resolution in July 1917, which called for an end to the fighting without punitive terms.

Taxes did not cover the costs of the war, so the German government took loans. By 1918, the national debt had risen to 250 billion marks. In January 1918, 500,000 went on strike in Berlin, demanding political change.

In September 1918, Hindenburg and Ludendorff persuaded the Kaiser to appoint a civilian government under Prince Max von Baden. This would create the appearance of a democratic government, and it was hoped that in armistice negotiations the Allies would be more lenient than if they were dealing with the Kaiser or the army. This step would also deflect blame for defeat on to the new government.

Kiel Mutiny and the German Revolution

The German revolution occurred in two stages:

1   3–26 October: The political stage. On 3 October, Prince Max asked president Wilson of the USA for an armistice. Wilson refused to negotiate with the generals or the Kaiser. The Kaiser therefore passed the October Reforms, transferring power to the Reichstag, creating a parliamentary monarchy.

2   28 October–9 November: The military stage. Wilhelm II and the head of the German navy ordered the German fleet to launch a huge naval assault. Angry at being sent into battle against the Royal Navy when the war was clearly lost, German sailors at the main naval bases of Kiel and Wilhelmshaven mutinied. Inspired by this and by the 1917 Russian Revolution, Workers' and Soldiers' Councils (Soviets) seized major cities. Protests, food riots and strikes followed in Berlin and other cities. The Kaiser abdicated and fled to the Netherlands.

On 9 November, von Baden gave control of the government to Friedrich Ebert, the leader of the largest party in the Reichstag. Ebert immediately asked for a ceasefire.

The proud German Army, after victoriously resisting an enemy superior in numbers for four years, performing feats unprecedented in history, and keeping our enemies from our frontiers, disappeared in a moment. Our victorious fleet was handed over to the enemy. The authorities at home, who had not fought against the enemy, could not hurry fast enough to pardon deserters and other military criminals, including themselves and their nearest friends. They and the Soldiers' Councils worked

with determination to destroy the whole military structure. Such was the gratitude of the new homeland to the German soldiers who had bled and died for it in millions. The destruction of Germany's power to defend herself – the work of Germans – was the most tragic crime the world has witnessed. A tidal wave had broken over Germany, not by the force of nature, but through the weakness of the Government, represented by the chancellor, and the paralysis of a leaderless people.

Source 8T: Erich von Ludendorff's war memoirs, published in 1920.

> **ACTIVITY 8.13**
>
> Study Source 8T and answer the following questions. Explain your answers, with reference to the source.
> - Whom does Ludendorff blame for Germany's defeat?
> - Whom does Ludendorff not blame for Germany's defeat?
> - How does Ludendorff describe the German army in 1918?
> - Why might Ludendorff have expressed these views in 1920?

Why was the Armistice signed?

The Armistice between the Allies and the Germans was signed at 5 am on the morning of 11 November 1918, and came into effect at 11 am Germany surrendered unconditionally. The terms of the Armistice were that:

- Germany would evacuate all occupied territories.
- Treaties already negotiated with Russia and Romania were annulled.
- Germany would hand over military equipment, including the entire submarine fleet.
- Germany's surface fleet would go to the British naval base at Scapa Flow in Scotland. (When they arrived, the German commanders scuttled their ships rather than hand them over.)

Many Germans thought the terms harsh, but the government wanted peace, so the Armistice was signed anyway.

After such a long and destructive war, why did the German war effort collapse? Even in 1919, it was not obvious: Field Marshal Haig asked a friend: 'Why did we win?'

Review your learning

Having gone through this chapter, and undertaken its tests and activities, you should be able to describe, assess, understand and explain the following:

- How the Schlieffen Plan was supposed to work, and the reasons for its failure.
- Why both sides introduced trenches on the Western Front before the end of 1914, and the main features of trench warfare and life for ordinary soldiers in the trenches.
- Why trench warfare led to stalemate, and why the major offensives of 1916 failed to break the deadlock on the Western Front, as well as how important new developments in technology were.
- Which side won the war at sea.
- Why the Gallipoli campaign was launched, and why it failed.
- The war on the Eastern Front, the impact of the war on Russia and why Russia pulled out of the war in March 1918.
- How civilian populations in the warring countries were affected by the war.
- What kind of impact America's entry into the war in 1917 had, and how the USA helped to win the war.
- Why Germany asked for and signed an armistice in 1918, and why a revolution broke out in October 1918.

If you can't, go back to the relevant section and revise.

Summary points

- The Schlieffen Plan was supposed to defeat France within six weeks and allow the Germans to avoid a war on two fronts, but it failed when the Belgians and the British intervened.

- Both sides introduced trenches on the Western Front before Christmas 1914. A line of trenches stretched from the English Channel to the Swiss border. Trench warfare was a new way of fighting, involving new weapons and tactics. Stalemate set in, and generals were slow to learn how to break the deadlock. Casualties were heavy on both sides.

- Important offensives by both the Germans and the British in 1916 failed to break the deadlock on the Western Front.

- The outcomes of sea battles were indecisive. The German submarine campaign and the British naval blockade each had the potential to win the war. Both sides were so worried about losing their expensive navies that they were reluctant to use their ships.

- The Allies tried to break the deadlock on the Western Front by defeating Germany's allies. The Gallipoli campaign was launched against the Ottoman Empire, but it was poorly planned and resourced, and was a costly failure.

- The war on the Eastern Front was different from the Western Front. The war was extremely costly for Russia and the government's failure to plan and fight the war effectively led to the March Revolution. The new Provisional Government was equally unable to cope, so when the Bolsheviks seized power they took Russia out of the war in March 1918.

- Every aspect of life for civilian populations in the belligerent countries was affected by the war. Government control was increased over areas such as work, food supply and access to information. The war particularly affected women, for whom the changes could be positive as well as negative.

- After remaining neutral for three years, America's entry into the war in 1917 had a significant impact. Although Americans did not fight in large numbers until late in 1918, their arrival was decisive.

- Germany's Spring Offensive almost won the war; its failure and the mounting problems at home led the government to request an armistice in 1918.

The Big Challenge

Study this list of possible reasons why Germany lost the war:

- Germany had to fight on two fronts for most of the war.
- The British naval blockade forced the German people into starvation by 1917. Shortages contributed to declining support for the war at home.
- Four years of devastating battles had weakened the German army and the spirit of the German people.
- Americans intervened at a crucial moment.
- Ludendorff's Spring Offensive exhausted Germany's reserves.
- This had been a war of attrition; German military and civilian morale and supplies had simply been worn down.
- The Allies had larger armies, better resources and more weapons in 1918:
  - 18,500 guns to Germany's 14,000.
  - 4,500 aircraft to Germany's 3,760.
- Germany had been outproduced in tanks by a ratio of approximately 320:1.
- Allied counter-attacking tactics were effective by 1918.
- Germany's allies were unreliable. Austria-Hungary needed continual support on the Eastern Front. In 1918, allies started surrendering and signing separate armistices: Bulgaria on 30 September, Turkey on 30 October, Austria-Hungary on 3 November 1918.

1 Is anything missing from this list? Add other reasons that you think are important.

2 Rank these reasons.

3 Show which reasons are connected with others. Several of these points are interconnected.

4 Write a paragraph to explain which one you think is most significant.

Exam-style questions

Questions in the style of Paper 1

1 a Describe trench warfare.

   b Why did the Schlieffen Plan fail?

   c How far was Haig a successful military leader?

2 a What were the aims of the Gallipoli campaign?

   b Why did Russia pull out of the war in March 1918?

   c 'Problems at home caused Germany to ask for an armistice.' How far do you agree with this statement? Explain your answer.

Questions in the style of Paper 4 - IGCSE only

1 How important was the fighting on other fronts in determining the outcome of the First World War?

2 How significant was America's contribution to the Allied war effort by 1918?

Chapter 9

Depth Study B: Germany, 1918–1945

What is this depth study about?

This chapter covers the period in German history from the revolution of 1918 through to the end of the Second World War. Germany was a well-developed and educated society – one of the most advanced in the world – yet it failed in its democratic experiment resulting in a dictatorship led by Adolf Hitler. Why was this? The first half of this chapter deals with the Weimar Republic, the reasons for its failure and the rise of the Nazis. The second half looks at life in the Third Reich, exploring the methods through which Hitler maintained control and the consequences of his rule for all groups in society.

The four investigative questions are:

1   Was the Weimar Republic doomed from the start?

2   Why was Hitler able to dominate Germany by 1934?

3   How effectively did the Nazis control Germany, 1933–1945?

4   What was it like to live in Nazi Germany?

9.1 Was the Weimar Republic doomed from the start?

Focus points

- How did Germany emerge from defeat at the end of the First World War?
- What was the impact of the Treaty of Versailles on the Republic?
- To what extent did the Republic recover after 1923?
- What were the achievements of the Weimar period?

How did Germany emerge from defeat at the end of the First World War?
The revolution of 1918 and the establishment of the Republic

By the end of 1918 Germany was losing the First World War. The army was retreating in disorder, attacked by the British, French and Americans. Kaiser Wilhelm II ordered the German Navy to attack the Allies. Considering it a suicide mission, the sailors based at Kiel mutinied on 9 November. The German revolution had begun.

Told clearly by the head of the War Office, General Groener, that he could no longer rely on the army, the Kaiser abdicated. He handed power to his chancellor, who in turn passed it to the leader of the largest party in the Reichstag, Friedrich Ebert of the Social Democrats

(SPD). Ebert knew that he needed the support of the army if he was to maintain control. He approached Groener. The two agreed the secret Ebert-Groener Pact. The army would support the new government, which in turn would support the army. Both sides wanted to avoid revolution.

On 11 November Ebert's colleague Matthias Erzberger signed the Armistice with the Allies. The conditions laid down by the French were strict. The German army had to leave France and abandon all their heavy weapons. An armistice is meant to be a ceasefire; this was a surrender.

The Weimar constitution

In January 1919, Germany adopted a new constitution. The new system was called the Weimar Republic after the town where the constitution was signed. With the militaristic rule of the Kaiser ended, the democratic institutions were strengthened and the country was a republic.

> **ACTIVITY 9.1**
>
> Look at Table 9.1 with the main features of the constitution. Assess its strengths and weaknesses.

Many observers thought the new constitution was the most democratic in the world. The emphasis on democracy and individual rights seemed to be exactly what American President Woodrow Wilson had demanded in 1918 as a precondition for a treaty. The Germans had played their part in removing the Kaiser so they expected Wilson to honour the terms of his 'Fourteen Points' which suggested minimal punishment for Germany.

What was the impact of the Treaty of Versailles on the Republic?
The Versailles Settlement and German reactions to it

In May 1919 the German government were simply given the provisional peace terms to accept or reject. Wilson's promises had not been kept. Not only was Germany to be heavily punished, they also had to admit responsibility for starting the war. The public were shocked and the government resigned in protest, but the Germans had no option but to accept. They were faced with possible mutiny, revolution, economic collapse, a continuing blockade and invasion. The Treaty of Versailles was signed on 28 June 1919.

Democracy	Everyone over the age of 20 could vote. Political parties were represented in a parliament called the Reichstag. Voting in elections was by **proportional representation**.
Rights	Every German citizen had freedom of speech, freedom of religion and equality before the law.
Chancellor	The chancellor appointed ministers and they ran the government on a daily basis. The support of the Reichstag was needed so normally the leader of the largest party was made chancellor.
President	The president was the head of state, head of the army and protector of the constitution. They could appoint and dismiss the chancellor. In a crisis the president could allow the chancellor to use **Article 48** to pass an emergency decree.
Regions	Germany was made up of 17 individual states called 'Länder' which had power over, for example, police and education.
Justice	The President appointed judges. Anyone who tried to overthrow the new system could be charged with treason.

Table 9.1: The constitution of the Weimar Republic.

KEY TERM

Proportional representation: a voting system in which the proportion of assembly seats won by parties closely resembles the proportion of the votes cast in the election.

CHECK YOUR UNDERSTANDING 9.1

Why was the new Weimar government held responsible for the position Germany was in?

186

ACTIVITY 9.2

The French and Allied military commander Ferdinand Foch said of the Treaty of Versailles: 'This is not a treaty, it is an armistice for twenty years.' What causes for a future war do you think Foch might have had in mind?

There were four commonly used phrases in 1919, and after, which summarised popular opinion:

1   Many ex-soldiers felt that the army had been betrayed by corrupt politicians in October and November 1918. They had not actually lost the war on the battlefield and were still in France when the armistice was signed. This became known as the 'stab in the back' (or 'Dolchstoss,' see Source 9A).

2   The politicians who had signed the Armistice in November 1918 were labelled the 'November criminals'.

3   Versailles was referred to as a 'Diktat' (a dictated peace).

4   Wilson's peacekeeping body, the League of Nations, was called 'the League of Victors' as it was believed to exist only to keep Germany weak.

Source 9A: A German cartoon from 1942 depicting the 'stab in the back' theory. Right-wing Germans believed Jews were not loyal Germans and had not fought in the war. Jews were blamed for Germany's defeat in the war. Here a German soldier is being knifed. Note the Star of David on the cuff to identify the hand as Jewish and the barbed wire to show a battlefield.

The main political divisions and the role of the army

At the end of the war, Germany was divided into three broad groups of political opinion. They are summarised in Table 9.2.

CHECK YOUR UNDERSTANDING 9.2

How did each grouping react to: a) the Treaty of Versailles and b) the new constitution?

Left-wing political developments

In January 1919, the Spartacist Party, led by Rosa Luxemburg and Karl Liebknecht, seized government buildings in a bid for power. President Ebert called on the army and the Freikorps to help crush the uprising. Liebknecht and Luxemburg were arrested by the police; both were violently beaten and shot. The first attempt at a communist revolution failed and the Ebert-Groener Pact had passed its first test of loyalty.

In February 1919, the leader of Bavaria (a large state in south Germany), Kurt Eisner, was killed. Communists seized power in March so Ebert again turned to the army. By May 1919 order had been restored with around 600 communists killed.

The third attempt at a communist uprising was made in 1920 in the Ruhr valley. Workers formed the Ruhr Army, which gained 50,000 members. They were defeated by the army and the Freikorps, with at least 1,000 workers and 250 soldiers and policemen killed.

Despite considerable support, communists failed to seize power. Even so, they continued to cause trouble in the form of strikes and demonstrations up to 1923.

CHECK YOUR UNDERSTANDING 9.3

Which of the three left-wing uprisings was the greatest threat to the Weimar Republic? Give reasons for your answer.

Right-wing political developments

The Freikorps supported the government in 1918 and 1919 because many former soldiers hated communists and blamed them for the 1918 defeat. Once the threat of revolution seemed over, Ebert ordered them to disband (in 1920).

One Freikorps leader, General Lüttwitz, refused and joined forces with the leader of the patriotic Fatherland Party, Wolfgang Kapp. With 12,000 Freikorps they marched on Berlin in the Kapp Putsch. This time the Ebert-Groener pact failed: the army, willing to shoot communists and strikers, refused to fire. Kapp was made chancellor of a new militaristic government but it had little popular support. Berlin workers opposed to Kapp organised a general strike. All public services, such as electricity and water, stopped working. The putsch collapsed after only four days and Kapp fled to Sweden, never to return.

As Hitler found out in 1923, many judges sympathised with the right wing: only one person involved in the Kapp Putsch was actually sent to prison. Freikorps men now founded a secret society called Organisation Consul, which assassinated government officials. By 1923 they had killed 354 politicians including Matthias Erzberger and Walther Rathenau. There were only 28 convictions for these, with one death penalty.

	Left	Centre left and centre right	Right
Beliefs	An equal society based on communism. They were inspired by Lenin's Bolsheviks in Russia who achieved a revolution in 1917.	Democracy and the new constitution. They wanted reform and democracy, not revolution.	Return of the monarchy, protection of private property, defeat of communism, strong government, rebuilt German prosperity and power.
Supporters	The working classes and the poor. They were represented by the Spartacist party (later the KPD).	Working and middle classes. Included Social Democrats, Centre and various liberal and conservative parties.	Conservatives, nationalists, monarchists, big business, the army and the Freikorps, people who had lost their savings in high inflation or their job during high unemployment.

Table 9.2: German political factions in 1919.

!

FACT FILE

Walther Rathenau was involved in the Versailles negotiations and was Jewish so he was hated by the Freikorps. He was the Foreign Minister and was killed by Organisation Consul in 1922. Approximately 700,000 people protested in Berlin and he was given a state funeral in the Reichstag. Until Hitler came to power, 24 June was a day of public commemoration for opponents of anti-Semitism.

The French occupation of the Ruhr 1923

In April 1921, the Reparations Committee set up by the Allies reported on the damages the Germans had to pay for the First World War. The amount announced was £6.6 billion. Germans were shocked and angry. In 1922 the government announced that it could not afford to pay the next instalment. Ebert tried to get concessions, but the French were not interested. When the payment deadline had passed in January 1923 French and Belgian troops entered the Ruhr valley to seize goods (mainly coal) in place of the payments.

The government ordered a policy of passive resistance, not fighting with the French and Belgians but not cooperating either. However, with no foreign support coming, Germans

Source 9C: Here, a woman is paying for her shoes to be repaired not with money but by bartering a sausage c. 1923. The notice on the wall announces in German 'Sales and repairs in exchange for food'.

in the Ruhr started to challenge the occupation forces. French soldiers killed approximately 100 protesters and expelled another 100,000 from the region.

The government turned to a radical solution. They owed money so they decided to print more bank notes. However, the debt was so high that huge amounts had to be printed. In the short term this worked as around £2.2bn of debt was paid off within Germany; the allies refused German currency. As time passed it led to high levels of inflation and hyperinflation.

Many people benefited as they were now easily able to pay off mortgages and loans. Many others lost out: workers' wages did not rise as quickly as prices and those with savings found that they were now worthless. Old people who lived off a fixed monthly pension were sent into poverty. Huge piles of banknotes were needed to buy simple things (see Table 9.3 and Sources 9B and 9C).

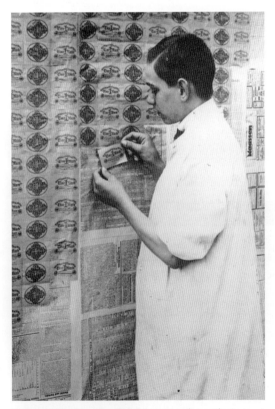

Source 9B: People did things to show their contempt for their almost worthless currency. Here you can see someone using bank notes as wallpaper in 1923.

Date	Value of $1 in marks
1914	4.2
1919	8.9
1920	14.0
1921	64.9
1922	191.8
1923 – Jan.	17,792
1923 – July	353,412
1923 – Sept.	98,860,000
1923 – Nov.	200,000,000,000

Table 9.3: The impact of hyperinflation.

Gustav Stresemann became chancellor in August 1923 and ended the campaign of passive resistance. He resumed reparations payments and abolished the worthless currency. The French and Belgian soldiers withdrew from the Ruhr. Despite these successes Stresemann was unpopular for giving in to the French. He resigned as chancellor in November but became foreign minister in the new government.

Source 9D: Gustav Stresemann giving a speech to the League of Nations shortly before his death in 1929.

FACT FILE

Gustav Stresemann was a politician with a doctorate in economics. Right-wing and pro-Freikorps after the war, the wave of political assassinations persuaded him that moderation was needed. He went on to become Weimar Germany's most influential politician. He shared the Nobel Peace Prize in 1926 with the French Foreign Minister Aristide Briand. His foreign policy successes are covered in Key Question 2.

ACTIVITY 9.3

Although many of Germany's problems were a result of the Treaty of Versailles, not all were. Many were more to do with domestic political struggles. Organise the information so far into two bullet-point lists:

1   Problems caused by the Treaty of Versailles.

2   Problems caused by German political developments.

Evaluate each list. Which side was more problematic? Decide for yourself if Germany's problems mainly resulted from Versailles or if they came from divisions within the country.

To what extent did the Republic recover after 1923?

Stresemann's new role as foreign minister allowed him to rebuild relations with the other European nations. French action over the Ruhr was widely seen as extreme, while Stresemann had compromised. This created the chance of discussing Germany's future with other governments.

In 1923 Stresemann had destroyed the old currency by claiming back all notes in circulation and burning them. In its place he introduced a new temporary form of money called the Rentenmark. Later in 1924 this was replaced with the Reichsmark, which solved Germany's cash problems.

In 1924 he negotiated the Dawes Plan with a committee appointed by the Reparations Committee. Germany would only pay an instalment of reparations when they could afford to and the occupation of the Ruhr would be ended. American banks loaned Germany 800 million Reichsmarks, which helped to kick-start economic growth. By 1928 German industry was back to level it had been at in 1914.

In 1929 another agreement was reached over reparations. Once again the Americans were involved. Reparations would be cut to £1.85bn and more loans were to be given. By the time the plan came into action Stresemann had died and the American economy had collapsed because of the Wall Street Crash of October 1929.

By 1929 Germany had been largely rehabilitated into the international community (see Source 9D).

What were the achievements of the Weimar period?

In the election of 1924, parties who supported the system won only 52% of the seats in the Reichstag. Opponents of the system won 39.4%. Yet by 1928, this had changed; support rose to 72.8%, opposition fell to 13.3%.

Culture and society were also changing. Berlin became a liberal city known for late-night clubs, cabarets and tolerance of different lifestyles. Cinema became popular, with Marlene Dietrich emerging as Germany's first film star. Modern music and jazz found audiences.

However, under the surface, problems remained. The economic recovery was based on American finance and while Stresemann had reduced reparations he had not changed Versailles. In fact, he had agreed to some of its harshest clauses, such as the demilitarisation of the Rhineland.

An worrying sign was the new president. Ebert died in 1925, one year before a presidential election was due. The Germans replaced centre-left Ebert with right-wing Paul von Hindenburg as their new president.

189

FACT FILE

Hindenburg served in wars against Austria and France before retirement in 1911. Recalled to service in 1914, he led the German army alongside Ludendorff until 1918. A monarchist, he became president in 1925, and he was re-elected in 1932. He despised Hitler – he called him 'the Bohemian corporal' or 'Austrian corporal' as a double insult of his nationality and rank – but eventually found it impossible not to appoint him chancellor (see Source 9E). His death in 1934 removed the last obstacle to Hitler's total authority.

Source 9E: Hindenburg pictured at a parade with Hitler in May 1933. His body language is particularly telling.

Source 9F: *Metropolis,* a film by Fritz Lang. This 1927 classic film shows how futuristic thinking had replaced the classical culture of the Kaiser's period. It popularised science fiction in world cinema and inspired many later films, for example the character C-3PO in *Star Wars* was based on the Maschinenmensch shown in this poster.

ACTIVITY 9.4

What do you think people mean when they call this a 'golden era'? How should historians respond to this kind of judgement? Should we focus on political and economic developments? How can we assess cultural and social developments, and the quality of life (see Source 9F).

Make brief notes indicating how you would answer the question 'Was the Weimar Republic doomed from the start?' You will need these later.

9.2 Why was Hitler able to dominate Germany by 1934?

Focus points

- What did the Nazi Party stand for in the 1920s?
- Why did the Nazis have little success before 1930?
- Why was Hitler able to become chancellor by 1933?
- How did Hitler consolidate his power in 1933–1934?

What did the Nazis stand for in the 1920s?

In January 1919, Anton Drexler, a railway worker in Munich (in Bavaria), founded the German Workers Party (DAP). It had at most 40 members and held meetings in beer cellars around the city. In September 1919, a 30-year-old army corporal named Adolf Hitler attended a DAP meeting. He worked for the army as an informant on the new political parties. Drexler was impressed and invited him to join the party. Hitler was put in charge of propaganda and in 1921 successfully challenged Drexler for the leadership.

Nazi ideas and methods

Hitler made significant changes to the DAP 1920–1922:

1. He changed its name to the National Socialist German Workers Party (NSDAP – or 'Nazi' for short) to attract more supporters.

2. He helped to write the party's **25-Point Programme** in 1920.

3. He introduced the swastika as the party's symbol.

4. He set up the Sturm Abteilung (SA) as the party's paramilitary wing (also known as the Brownshirts because of their uniform).

5. He bought a Munich newspaper called the *Völkischer Beobachter* to spread party ideas and propaganda.

6. He introduced the Hitler salute = ('Heil Hitler!').

KEY TERM

The 1920 **25-Point Programme** set out Hitler's early ideas. It opposed the Versailles Treaty. Only pure Germans could be German citizens; Jews could not be. It also opposed large-scale capitalism.

CHECK YOUR UNDERSTANDING 9.4

Organise Hitler's reforms into a hierarchy of significance, with the most important at the top.

Why did the Nazis have little success before 1930?

Munich Putsch 1923: the 'Beerhall Putsch'

By 1923 the Nazis had 20,000 members, mostly in Bavaria. Hitler decided to seize power. To succeed he needed the support of the Bavarian state government led by Gustav von Kahr and the army led by General Otto von Lossow. The strategy was to lead a march on Berlin, where he would use the army to overthrow the Weimar Republic.

On 8 November 1923, Kahr was giving a speech in a Munich beer hall. Hitler entered the room and fired a gun in the air and announced that a 'national revolution' had begun. Men from the SA surrounded the building. However, Kahr and Lossow were not convinced, even when First World War general Ludendorff appeared in support. After some time waiting Hitler was persuaded by Ludendorff to let the men go home and put off the march. On the morning of 9 November 2,000 Nazis marched towards the city centre. Kahr and Lossow had alerted the police and army, who were waiting. At Odeonsplatz the police opened fire killing 16 Nazis. The leaders were arrested.

CHECK YOUR UNDERSTANDING 9.5

Compare and contrast the events of the Kapp Putsch and the Munich Putsch. What similarities and differences do you notice?

Hitler's trial and sentence

Hitler went on trial in February 1924, where he made speeches that were widely reported.

For, gentlemen, it is not you who pronounce judgment upon us, it is the external Court of History which will make its pronouncement upon the charge which is brought against us. The verdict that you will pass I know. But that Court will not ask of us, 'Did you commit high treason or did you not?' That Court will judge us as Germans who wanted the best for their people and their fatherland, who wished to fight and to die. You may pronounce us guilty a thousand times, but the Goddess who presides over the Eternal Court of History will with a smile tear in pieces the charge of the Public Prosecutor and the verdict of this court. For she acquits us.

Source 9G: The conclusion to Hitler's trial speech.

The trial made his name known outside Bavaria for the first time. In the 1924 elections, Nazis won 32 seats in the Reichstag with 6.5% of the national vote. He was guilty of high treason (for which he could have been executed), but the right-wing judge gave him a lenient sentence of five years, of which he served nine months. Ludendorff was released. Landsberg Prison was very comfortable and Hitler used his time to write *Mein Kampf* ('My struggle') which set out at length his political beliefs.

CHECK YOUR UNDERSTANDING 9.6

Evaluate Source 9G. How would it be received by the public in 1924? Think about the political context after the events of 1919–1924.

Changing methods: the legal strategy

Hitler was released in December 1924. With him in prison the NSDAP had fallen into disarray. He reorganised the party and announced a new strategy. Violent revolution had failed; the Nazis would instead campaign in elections to become the most popular party in Germany.

We shall have to hold our noses and enter the Reichstag against the Catholic and Marxist deputies. If outvoting them takes longer than outshooting them, at least the result will be guaranteed by their own constitution

Source 9H: Hitler's justification of his new strategy.

CHECK YOUR UNDERSTANDING 9.7

What did Hitler mean by the justification in Source 9H?

Hitler divided Germany into different regions, each called a 'Gau'. Each would have a leader, a Gauleiter, who was responsible for winning support and spreading the party message.

Hitler also founded a number of new organisations to appeal to different social groups:

- The Hitler Youth.
- The Order of German Women.
- The Nazi Teachers' Association.
- The Union of Nazi Lawyers.

From 1925 to 1928 the number of party members increased from 27,000 to 108,000.

In 1926 Hitler set out the idea of the Führerprinzip ('leader principle') at the Bamberg Conference. This meant that his authority was unquestionable. This was important as some members argued for more left-wing policies that appealed to workers instead of right-wing racist policies. This left-wing group was led by two brothers, Gregor and Otto Strasser.

The work of the SA and SS

The Sturm Abteilung (SA) had been formed in 1920 as a unit to protect Nazi speakers at meetings (see Source 9I). Under Ernst Röhm's leadership it grew quickly and was heavily involved in the street-fighting of 1920–1923. After the Munich Putsch Röhm left for Bolivia, so Hitler had to re-establish the SA in 1925.

Approximately half of their members were unemployed young men, to whom membership offered a purpose, a uniform and hot meals. The Party also had SA hostels where they could stay. From 1927 there was an annual rally at Nuremberg, which was useful for propaganda. The filmmaker Leni Riefenstahl made a famous documentary on the 1934 rally called *The Triumph of the Will*.

In 1925, Hitler created his own personal bodyguard, the Schutzstaffel ('protection squad', SS), led from 1929 by Heinrich Himmler. They later became the most significant organisation in the Nazi state.

Campaign against the Young Plan

Despite the changes, the Nazis only won 12 seats in the 1928 elections, only 2.6% of the national vote. This was

Source 9I: SA men marching in 1933.

significantly down from the previous election of 1924. The Nazis needed more publicity and popularity. They needed something to bring them publicity and respect.

An opportunity arose in 1929 over the Young Plan. This followed on the Dawes Plan, and would reduce reparations payments and spread them over 59 years. However, nationalists felt the deal implied acceptance of the principle of reparations, and therefore German war guilt.

A national campaign against the plan was led in 1929 by a wealthy cinema magnate Alfred Hugenburg, leader of the German National People's Party (DNVP). The Nazis took part in Hugenberg's campaign against the Young Plan and successfully won the publicity and respectability that would be crucial in the 1930s.

ACTIVITY 9.5

Are you surprised by Hitler's new strategy? Give reasons for your answer.

FACT FILE

Alfred Hugenberg, the wealthy leader of the DNVP, joined Hitler's cabinet in 1933. That party lost members and voters to the Nazis after 1930.

192

ACTIVITY 9.6

Why did the Nazis make few gains before 1930? List three reasons why Hitler's legal strategy failed to make a significant impact in the 1920s.

KEY TERM

Stock market: the place where stocks and shares (ownership of companies) are bought and sold

Leading Nazis

Hitler was supported by several crucial figures. These included:

- Ernst Röhm: a First World War captain and leader of the SA. He was arrested in the Munich Putsch but released.
- Joseph Goebbels: head of propaganda and a deputy in the Reichstag. He originally supported Gregor Strasser but became a Hitler loyalist after the Bamberg Conference. He edited a Nazi newspaper called *Der Angriff* ('the attack') and was made Gauleiter of Berlin.
- Herman Göring: a First World War pilot who was also involved in the Munich Putsch. He was a deputy in the Reichstag and helped Hitler make important contacts in business circles.
- Heinrich Himmler: head of the SS from 1929. He took part in the Munich Putsch and assisted with party propaganda. His influence grew after Hitler came to power.

ACTIVITY 9.7

Do more research on Röhm, Goebbels, Göring and Himmler. Select information to create a profile of each man:
- Name, date and place of birth.
- Career before joining the party.
- Role in the party.
- Useful facts about them.

Why was Hitler able to become chancellor by 1933?

Impact of the Depression on Germany

Germany's economic recovery was built on borrowing from American banks. When the USA **stock market** crashed in October 1929, the USA banks loaning money to Germany wanted it back to meet their cash crisis. The effects were disastrous. In 1931 a major Austrian bank, Kredit Anstaldt, collapsed. This had a knock-on effect on German banks so the crisis deepened. Unemployment increased significantly. In 1929 1.4 million Germans were out of work. By 1933, this had increased to 6 million.

Hitler's message in the 1920s was that Germany shouldn't take money from the USA. This now looked intelligent to all Germans ruined by the Wall Street Crash. In the election of 1930 the Nazis made their first big breakthrough by winning 107 seats, second only to the SPD.

Several key methods were used to exploit the widespread feelings of distress:

- Propaganda: Goebbels used cinema and radio to spread the Nazi message. It was carefully crafted to appeal to specific groups. Posters were designed with simple but effective slogans that emphasised Hitler as the man who would save Germany.
- Speeches: Hitler was a very persuasive speaker and seemed to express the anger and frustration that so many Germans felt. In addition, 6,000 Party members had been trained by 1933 to deliver messages that would appeal to their audience. In the countryside they would talk about problems facing farmers; in the city they would talk about unemployment. Nazi policies were flexible, so many Germans could find something that appealed to them.
- Political violence: Röhm returned from Bolivia in 1931 to lead the SA and expanded their numbers dramatically. By the end of 1932 they had 425,000 men – over four times the size of the army. They frequently beat up communists and disrupted Communist Party (KPD) meetings. In the summer of 1932, 82 people died in street fighting in Berlin.

The success of these methods is reflected in the increase in votes for the Nazis from 1928 to 1933 (Table 9.4).

Date	Nazi % of the vote	Nazi seats in the Reichstag	SPD seats	KPD seats
1928 – May	2.6	12	153	54
1930 – Sept.	18.3	107	143	77
1932 – July	37.3	230	133	89
1932 – Nov.	33.1	196	121	100
1933 – Mar.*	43.9	288	120	81

* After Hitler was appointed chancellor

Table 9.4: Increase in Nazi votes.

TOP TIP

The percentage of votes and number of seats are excellent evidence to use in answers about Hitler's rise to power. Practise recalling these statistics with a partner so you can show your detailed knowledge in a written answer.

What these results show is a huge increase in the Nazi vote after the Wall Street Crash. However, the KDP also increased up to November 1932. Like the Nazis, they wanted to end the Weimar Republic. The SPD were the largest party who supported democracy. In the last three elections half the electorate backed the two parties that proposed to end Weimar democracy.

Weimar chancellors 1930–1933

The man in charge when the Wall Street Crash first hit Germany was SPD leader Herman Müller. He led a coalition government that disagreed over how to tackle the depression. Müller resigned as chancellor in 1930, dying a year later. Although the SPD was the largest party in the Reichstag they lacked leadership after this.

The 1932 presidential elections

Hitler decided to challenge Hindenburg in the 1932 presidential election. Goebbels organised an election campaign in which Hitler flew around Germany to address crowds in different cities on the same day.

No candidate won 50% of the vote, so a second round was staged with the three most successful

candidates – Hindenburg, Hitler and the communist leader Ernst Thalmann.

Candidate	Hindenburg	Hitler	Thälmann
% of votes	53%	36.8%	10.2%
Number of votes	19.4 million	13.4 million	3.7 million

Table 9.6: Results of the 1932 presidential election run-off.

TOP TIP

Make sure you know the events of 1932 and 1933 in detail. A lot happens here, and there are several key leaders. Allow some additional time to revise this before the exam.

How did Hitler become chancellor?

In the election of July 1932, the Nazis won 230 seats and overtook the SPD to become the largest party. Hindenburg still refused to make Hitler chancellor, but six months later he was persuaded to change his mind. What caused this? The answer lies in political deals that were done behind the scenes.

Von Papen was not a popular choice as chancellor in 1932. He had less Reichstag support than Müller or Brüning, and he resigned from the Centre Party (which distrusted him) shortly after being appointed chancellor. Schleicher thought he would follow the army line but soon realised that von Papen lacked authority. Hindenburg agreed to sack von Papen and make Schleicher chancellor instead.

Name	Background	Time as Chancellor	Policies
Heinrich Brüning	Leader of the Centre Party	1930 (March) to 1932 (May)	Cut government spending and increased taxes. This decreased Germany's debt but was unpopular: people called him the 'hunger chancellor'. He ruled using Article 48 as he had little support in the Reichstag. He used this to ban the SA.
Franz von Papen	Centre Party aristocrat. An officer and diplomat in First World War	1932 (June to November)	Right-wing and a Hindenburg adviser. He tried to bring the Nazis into his government and lifted the ban on the SA. The KPD and the Nazis voted together to bring down his government.
Kurt von Schleicher	General and political adviser to Hindenburg	1932 (November) to 1933 (January)	Undermined Brüning. Although defence minister under von Papen, he decided Germany needed a strong man to deal with the crisis. Thought he could split and use the Nazis.

Table 9.5: The 1930s chancellors before Hitler.

Schleicher's plan was to split the Nazis. He knew that some Nazi members preferred the Strasser brothers to Hitler, so he offered Gregor Strasser the role of vice-chancellor. The Nazis had lost votes in the election of November 1932, dropping to 196 seats, so Hitler's methods didn't seem to be working. All the election campaigns of 1932 also left them short of money. Strasser wanted to take the job and Hitler's authority was openly questioned.

At a meeting of the Nazi leadership in December 1932 Hitler made an emotional appeal for support. He attacked Strasser's disloyalty and won the backing of the Gauleiters. It was a vital moment. The Strassers resigned from the party and Schleicher's plan failed.

Von Papen now saw an opportunity to gain revenge on Schleicher. He went to Hindenburg with a plan that Hitler should be made chancellor, but in a government that had few Nazi ministers. Von Papen would be vice-chancellor and there were would be many conservative ministers to limit Hitler's power. This would have one of two consequences:

1   Hitler would do well and the financial crisis would end so Hindenburg could take the credit for appointing him.

2   Hitler would do badly and the crisis would get worse causing Nazi support to collapse.

This seemed a win-win situation. Fearing a revolutionary uprising by either the Nazis or the KPD, appointing Hitler as chancellor seemed to be the least dangerous option. Hindenburg invited him to form a government on 30 January 1933 – just nine years after being jailed for treason.

ACTIVITY 9.8

Why did Hitler become chancellor? Select the most important information and organise it into a mind map showing the reasons why Hitler was appointed. Cover these key points:
- The impact of the Depression.
- The weakness of Weimar chancellors.
- Hitler's leadership.
- The role played by other Nazi leaders.

How did Hitler consolidate his power in 1933–1934?

When Hitler was appointed chancellor there were several limitations to his power:

1   Hindenburg had the power to sack him.

2   He didn't control the army.

3   There were only three Nazis in a cabinet of 14 ministers – Hitler, Göring and Wilhelm Frick.

4   The economy was still weak.

5   With 196 of the 584 seats he lacked a majority in the Reichstag.

Despite these problems Hitler managed to turn Germany into a dictatorship by the summer of 1934. There were four important steps that destroyed the Weimar Republic and turned Germany into the Third Reich.

Step 1: The Reichstag fire

Hitler's first act as chancellor was to call a new election as he hoped to win a majority in the Reichstag. Street-fighting left 69 people dead. He blamed the violence – like Germany's other problems – on the KPD.

On 27 February, just a week before the election, the Reichstag burned down. A Dutch communist named Marinus van der Lubbe was found at the scene and confessed. Some historians believe the Nazis were guilty and that van der Lubbe was merely a scapegoat (and so did some people at the time, see Source 9J). Whatever the real cause, Hitler persuaded Hindenburg to sign the 'Decree For The Protection Of People And State' the next day. This cut individual rights and gave the government more power. The leaders of the KPD were arrested as Hitler claimed they were attempting a revolution.

Following the fire, hundreds of the Nazis' opponents were arrested. Hitler won the election gaining 288 seats, too few to rule without a coalition and far less than the 434 seats needed to change the constitution.

Source 9J: Protestors outside the German legation in New York, 1933. One banner reads 'Nazi Leaders Set Reichstag Fire'.

195

ACTIVITY 9.9

Investigate the Reichstag fire. First, decide whether the Nazis were responsible. Second, what does your verdict tell us about Hitler's decision making?

Step 2: The Enabling Act

When the Reichstag deputies met in the Kroll Opera House on 23 March, Hitler proposed a measure to grant dictatorial power to the government for the next four years. He made a speech to the deputies in an atmosphere of intimidation with SA men surrounding the building. The SPD opposed the measure but the banned KPD could not take part. The DNVP naturally supported the Nazis, but Hitler needed a two-thirds majority vote as this would change the constitution. This left the Catholic Centre Party holding the balance of power. Hitler promised to protect the Catholic Church and Catholic schools so they supported the Enabling Act. It was passed by 444 to 94.

The passing of the Enabling Act gave Hitler enormous power. He no longer needed the support of the Reichstag to make laws or decisions, just Hindenburg's backing. He had achieved what he set out to do in 1924.

Step 3: The Night of the Long Knives

By June 1933, opposition parties had been banned. The trade unions were outlawed in May, workers being represented by the Nazi-led German Labour Front. The opposition Hitler still had to fear lay within his own party.

Once in power, radical Nazi members expected action, particularly against Jews, the Treaty of Versailles and big business. Hitler knew it was too early to make any bold moves for fear of alarming business leaders and foreign governments.

The SA was not happy with Hitler's caution. It had 2.5 million members by 1934 and Röhm was increasingly outspoken in his criticism. He felt Hitler was too friendly with rich conservatives and had lost touch with ordinary Nazis. Himmler hated Röhm and fed Hitler rumours of his disloyalty. He claimed Röhm was planning a putsch and even forged evidence to prove this.

On 30 June, Hitler made his move on what became known as 'the Night of the Long Knives'. The SA were given a holiday; so Röhm and his entourage were staying at a hotel in Bavaria. Hitler travelled there with a group of SS men. Röhm was arrested and executed. An estimated 200 people were killed, including, Schleicher, Gregor Strasser and von Kahr.

The cabinet issued a decree that said simply: 'The measures taken on 30th June and 1st and 2nd July to suppress the acts of high treason are legal, being necessary for the self-defence of the state.' Hitler had legalised murder.

Step 4: The presidency

When Hindenburg died on 2 August 1934, Hitler became president while also remaining chancellor. He was simply the 'Führer' (leader). This was approved in a country-wide referendum by over 90% of those who voted. The army swore an oath of allegiance to Hitler personally. The last obstacle to his complete control of power had been removed.

CHECK YOUR UNDERSTANDING 9.8

Which of the four steps was the most significant turning point in Hitler's quest to establish a dictatorship?

TOP TIP

To help you remember the many important events in 1932–1934, use this chapter to create a flow diagram so you know in which order they go.

Make brief notes indicating how you would answer the question 'Why was Hitler able to dominate Germany by 1934?'

9.3 How effectively did the Nazis control Germany, 1933–1945?

Focus points

- How much opposition was there to the Nazi regime?
- How effectively did the Nazis deal with their political opponents?
- How did the Nazis use culture and the mass media to control the people?
- Why did the Nazis persecute many groups in German society?
- Was Nazi Germany a totalitarian state?

How much opposition was there to the Nazi regime?

The arrest of rival political leaders in 1933 and the economic recovery by 1936 both undermined opposition to the regime. Hitler's more radical foreign policies from 1938 and the attacks on Jews increased some people's concerns about the nature of his government. When the war began this opposition became much more evident. Although fear silenced much criticism, secret police reports reveal gradually increasing resentment and mockery by the general public as the war went on.

We can organise the types of opposition between 1933 and 1945 into four categories.

Churches

The Roman Catholic Bishop of Münster August von Galen gave a sermon that condemned the **Aktion T-4** programme. Hitler wanted Galen arrested but Goebbels warned he was too popular a figure to persecute. Galen was sent to a **concentration camp** in 1944, but survived.

KEY TERMS

Aktion T-4: a euthanasia programme. It started at the beginning of the war and ran officially until August 1941. It involved the killing of mentally handicapped, mentally ill and terminally ill people by doctors administering lethal injections; 70,000 died.

Concentration camp: prisons for political opponents up to 1939 and in the Second World War Jews were sent to them as well. The idea was that opponents would be 'purified' by hard labour, so the slogan 'Arbeit Macht Frei' ('work sets [you] free') was written above the gates (Source 9N).

Protestant pastor Dietrich Bonhoffer was a vocal critic of Nazism and was arrested in 1943. He was active in the resistance and helped many Jews to escape Germany. He was executed in April 1945 at Flossenbürg concentration camp, two weeks before it was liberated by the Americans.

First they came for the Communists
And I did not speak out
Because I was not a Communist
Then they came for the Socialists
And I did not speak out
Because I was not a Socialist
Then they came for the trade unionists
And I did not speak out
Because I was not a trade unionist
Then they came for the Jews
And I did not speak out
Because I was not a Jew
Then they came for me
And there was no one left
To speak out for me.

Source 9K: A statement by Martin Niemöller.

CHECK YOUR UNDERSTANDING 9.9

Analyse Sources 9K and 9L. Write down your initial thoughts and reflections on them. How do each of them help you understand the mentality of many Germans in the 1930s?

Youth

Galen's example provided inspiration for the White Rose group in Munich. This was founded in 1942 by Hans and Sophie Scholl, siblings who attended Munich University. With their followers they distributed leaflets on the university campus which openly attacked the Nazis. These were smuggled out of Germany, reprinted and dropped by allied planes over cities. However, it was not hard for the authorities to crack down on the group. The Scholls and their accomplices were arrested, tortured and beheaded in February 1943.

Somebody, after all, had to make a start. What we wrote and said is also believed by many others. They just don't dare express themselves as we did.

Source 9L: Sophie Scholl speaking at her trial in 1943.

Political

The SPD's underground movement has already been noted and they set up an exile group called SOPADE. They were based in Prague until Hitler invaded Czechoslovakia. They tried to report to the outside world what was happening in Germany. Also on the left, the Red Orchestra was a spy network that sent information to the USSR from 1936. Many of their spies were tortured and killed by the Gestapo.

A small group of conservatives formed an opposition discussion group about how to run Germany after Hitler was gone. The Gestapo knew them as the Kreisau Circle and several members were executed in 1944 after the army bomb plot.

Military

Key figures within the army shared Hindenburg's doubts about Hitler. This increased as the war went on leading to an assassination attempt codenamed **Operation Valkyrie**. The man chosen to plant the bomb was Colonel **Claus von Stauffenberg**. He turned against Hitler after witnessing the savagery of Russian front in 1942. Stauffenberg attended a meeting with Hitler on July 20th 1944. He placed a briefcase bomb on the floor and left the room. However, the bomb was moved just before it went off. Four people were killed but Hitler's only injury was a perforated eardrum from the sound of the explosion. A planned uprising in Berlin failed and 5,000 conspirators were executed in the aftermath.

197

ACTIVITY 9.10

There were at least 40 assassination attempts on Hitler. Research Georg Elser online and write a brief summary of his plot. What do you think motivated him? What does his story tell us about opposition to Hitler?

ACTIVITY 9.11

Make a spider diagram of the types of opposition. Evaluate how serious each group was. Clearly label your diagram to show the level and nature of threat posed to the Third Reich.

How effectively did the Nazis deal with their political opponents?

Hitler's consolidation of power is known as Gleichschaltung, which means 'coordination'. It meant that Germany was now a dictatorship ruled by one party and one man. There were still limits to Hitler's power but only those willing to risk their lives showed open opposition. Authority was maintained through the police state. There were several levels to this:

1   The Ordo and Kripo: the regular police.
2   The Gestapo – the secret police who dealt with moral and political opposition.
3   The SA – under Himmler's control after 1934.
4   The SS – they expanded to take over many aspects of the Nazi regime.
5   The army.

The most important individual in all of this was Heinrich Himmler. In 1936 he was put in charge of all police in Germany, so wielded immense power. His deputy, Reinhard Heydrich, was head of the SD, the party's internal security police and main source of intelligence.

FACT FILE

Reinhard Heydrich (Source 9M) was one of the few Nazis who conformed to the racial ideal of being blond-haired and blue-eyed and was tipped to be a future leader after Hitler. He ran the SD, assisted in the Gestapo and was in charge of Bohemia and Moravia after the fall of Czechoslovakia. He died in 1942 after an assassination attempt by Czechoslovak patriots; in retaliation the SS murdered the population of an entire town, Lidice.

Source 9M: Heydrich (on the right, pictured in 1934) was one of the leading Nazis. A key figure in the SS, he was a major architect of the Holocaust.

Source 9N: The gates at Sachsenhausen, just outside Berlin. All concentration camps had this sign at the entrance.

The Gestapo had a network of informers but they were overwhelmed with information from the public. Neighbours often reported on people they didn't like as a way of settling personal rivalries. Anyone found guilty of 'deviant behaviour' could be sent to a concentration camp. The first of these was Dachau, which was opened in March 1933. Goebbels made sure it was heavily publicised so that potential opponents knew what would happen to them.

How did the Nazis use culture and the mass media to control the people?

The state controlled the radio but newspapers were privately owned. The Editors' Law of October 1933 made editors responsible for everything published in their newspaper. If a journalist wrote something critical of the Nazis, the editor would be punished. Consequently, editors ensured no such articles were published.

In March 1933, the Ministry for Popular Enlightenment and Propaganda was created, with Goebbels in charge. He ensured that all art and entertainment conformed to Nazi values. A cheap radio called the 'People's Receiver' was mass-produced so that more Germans could receive entertainment and propaganda. By 1939, 70% of the population had a radio, the highest level of ownership in the world.

In 1937 Goebbels arranged an exhibition called 'Degenerate Art' (Source 9O). It was intended to educate the public by showing art that was immoral and repulsive to Nazi values – mainly modern art. It included works by Picasso, Matisse and Van Gogh. It was enormously popular as over 4 million people went to see it by 1940.

Source 9O: Hitler and Goebbels touring the exhibition on 'Degenerate Art' in 1937.

CHECK YOUR UNDERSTANDING 9.10

Assess the importance of propaganda in maintaining the Nazis' authority in Germany. Was it more important than other factors, such as the use of terror?

Why did the Nazis persecute many groups in German society?

There were two main reasons for the persecution of particular groups in society.

Ideological

The 25-Point Programme of 1920 and *Mein Kampf* showed hostility to Jews, foreigners, communists and anyone who was deemed to be against the national interest. Nazi notions of racial purity (the study of 'eugenics') meant they discriminated against people who were mentally or physically handicapped.

Political

Hitler never won a majority of the vote in an election. Even in March 1933, with KPD leaders under arrest and the SA intimidating all opposition parties, the Nazis won 43.9%. This meant that 56.1% of Germans voted for other parties even after Hitler became chancellor. He knew that he either had to win over the doubters, or intimidate them.

Churches

The churches' moral principles led some to challenge the Nazis. In addition, church leaders offered a rival influence for Germans. Churches could not simply be shut down, like the KPD, but they could be neutralised. In July 1933, von Papen as Vice-Chancellor signed a Concordat with the Catholic Church, which guaranteed its freedom, rights and property would be protected.

To gain the support of Protestants a new organisation called the German Christians was created, led by a Reich bishop. This aimed to blend Christian and Nazi principles, but had little success. In 1934 Martin Niemöller and Dietrich Bonhoffer helped to set up the Confessing Church for non-Nazi ministers. It gained the support of 7,000 of Germany's 17,000 pastors. In response, priests and pastors were arrested, church schools were closed and funds confiscated. Niemöller was sent to a concentration camp in 1937 and remained there until 1945.

Jews

Although there were only 503,000 Jews in Germany in 1933, fewer than 1% of the population, the Nazis saw them as a threat. Hitler's priority was to revise the Treaty of Versailles, which meant making a good impression with foreign nations. This explains why there was limited official action against Jews up to 1937. There was a one-day boycott of Jewish shops on 1 April 1933, but this was mainly to please the SA and had little impact. In 1935 the **Nuremberg Laws** deprived Jews of their citizenship.

KEY TERM

Nuremberg Laws: were two laws called the 'Reich Citizenship Law' and the 'Law for the Protection of German Blood and German Honour'. Jews could not be citizens of the Reich and were forbidden from marrying – or having sexual relations with – a German. Jews were defined as anyone with three or four Jewish grandparents, irrespective of whether or not they were religious.

The 1936 Olympics were held in Berlin, so again Hitler and Goebbels put aside anti-Semitism to make a big propaganda impression to the world about how advanced Germany was. Many Jews, having emigrated in 1933, actually came back to Germany because it appeared that things were not as bad as they originally feared.

ACTIVITY 9.12

Research the 1936 Berlin Olympics. To what extent was it a propaganda triumph for Goebbels and Hitler?

In 1938 Hitler's foreign policy became more aggressive. As Austria was invaded, Jews in Vienna were mistreated (see Source 9P) and Heydrich's assistant, Adolf Eichmann, deported thousands. Later that year, on 7 November, Herschel Grynszpan went into the German embassy in Paris and shot a minor official called Ernst vom Rath. Grynszpan's parents were Polish Jews and had been deported from Germany against their will in October, along with 17,000 others.

Source 9P: Jews in Vienna in 1938 are forced to scrub the streets while Austrians and Nazis shout insults and look on.

Goebbels persuaded Hitler that the time was right to attack German Jews. The order was given for SS men (dressed in plain clothes) to attack Jewish homes, shops and synagogues. At least 100 people were killed in the violence. The next morning city centres were littered with broken glass and debris from the night before, hence the events of 9th to 10th November 1938 became known as Kristallnacht – the 'Night of Broken Glass'.

Jews were blamed for these events and fined 1 billion marks. They were continually persecuted. Their businesses were confiscated, their children excluded from schools and universities.

TOP TIP

The website of United States Holocaust Memorial Museum in Washington DC is useful for learning about all aspects of the Nazi regime. You can find it by searching for USAHMM.

Was Nazi Germany a totalitarian state?

A totalitarian state is one in which the government has total power over all individuals and institutions. Two American historians have identified six key features of such a state:

1   an official ideology
2   a single party state, led by one person
3   total control of the military
4   total control of media and communication
5   a police state that uses terror to suppress opposition
6   total control of the economy.

ACTIVITY 9.13

Look at the six criteria listed. How far do they apply to the Third Reich? For each one select at least three pieces of evidence that argue for or against it applying to Germany.

Make brief notes indicating how you would answer the question: 'How effectively did the Nazis control Germany, 1933–1945?' You will need these later.

9.4 What was it like to live in Nazi Germany?

Focus points

- How did young people react to the Nazi regime?
- How successful were Nazi policies towards women and the family?
- Did most people in Germany benefit from Nazi rule?
- How did the coming of war change life in Nazi Germany?

How did young people react to the Nazi regime?

The NSDAP was keen to indoctrinate young people with Nazi principles to secure Germany's future. Jewish and politically suspect teachers were removed. The curriculum was changed: subjects such as biology were used to emphasise German racial superiority. Teachers went on Nazi ideology courses.

Outside school, indoctrination continued. For boys there was the Hitler Youth led by Baldur von Schirach. They went camping, sang songs and did athletics, which was meant to prepare boys for the army. By 1938 it had 7.1 million members. In 1939 membership was made compulsory. Girls went to the League of German Maidens where they learned cooking and domestic skills. The result of this was that children were brought up to be loyal to Hitler and the nation before anything else. Some children even informed on their parents to the Gestapo if they said something that contradicted what they had been taught in school or the Hitler Youth.

Not all children blindly followed. Many formed their own opposition groups, like the Edelweiss Pirates. They listened to American jazz ('black music' the Nazis accused of being racially inferior) and dressed in their own style. They attacked the Hitler Youth and caused so much concern that 12 Pirates were publicly hanged in Cologne in 1944 as a warning to others.

Sources 9Q and R: An Edelweiss Pirate group (top) and the executions in Cologne in November 1944 (bottom).

ACTIVITY 9.14

Change and continuity: look at Sources 9Q and 9R. In what ways had life changed for young people in Germany since the Weimar Republic, and what had remained unchanged?

How successful were Nazi policies towards women and the family?

The First World War and the Weimar era saw massive changes for German women. They worked in factories and could vote under the Weimar constitution. Young women used the freedom of the 1920s to go to clubs and socialise. The Nazis were appalled by this trend. Many older women were also unimpressed by the younger generation and they worried more about family stability and employment for their husbands. Initially, such women tended to vote for conservative parties and backed Hindenburg instead of Hitler for the presidency in 1932. It was only by the July 1932 election that large numbers of women had shifted their support to the NSDAP.

> **His words had power. He was emotional. He was sentimental, he was never intellectual ... The lonely bachelor, the non-smoker, the crusading teetotaller – the glorious fighter for Germany's honour who had gone to prison for his convictions. It was a richly emotional picture for the women to gaze on.**

Source 9S: Katherine Thomas was a British visitor to Germany and published a book on German women in 1943. She wrote this extract after hearing Hitler speak in public.

CHECK YOUR UNDERSTANDING 9.11

What does Source 9S tell us about the nature of Hitler's appeal to women in Germany?

Nazi policies towards women were summed up in the slogan 'Kinder, Küche, Kirche' ('children, kitchen, church'). Women could only have specialist jobs that men should not do, such as being a midwife. Only 10% of university places were available for females. As political parties and trade unions had been banned, women had no outlet for protest against these policies.

Young women were encouraged to marry a German man of pure blood and have as many children as possible. The Honour Cross of the German Mother was awarded for having several children: bronze for 4, silver for 6 and gold for 8. In 1936 the SS went a step further and established the Lebensborn programme where officers would have children with unmarried women who were deemed racially pure. There was no obligation to act as a responsible father and the women were given financial support to raise the child.

Things changed in the Second World War. As the war progressed there was a greater need for workers. As 12.5 million men served in the armed forces women were needed to perform war-related work. This was mainly in weapons factories and on farms.

However, many brave women joined the resistance. They used Nazi stereotyping to escape questioning by feigning deference, or pretending to be pregnant. Some suffered for opposing Nazism: a female-only concentration camp was set up at Moringen in November 1933. The largest of the female camps was established at Ravensbrück in 1938, where an estimated 50,000 women died.

ACTIVITY 9.15

Explore female opposition to Nazism by researching: Minna Cammens, Maria Terwiel, and Gertrud Staewen. How significant were their actions?

Did most people in Germany benefit from Nazi rule?

One of the key reasons why the Nazis were able to win support was through establishing economic stability. Hitler was fortunate as the Depression had actually peaked in December 1932, just before he came to power. Economics Minister Hjaldmar Schacht (who wasn't a Nazi) was an experienced banker and had helped Stresemann end hyperinflation in 1923. His New Plan of 1934 created jobs through public works schemes such as the building of the Autobahn (the motorway). Another significant project was building the Volkswagen (meaning 'people's car'). The government spent a lot of money to create these jobs but it stimulated industry. In 1935 Hitler announced the army would expand from 100,000 to 500,000 and that an airforce (the Luftwaffe) would be built, which created new jobs in manufacturing.

ACTIVITY 9.16

How useful is Source 9T to an historian investigating the Nazi economy in the 1930s?

Source 9T: Hitler speaking at the opening of a Volkswagen factory in 1938, with the iconic cars in front of the podium.

With unemployment back down to pre-Depression levels in 1936, Hitler set up the Four-Year Plan Office under Göring. This was to make Germany ready for war with more weapons and materials and a drive towards **autarky**. Schacht opposed this, but lost the argument and was removed from office in 1937.

KEY TERM

Autarky: complete economic self-sufficiency. A state that is autarkic has no need of imports or exports and produces everything it needs by itself. This is virtually impossible in a modern economic setting.

Göring was no economist. The Four-Year Plan Office was chaotic and failed to achieve its targets for production (see Figure 9.1). In particular the Nazis lacked oil and rubber which were essential war materials.

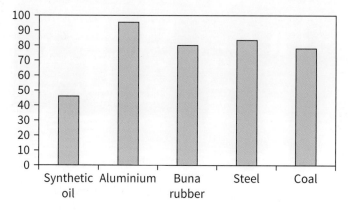

Figure 9.1: % of target met by the Four-Year Plan by 1942.

Policy towards workers

The Nazis distrusted the workers, most of whom had voted for the SPD and KPD. The 'Strength Through Joy' programme was established with two key aims.

1 To win workers' support by providing leisure and holiday activities they might not otherwise be able to afford, such as skiing or theatre trips.

2 To fill workers' spare time with activities, limiting their ability to think about politics, thereby reducing opposition.

By 1936 there were 30 million workers enlisted in the programme but there was little evidence that it converted the working class. Both internal SD reports and SOPADE sources reveal that workers were happy to accept the free holidays but didn't necessarily adopt Nazi ideology.

ACTIVITY 9.17

Hold a class debate about the reasons why Hitler was able to maintain power in the period from 1933 to 1939. In particular, debate these reasons:

- Goebbels' propaganda.
- Himmler's police state.
- Schacht's economic policies.

Discuss the relative importance of each factor.

How did the coming of war change life in Nazi Germany?

In the first two years of the Second World War, campaigns went well for the Nazis and there was little disruption to life on the home front. Food rationing, introduced in 1939, was not too severe. However, as autarky failed, more restrictions were put in place. With the 1941 invasion of the USSR, Germany began to struggle so the transition was made to **total war**. The economy was oriented to the war: by 1944 61% of the workforce were in war-related employment.

TOP TIP

The BBC documentary *The Nazis: A Warning from History* covers Hitler's rise to power and life in Nazi Germany. The interviews with Germans who lived through the period are revealing.

KEY TERM

Total war: a war that uses the full economic and military capacity of a nation. Every person is involved in supporting the war effort: for example through conscription to the military. Food is rationed and individual rights are restricted.

The biggest problem was producing weapons. The Four-Year Plan failed spectacularly to produce the amount of equipment that the Wehrmacht (army) needed. In 1942 Hitler appointed Albert Speer as Minister of Armaments. Despite his inexperience – he was Hitler's personal architect with no background in industry – he reorganised German industry and by 1944 there was a 300% increase in production. Even this wasn't enough. In the vital year of 1944 Germany could only produce 40% of the tanks and 25% of the planes that the USA, USSR and Britain together could.

Effects of Allied bombing

Britain and Germany started bombing one another's cities in 1940. Britain aimed at economic and military targets such as the Ruhr valley coal fields and naval bases. In February 1942 British Bomber Command decided to target cities to undermine German civilian morale. They used incendiary bombs that started fires on the ground as this was the most effective method of destroying a city. American planes also took part.

One of the most infamous raids was on Hamburg in July 1943, where an estimated 30,000 people were killed and one million left homeless by a huge blaze caused by incendiary bombs. Another was on Dresden in February 1945, just before the end of the war. A recent commission claimed that between 18,000 and 25,000 people were killed; previous estimates were higher. By the end of the war British and American planes had killed about 300,000 German civilians.

FACT FILE

American author Kurt Vonnegut was held as a prisoner of war in Dresden when the city was fire-bombed. He survived and wrote the surreal cult novel *Slaughterhouse-Five* about his experiences.

CHECK YOUR UNDERSTANDING 9.12

Look at Source 9U. Do you think the Allies succeeded in their strategy to weaken German morale? Do you think it reduced support for Hitler?

Source 9U: Dresden after the bombing by Allied planes in 1945.

The impact of the war on Jews

On 1 September 1939, the Wehrmacht (the army) invaded Poland. Now 3 million additional Jews were living in German-occupied territory. This presented its own problems. Jews were banned from working or living freely so the Reich had to provide for them. The first **ghetto** was set up in Poland in October 1939.

KEY TERM

Ghetto: an area in which a specific ethnic group is forced by law or informal threat of violence to live. By the end of the war the Nazis had set up more than 1,000. The largest was the Warsaw ghetto, which held over 400,000 people.

The June 1941 invasion of the Soviet Union further increased the number of Jews under Nazi control. German intentions in this invasion were clear. Just behind the Wehrmacht were four Einsatzgruppen ('action groups'), which totalled around 3,000 men. Their orders were to murder Jews and dump their bodies in mass graves. By the end of the year they had killed 700,000 people. The war with the USSR was draining money and manpower. Staffing the ghettos was costly. Killing the Jews was the solution chosen. The SS were the driving force behind this. However, by the end of 1941 there were concerns about the efficiency of the operation. A new method was required.

The Wannsee Conference and the Final Solution

On 20 January 1942, a meeting was held in Wannsee, just outside Berlin. It was chaired by Heydrich and arranged by his deputy Eichmann. This planned the 'Final Solution of the Jewish question'. Heads of government departments,

Land	Zahl
A. Altreich	131.800
Ostmark	43.700
Ostgebiete	420.000
Generalgouvernement	2.284.000
Bialystok	400.000
Protektorat Böhmen und Mähren	74.200
Estland – judenfrei –	
Lettland	3.500
Litauen	34.000
Belgien	43.000
Dänemark	5.600
Frankreich / Besetztes Gebiet	165.000
Unbesetztes Gebiet	700.000
Griechenland	69.600
Niederlande	160.800
Norwegen	1.300
B. Bulgarien	48.000
England	330.000
Finnland	2.300
Irland	4.000
Italien einschl. Sardinien	58.000
Albanien	200
Kroatien	40.000
Portugal	3.000
Rumänien einschl. Bessarabien	342.000
Schweden	8.000
Schweiz	18.000
Serbien	10.000
Slowakei	88.000
Spanien	6.000
Türkei (europ. Teil)	55.500
Ungarn	742.800
UdSSR	5.000.000
Ukraine 2.994.684	
Weißrußland ausschl. Bialystok 446.484	
Zusammen: über	11.000.000

Source 9V: A document from the Wannsee Conference showing the Nazi estimates on the Jewish populations in each country.

the SS and the Wehrmacht were ordered to focus on killing all Europe's Jews. Special camps had been built where Jews would be murdered using Zyklon B (hydrogen cyanide) and their bodies cremated.

TOP TIP

The film *Conspiracy* made by the BBC and HBO is about the Wannsee Conference. It was filmed on location at the actual villa where the meeting took place and is worth watching.

ACTIVITY 9.18

Research the term 'genocide'. When was it first used? Why does the Holocaust qualify as an act of genocide? What other examples are there? Study Source 9V: what does it tell us about the Nazi approach to the killing of Jews by this stage?

What the Nazis termed the Final Solution later came to be known as the Holocaust. Approximately 6 million people were killed. Around half of the victims died in the peak period of murder, from the spring of 1942 to February 1943. By 1944 the war against the USSR was failing so this gradually brought an end to the Holocaust by spring 1945.

Name of camp	Estimated no. of victims
Auschwitz	1.5 million
Treblinka	750,000
Belzec	600,000
Majdanek	360,000
Chełmno	250,000
Sobibor	250,000

Table 9.7: Death camp victims.

ACTIVITY 9.19

All the death camps were outside Germany's pre-war borders (see Source 9W): why do you think this was?

As well as Jews, the Nazis targeted other marginalised social groups such as homosexuals, the homeless and Balkan Muslims. The Soviet army discovered the six death camps, four in the summer of 1944, Chełmno and Auschwitz in January 1945. Holocaust Memorial Day is on 27 January every year – the day that Auschwitz was liberated.

Country	No. of victims
Poland	2.9 million
Ukraine	900,000
Hungary	450,000
Romania	270,000
Belarus	245,000
Lithuania	220,000
Germany	130,000
Russia	107,000
Holland	106,000
France	90,000

Table 9.8: Countries with the highest number of Holocaust victims.

205

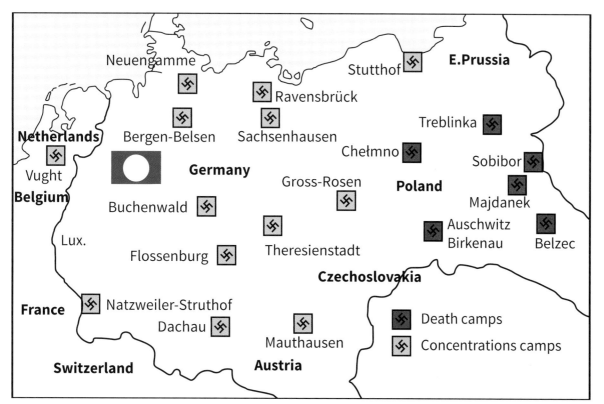

Source 9W: A map showing the location of the six death camps that accounted for more than half of all Holocaust victims. Concentration camps were for hard labour and were intended to contribute to the war economy. The death camps were specifically to murder people.

TOP TIP

There are many excellent films on the Holocaust. *Schindler's List, The Pianist* and *Life Is Beautiful* are all strongly recommended.

ACTIVITY 9.20

Make brief notes indicating how you would answer the question, 'What was it like to live in Nazi Germany?' You will need these later.

Review your learning

We began with these four investigative questions:

1 Was the Weimar Republic doomed from the start?

2 Why was Hitler able to dominate Germany by 1934?

3 How effectively did the Nazis control Germany, 1933–1945?

4 What was it like to live in Nazi Germany?

Having undertaken several activities and tests, you should now be able to describe events, assess their significance, discuss causes and consequences in each case, and offer opinions supported by evidence. If you feel that you cannot do this for any of these four questions, you should revise the relevant section. Then read the summary points – and turn to the Big Challenge!

Summary points

- The Weimar Republic had a problematic start but recovered and enjoyed some prosperity from 1924 to 1929.

- Hitler established a political movement in the 1920s that made little progress before 1929 but thereafter was more popular than any other German party.

- The Nazis maintained control over Germany after 1933 through use of the police state, heavy propaganda and the benefits of a stronger economy.

- German society was divided between those the regime favoured and those who were persecuted. Some benefitted; many others suffered.

The Big Challenge

In the four investigative questions for this chapter you will have noticed that judging the significance of an event or a person in a wider process is an important skill. Here we need to put this into practice. Look at the following two examples:

1 The Kapp Putsch 1920
2 The Nuremburg Laws 1935

We know these events are important, but how important are they? To make this decision, we need to consider first what they are important for. Then

we need to consider what other events might be important in this wider process. Let's take the first example and expand it.

The Kapp Putsch is an example of right-wing opposition to the Weimar government. So how important was it as an example of opposition to the government? Let's consider all the examples of this:

- The Kapp Putsch
- Organisation Consul
- The Munich Putsch

Event	Who was affected?	Challenge to government?	Long term consequences	Evaluation of significance
Kapp Putsch				
Organisation Consul				
Munich Putsch				

Which of these events was the most significant challenge to the Weimar government? We need some criteria to judge this. Think about how many people were affected, how close the government came to collapsing, and whether there were long-term consequences of the event. Set up a table like the one given.

Add a sentence in each box then reach a decision about the overall significance of the event. Which was most important and why?

Now try it with the second example of the Nuremberg Laws. This is an example of Nazi anti-Semitism. How important was it for Jewish people in the 1930s? Think of all the examples of anti-Semitism in the period from 1933 to 1939. Now think of criteria to judge this on. Construct a table again, but make sure to come up with new criteria as the investigation is different. Now come to a conclusion based on the overall significance of the Nuremberg Laws. Were they the most significant development for Jews in the 1930s? Or were there other changes which were more important?

Exam-style questions

Questions in the style of Paper 1

1   Describe Nazi policies towards young people in Germany.

2   What were the main features of the Four-Year Plan?

3   Why was there a threat to the Weimar Republic from the left wing from 1919–1920?

4   Why did Hitler purge the SA in the Night of the Long Knives?

5   To what extent did Germans benefit from Nazi rule in the period from 1933 to 1939?

6   'From 1919 to 1929 the Weimar Republic was a success.' How far do you agree with this statement? Explain your answer.

Questions in the style of Paper 4 - IGCSE only

1   How important was the War Guilt Clause in German opposition to the Treaty of Versailles?

2   How significant was the collapse of the German economy after 1929 in Hitler's rise to power?

3   How significant was Hitler's invasion of the Soviet Union in 1941 in the development of the Holocaust?

Chapter 10
Depth Study C: Russia, 1905–1941

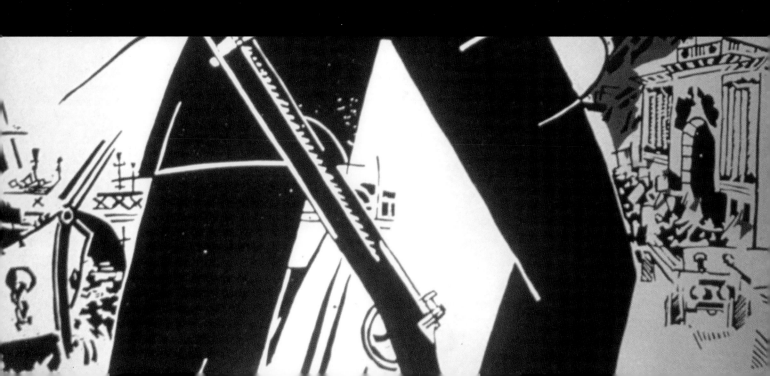

What is this depth study about?

In 1913, the Russian Empire covered one-sixth of the world's land surface. With Tsar Nicholas II celebrating the 300th anniversary of his family's reign, the Russian monarchy seemed secure. Yet, within five years Russia had experienced two revolutions, and Nicholas II and his immediate family were killed. A **communist** government was led first by Vladimir Lenin and then by Joseph Stalin. Despite these dramatic changes, Russia's economy and society continued to be largely rural. Under a cruel dictatorship, the USSR modernised, affecting millions of people's lives.

As historians, your challenge is to study this turbulent period of Russian history and consider the causes and consequences of these events.

The key questions we will be examining are as follows:

1 Why did the tsarist regime collapse in 1917?
2 How did the Bolsheviks gain power, and how did they consolidate their rule?
3 How did Stalin gain and hold onto power?
4 What was the impact of Stalin's economic policies?

Source 10A: A photograph of Tsar Nicholas II and his family, taken in 1913 at the time of the Romanov 300th anniversary celebrations.

KEY TERM

Communists: believers in communism, a social, political and economic theory based on the common ownership of wealth and the means of producing and distributing goods.

209

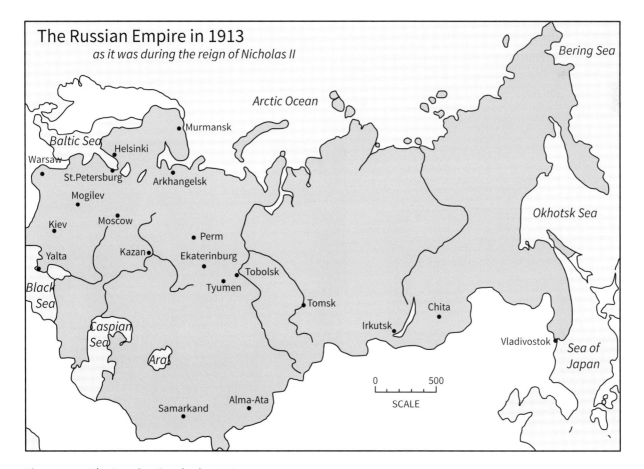

Figure 10.1: The Russian Empire in 1913.

FACT FILE

Nicholas II was concerned that **Tsarevich** Alexei, who suffered from **haemophilia**, might die. He was influenced by his wife, Tsarina Alexandra, who in turn was influenced by Gregory Rasputin (see 'Political impact').

ACTIVITY 10.1

Study and interpret Source 10A. What do you think was the purpose of this photograph in 1913?

10.1 Why did the tsarist regime collapse in 1917?

Focus points

- How well did the tsarist regime deal with the difficulties of ruling Russia up to 1914?
- How did the tsar survive the 1905 Revolution?
- How far was the tsar weakened by the First World War?
- Why was the revolution of March 1917 successful?

How well did the tsarist regime deal with the difficulties of ruling Russia up to 1914?

There were no legal restrictions on the tsar's power. He could ignore the Imperial Council's advice or dismiss its members. Nicholas II did not trust his government ministers. He took advice from his German-born wife, who disliked public appearances. Russia had:

- no elections
- no parliament
- no political opposition.

Russian society under the tsarist regime was hierarchical and there was great inequality.

- Aristocracy: 1.5% of the population, but owned 25% of the land, often wealthy and influential.
- Capitalists: few but influential, always in favour of economic progress, often of political progress.
- Peasants: 80% of Russia's population.

After the 1861 abolition of **serfdom**, peasants bought their land over 49 years but still lacked civil rights. In 1897, Russia's peasants largely lived in **communes.** Some were successful farmers (**kulaks**) but most were poor because of:

- large families
- small farms

- poor education
- outdated farming methods
- harvest failures.

Russia's urban workers suffered 12-hour shifts in unsafe conditions for low wages. Trade unions were illegal. The army could be used to end strikes. Such **repression** encouraged support for revolutionary opposition.

KEY TERMS

Tsarevich: the official title of the son of the tsar.

Haemophilia: a hereditary disorder that causes bleeding and is potentially fatal.

Serfdom: a condition similar to slavery in which peasants are owned by a landowner and have few rights

Commune: a village in which people share property, resources and labour

Kulak: prosperous peasant

Repression: the use of spies and harsh punishments to crush opposition

CHECK YOUR UNDERSTANDING 10.1

What were the main features of life for peasants in the years before 1914?

Source 10B: Russian peasant village, c.1900.

Source 10C: Photograph of a rural scene in 1909 taken by Sergei Prokudin-Gorsky.

ACTIVITY 10.2

Compare and interpret Sources 10B and 10C. What similarities and differences do you notice and how reliable are they as evidence?

CHECK YOUR UNDERSTANDING 10.2

1 Create three lists showing which of Russia's difficulties you think were:

- unavoidable
- created by the government
- worsened by the government.

2 Russia's long-term problems had been building for many years. For each group, write a sentence about why there were grievances:

- workers
- peasants
- national minorities
- the middle classes
- revolutionaries.

The Emperor of all the Russias is an autocratic and unlimited monarch. God commands that his supreme power be obeyed out of conscience as well as fear.

Source 10D: The Fundamental Laws of Tsarism.

I am not prepared to be a Tsar. I never wanted to become one. I know nothing of the business of ruling.

Source 10E: Nicholas II, on the death of his father.

ACTIVITY 10.3

Compare and interpret Sources 10D and 10E. What can you learn from these sources about the reasons why Nicholas II found ruling Russia difficult?

Russia was large and potentially wealthy, but difficult to govern. Its size slowed communications; its long land borders with different countries made it vulnerable to attack. The Empire was **multi-ethnic,** containing over 200 nationalities. Only 44% of the population were Russian. Government officials were poorly paid, which led to corruption. Central government found it hard to enforce its decisions; local officials ruled almost independently. Minister of Finance Sergei Witte had begun modernisation and Russia's economy had the fastest growth rate in the world in the period 1900–1914. However, Russia remained one of the least industrialised economies in Europe in 1914.

The government was based in the capital, St Petersburg. Russia's rulers tried to unite the Empire through **Russification**. This policy led many to desire greater independence.

KEY TERMS

Multi-ethnic: made up of multiple different ethnic groups

Russification: forcing Russia's ethnic and religious minorities to speak Russian and adopt Russians ways.

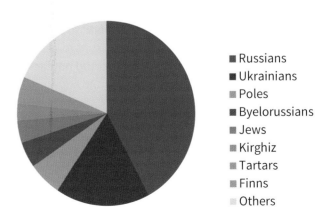

- Russians
- Ukrainians
- Poles
- Byelorussians
- Jews
- Kirghiz
- Tartars
- Finns
- Others

Figure 10.2: Russia's population in 1900.

211

ACTIVITY 10.4

List the problems Nicholas II faced in ruling Russia before 1905. Put your points in order of seriousness.

The Russian Orthodox Church was a powerful spiritual force, closely tied to the monarchy. Research its role under Tsar Nicholas II.

How did the tsar survive the 1905 Revolution?

The revolution was brought on by a mixture of errors and reforms:

- Censorship was relaxed, encouraging political discussion and opposition.
- The defeats, economic effects and accounts of official incompetence in the 1904/5 Russo-Japanese War all damaged the government.

Over 100,000 workers went on strike in January 1905. On 22 January 1905, 200,000 protesters marched through St Petersburg to the Winter Palace. The strikers were led by a priest, Father Gapon, a double-agent working for the police.

> Sovereign! We, workers and inhabitants of the city of St Petersburg, our wives, children, and helpless old parents, have come to you, Sovereign, to seek justice and protection. We are treated like slaves who must suffer a bitter fate and keep silent. And we have suffered, but we only get pushed deeper and deeper into an abyss of misery, ignorance, and lack of rights.
>
> Our first request was that our employers discuss our needs together with us. But they refused to do this on the grounds that the law does not provide us with such a right. Also unlawful were our other requests: to reduce the working day to eight hours; for them to set wages together with us and by agreement with us; to examine our disputes with lower-level factory administrators; to increase the wages of unskilled workers and women to one ruble per day; to abolish overtime work; to provide medical care attentively and without insult; to build shops so that it is possible to work there and not face death from the awful draughts, rain and snow.
>
> Sovereign, this is what we face and this is the reason that we have gathered before the walls of your palace. Do not refuse to come to the aid of your people. Tear down the wall that separates you from your people and let it rule the country together with you.

Source 10F: The petition carried by protesters on Bloody Sunday, 1905.

The protesters never delivered their message to the tsar, who was not even at the Winter Palace that day. Instead, the protesters were met by soldiers who opened fire, killing 200 and wounding another 800 people. This was 'Bloody Sunday'. It marked the beginning of a year of revolutionary events.

ACTIVITY 10.5

Look at the petition delivered by Father Gapon on Bloody Sunday in Source 10F.

1 What complaints does it list?
2 What are the protesters' demands?
3 Describe the tone of the petition.
4 Do you think the tsar would have been more concerned by the content or the tone of the petition? Explain your answer.

Research Bloody Sunday 1905 and describe the key events.

Source 10G: A revolutionary cartoon from 1905.

ACTIVITY 10.6

Study and interpret Source 10G. What message was this cartoon intended to convey in 1905?

Timeline of events in 1905

January	Strikes spread across every major town and city.
February	Grand Duke Sergei killed by a revolutionary. Moscow University students protested. The government closed down all universities.
	Peasants began stealing from aristocrats' lands. The army was used 2,700 times to control peasant uprisings before October 1905.
June	Maggoty meat caused a mutiny on the battleship *Potemkin*. The captain shot the rebels, so the crew shot their officers and sailed the ship to Odessa, where thousands assisted the sailors. Soldiers killed 2,000 people. The mutiny did not spread, but it caused major embarrassment for the government.
	National minorities demanded change. In Poland there were more strikes than in all the rest of the empire. Georgia declared itself independent.
July	A Peasants' Union was formed, with similar demands to Gapon's union.
October	Strikes brought Russia to a standstill. Transport stopped, lights went out, telephone lines went dead, shops closed, food was scarce, robberies and lootings increased and the Moscow water system failed.
	As state censorship failed, newspapers critical of the government sprang up.
	The St Petersburg **Soviet** was created to direct the strikes. Dominated by Leon Trotsky, it organised strikers, published a newspaper (*Izvestiia*), established an army and distributed food. Similar soviets appeared in 50 other cities.

ACTIVITY 10.7

Study the timeline of events in 1905.

1 List the groups involved in protest, strikes or political opposition in 1905.

2 What motivated each of these groups?

3 Which of the events of 1905 do you think represented the most serious threat to tsarism?

KEY TERM

Soviet: Russian for 'council' or 'committee'.

On the improvement of order in the state

The disturbances and unrest in St Petersburg, Moscow and in many other parts of our Empire have filled Our heart with great sorrow. The disturbances could give rise to national instability and present a threat to the unity of Our State. The oath which We took as Tsar compels Us to use all Our strength, intelligence and power to put a speedy end to this unrest. The relevant authorities have been ordered to take measures to deal with outbreaks of disorder and to protect people.

(i) Fundamental civil freedoms will be granted to the population, including real personal inviolability, freedom of conscience, speech, assembly and association.

(ii) Participation in the Duma will be granted to those classes of the population which are at present deprived of voting powers, and this will lead to the development of a universal franchise.

(iii) It is established as an unshakeable rule that no law can come into force without its approval by the State Duma and representatives of the people will be given the opportunity to take real part in the supervision of the legality of government bodies.

Source 10H: The October Manifesto, 1905.

Defeating the 1905 revolution

In August 1905, Sergei Witte ended the Russo-Japanese War, reducing pressure on the government. From September 1905, pro-tsarist organisations such as the Black Hundreds carried out violent attacks on Nicholas's opponents. Over 3,000 people were killed.

In October 1905, Nicholas issued the October Manifesto, granting certain civil freedoms (see Source 10H). This satisfied many liberals, conservatives and democratic socialists. In November 1905, Nicholas issued the November Manifesto, which cut peasants' redemption payments in half for 1906, and ended them in 1907. It also

ACTIVITY 10.8

Study and interpret Source 10H. What concessions did Nicholas grant?

213

promised financial assistance for buying land. For most, this was not enough. A poor harvest in 1905 led to more protests.

Minister of the Interior Peter Stolypin was appointed prime minister in 1906. He sent the army into the countryside with orders to show no mercy: 15,000 peasants were executed, 45,000 were deported and the rebellion ended.

In December, troops arrested the St Petersburg Soviet. A Bolshevik uprising in Moscow was crushed. The **Okhrana** targeted revolutionary leaders, and by 1917 the most important ones were dead, in Siberian exile or in hiding abroad. This did not stop the murder by revolutionaries of 2,000 government officials in 1906.

Opponents of tsarism were not united. Different social groups had little in common but anger and no agreed leadership. The tsar's ministers skilfully used a mixture of concessions and force to deal with different groups. Key parts of society – especially the army – remained loyal to the tsar.

CHECK YOUR UNDERSTANDING 10.3

How effectively did the October and November 1905 manifestos respond to the concerns of that year's demonstrators?

214

After the 1905 revolution: Dumas

By April 1906, with the government back in control, Nicholas issued his Fundamental Laws, restating the principles of tsarism and revising some of the promises in the October Manifesto. Voting laws were redesigned to ensure that pro-tsarist representatives would be elected. A week later, the Duma met for the first time.

Many of the first Duma deputies were optimistic about the prospects for democratic government in Russia, but quickly realised that Tsar Nicholas had no intention of allowing them real power. Four Dumas met during 1906–1914. The first two were highly critical of Nicholas and the tsar **dissolved** both. After electoral law changes, the 3rd Duma from November 1907 was much less critical. Allowed no significant power, it gradually came to oppose the government. The 4th Duma supported Nicholas II at the outbreak of the First World War.

KEY TERMS

Dissolved: parliament is ended; elected officials are sent away.
Okhrana: a tsarist Russian political police force formed to combat anti-government activity.

After the 1905 revolution: peasants

Stolypin tried to win over the peasantry by addressing some of their grievances. He allowed kulaks to leave the communes and offered incentives for peasants to buy farms or move to farms in Siberia to increase the amount of land available. By 1914:

- almost 2 million peasants had left communes
- peasants owned almost half of Russia's land
- agricultural productivity was increasing
- five consecutive harvests had been good
- peasant violence was declining.

Stolypin's policies benefited many, but most of Russia's farms were small and inefficient, and peasants' conditions remained poor. Russia's population increased by 21% during the period 1900–1910, worsening the problem of land-hunger.

CHECK YOUR UNDERSTANDING 10.4

How far do you think the situation in the Russian countryside changed after the 1905 revolution?

After the 1905 revolution: workers

Stolypin improved industrial output, but Russia still lagged behind Britain, Germany and the USA. He had plans for basic education programmes and intended to introduce regulations on factory work. However, workers' basic living costs remained high and their conditions were still poor. There were increasing numbers of workers, and increasing numbers of them were literate and politicised. The number of political strikes increased. Meanwhile, the state remained repressive: in one strike in the Lena goldfields in Siberia in April 1912, soldiers killed 270 workers and injured many more.

	Number of strikes	Number of strikes classed by government as 'political'
1911	466	24
1912	2,032	1,300
1913	2,404	1,034
1914 (Jan–July)	3,534	2,401

Table 10.1: Strikes in Russia between 1911 and 1914.

After the 1905 revolution: middle classes and aristocracy

Economic modernisation led to increasing wealth for the middle class, but their power did not increase after 1905. Although increases in industrial production made capitalists rich, government reforms in the countryside angered wealthy landowners.

CHECK YOUR UNDERSTANDING 10.5

Which of the following statements do you most closely agree with? Explain your answer in a paragraph.

a Tsarism was as strong as ever in July 1914.

b Tsarism looked strong, but was weak in reality in July 1914.

c Tsarism was weak – revolution was near in July 1914.

How far was the Tsar weakened by the First World War?

To support Russia's ally Serbia against Austria-Hungary, the tsar ordered his army to mobilise in July 1914, prompting Germany to declare war. The outbreak of war sparked an outburst of patriotism in Russia; the Duma passed a vote of loyalty to Nicholas.

Military impact

Russia's army of 1.4 million men was the largest in Europe in 1914; a further 4 million had been conscripted by 1915. By January 1915, 25% of the Russian army had been killed, wounded or captured in a disastrous campaign. Defeats at the Battles of Tannenberg and Masurian Lakes were especially costly. During 1915, the Russian army was forced to retreat nearly 1000 km into Russia, and two million soldiers were lost. A major offensive in 1916 was very successful until supply and reinforcement problems forced the Russians to retreat. The army's leadership was extremely incompetent. Severe supply shortages meant that thousands of soldiers were sent into battle barefoot before 1916.

Economic impact

The First World War had a huge impact on Russia's economy. Government spending rose from 4m **roubles** a year to 30 million, while income fell because the war reduced foreign trade, and because Nicholas tried to ban vodka (30% of government income came from alcohol tax). The government printed more money, but this caused inflation. Between July 1914 and early 1917, average wages increased by 100% but prices rose faster.

KEY TERM

Roubles: Russia's currency.

	Petrograd price increases between August 1914 and late 1916
Milk	150%
Shoes and clothing	500%
White bread	500%
Butter	830%
Meat	900%

Table 10.2: Petrograd price increases between August 1914 and late 1916.

Labour shortages caused factory closures and severe shortages. Food production fell, and transport problems worsened things dramatically. In 1917 Petrograd received only 48% of the grain it required.

Social impact

Large numbers fled the areas in which fighting occurred. The population of St Petersburg and Moscow swelled. Meanwhile, 13 million peasants were conscripted into the army, causing rural labour shortages, which affected aristocrats' incomes. The government seized horses, harming agriculture. In 1914–1915, the Russian army suffered a huge loss of officers, the sons of aristocratic families. Half of the peasant families lost sons. Russia contained millions of discontented people and, as a result of conscription, large numbers of them were armed.

Political impact

The Duma demanded to be recalled. It criticised the handling of the war and offered to form a new government; Nicholas refused. In August 1915, liberal and reform Duma members formed a 'Progressive Bloc', requesting political reform. Once Nicholas II took personal command of the army in August 1915, all defeats reflected badly on him.

In his absence at the front, Tsarina Alexandra ran the government. Rumours spread that she was a German spy, or that she was having an affair with a man called Gregory Rasputin. He was believed by many Russian aristocrats to be a holy man. His apparent ability to cure the Tsarevich gave him huge influence over the Tsarina. Most damaging, however, were the stories that she was taking his advice on politics. Several aristocrats became so concerned about

215

Rasputin's influence that they murdered him in December 1916. A few months later, a revolution broke out on the streets of Petrograd.

Why was the revolution of March 1917 successful?

The March 1917 Revolution began as a series of spontaneous and peaceful protests on the streets of Petrograd, and it ended with the abdication of Tsar Nicholas II. The people who began protesting in early March 1917 would never have imagined that two weeks later the tsar would be gone, with political power in the hands of some Duma deputies. As historians, your job is to explain why this happened.

Source 10I: Protesters in Petrograd on 8 March 1917 International Women's Day.

Source 10J: People looking at the head of a destroyed statue of Tsar Alexander III after the March revolution in 1917.

Timeline of events in March 1917

7 March:	Workers in Petrograd's largest factory went on strike over low wages, poor working conditions and rising prices.
8 March:	More Petrograd workers went on strike. Many celebrated International Women's Day. Perhaps 250,000 participated in peaceful demonstrations. Soldiers were on the streets, but there was no violence.
9 March:	Strikes spread and factories came to a standstill. Rumours about bread shortages caused some violence, but protesters – with slogans like 'Down with the war' and 'Bread' – were generally peaceful (see Source 10I).
10 March:	Nicholas ordered the Petrograd garrison to put down the protesters using force.
11 March:	Some soldiers ignored orders to shoot at demonstrators and began siding with the crowds. Other troops opened fire and killed 50 protesters. Duma ministers sent a message to Nicholas, saying 'the situation is serious ... the capital is in a state of **anarchy**' and demanding that a new government be formed. Nicholas disagreed, ordered the army to end the disturbances and suspended the Duma.
12 March:	Up to 170,000 soldiers refused to shoot protesters. Soldiers and strikers seized weapons, opened the prisons and rounded up those who were loyal to the tsar. The government resigned. Duma members formed a Provisional Government in the Tauride Palace. In the same building, the Petrograd Soviet of Workers', Sailors' and Soldiers' Deputies was elected.
13 March:	Most Petrograd soldiers joined the revolution. The Provisional Government assumed control and ordered the arrest of tsarist ministers. Nicholas decided to return to Petrograd.

14 March:	The revolution spread to the Kronstadt naval base outside Petrograd, and Moscow. Nicholas's train was stopped by railway workers and soldiers. His generals advised him to abdicate.
15 March:	The Provisional Government was in control, with conditional support from the Soviet. Nicholas abdicated.

KEY TERM

Anarchy: a situation where no one is in control

CHECK YOUR UNDERSTANDING 10.7

1 Which group was the most significant in bringing about a revolution in March 1917? Give your reasons.

- working men
- women
- soldiers
- Tsar
- Duma
- Petrograd Soviet
- generals.

2 List the key reasons for Nicholas II's abdication. Explain the importance of each one.

3 Write a defence of each of these two statements:

- The First World War made little difference to Tsarism, which was doomed even before 1914.
- The First World War directly caused the 1917 revolution and the tsar's abdication.
- Which do you agree with and why?

10.2 How did the Bolsheviks gain power, and how did they consolidate their rule?

Focus points

- How effectively did the Provisional Government rule Russia in 1917?
- Why were the Bolsheviks able to seize power in November 1917?

- Why did the Bolsheviks win the Civil War?
- How far was the New Economic Policy a success?

How effectively did the Provisional Government rule Russia in 1917?

The Provisional Government was made up of Progressive Bloc members. The most important were:

- Prince Lvov, a liberal politician from a landowning aristocratic family: prime minister.
- Paul Milyukov, a liberal politician from a prosperous middle-class family: foreign minister.
- Alexander Kerensky, a democratic socialist politician from a middle-class, son of a schoolteachers: justice minister.

The March revolution created an atmosphere of goodwill and the Provisional Government had the support of many, though as it had appointed itself, and not been elected, it faced questions of legitimacy. Most pressing of all, it had inherited the key challenges that had faced Nicholas II.

CHECK YOUR UNDERSTANDING 10.8

1 How strong was the Provisional Government in April 1917?

2 Which was the most serious of the problems that the Provisional Government faced in the summer of 1917? Explain your answer.

3 How effective were the Provisional Government's policies?

The Provisional Government passed some significant political reforms:

- The Okhrana was abolished.
- Political prisoners were released.
- Press censorship was abolished.
- The police were replaced by a people's militia.
- Independent judges and trial by jury were introduced.
- Capital punishment and exile were abolished.
- All men and women over age 20 were given the vote.
- Discrimination on the grounds of class, religion, race, gender or belief was made illegal.

However, by September 1917, the Provisional Government and the parties in it – liberals, Mensheviks and Socialist

What were the Provisional Government's problems in summer 1917?	What policies did the Provisional Government follow?	What were the consequences of these policies?
The Petrograd Soviet: made up of 3,000 members, this was elected by soldiers, sailors and workers, and it had their support. It controlled the railways, the postal and telegraph communications systems, the factories and the armed forces. The Soviet had published Order No. 1 on 1 March, taking over the army.	Kerensky (who was also a member of the Soviet) negotiated on behalf of the Provisional Government. The Soviet would support the Provisional Government, if it granted reforms: an **amnesty** for prisoners, civil liberties, the end of official discrimination and granting workers' rights to join unions and strike. The Provisional Government also agreed not to send the Petrograd soldiers to fight at the front line.	The Provisional Government and the Soviet cooperated for several months in the 'Dual Power'. The Provisional Government was relieved that the Soviet did not make more radical demands, and grateful that the Soviet brought the army under control. Moderates in the Soviet had no wish for more radical change.
The First World War: most members of the Provisional Government wanted to continue fighting, but while some wanted to make territorial gains if the Allies won, the moderates only wanted to fight to protect Russian territory.	In June 1917, the Provisional Government ordered a massive new offensive. For three days things went well, then the attack fell apart. Soldiers shot their officers, and up to 2 million Russian soldiers deserted.	The army was disintegrating. Many soldiers turned to the Bolsheviks.
The land problem: by summer 1917 the countryside was in revolt. The breakdown in social and political order left the countryside without the means to stop peasants from seizing landlords' property. Violence was increasing.	The Provisional Government wanted Russia's land to be redistributed fairly and in an orderly fashion.	The Provisional Government urged the peasants to wait for national elections and the calling of a Constituent Assembly, so that the land redistribution process could be supervised. The peasants ignored them and the land seizures continued.
National minorities' demands: these demanded more power as soon as Nicholas abdicated, and the Provisional Government could not agree on how to respond.	When Ukraine demanded self-government, socialists in the Provisional Government were prepared to grant it.	Liberals feared that the Russian Empire was about to break up. Prince Lvov resigned, leaving Kerensky to become prime minister.
Russia's economic problems: food shortages, inflation, high prices and supply problems were causing tremendous hardship in the cities. As conditions worsened, more strikes broke out.	The government promised to double the amount it paid peasants for grain, but the supply did not improve. Liberals in the Provisional Government supported the capitalists, while socialists supported the workers, but neither had plans for how to improve things.	Factory committees became more powerful, and began taking control to keep the factories working. Workers became disillusioned with the Provisional Government. One million people took part in strikes in Russia in September 1917, and many turned to the Bolsheviks.

KEY TERM

Amnesty: a blanket official pardon.

Revolutionaries – had become discredited. While the Bolsheviks became more powerful, the Provisional Government made several fatal mistakes.

ACTIVITY 10.10

Why do you think the Provisional Government failed to gain the support of:
1 peasants
2 workers
3 soldiers and sailors
4 aristocrats
5 capitalists
6 national minorities?

Why were the Bolsheviks able to seize power in November 1917?

In March 1917, the Bolsheviks were a Marxist revolutionary party with around 10,000 members. Almost all their leaders were in exile or abroad; they did not participate in the March revolution.

In April 1917 the German government arranged for Lenin to return to Petrograd by train, hoping he would create enough trouble to force Russia to pull out of the war. His policies in 1917 were different from other parties and meant a change from the Bolshevik line adopted before his arrival:

- 'All Power to the Soviets'
  - The Bolsheviks would stop cooperating with the Provisional Government and other parties.
  - The Soviets should seize power in the name of the working class at once.
- 'Peace, Land and Bread'
  - An immediate end to the war.
  - Give the peasants the right to seize landlords' land.
  - Give the workers and peasants control of food supplies.

As the Provisional Government grew less effective, the Bolsheviks won majorities in the Petrograd Soviet, the Moscow council elections, the key Petrograd Vyborg district and the Kronstadt naval base. Trotsky (who had been a Menshevik, but joined the Bolsheviks after Lenin's return in 1917) was elected Chairman of the Petrograd Soviet in September. They had over 250,000 supporters by October 1917, and their support was strongest among soldiers, sailors and workers.

Two events helped the Bolsheviks to decide the time was right for them to seize control.

The 'July Days', July 1917

Bolsheviks led protests against the Provisional Government. Troops loyal to the Provisional Government opened fire on protesters, and they all fled. The Provisional Government issued arrest warrants for leading Bolsheviks and captured Trotsky, while Lenin escaped to Finland in disguise. He stayed in hiding until it was safe to return.

Source 10K: Protesters flee after troops open fire during the 'July Days'.

ACTIVITY 10.11

Study Source 10K. What can you learn from this image about the nature of the protests in the 'July Days'?

CHECK YOUR UNDERSTANDING 10.9

Why did the July Days help leading Bolsheviks to realise that the time was right for an uprising?

The Kornilov Affair, September 1917

In August, Prime Minister Kerensky appointed General Kornilov to lead the army. Kornilov agreed to send soldiers to defend Petrograd, but then Kerensky worried that the army would overthrow the Provisional Government. As Kornilov's men approached, Kerensky panicked. He requested support from the Soviet, who controlled the military units in the capital, and he released imprisoned Bolsheviks. The government armed 25,000 Bolsheviks volunteers. Kornilov and his men were captured, but Kerensky and the Provisional Government were discredited. The Bolsheviks were seen as defenders of the revolution, and won majorities in elections to Soviets all over Russia.

How did the Bolsheviks become so powerful during 1917?

The October Revolution

From Finland, Lenin wrote to the Bolshevik leadership that the time was right for revolution. Kamenev, Zinoviev and even Trotsky remained unconvinced. When he returned to Petrograd, Lenin overruled them.

Timeline of the October 1917 Revolution

2 November: The Soviet set up a Military Revolutionary Committee – Trotsky was one of its leaders. Petrograd garrisons came under MRC control.

5 November: Kerensky shut down Bolshevik newspapers. Lenin argued Kerensky was starting a counter-revolution.

6 November: Lenin ordered the arrest of the Provisional Government. At dawn, Trotsky ordered Bolsheviks to take control of Petrograd's bridges and railway stations.

7 November: The Bolsheviks controlled Petrograd, but the Provisional Government was still inside the Winter Palace. Kerensky escaped. The battleship *Aurora* fired a shot, the Bolsheviks stormed the Winter Palace and Provisional Government members were arrested.

ACTIVITY 10.12

Look back at the timeline of the October Revolution:
1 Find evidence of how important Lenin was.
2 Find evidence of how important Trotsky was.
3 Which Bolshevik leader was more important, in your opinion?

The Bolsheviks immediately began securing their power. Why were they successful?

Reasons for the failure of the Provisional Government	Reasons for the success of the Bolsheviks
• It was weakened by its temporary nature and the existence of the Soviet. • Its policies made it increasingly unpopular. • Kerensky made several mistakes in the summer of 1917. • It lost the support of key groups and was defenceless by November 1917.	• Their policies set them apart from the other parties and won them support. • They were led by determined, charismatic and skilful leaders such as Lenin and Trotsky. • They were lucky on several occasions. • They gained control of key institutions such as the Moscow and Petrograd Soviets.

Table 10.3: Why were the Bolsheviks successful?

CHECK YOUR UNDERSTANDING 10.11

'The Bolsheviks were successful in November 1917 because of the failures of the Provisional Government.' How far do you agree with this statement? Explain your answer.

ACTIVITY 10.13

Look at Table 10.3:
1 Provide an example for each Provisional Government failure and each Bolshevik success.
2 Rank them in order of importance.
3 Write a sentence commenting on each one.

Why did the Bolsheviks win the Civil War?

Lenin created a new government and they issued their first decrees:

8 November: Decree on Land: peasants could seize any land previously belonging to the tsar, the Church and aristocracy

Decree on Peace: Russia asked Germany for an armistice

12 November: Maximum eight-hour day for workers, 48-hour week

14 November: Social insurance (old age, unemployment, sickness benefits) introduced

December: Non-Bolshevik press banned

Rights of self-government for all parts of the Russian Empire

Workers' control of factories introduced

Equal rights to property ownership

Democratisation of the army – officers to be elected, soldiers' soviets assumed control of the army, and ranks, saluting and decorations were abolished

Banks nationalised

Cheka (secret police) set up

Marriage and divorce became civil matters, equal rights for women wanting a divorce.

ACTIVITY 10.14

1 What measures, if any, did the Bolsheviks take in order to please:

2 **a** peasants
   b workers
   c soldiers and sailors
   d aristocrats
   e capitalists
   f national minorities?

3 Which ones made Russia fairer and more democratic? Explain.

4 Were there any that suggested that Russia might become less free and fair? Explain.

Constituent Assembly

Many Bolshevik measures were popular, but in 1917 and 1918, Lenin's government also took unpopular steps. Lenin had promised to allow elections for the Constituent Assembly to go ahead, expecting a Bolshevik majority. When the results came in, the Bolsheviks were shocked. For a party that had been relatively unknown until recently they did very well, with 23.5% of the vote and 168 seats. But while the Bolsheviks proved popular in the big towns and cities and among soldiers, the Socialist Revolutionaries, slightly less radical than the Bolsheviks, were better known in the countryside and won 41% of the vote and 380 seats.

The remainder went to a range of other socialist, liberal and regional parties, including some had featured in the Dumas.

The Constituent Assembly met for the first and only time on 18 January and refused to support Lenin's proposals. The following day he sent soldiers to close it down. From now on, Lenin ruled by decree or used Bolshevik control in the Congress of Soviets to pass his laws. He admitted that he was establishing a dictatorship, but called it a 'dictatorship of the **proletariat**'.

ACTIVITY 10.15

Why was the closing down of the Constituent Assembly an important turning point in the revolution?

The Treaty of Brest-Litovsk, March 1918

Lenin had promised an immediate end to the war. When peace talks began in December 1917, Trotsky intended to prolong negotiations until a communist revolution broke out in Germany. The Germans, frustrated, restarted the war and advanced 150 miles into Russia in five days, so a treaty was signed at Brest-Litovsk in March. Russia lost:

- 34% of the population, 60 million people
- 32% of agricultural land
- 54% of industry
- 89% of coal mines
- 26% of railways.

Russia also had to pay reparations of 300 million gold roubles.

Brest-Litovsk showed Lenin's willingness to make sacrifices in order to achieve his aims. Many Russians were horrified by the treaty's harshness. A Socialist Revolutionary tried to kill Lenin in August 1918. By the end of 1918, a civil war had broken out.

KEY TERMS

Cheka: the Bolsheviks' political police.
Proletariat: Marxist term for the working classes.

What happened in the Russian Civil War?

The Russian Civil War lasted from summer 1918 until spring 1921. It was actually several small wars, fought by twenty different armies. Bolshevik forces (the Red Army, or Reds) fought various armies:

- The Whites: a broad group, including anti-Bolshevik socialists, liberals, tsarists and nationalists. Few wanted tsarism, some wanted the Constituent Assembly recalled, but all wanted to beat the Bolsheviks. Otherwise, they had little in common, and sometimes even fought each other.
- The Greens: local peasant armies who fought to defend their own areas.

- Foreign armies, including the Czech Legion, a unit of Czech nationalists who had been fighting the Austrians on the Eastern Front.

Trotsky, as Commissar for War, was in charge of the Red Army. He turned them into a ruthless force of 3.5 million men by the end of 1920 by:

- employing ex-imperial army officers, while taking their families hostage to ensure loyalty
- attaching Political Commissars to each unit to ensure loyalty

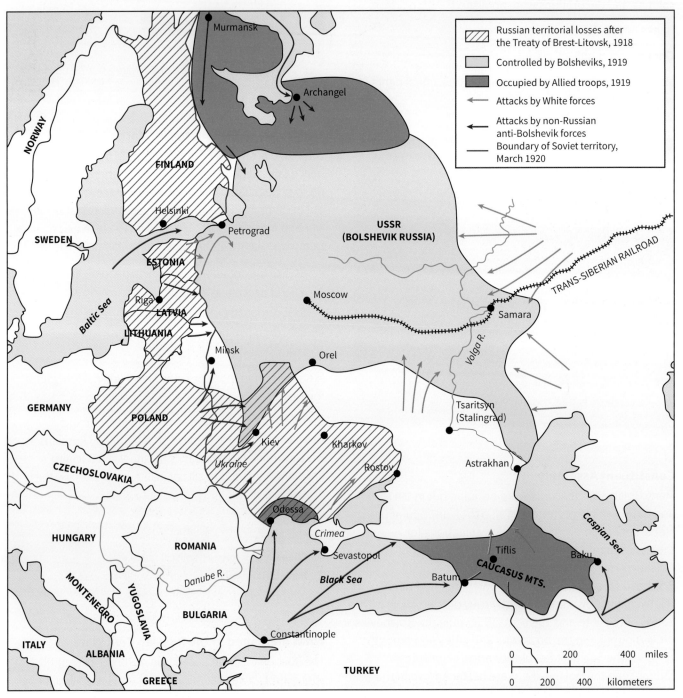

Figure 10.3: The Russian Civil War.

- reintroducing ranks, saluting, and discipline, including the death penalty for cowardice.
- not interfering in military decisions, but using his War Train (see Source 10L) to travel to where fighting was heaviest to inspire his men.

Source 10L: An armoured train, like the one Trotsky used in the Civil War. The slogan on the side of the train reads 'United Russia'.

ACTIVITY 10.16

Study and interpret Source 10L. What does the image tell you about the Bolsheviks' advantages in the Russian Civil War?

War Communism

The Bolshevik government introduced 'War Communism' – harsh measures to regain control, including:

- government control of all industries
- strict worker discipline, including execution for strikers
- rationing food
- outlawing private trade
- forcing peasants to hand over grain and hanging any who resisted: this policy, and poor harvests in 1920–1921, led to a famine that killed an estimated 7 million people
- the 'Red Terror': the Cheka arrested or executed people suspected of being the Reds' enemies – in July 1918, the royal family were shot.

There were three phases of fighting:

- **June–November 1918:** The Reds fought Green armies and the Czech Legion. Two Socialist Revolutionary uprisings occurred, which the Whites defeated.
- **November 1918–December 1920:** Several White and foreign armies threatened the Reds.
  - Admiral Kolchak's White army was defeated by the Reds at the end of 1919.
  - General Denikin's White army got within 200 miles of Moscow and almost defeated Stalin's army at Tsaritsyn but was beaten in 1920.
  - General Yudenich's White army attacked Petrograd through Estonia in October 1919, but was beaten by the Reds.
  - British forces went to Murmansk and the French fleet to the Black Sea, Japanese forces captured Vladivostok and US troops were sent to watch closely the Japanese. These foreign armies did little fighting and withdrew by 1920.
  - Polish forces attacked Russia in 1919–1920 and captured Kiev. The Reds pushed them back, but Poland gained large areas of territory in the 1921 Treaty of Riga.
- **August 1920–December 1921:** For over a year the Reds resisted outbreaks of violence all over the country.
  - Peasants attacked Reds in Tambov region in late 1920. A Red army of 100,000 men was sent to crush the rebels in 1921.
  - In February 1921, sailors in the Kronstadt naval base rose up in rebellion in protest at the Bolsheviks' harsh methods, and War Communism in particular. Kronstadt sailors had been at the head of the November revolution (see Source 10M) and now they demanded political freedoms. It took 50,000 Red Guards two weeks to defeat the revolt. Over 2,000 were killed or executed and almost 5,000 injured.

223

Source 10M: A Soviet poster that glorifies the role of the Kronstadt sailors from 1920.

How far was the New Economic Policy a success?

The Kronstadt uprising and the failures of War Communism forced Lenin to rethink. At the Communist Party Congress in March 1921, Lenin announced the New Economic Policy (NEP):

- State ownership of heavy industry, transport and banking remained.
- Private businesses were allowed – people could produce goods and sell them.
- Grain requisitioning ended – the state took 50% of a peasant's grain, and peasants could sell the rest for profit.
- Rationing was reduced. People had to buy food, but they had more income and there was more food available because private peasant farms were allowed.

Lenin stated that the NEP was a tactical retreat – not a defeat. There was still opposition from inside the party, but the NEP was popular because the economy began to recover.

CHECK YOUR UNDERSTANDING 10.12

Why did Lenin introduce the NEP?

How was the NEP different from War Communism?

	1921	1922	1923	1924	1925
Grain harvest (m tons)	37.6	50.3	56.6	51.4	76.8
Coal (m tons)	8.9	9.5	13.7	16.1	18.1
Electricity (m kWhs)	520	775	1,146	1,562	2,925
Steel (thousand tons)	183	392	709	1,140	2,135

Table 10.4: Economic recovery under the NEP.

ACTIVITY 10.17

Why was the defeat of the Kronstadt Rebellion an important turning point in the revolution?

Complete the table that follows, using the information in this section:

	Red strengths	Opposition weaknesses
Geography	The Bolsheviks controlled the centre of western Russia, including Moscow and Petrograd. This gave them control of: • most of the railway system • industry • weapons and supplies • the densely populated areas.	Opposition armies were separated by hundreds of miles, which made co-ordination impossible. The areas they held were thinly populated so recruitment was hard. They had little industry and poor transport links.
Strength		The opposition armies were small and poorly resourced. They received little assistance from the Russian peasants, who did not want to lose their land.
Leadership		White generals treated their armies with disgust – many White soldiers deserted.
Unity		They had no common aims, and did not cooperate.
Propaganda	The Bolsheviks used propaganda very effectively. They used posters, films, loudspeakers and trains travelled around the country producing new material for local areas to keep morale high.	Opposition forces did not use propaganda to win support. Bolshevik propaganda about what would happen if the Whites won hurt the opposition forces.
Foreign help	Foreign help for the Whites allowed the Reds to portray themselves as the patriots.	

By 1923, 75% of all trade was in private hands, and traders called 'Nepmen' supplied all kinds of goods. They were harassed by the Cheka (now renamed the GPU). Peasants thrived under the NEP, but urban workers struggled. Unemployment rose, wages remained generally low and working conditions did not improve. Many wondered whether Lenin had abandoned the idea of creating a workers' paradise.

Source 10N: Lenin and Stalin, shortly before Lenin's death in January 1924.

225

> **CHECK YOUR UNDERSTANDING 10.13**
>
> 1 'Lenin's New Economic Policy was unsuccessful.' How far do you agree with this view?
> 2 Which of the following reasons explain how the Bolsheviks were able to consolidate their control in 1917–1922? Comment briefly on each one:
>   a Bolsheviks' early decrees
>   b leadership of Lenin and Trotsky
>   c crushing of opposition by the Cheka
>   d defeat of enemies in the Russian Civil War
>   e War Communism
>   f New Economic Policy
>   g Treaty of Brest-Litovsk.

10.3 How did Stalin gain and hold onto power?

Focus points

- Why did Stalin, and not Trotsky, emerge as Lenin's successor?
- Why did Stalin launch the purges?
- What methods did Stalin use to control the Soviet Union?
- How complete was Stalin's control over the Soviet Union by 1941?

Why did Stalin, and not Trotsky, emerge as Lenin's successor?

Lenin had led the Bolshevik party from obscurity to success in revolution and war. In 1922–1923, he suffered a series of strokes that left him paralysed and unable to speak. When he died in January 1924, there were several contenders for the leadership. Lenin had written critically about each of them, but they agreed to keep this a secret. With hindsight, we can see that there were two strong candidates for the leadership.

	Josef Stalin	Leon Trotsky
Real name	Josef Djugashvili	Lev Bronstein
Background	Born to poor working family in Georgia and attended Christian school. Expelled from school for reading banned political literature.	Born to a prosperous family in Ukraine. Spent time in prison, where he adopted the name of one of his jailers as his alias, and in exile abroad.
Personal qualities	Seen as an efficient bureaucrat, he kept his ambitions to himself and was regarded as a potential ally for others, not a leadership contender himself.	Independent, arrogant, intelligent and a brilliant speaker. Distrusted by colleagues, who feared he would seize power.

	Josef Stalin	Leon Trotsky
Career in the Communist Party	Joined the Bolshevik Party when it was founded in 1898 and became involved in hijackings, bank robbery and gun-running, extortion and murder. His dedication and working-class origins impressed Lenin. Editor of party newspaper *Pravda* in 1917. Did not play a leading role in the October Revolution.	Sided with rivals the Mensheviks until 1917, when he joined Lenin's Bolsheviks. Prominent in the 1905 Revolution. Planned the October Revolution, was a leading member of the Party's Central Committee, and was Commissar for War.
Support base	New members. As General Secretary of the Party, controlled invitations to party congresses, where the Central Committee was chosen and major policies were discussed.	The Red Army, where he was popular after the Civil War. Also younger party members especially students.
Lenin's funeral	Organised it.	Missed it.
What Lenin wrote in his 'Political Testament'	'Comrade Stalin, having become Secretary-General, has unlimited authority concentrated in his hands, and I am not sure whether he will always be capable of using that authority with sufficient caution.' 'Stalin is too rude and this is intolerable in a Secretary-General. I suggest that comrades think about a way of removing Stalin from that post and appointing another man [who is] more tolerant, more loyal, more polite, and more considerate.'	'Comrade Trotsky … is distinguished not only by outstanding ability. He is personally perhaps the most capable man in the present Central Committee, but he has displayed excessive self-assurance and shown excessive preoccupation with the purely administrative side of the work.' 'He should not be blamed for not being a member of the party before 1917.'

The leadership struggle was decided by events between 1924 and 1929.

In addition to the NEP, there was disagreement about relations with communists abroad. Trotsky believed that the USSR should be pursuing a policy of 'Permanent Revolution', helping communists abroad because revolutions worldwide would strengthen the USSR. Stalin instead proposed 'Socialism in One Country', strengthening Soviet communism and creating a country superior to the capitalist West. Stalin's ideas were much more popular.

Source 10O: Leon Trotsky c. 1930.

ACTIVITY 10.18

Why did Stalin win the leadership struggle and not Trotsky? Write a sentence, with examples, about each of the following factors:

1 policies
2 luck
3 role
4 personality and background
5 mistakes.

Timeline of events 1924 and 1929

January 1924: Stalin was a coffin-bearer and made a speech at Lenin's funeral. He implied that he had been Lenin's closest friend (see Source 10N). Stalin deceived

	Trotsky, who was unwell, about the date of the funeral; Trotsky's resulting absence seemed disrespectful.
April 1924:	Stalin created a 'Cult of Lenin', changed Petrograd's name to Leningrad and published a book on Lenin, which implied that he was a close colleague. He also recruited one million young, uneducated urban workers into the party: they liked Stalin's approach and thought Trotsky too intellectual.
May 1924:	The Central Committee, including Trotsky, voted to keep Lenin's 'Political Testament' secret at the 13th Party Congress because it was unflattering about all of them. During the Congress, Trotsky made a series of attacks on Stalin's running of the party. Stalin sided with powerful Central Committee members Kamenev and Zinoviev, and their supporters outvoted Trotsky.
December: 1925	Zinoviev and Kamenev attacked Trotsky before the 14th Party Congress, and Trotsky retaliated. Stalin happily let his rivals discredit each other. At the Congress Zinoviev and Kamenev criticised the NEP and called for rapid industrialisation. Stalin's supporters outvoted them easily.
1926 and 1927:	In 1926, Zinoviev, Kamenev and Trotsky formed the 'United Opposition'. They demanded an end to the NEP, rapid industrialisation and harsh measures against the peasants. Stalin and Bukharin, a prominent central Committee Convert to the NEP, defended the new economics. Stalin controlled the programme for the 15th Party Congress, and the United Opposition were not allowed to present their ideas. Growing desperate, they appealed directly to Moscow workers. Kamenev, Zinoviev and Trotsky were expelled from the party for acting illegally.
1928:	Stalin criticised the NEP, using the arguments of the 'United Opposition'. Stalin's supporters voted Bukharin and his supporters out of the Politburo – Stalin's position was now secure.

Why do you think that 'Socialism in One Country' was a more popular policy than 'Permanent Revolution'?

What mistakes did Trotsky make in his struggle for power with Stalin?

Why did Stalin launch the purges?

As you will see from your study of the impact of Stalin's economic policies, by 1933 the Communist Party had lost support. The Soviet state always used force to achieve its aims, but in the period 1934–1938 up to 18 million people were imprisoned, and perhaps 1.5 million were executed by the NKVD (the Cheka's new name). These events are known as 'the purges', and the period 1936–1938 is specifically referred to as 'The Great Terror'. In 1938 alone Stalin personally approved the execution of 44,000 people. Stalin also intervened to save certain people (including his old history teacher).

Victims were arrested (usually at night), given trials that might be long and high profile ('show trials') or secret and brief, depending on the individual, and then either executed immediately or sent to a prison camp. As Source 10P shows, even the victims didn't know or understand why they were being punished.

Source 10P: Bukharin's last message to Stalin, shortly before his execution in March 1938, read:

> **'Koba, why do you need me to die?'**
>
> **('Koba' was one of Stalin's aliases before 1917.)**

Historians have suggested many reasons for the purges:

- to destroy opposition and terrorise the population
- to destroy other, potentially rival, Bolshevik leaders
- as the only reliable response to enemies
- the growing threat from Nazi Germany after 1933 causing fear of war in USSR, which prompted the removal of anyone critical of Stalin
- to deflect criticism from the government and on to scapegoats: for example economic failures
- to provide slave labour for the logging, gold-mining and canal-building needed to finance imports.

The purges began after December 1934 following the assassination of Sergei Kirov, party boss in Leningrad. Many have suggested that Stalin was responsible for Kirov's murder. Kirov won more votes than Stalin at the

17th Party Congress, and some wanted Kirov to be made party leader. The following campaign led, within two years, to the deaths of many leading party members.

The purges and their victims

- Party members, 1934–38: one million people were arrested in connection with Kirov's murder. Most of the senior party leaders were arrested and executed. Zinoviev and Kamenev (1936) and Bukharin (1938) were given show trials before their executions. They were forced to confess to false charges and false evidence was provided. Trotsky was murdered by an NKVD agent in Mexico in 1940. Around 500,000 lower-ranking party members were also arrested.

- Secret Police: over 3,000 NKVD members were purged. NKVD chief Yagoda was given a show trial and executed. His replacement, Yezhov, was executed in 1939. He was replaced by Beria, who survived Stalin.

- Anti-Soviet spies, 1937: several politicians were accused of spying for Nazi Germany.

- The army, 1937: 3 out of 5 Marshals in the Red Army, 14 of 16 Army Commanders, 60 of 67 Corps Commanders, and 35,000 officers were tried for treason and executed. Only one senior Soviet Air Force commander survived the purges.

- The people: colleagues, friends and family of those arrested were also likely to be targeted. One in 18 of the Soviet population was arrested during the purges.

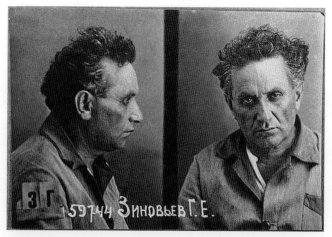

Source 10Q: Zinoviev's NKVD file photo, taken shortly before he was shot in 1936.

ACTIVITY 10.19

Study Sources 10N, 10O and 10Q. In what ways do they contrast with one another? What different messages do they communicate? Now read Source 10P: what do you think is the answer to Bukharin's question?

CHECK YOUR UNDERSTANDING 10.15

What were the effects of the purges on the Soviet Union by 1941?

Why do you think that Stalin forced people to go through show trials?

What methods did Stalin use to control the Soviet Union?

Stalin's control of the USSR was not solely dependent upon forcing people to obey.

The 1936 Constitution

Every citizen over 18 had a vote, and there was freedom of the press, religion and organisation. There was also guaranteed employment. In practice, however, the Constitution restricted the rights ensuring that only communist candidates could stand in elections.

CHECK YOUR UNDERSTANDING 10.16

How democratic was the Soviet Constitution? Did the reality of life in the USSR match what the Constitution promised?

Personality cult and propaganda

The cult of Lenin appeared in newspapers, statues and the cinema to motivate the population to imitate his commitment to the revolution. A cult of Stalin was also developed. As early as 1923 the town of Tsaritsyn was renamed Stalingrad in memory of Stalin's civil war heroics there. Stalin was portrayed as the saviour of socialism in propaganda. By 1941 Stalin dominated the USSR physically as well as politically. He was presented as the heir of Lenin and sole interpreter of party ideology, with a god-like status. There was genuine enthusiasm for Stalin in the 1930s.

Rewriting history

The History of the All-Union Communist Party or *Short Course* was published in 1938. Stalin's role in the revolution and the Civil War were boosted, while other Bolsheviks were relegated to minor roles. Photos were altered with old heroes airbrushed out.

Supervision of art and culture

Government control over news, art and culture ensured that Soviet people received a narrow range of views. Leading newspapers were used for propaganda, highlighting the state's achievements. Radio stations were controlled by the government. Cinema became a popular form of entertainment in the 1930s: towns built huge new cinemas, propaganda trains with travelling cinemas took film into rural areas. After 1934, Socialist Realism meant all art films, books, theatre and music had to be straightforward, optimistic, easily understood, and feature plausible but idealised heroes.

Religion
The Bolsheviks intended to make Russia a secular state. The teaching of religion was banned, hundreds of churches were destroyed and religious schools were closed. Although they suppressed it, the Bolsheviks did not succeed in destroying religion.

CHECK YOUR UNDERSTANDING 10.17

Which method of control do you think would have been most effective?

How complete was Stalin's control over the Soviet Union by 1941?
Stalin certainly had a large degree of control over the Soviet Union by 1941. However, his control was limited by several factors:

- Personal limits: no single person could have controlled everything in an empire as large as USSR.
- Political limits from colleagues: members of the Politburo did oppose Stalin sometimes.
- Political limits from below: more junior officials could obstruct policies.

ACTIVITY 10.20

Gather evidence to show that Stalin had almost total control over the USSR.

Gather evidence to show that Stalin was not in complete control.

10.4 What was the impact of Stalin's economic policies?

Focus points
- Why did Stalin introduce the Five-Year Plans?
- Why did Stalin introduce collectivisation?
- How successful were Stalin's economic changes?
- How were the Soviet people affected by these changes?

Why did Stalin introduce the Five-Year Plans?

We are fifty or a hundred years behind the advanced countries. We must make good this distance in ten years. Either we do it, or they will crush us.

Source 10R: Stalin, speaking in 1931.

Stalin's economic policies aimed to industrialise and modernise the USSR as quickly as possible (see Source 10R). He wanted to do this in order to:

- Increase the USSR's military strength: the USSR needed a well-developed industrial base to protect itself from an attack.
- Make the USSR self-sufficient: Stalin did not want the USSR to be dependent upon foreign countries.
- Increase food supplies: the USSR's agriculture was backward. Stalin wanted to produce a surplus to guarantee food supplies, and sell grain abroad to raise cash for industrial equipment.
- Create a socialist society: according to Marx, communism could be built in an industrial society, but in 1928, only about 20% of Soviet people were industrial workers. Stalin wanted people to move from the countryside into the factories.
- Improve living standards: communism was supposed to bring higher living standards, but industrialisation, which creates wealth, needed to come first.
- Secure his position: Stalin imagined that his economic changes would create a second revolution comparable with Lenin's and so secure his reputation as a great leader.

At the 15th Party Congress in 1927, Stalin ended the NEP and announced the first Five-Year Plan. There would be three Five-Year Plans before 1941. They were all centrally planned, meaning:

- Government planning agencies like GOSPLAN set overall targets.
- Government departments allocated targets to different regions.
- Local bosses set targets for each factory.
- Factory managers set targets for workers.

CHECK YOUR UNDERSTANDING 10.18

What did Stalin want to achieve when he introduced the Five-Year Plans?

229

First Five-Year Plan, 1928–1932

The emphasis was on heavy industry. The labour force doubled to 23 million by 1932, and the production increases were dramatic. This plan was supposed to build foundations for future development, so 1,500 factories and many cities were built from scratch. In 1929 there were only 25 people living at Magnitogorsk, but by 1932, when a gigantic iron and steel works had been built, this had risen to 250,000.

Source 10S: Modern and traditional technologies at Magnitogorsk in the 1930s.

Second Five-Year Plan, 1933–1937

Heavy industry was the priority in the second Five-Year Plan, but new industries were created, and there was more emphasis on rail links (notably Moscow's spectacular

Source 10T: The Dnieprostroi hydroelectric dam. This was the largest dam in Europe when it was built in 1932. It was destroyed by the Germans in 1943.

Source 10U: Mayakovsky Moscow Metro station, opened in 1938.

ACTIVITY 10.21

Study and interpret Sources 10S, 10T and 10U. What do the images have in common? Why do you think that the Moscow Metro stations were built to look so grand?

underground rail system) and some big projects such as the Dnieprostroi hydroelectric dam. The USSR became almost self-sufficient in machine-making. Food rationing was ended and families had more spare money.

Third Five-Year Plan, 1939–1941

The third Five-Year Plan was supposed to deliver more consumer goods, but when the Second World War began the government ordered increases in heavy industry. Machinery and engineering production grew, but steel, oil and consumer goods did not. The purges and the change of priorities caused chaos.

The Five-Year Plans caused huge problems for the Soviet government. There were shortages of vital supplies and production was handicapped by unskilled and unreliable workers. The government therefore took several measures:

- Bonuses and incentives, such as better housing or clothes encouraged workers to stay in their jobs.
- Skilled workers received higher wages.
- Workers were paid according to how much they produced, in order to increase productivity.
- Workers were encouraged to break production records. In 1935, Alexei Stakhanov mined 102 tons of coal in one shift – sixteen times more than usual. Propaganda encouraged workers to compete to produce more.
- Training and education were offered to workers.

- Workers who failed to follow rules could be fined. Causing damage or leaving without permission could lead to a prison sentence.
- Slave labour was used on the most dangerous projects. Around 300,000 prisoners worked on the Baltic-White Sea Canal, and 25,000 died.

Why did Stalin introduce collectivisation?

In 1928, the USSR had less grain than it needed, by around 2 million tons. The state could not get the peasants to give the grain they had harvested. Soviet agriculture was extremely backward – there were still an estimated 5 million wooden ploughs in the USSR. Stalin's solution was collectivisation. The peasants would merge their individual farms and create large collective farms – 'kolkhoz'. All their tools and animals would be shared, they would live together and share any profits. This was considered to be a good idea because:

- It was a more efficient way of farming. The government supplied fertilisers and Machine and Tractor Stations (MTS), and expertise and labour could be shared.
- Greater agricultural efficiency would release people for industrialisation. Collectivisation would therefore help to achieve the Five-Year Plan's targets.
- The state would be able to collect the grain it needed. Grain collection and distribution would be easier, and the surplus could be sold abroad.
- Grain requisitioning had been used successfully in 1927–1928.
- Collectivisation was the socialist way to farm. It would teach the peasants how to live and work communally.
- Rich peasants were blamed for hoarding grain. Stalin imagined that richer peasants wanted to destroy the communist state. Collectivisation offered the opportunity to attack these kulaks.

The logic of collectivisation

Kolkhozes were supposed to have many benefits for peasants. They had schools, libraries and hospitals attached to them. They ran technical lectures on modern farming techniques.

Initially, collectivisation was voluntary, but few peasants volunteered to join collectives so the state began using

force. In December 1929, Stalin announced that the kulaks would be eliminated. An army of 25,000 (The 'Twenty-five Thousanders') urban workers was sent to find kulaks and persuade poorer peasants to join the collectives. Each region was given a quota of kulaks to find. Usually these were ordinary peasants who were harder working and brighter; arresting or murdering them merely deprived localities of their best farmers.

Source 10V: Peasants signing up for a collective farm in 1932.

The supposed kulaks were divided into three categories:

- counter revolutionaries: shot or sent to labour camps
- opponents of collectivisation: deported elsewhere in the USSR
- less troublesome: expelled from their land but not from the region.

Up to 10 million were deported or sent to prison camps after 1930. Some peasants resisted. Many destroyed their property, or killed themselves or their livestock.

At the end of 1934, the government announced that 70% of households had been collectivised, a figure that rose to 93% by 1937. The effects on agriculture were disastrous.

CHECK YOUR UNDERSTANDING 10.19

1 How was collectivisation intended to aid the Five-Year Plans?
2 Why did Stalin use force to get peasants to join collective farms?

How successful were Stalin's economic changes?

As Table 10.5 shows, the Five-Year Plans achieved some significant increases in industrial production.

	1928	1932	1936	1940
Electricity (m kWhs)	5.05	13.5	32.8	48.3
Coal (m tons)	35.5	64.4	126.8	165.9
Oil (m tons)	11.6	21.4	27.4	31.1
Pig iron (m tons)	3.3	6.2	14.4	14.9
Steel (m tons)	4.0	5.9	12.5	13.1
Locomotives	478	828	1566	1220

Table 10.5: Output figures for Soviet industry during the Five-Year Plans.

What are the results of the Five-Year Plan in four years in the sphere of *industry*?

Have we achieved victories in this sphere?

Yes, we have. We did not have an iron and steel industry, the basis for the industrialisation of the country. Now we have one.

We did not have a tractor industry. Now we have one.

We did not have an automobile industry. Now we have one.

We did not have a machine-tool industry. Now we have one.

We did not have a big and modern chemical industry. Now we have one.

We did not have a real and big industry for the production of modern agricultural machinery. Now we have one.

We did not have an aircraft industry. Now we have one.

In output of electric power we were last on the list. Now we rank among the first.

In output of oil products and coal we were last on the list. Now we rank among the first.

And we have not only created these new great industries, but have created them on a scale and in dimensions that eclipse the scale and dimensions of European industry.

Source 10W: Stalin, speaking about the results of the first Five-Year Plan in 1933.

ACTIVITY 10.24

Compare Table 10.5 with Source 10W. Do you think that Stalin was exaggerating the success of the Five-Year Plans? Explain your answer.

There were some big problems with the Five-Year Plans, and some historians claim that the production figures were falsified. Factory managers were under huge pressure, and there was widespread corruption.

Results of collectivisation

Collectivisation was a disaster. Grain harvests dropped below 1928 levels for five of the following seven years. Stalin refused to believe there was not enough grain – he believed that kulaks were hiding it. He ordered that all grain found was to be confiscated. The result was catastrophic. Peasants could not sow crops the following year. They did not have enough food for their animals, so 10 million horses died in five years. In the Ukraine, collectivisation caused a famine that killed 3–7 million people in 1932–1934.

ACTIVITY 10.25

List the following: a) Stalin's economic successes, b) Stalin's economic failures.

CHECK YOUR UNDERSTANDING 10.20

1 In what ways had Stalin's economic policies made the Communist Party unpopular by 1934?
2 How successful were Stalin's economic policies? Explain your answer.

How were the Soviet people affected by these changes?

For most groups, Stalin's economic policies had both positive and negative effects.

	1928	1929	1930	1931	1932	1933	1934	1935
Grain harvest (million tons)	73.3	71.7	83.5	69.5	69.6	68.4	67.6	75.0
State procurement of grain (m tons)	10.8	16.1	22.1	22.8	18.5	22.6		
Grain export (m tons)	0.03	0.18	4.76	5.06	1.73	1.69		
Cattle (million)	70.5	67.1	52.3	47.9	40.1	38.4	42.4	49.3
Pigs (million)	26.0	20.4	13.6	14.4	11.6	12.1	17.4	22.6
Sheep and goats (million)	146.7	147.0	108.8	77.7	52.1	50.2	51.9	61.1

Table 10.6: The results of collectivisation.

Workers

Many urban workers – 33% of the population by 1939 – supported the Five-Year Plans. Some benefited from better education opportunities. Exceeding targets brought rewards such as higher pay, and better conditions and housing. For most, overcrowding, shortages and inadequate facilities meant that living standards fell. Average incomes fell by about 50% after 1928. Fresh foods, luxury goods, housing, shoes and clothing were not available.

Women

Stalin's social policies had a significant impact on women. The revolution had promised liberation and equality, but most still had their traditional roles. Also, collectivisation left women to do much of the work in the countryside, and the Five-Year Plans saw the female workforce increase by 10 million after 1928. Women gained higher education opportunities – 40% of engineering students were women by 1940. However, Stalin disliked and reversed many of the early reforms:

- marriage became more important
- divorce became more expensive
- awards were given to 'mother-heroines' who produced 10 or more children
- abortion became illegal.

Youth

Education policies had significant results:

- In 1930, universal primary education for four years was introduced.
- Numbers in secondary education increased from 1.8m in 1926 to 12m by 1938.
- In 1913, 78% of the population were illiterate, but by 1934 it was just 8%.

In addition to the opportunities provided through education, the state ensured that communism was taught to young people through membership of a youth organisation: the Komsomol. Members were organised in brigades and had their own banners, flags, uniforms and songs. There was a wide range of activities, including demonstrations, editing newspapers, voluntary work, plays and concerts.

Source 10X: A poster advertising the Komsomol, 1933. The slogan declares 'Leninist Komsomol, decent change'

ACTIVITY 10.26

With a partner study Source 10X; discuss why many young people joined the Komsomol.

National minorities

Despite being Georgian, Stalin had no sympathy with the non-Russian regions of the USSR. His policies were similar to the tsars' Russification policies. In the 1930s, whole populations, including Poles, Finns and Koreans, were relocated because Stalin did not trust them.

ACTIVITY 10.27

1 Compare the situation under Nicholas II and Stalin. How far had things changed for:

a workers

b women

c youth

d national minorities?

2 For each of the social groups mentioned in this section, explain how much you think they benefited from Stalin's rule.

Review your learning

Russia was a difficult country to rule, with a number of political, social and economic problems. Removing the tsar did not solve many of them. The failure of the 1905 Revolution shows that tsarist structures had some strength left in them. However, the impact of the First World War was unprecedented, creating a series of shocks far greater than the earlier controversial Russo-Japanese War. The fact that the poorly organised Duma itself could even briefly form a Provisional Government shows the weakness of tsarism by March 1917. The better organised Bolsheviks, efficiently led by the more ruthless Lenin, were able to seize power in November 1917. The same ruthlessness shaped their victory in the Civil War and their style of government. In such a system, it is not surprising, in retrospect, that the more ruthless Stalin outwitted Trotsky to become the party's and country's leader. Once in charge, Stalin favoured radical change in the economy, but in some issues was socially conservative.

Summary points

- The tsarist government was backward and inefficient.
- Nicholas II survived the 1905 Revolution because of the weakness of his opponents and the loyalty of the army.
- The First World War discredited Nicholas II and his regime.
- The revolution in March 1917 was popular, but the army was central.
- The Provisional Government faced difficulties and made mistakes.
- Organisation, ruthlessness and military power enabled the Bolsheviks to seize power in November 1917.
- The Bolsheviks won the Civil War in Russia because of the divisions among their opponents, geographical advantages and Trotsky's leadership.

- The NEP was a success in the short term, but caused political problems.
- Stalin's cunning and Trotsky's mistakes combined to ensure that Stalin won the leadership struggle after Lenin died.
- Stalin launched the purges to rid the USSR of all those he considered his enemies.
- Stalin used a mixture of repression, rewards and propaganda in order to control the USSR.
- Stalin's Five-Year Plans were intended to modernise Soviet industry, and collectivisation agriculture.
- Stalin's economic policies changed society, increased industrial production and wrecked agriculture.

The Big Challenge

This list includes aspects of Russia 1905–1941:

- Tsarism was replaced with communism.
- The government relied on repression.
- Industry was modernised and expanded.
- Religion was banned and the church persecuted.
- Agriculture was backward and inefficient.
- Agriculture was collectivised.
- People had little or no choice who governed.
- Most people prayed and worshipped God.

Divide it into two lists: issues where things changed; issues where things stayed the same. Which issues:

1 are you unsure about? Why do you think that is?

2 are missing from the lists?

3 do you think are most important and why?

Now write explaining how far you think Russian society and economy changed in the period 1905–1941.

Exam-style questions

Questions in the style of Paper 1

1   a   What happened on Bloody Sunday, 1905?

    b   Why was the tsar able to survive the 1905 Revolution?

    c   'Discontent among the working classes was the main reason for the downfall of the tsar in March 1917.' How far do you agree with this statement?

2   a   What was the Stalin Cult?

    b   Why did Stalin carry out the purges?

    c   'Stalin's rule was a disaster for the Soviet Union.' How far do you agree with this view?

Questions in the style of Paper 4 - IGCSE only

1   How important was the dissatisfaction of the peasantry in causing the 1905 Revolution?

2   How significant were changes brought about by Stalin's policies after 1929?

Chapter 11
Depth Study D: The USA, 1919–1941

What is this depth study about?

In this chapter you will be learning about the United States in a time of great change, from the end of the First World War up to its entry into the Second World War. We will be looking at the reasons for the economic prosperity of the 1920s, how this affected the American people and the extent to which different groups in society enjoyed the benefits of the 'boom years'. We will then examine the reasons why, in 1929, the country experienced the Wall Street Crash, followed by a long period of business failure, mass unemployment and poverty. Finally, the chapter looks at the policies of Franklin Delano Roosevelt, president from 1933 to 1945, who introduced the 'New Deal' in an attempt to bring about recovery from the crisis.

The key questions we will be examining are as follows:

1   How far did the US economy boom in the 1920s?

2   How far did US society change in the 1920s?

3   What were the causes and consequences of the Wall Street Crash?

4   How successful was the New Deal?

11.1 How far did the US economy boom in the 1920s?

The USA and the First World War

The US reluctantly joined the First World War in April 1917, almost three years after the European powers had started fighting. It contributed almost one million troops and gave financial support to Britain and France.

The end of the war in November 1918 left the US in a strong position. Its losses were relatively small and there was no damage to its own land. In fact, the US economy benefited in several ways. Its European allies received food and goods from American farms and factories, and almost $10 million in loans from US banks during and immediately after the war. The US expanded into new overseas markets as its competitors struggled to recover from the war.

Another effect of the war was the US policy of isolationism. It refused to join the League of Nations, preferring to stand aloof from overseas quarrels. Congress imposed tariffs on imports, in order to protect US industries and encourage the buying of American-made goods.

CHECK YOUR UNDERSTANDING 11.1

List three ways in which the United States benefited from its involvement in the First World War.

On what factors was the economic boom based?

After a brief slump in the immediate post-war period, the 1920s saw a sustained economic boom. The annual **Gross National Product** increased by 40% in the period 1922–1929. There were a number of reasons for this. The First World War gave the US several advantages over competitors. It had plentiful natural resources such as oil, coal and iron. Immigration provided an abundant supply of cheap labour: almost 14 million people arrived in the US during 1900–1920, mostly from Europe.

KEY TERM

Gross National Product: the total value of all the goods and services produced by a country.

There were also several new factors that promoted economic growth after the war.

Mass production and standardisation

Car maker Henry Ford used an assembly line method of production. The body of the car was moved on a conveyor belt past a series of workers, each of whom carried out a specific task as part of the manufacturing process. This speeded up the work – by the mid-1920s, 7,500 cars were being produced every day – and reduced manufacturing costs. Ford explained that it was important to 'keep everything in motion and take the work to the man and not the man to the work'. This 'mass production' technique was adopted by other industries.

Ford also made sure factories made just one type of car to a standardised specification. These developments meant that the car ceased to be a luxury item and became affordable to ordinary Americans. The best known car of the period, the Model T Ford, cost almost $1,000 when it was introduced in 1908 but by 1927 its price had fallen to less than $300. By the mid-1920s there was a car for one in every five Americans, whereas the figure in Britain was one to 43.

The mass production of cars affected the whole economy, creating a demand for rubber for tyres, glass for windscreens

237

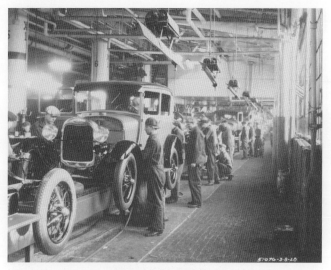

Source 11A: An assembly line in one of Henry Ford's car factories in the 1920s, showing how cars were constructed in stages as they passed along a conveyor belt.

and other materials. Garages were built to provide petrol, servicing and repairs; hotels and restaurants appeared to meet the needs of travellers. Suburbs expanded, as people could travel further to their workplace; rural areas became less isolated.

238

ACTIVITY 11.1

Using Source 11A and other evidence in this section, write your own explanation of how Henry Ford made his factories work efficiently.

Consumer culture

The average wage rose by 8% between 1923 and 1929. At the same time the price of consumer goods fell, so people's spending power grew, increasing demand. Newspapers, magazines and the radio carried advertisements designed to make people feel that they needed items such as refrigerators, washing machines and vacuum cleaners. Many targeted women, who were responsible for housework, to encourage them to purchase labour-saving devices. Salesmen sold goods directly to people in their homes.

CHECK YOUR UNDERSTANDING 11.2

Study Source 11B. How does this advertisement make the product appear more attractive to potential purchasers?

The purchase of these goods was made easier by the spread of **hire purchase** – buying of goods on credit through a series of instalments. Before the war there had

Source 11B: An advertisement for a refrigerator in the mid-1920s.

been shame attached to buying something if you could not afford to pay for it entirely. This now disappeared as people accepted increasing levels of debt. This would be one cause of future problems, as people's ability to make repayments was dependent on continued economic growth. As we will see in Section 11.3, this stopped after the Wall Street Crash of October 1929.

Table 11.1: The growth of mass consumption in US households, 1920–1930.

Consumer item	Percentage of homes in 1920	Percentage of homes in 1930
Radio sets	0	40
Vacuum cleaners	9	30
Washing machines	8	24

ACTIVITY 11.2

How useful is Table 11.1 for studying the economic boom of the 1920s? What other information would you need in order to understand how far American people benefited from the increased production of manufactured goods?

Republican government policy

Republican presidents Warren Harding, Calvin Coolidge and Herbert Hoover, in power from 1921 to 1933, reduced taxes and left businesses to make their own decisions, a policy known as **laissez-faire**. Hoover called for 'rugged individualism': people should succeed through their own talents and work. The tax cuts left people with more money, fuelling a spending boom.

Governments did abandon laissez-faire on one issue. The 1922 Fordney-McCumber Act raised tariffs to their highest ever level and allowed the government to increase them annually. This made imports more expensive, protecting US industries from foreign competition.

> **KEY TERM**
>
> **Laissez-faire:** French term meaning 'leave alone', a policy of minimising government involvement especially in the economy.

> **ACTIVITY 11.3**
>
> Consider the main reasons for the economic boom of the 1920s:
>
> - impact of the First World War
> - plentiful natural resources
> - cheap labour
> - mass production
> - advertising
> - hire purchase
> - Republican government policies.
>
> In your opinion, which of these were the most important causes of growth? Give reasons for your answer. Can you link the various factors together in your answer?

Why did some industries prosper while others did not?

The automobile industry was a success story and drove successes in related industries such as road-building: the US road network had doubled in length by 1930. Among new industries, commercial flying became feasible with the appearance of larger and more comfortable aeroplanes. Aviator Charles Lindbergh became the first person to fly solo across the Atlantic in 1927, making flying seem glamorous.

Electricity was supplied to many homes and factories in the 1920s, encouraging the growth of industries that produced electrical consumer goods. Department stores, which stocked these, appeared in cities. This all generated new jobs, and the workers spent their wages on buying goods, thus stimulating further production.

The decade also saw the construction industry enjoying a period of strong growth, as the success of big business produced a demand for new office buildings. New building materials and techniques enabled the construction of skyscrapers, which now became a familiar part of the urban landscape. The Chrysler Building in New York, 319 metres high (1046 feet) the tallest in the world when completed in 1930, was overtaken by the Empire State Building (381 metres or 1250 feet high).

Source 11C: Construction work on a skyscraper in the 1920s, showing workmen on the scaffolding high above the city streets.

> **CHECK YOUR UNDERSTANDING 11.3**
>
> What do Table 11.1 and Source 11C tell you about the booming US economy of the 1920s?

Not all industries were able to adapt to change by introducing new methods such as assembly-line production. Some older industries only grew slowly, partly because of competition from new technology. Demand for coal declined as oil, gas and electricity became more widely used. Railways struggled to compete with the expansion of road traffic. Rail still transported freight, but road transport was becoming increasingly important.

The textile industry faced a number of challenges. Shorter dresses were fashionable, requiring less material than pre-war designs. The introduction of cheap synthetic fibres such as rayon, made in factories requiring fewer workers, was a threat to older textiles such as cotton.

ACTIVITY 11.4

What do you think were the main reasons why some US industries performed better than others in the 1920s?

Why did agriculture not share in the prosperity?

Agriculture experienced a boom during the war. However, as European producers began to recover and competition from Canada, Argentina and elsewhere emerged, prices for American farm produce fell. Wheat went from $183 a **bushel** in 1920 to 38 cents in 1929. Farmers who had taken out loans in order to increase the size of their farm and buy tractors and combine harvesters could not repay the banks. Mechanisation enabled farmers to produce more, but this only drove prices down further. By 1924 600,000 farmers were bankrupt and over one million farm workers had left the land in search of other jobs.

> Nearly everything was done on credit … the small farmers back at that time … They all had to borrow money every year to make a profit. So, if they had a bad crop year, a lot of them, that's the way they lost their farms. The bad times back there, was 1920 and you just can't imagine the number of people then that was big men the year before who had lost everything they had.

Source 11D: Clay East, who ran a petrol station in a rural community in Arkansas, recalls the problems faced by tenant farmers in the 1920s.

ACTIVITY 11.5

How useful is Source 11D for a study of agriculture in the US in the 1920s?

Attempts by the government to help farmers made things worse. Increasing tariffs on imported food in the early 1920s caused other countries to retaliate with tariffs of their own, thereby making American produce less competitive. The McNary-Haugen Farm Relief Bill was introduced by Congress in 1924. This would have created a **Federal** Farm Board to buy up surplus food. However, president Coolidge, who believed that government intervention in the economy was undesirable, vetoed the bill.

Demand for cotton and wool declined as artificial fibres were increasingly used. Fewer animals were needed as the car industry boomed, so reducing the demand for animal foodstuffs such as hay and oats.

Rural communities lagged behind the towns. In 1930 more than 90% of American farms were still not connected to the electricity network.

Nearly half the US population lived in the countryside in the 1920s and so the effects of the farming crisis were severe. There were, however, some exceptions. Large-scale wheat farmers in the Mid-West, and fruit growers in California and Florida, continued to make a good living.

KEY TERMS

Bushel: a dry measure of 8 gallons, roughly equivalent to 36 litres.

Federal: the central government of the US, based in Washington DC, which deals with national issues such as taxation, defence and foreign policy. Each state has its own government, responsible for local matters such as education.

ACTIVITY 11.6

Make a mind map to show the various reasons why farmers experienced problems in the 1920s.

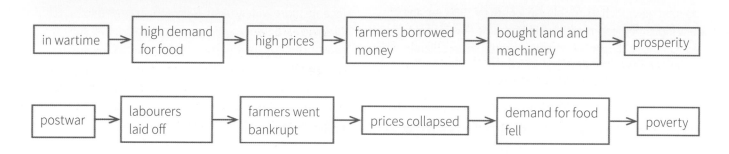

in wartime → high demand for food → high prices → farmers borrowed money → bought land and machinery → prosperity

postwar → labourers laid off → farmers went bankrupt → prices collapsed → demand for food fell → poverty

FACT FILE

People in newer and older industries, or in urban and rural US, or in different social classes or ethnic groups, had different experiences. While farm-workers' wages were falling, skilled factory workers' pay rose. There were variations across the country, with the South doing worse than the North. Any analysis of the period has to take account of this variation.

Did all Americans benefit from the boom?

The US remained an unequal society in the boom years. A survey in 1929 found that 18 million people (just under 15% of the total population) lived in poverty, and that 78% of profits from industry went to 0.3% of the population.

Unskilled and casual workers, and the two million unemployed, were unable to purchase the goods available to better-off Americans. For them, life was a matter of survival rather than of participation in the consumer boom.

New immigrants often had a lower standard of education than more established Americans. They had to take whatever work was available.

Workers in older industries faced unemployment or wages that failed to keep up. Coal miners' standard of living dropped: by 1929 their wages had fallen to a third of the national average. Textile industry employers, faced with rising competition, employed cheaper female or child labour in order to reduce costs. Strikes for higher wages were rarely successful, partly because the police suppressed disturbances. Trade-union power remained limited. Some firms only hired non-union labour to avoid strikes.

Farmers and farm workers were badly affected by the agricultural slump of the 1920s. Many farmers who had overextended themselves by taking out loans had their farms repossessed by the banks to whom they owed money. Bankruptcy turned some into tenants on their own land. Others moved to industrial cities or to California, where fruit farms were creating employment. Some travelled the country in search of work. Share-croppers rented farmland; when prices of farm produce fell, they struggled to pay the rent. Eviction brought both unemployment and homelessness.

Black Americans formed a disproportionate part of the country's poor. In cities such as New York or Chicago

Table 11.2: Changing average weekly pay of farm and factory workers, 1919–1930.

	1919	1930
Average farm-worker	$13.5	$7.5
Skilled factory worker	$22.3	$28.6

they tended to be confined to poorly paid employment, often living in overcrowded conditions in segregated areas known as ghettoes. Many farm workers in the South were black, and one million of them lost their jobs in the 1920s.

ACTIVITY 11.7

Sort the following groups into those which benefited from the boom of the 1920s, and those which did not:

- coal miners
- car-factory workers
- small farmers
- black Americans
- California fruit growers
- department store employees.

Make a chart with two columns to show your findings, and for each group outline the reasons why they either prospered or did not do well in the 1920s.

11.2 How far did US society change in the 1920s?

What were the 'Roaring 20s'?

The prosperity created by the economic boom of the 1920s led to major changes in American society. There were new opportunities for entertainment. Women enjoyed greater freedom. On the other hand, there was a backlash from older and more conservative people, and life changed much less in the countryside than in the cities.

Consumer boom

Better-off people bought new consumer goods and services. With wages rising for those who were employed in the newer industries, and factories producing more products for them to buy, this was a good time to be young and with money to spare.

New inventions

Radios, refrigerators and record players improved the material quality of life. Labour-saving devices in the home such as vacuum cleaners created more leisure time. Advertising in newspapers and magazines, and on the radio and at the cinema, made people aware of what they could spend their money on.

Social and cultural change

Jazz originated among the black population of the southern states, spreading to northern cities after the First World War. This music was sometimes condemned as immoral, perhaps only serving to make it more popular. Band leaders such as Duke Ellington and Louis Armstrong became well known and eventually jazz became part of the cultural mainstream in the US.

Source 11E: A jazz band giving a performance circa 1924.

Spectator sports attracted large crowds. By 1930 40% of American homes had a radio set and radio reporting generated interest in sporting stars. 'Babe Ruth', the most successful baseball player of his time, became a celebrity. Cheaply available motor cars enabled people to travel further for pleasure as well as for work. New crazes such as jazz and dances like the Charleston were fashionable. This was also the golden age of cinema, with the rise of Hollywood. Films were silent, cinemas hiring a pianist or an orchestra to play suitable music to accompany events on the screen. From 1927, with the success of Al Jolson's *The Jazz Singer*, 'talkies' appeared, in which the actors' voices could be heard. By 1930 more than 100 million cinema tickets were being sold each week.

Young people enjoyed greater freedom. Shorter skirts and smoking in public became common. Women with a more independent lifestyle were known as 'flappers'. The term implied immorality.

Not all Americans welcomed these developments. Some feared that new musical styles and dance crazes encouraged immoral contact between unmarried young people. They thought that the depiction of smoking, drinking and violence in films would be copied by impressionable viewers, leading to a decline in moral standards.

ACTIVITY 11.8

Research one of the following, and make a PowerPoint presentation for your class on how it contributed to social change in the 1920s:

- film
- sport
- music and dance.

How widespread was intolerance in US society?

The 1920s were a time when a number of minority groups faced intolerance, discrimination and persecution.

Immigrants

The US had been founded on the idea of immigration. The inscription on the Statue of Liberty in New York harbour famously welcomes the world's 'huddled masses' to a new life of freedom and opportunity. However, immigrants became less welcome in the early twentieth century for several reasons.

Whereas most early immigrants had originally come from parts of northern Europe such as Germany and Scandinavia, a growing number now came from Eastern Europe or Asia. Many people feared that these immigrants would not be easily assimilated into society because their racial and cultural background was different from that of established American citizens. Working-class Americans feared competition for jobs, at a time when employment opportunities were reduced by mechanisation in industry.

Congress responded to these fears by introducing quotas for immigrants in 1921. This meant that the number of immigrants admitted from a particular country must be proportional to the number of people from that country living in the US ten years earlier. This was intended to reduce the number of people coming from Eastern Europe, because there had been relatively few immigrants from there before the First World War. The quota was reduced from 3% to 2% in 1924, and in 1929 a further measure allowed the entry of only 150,000 immigrants a year. The entry of Asians was completely banned.

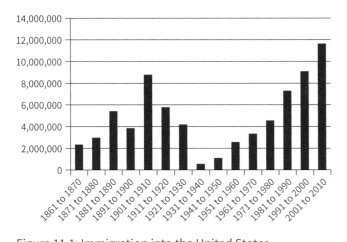

Figure 11.1: Immigration into the United States.

Communists and anarchists

Fear of immigrants was linked to the 'Red Scare'. The 1917 Russian revolution led many Americans to make a link between extreme political ideas and the arrival of immigrants from Eastern Europe. The atmosphere of suspicion was heightened by a series of bomb outrages associated with **anarchists,** including in 1919 an attack on the home of the government's chief law officer, Attorney-General Mitchell Palmer. Up to 6,000 suspected communists and anarchists were arrested in the 'Palmer raids' of 1920. Conservative Americans feared that their capitalist system was under attack from a foreign-inspired conspiracy.

KEY TERMS

Communists: people who believe that government should take over all private businesses and land.

Anarchists: people who believe in the abolition of government.

The vulnerability of immigrants was highlighted by the Sacco and Vanzetti case. This was a notorious criminal trial in 1921, in which two Italian anarchists, Nicola Sacco and Bartolomeo Vanzetti, were accused of murder during an armed robbery. The case was a controversial one, with unclear evidence and significant differences in the stories given by witnesses. They were found guilty and both were executed in 1927. Although the case revealed widespread prejudice against foreigners, there was also considerable support for the men's appeals and many felt that they were victims of a miscarriage of justice.

African Americans

Black Americans suffered from discrimination across the US. Although slavery had been ended as a result of the American Civil War (1861–1865) many southern states found ways to limit the freedom of black people. The 'Jim Crow' laws, named after a popular depiction of a black character, enforced segregation – the separation of black and white people in public facilities such as cafes and public transport. In some states, literacy tests or other qualifications were imposed to make it more difficult for black people to register to vote.

The North had no formal segregation, and many black people moved to northern cities in the 1920s in the hope of finding employment and better treatment. Nonetheless, black people tended to live in specific areas, and experienced poorer housing and education. Black people across the US suffered violence, especially in the South. The authorities often paid no attention to **lynchings**.

White fears can be seen in the growth of the **Ku Klux Klan**. By 1925 the Klan had an estimated five million members and enjoyed the private support of a number of politicians, judges and senior policemen in some southern states. One Klan leader, David Stephenson,

243

KEY TERMS

Lynchings: executions carried out by mobs, not by judicial process.

The Ku Klux Klan: a white supremacist organisation founded in the South following its Civil War defeat. Its aim is to ensure continued white power in part by making black people too frightened to participate in elections, strikes or demonstrations. It has also been hostile to Catholics, Jews, immigrants, communists and anarchists.

Source 11F: Ku Klux Klan officers in their robes and hoods, initiating a new member (seen kneeling) into their secret rituals in November 1922.

declared, 'I am the law in Indiana.' He was put on trial for raping and assaulting a woman who later died. This scandal affected the Klan's standing and its membership and influence declined in the second half of the decade.

CHECK YOUR UNDERSTANDING 11.5

Use the evidence in this section, including Source 11F, to explain why the Ku Klux Klan had such a fearsome reputation.

Despite all this, African Americans made advances in this period. Jazz was only one part of a flowering of African American culture (see Source 11E). Black artists and performers became well known, notably the dancer Josephine Baker. There was a growing black middle class in Chicago and New York. The National Association for the Advancement of Coloured People (NAACP), founded in 1909, continued to campaign for the rights of black people, and its investigations into lynchings helped to reduce the number of attacks. There was, though, little change in African Americans' political, economic and social position until the 1950s and 1960s.

Religious intolerance in the 1920s

Another area in which some Americans sought to suppress the freedom of others was the attempt by Christian fundamentalists to ban the teaching of the **theory of evolution**. Fundamentalists, who were numerous in the **Bible belt** of the South, argued that God created the world in six days. In 1925, the so-called 'monkey trial' took place in the Tennessee town of Dayton. A teacher named John Scopes taught evolution so that a test case could

be brought against him and the issue aired in public. The fundamentalist point of view was put by William Jennings Bryan, who had stood for the presidency on two occasions. The court found against Scopes but the trial exposed the lack of coherence of his opponents' arguments.

Tennessee, Arkansas and Mississippi continued to outlaw the teaching of human evolution – the ban was not overturned for 40 years. The remaining 45 states making US in the 1920s did not impose such restrictive laws.

KEY TERMS

Theory of evolution: the idea, put forward by biologist Charles Darwin in the 19th century, that life on earth developed over millions of years and that humans and apes were descended from a common ancestor.

Bible belt: approximately the south-east quarter of the US, so called because of the large number of socially-conservative evangelical Christians living there.

ACTIVITY 11.9

Jews are both a religious and an ethnic minority in the US. Research their situation there in the 1920s, making connections with what you have learned about East-European immigration, and religious and racial prejudice.

ACTIVITY 11.10

Does the evidence of this section suggest that intolerance was universal in American society in the 1920s? Remember to take account of different social classes, ethnic groups and regions in the US.

Why was Prohibition introduced, and then later repealed?

Religious campaigners, such as the Anti-Saloon League, had argued since the late 19th century that alcohol created poverty and undermined family life and morals. Some industrialists believed that alcohol impaired workers' efficiency. These feelings gained strength during the First World War, partly because many brewers were of German origin, so prohibition of beer became regarded as a patriotic issue. Several individual states passed their own laws banning alcohol.

After the war, anti-drink campaigners had enough support in Congress to secure the passing of the Eighteenth Amendment to the US Constitution in 1919, banning the 'manufacture, sale or transportation of intoxicating liquors'. The Volstead Act of 1920 defined 'intoxicating liquors' as anything containing more than 5% alcohol.

What were the effects of Prohibition?

Legal breweries and distilleries quickly closed down and the consumption of alcohol dropped. However, continuing demand financed illegal 'stills' that produced often poor-quality 'moonshine' whisky, leading to increased alcohol-related deaths. Previously law-abiding Americans now bought alcohol in illegal bars known as 'speakeasies', which charged high prices. Illegal traders known as 'bootleggers' flourished. The US's long land and sea borders made alcohol smuggling impossible to prevent.

Organised criminal gangs fought for control of the now illegal drink trade. With too few government agents to enforce the law, and widespread police and official corruption, the gangsters thrived. Al Capone (1899–1947, see Source 11G) was a gang leader who gained control of the illegal drink trade in Chicago, and dominated the city's political scene through bribery and election fixing. In the 1929 St Valentine's Day Massacre, his gang killed seven members of a rival gang in a Chicago garage. He was eventually prosecuted and imprisoned not for his gangster activities but for income tax evasion.

Source 11G: Al Capone pictured after his conviction in November 1931.

Prohibition thus unintentionally damaged people's health, turned law-abiding citizens into law breakers, and promoted corruption and violence.

Why did Prohibition come to an end in 1933?

Even after the Federal Bureau of Investigation (FBI) was brought in to combat the gangsters, the law proved impossible to enforce. A committee set up by president Hoover in 1929 concluded that Prohibition was not working. The government was fighting a losing battle, and the rule of law was being brought into disrepute. Following the beginning of the Depression and the election of Franklin Roosevelt, the Eighteenth Amendment was repealed.

The government hoped that making alcohol legal once again would create jobs, stimulate economic recovery and create a legal industry that could be taxed and regulated.

> **CHECK YOUR UNDERSTANDING 11.6**
>
> What were the main reasons for the failure of Prohibition?

How far did the roles of women change during the 1920s?

Greater political rights?

Before the First World War, women could vote in some state elections, but not in federal ones. In 1920 the Nineteenth Amendment to the Constitution gave women equal voting rights with men. This is often said to be the result of many women having successfully worked in what had traditionally been men's jobs during the First World War. Also, a campaign for voting rights had been gaining in strength before the war, including groups such as the Congressional Union (later the National Women's Party), founded in 1912 by Alice Paul and Lucy Burns.

Following the passing of the Nineteenth Amendment, few suffrage campaigners continued to pursue active political careers. Women such as Nellie Tayloe Ross of Wyoming, the first female state governor, were the exception rather than the rule. Hers was a special case in that she was elected to replace her husband, who died suddenly in 1924 whilst in office, and she refused to campaign for the post.

More independent lifestyles?

The 1920s saw the appearance of a new kind of young urban woman, sometimes known as the 'flapper'. Flappers wore fashionably short skirts without the restrictive undergarments of the pre-war era, and cut their hair short. Some went out to work and engaged in activities such as smoking and drinking in public, socialising openly with men and enjoying greater personal freedom.

Source 11H: A 'flapper' striking a pose daring for the 1920s.

Women in rural areas did not usually enjoy the same amenities as urban women; their lives remained hard. Most women continued to be dependent first on fathers and then husbands. They could not get credit independently of their husbands and had no legal protection against domestic abuse. Access to contraception was improving, with campaigner Margaret Sanger establishing the first birth-control clinic in 1923, but was still limited in availability and efficiency, and still controversial. Married women were still responsible for domestic life including child-care.

The proportion of women in the workforce did rise in the 1920s, but only from 20.4% to 22%. Women were generally paid less than men, and employment tended to occur in areas traditionally seen as 'female', such a teaching, nursing and librarianship.

CHECK YOUR UNDERSTANDING 11.7

Do you agree that the overall position of women in American society did not improve significantly in the 1920s? What do you think Source 11H can tell us about the situation of women in American in the 1920s?

11.3 What were the causes and consequences of the Wall Street Crash?

How far was speculation responsible for the Wall Street ICrash?

During the boom years of the 1920s many people made money by buying stocks and shares in US companies and selling them for a profit. This practice is known as speculation. It relied on the expectation that the companies would continue to perform well and therefore the value of shares would keep rising. This was the case until October 1929 when the Great Crash occurred and, almost overnight, the value of shares collapsed, leaving many investors facing huge losses. This was the start of a period known as the Great Depression, when millions of people lost their jobs as banks and businesses failed.

Source 11I: Anxious investors milling around in Wall Street, New York's financial district, at the time of the 1929 Crash.

Wall Street in New York is where the stock market is based. In the 1920s, when its activities were not regulated by government, growing numbers of ordinary people bought shares in the hope of making money. Many borrowed money to do so. When share prices rose, they could sell their shares, repay the loan and still make a profit. By 1929 20 million Americans owned shares. More people bought shares, pushing share prices beyond their real value. Too little attention was paid to the actual performance of the companies themselves, and too much to the performance of their shares on the stock market. In addition, the rising stock market was based on shareholders' confidence.

With the value of shares rising even when the demand for goods was falling, US companies were extremely overvalued. In the autumn of 1929, people who understood the situation became worried enough to begin selling shares. As prices came down small investors panicked (see Source 11I). On 'Black Thursday', 24 October, almost 13 million shares were sold in one day. Fewer people were willing to buy shares and their prices fell alarmingly. The low prices made some people think there were bargains to be picked up and the stock market briefly rallied, only to have its worst ever day on 29 October, when more than 16 million shares were traded. There were too many sellers and too few buyers; the value of the shares collapsed, causing large numbers of people to lose their money.

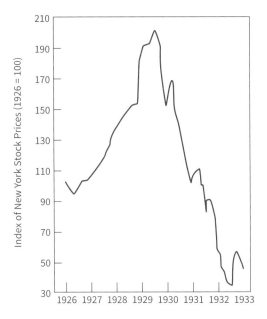

Figure 11.2: The changing value of shares on Wall Street, 1926–1933.

CHECK YOUR UNDERSTANDING 11.8

What can you learn from Figure 11.2 about the background to the Wall Street Crash?

ACTIVITY 11.11

Make a flow chart showing the different factors leading up to the Wall Street Crash. Highlight in different colours the factors that relate to the stock market, and those that have to do with the wider problems of the US economy.

Was the Wall Street Crash the only cause of the Depression?

The US economy had problems even before October 1929. Older industries such as coal and textiles, and agriculture, were struggling from the early 1920s onwards.

By the late 1920s mass production, a crucial component of the boom, led to overproduction and so demand for manufactured goods slowed. Once households had bought an item, they did not rush to buy an additional or replacement one. As firms found that they could not sell goods, they cut their employees' wages or reduced the size of their workforce.

Similarly, in the countryside, farmers faced falling prices throughout the decade because they were producing more than the market could absorb.

US companies had benefited from the tariffs which reduced foreign competition. At the same time, retaliatory tariffs reduced the companies' income from exports. In addition, European countries, struggling to repay the money the US had lent them during the First World War, were buying less.

What impact did the Crash have on the economy?

Many banks had invested their customers' money in shares, which were now worthless. To try to avoid their own collapse, these banks began calling in loans for repayment. Many firms and private individuals could not repay the money they had borrowed. Seeing the banks in trouble, people lost confidence in them and queued to withdraw their money. By 1933 more than 4,000 banks had gone out of business.

A vicious cycle developed:

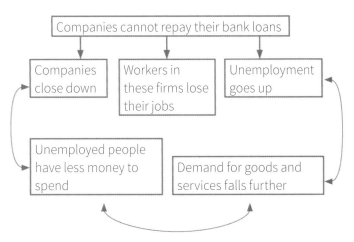

Unemployment reached 4.3 million (almost 9% of the workforce) in 1930, by 1932 it had rocketed to 12 million (almost 24% of the workforce). Those who found a job usually had to work for lower wages, making worse the problem of falling demand.

Additional factors added to the misery. In 1930 the government introduced the Smoot-Hawley tariff, which was higher than previous **import tariffs**. Other countries did the same for US imports, causing world trade to shrink, further damaging US industry. At home, the unequal distribution of wealth played a part. Poorer people who might have spent money on goods did not have the means to do so. For all these reasons the amount of money circulating in the economy contracted.

This was the Great Depression.

TOP TIP

Events are not experienced in the same way by different groups in society. Would a poor farmer or coal miner, for example, have agreed that the Depression had begun in 1929?

What were the social consequences of the Crash?

The Depression in the cities

Unemployment rose steadily until, by 1933, almost a quarter of the workforce was jobless. The industrial areas of the North and West, where entire factories closed, were worst hit. It was almost impossible to find another job in these areas.

One consequence of unemployment was homelessness as householders became unable to meet mortgage or rent payments. Many slept on the streets or resorted to travelling in search of work. In 1932 an estimated two million **hobos** risked their lives by hitching rides on long-distance trains. Several hundred thousand people built shanty towns of wood and cardboard on the edges of cities. These were known as 'Hoovervilles' in mockery of Herbert Hoover, president at the time of the Wall Street Crash. These were unhealthy places without running water and sewage systems.

KEY TERMS

Import tariffs: taxes on goods imported into a country.

Hobos: homeless, unemployed people travelling in search of work.

Jesse Jackson, the self-declared mayor of Hooverville, was one of the men who had a strong distaste for organized charity ... Jackson and his friends rounded up whatever they could find and began to create shelters. Seattle city officials were not thrilled

about this new development. In an original attempt to disband these shantytowns and unemployed 'jungles', city officials burned down the entire community, giving the men only seven days' eviction notice ... Hooverville residents, for their part, were not thwarted by the city's attempt to disband them. They simply dug deeper embankments for their homes and re-established the community.

Source 11J: From an account of a Hooverville in Seattle, Washington State, on the North-West coast of the USA.

ACTIVITY 11.12

What does Source 11J tell you about the attitudes of the unemployed towards the Great Depression?

The Depression affected family life. It discouraged people from marrying and having children. Marriages fell from 1.23 million in 1929 to 982,000 in 1932. The suicide rate went up from 14 per 100,000 people to 17 between 1929 and 1932.

The social problems of the Depression were worsened by the absence of a **welfare state** run by the federal government. Instead, individual towns and cities ran limited programmes of assistance, and there were also charities that provided soup kitchens. In some cases unemployed people joined together to help themselves. Sometimes farmers allowed them to collect food that could not be sold. Desperate people begged or stole.

The Depression in rural USA

The Depression worsened the problems of US farmers. Customers had become so poor that they struggled to afford their produce. Prices of farm produce fell further, sometimes making the harvesting of crops pointless. In Oregon, farmers killed thousands of sheep because the price they would fetch at market would not cover the cost of transporting them there. Banks repossessed the farms of those who could no longer pay their mortgages. Some farmers physically resisted the agents who came to evict them, but eventually they too had little option but to leave and move on.

In Kansas, Oklahoma, Texas, New Mexico and Colorado, farmers faced an additional challenge from nature.

A combination of poor farming methods, drought and strong winds led to severe soil erosion in the 1930s. The resulting dust storms ruined thousands of farmers: many sold and left.

Many farmers from the 'Dust Bowl' areas of Oklahoma and Arkansas, known respectively as 'Okies' and 'Arkies', moved to the west coast in search of work, but they rarely found the opportunities they expected. Locals often viewed them suspiciously as potentially criminal outsiders. The newcomers usually had to work for low wages, living in temporary camps.

Source 11K: A still from the film adaptation of John Steinbeck's 1939 novel *The Grapes of Wrath*. This tells the story of a farming family who move from Oklahoma to California in search of work picking fruit.

ACTIVITY 11.13

How would you assess the reliability of a novel like *The Grapes of Wrath* as an historical source? What message or information does the image in Source 11K give us?

Did all Americans face hardship?

Although they were affected by the Wall Street Crash, the rich tended to suffer less than the rest of society. Some had not invested everything in stocks and shares but had kept a proportion of their wealth in gold and property, which retained their value. Some

bought the property of the less fortunate quite cheaply. Nevertheless, most people experienced a crisis in the early 1930s.

 KEY TERM

Welfare state: a government-run system of national assistance to tackle poverty.

CHECK YOUR UNDERSTANDING 11.9

Did the Depression affect all Americans equally? Give reasons for your answer.

Why did Roosevelt win the election of 1932?

Franklin Delano Roosevelt (FDR), the Democratic Party's candidate, defeated the sitting president, Republican Party leader Herbert Hoover, in the November 1932 election. FDR went on to become the US's longest serving president, winning three further terms in 1936, 1940 and 1944. He was the US's leader in the Second World War, dying in office in April 1945, shortly before the allied victory over Germany.

Roosevelt took over the government when the Depression was at its worst. He was popular because he offered a message of hope at a time of great crisis. By contrast, his predecessor seemed to have no answers to the misery of his fellow Americans.

Source 11L: Roosevelt (right) greeting his defeated predecessor, Herbert Hoover, on the day he took over as president, March 1933.

Hoover's policies

Herbert Hoover (1874–1964) was a self-made man who became wealthy as a mining engineer. A first-rate administrator, he organised the distribution of food to people in Europe affected by the fighting in the First World War. After serving as Secretary of Commerce in the Republican administrations of the 1920s, he was elected president in 1928. He believed that hard work was the key to continued prosperity. This was an appealing message while the boom lasted, but after the Great Crash, people wanted positive action from the government.

Hoover seemed complacent about the problems of those whom the Depression had hit. In the first year of the Depression he insisted that the good times would return if government maintained its traditional laissez-faire approach. Individual states and charities could relieve poverty, not the federal government. If government intervened, it would undermine people's self-reliance.

Hoover was willing to increase public spending but refused to incur large debts. He set up a Farm Board to help farmers by buying up surplus food. His Reconstruction Finance Corporation, created in 1932, provided $2 billion in loans to businesses. His government financed public works schemes, including the Boulder Dam on the Colorado River, which was completed after he had left office and was later renamed the Hoover Dam. Yet these measures were not enough to deal with the scale of the problems that the US economy faced. As we have seen, the 1930 Smoot-Hawley tariff actually caused as many problems as it solved.

As a result, Hoover seemed not to care about the plight of many ordinary Americans. 'In Hoover we trusted, now we are busted' was one well-known farmers' protest slogan. He was criticised in particular for his handling of the 'Bonus Marchers', 20,000 army veterans who had been promised an extra payment in 1945. In 1932 some of them came to Washington to call for the money to be paid early, as they were in desperate need. They set up a camp on the edges of the city with their families. Hoover misread the situation and, acting in the belief that communist revolution would occur unless he took drastic action, he sent in the army with tanks and tear gas to disperse the bonus marchers. Many saw this as unnecessarily harsh.

CHECK YOUR UNDERSTANDING 11.10

Why did Hoover fail to appeal to American voters in the 1932 election?

What did Roosevelt offer?

Franklin Roosevelt (1882–1945) came from a privileged background and was noted for his easy charm as well as his skill as a politician (see for example Source 11L). He served as Assistant Secretary of the Navy in Woodrow Wilson's administration. Personal tragedy struck him just before the age of 40, however, when he contracted polio, which left him unable to walk. Roosevelt was a man of great determination. In 1928 he was elected governor of New York State and in 1933 became the US's first disabled president.

Roosevelt did not explain his policy proposals for dealing with the Depression in much detail. The measures he introduced turned out to be an extension of Hoover's. The key difference between the two was that Roosevelt created the impression that if elected, he would lead an active, energetic government. He emphasised his support for 'the forgotten man at the bottom of the economic pyramid' and travelled the country to make himself known to the people. He spoke of a 'new deal' for the US, making it clear that he would take whatever action was necessary to get the economy moving again.

FDR offered hope to poor people but also reassurance to the many middle-class Americans who feared that without urgent action, the country might slide into revolution. Roosevelt seemed best placed to avert such a catastrophe. He won with the support of 23 million people, equivalent to 57% of the vote, and carried all but six of the 48 states of the US.

ACTIVITY 11.14

Write election leaflets for Hoover and Roosevelt in the 1932 election, setting out their policies and why people should vote for them.

11.4 How successful was the New Deal?

What was the New Deal, as introduced in 1933?

The New Deal was not a fully worked out plan when Roosevelt came to office. It evolved over time, reflecting his election statement that what the country needed was 'bold, persistent experimentation'. Historians speak of a 'First New Deal' in 1933, followed by a second one in 1935. Roosevelt's first year in office was a period of intense government activity, focused on reviving the economy, getting people working again and stopping them from losing their homes and farms. Its purpose was summed up in the 'three Rs' – relief, recovery and reform.

Roosevelt's inaugural speech, March 1933

Each new US president makes a speech at the inauguration ceremony when they are installed in office. Roosevelt's is one of the most famous and important of all time. Words would not solve the US's problems, but it was important to give the country a lead and generate a spirit of optimism. This he succeeded in doing. He told his audience that 'the only thing we have to fear is fear itself'. Roosevelt followed this up with a series of radio addresses, known as 'fireside chats' for their informal manner, in which he explained his policies and encouraged people to look to the future. Radio was a relatively new medium and Roosevelt was the first president to master it as a means of communicating with the people.

> **We are working toward a definite goal, which is to prevent the return of conditions which came very close to destroying what we call modern civilization. The actual accomplishment of our purpose cannot be attained in a day. Our policies are wholly within purposes for which our American Constitutional Government was established 150 years ago.**
>
> **I know that the people of this country will understand this ... I do not deny that we may make mistakes of procedure as we carry out the policy. I have no expectation of making a hit every time I come to bat. What I seek is the highest possible batting average, not only for myself but for the team.**

Source 11M: Roosevelt addresses the nation in his second 'fireside chat', 7 May 1933.

CHECK YOUR UNDERSTANDING 11.11

How effective do you think the extract from Roosevelt's broadcast in Source 11M is? Look at the use of language and the tone of the passage. Bear in mind the mood of the people listening to Roosevelt at a time of great national uncertainty.

The Hundred Days

The economic crisis actually worsened in the early months of 1933. Strengthened by his election victory, Roosevelt persuaded Congress to give him the necessary emergency powers to tackle the most immediate problems in his first hundred days in office. The first task was to restore confidence in the banking system, which was nearing collapse as so many people had withdrawn their savings and businesses had been unable to repay loans. Roosevelt imposed a temporary closure of the banks and only allowed those banks to reopen that the government had certified as sound and properly run. He succeeded in getting people to start saving money in the banks once again. This was followed by the Glass-Steagal Act, which introduced government regulation of Wall Street and protected ordinary people from having their savings wiped out by the reckless investment decisions of the banks. Another decision was the ending of Prohibition. This cut the ground from under the bootleg gangs and provided the government with a new source of tax revenue.

The alphabet agencies

Roosevelt set up a number of government bodies known by their initial letters, which, for this reason, were called the 'alphabet agencies'. Their aim was to drive economic recovery and to provide assistance to the most vulnerable groups in American society. This dramatically extended the role of the federal government in people's lives. It brought relief to millions but aroused opposition from conservatives who saw it as undue interference in the working of the market and the lives of individuals. Another criticism was that the New Deal was not fully planned in advance, and some of the agencies overlapped with others in what they did.

The alphabet agencies were important in three main areas:

Helping the poor and unemployed

- Civilian Conservation Corps (CCC): provided men aged 18–25 with work on conservation projects such as planting trees to combat soil erosion. More than 2 million men had taken part in this work by the time the US entered the Second World War. It developed useful practical skills and gave participants a sense of purpose.
- Federal Emergency Relief Administration (FERA): provided assistance for the poor, in the form of grants to state governments.
- Civil Works Administration (CWA): provided employment for 4 million people for a short-term period in 1933–1934. Its job-creation schemes varied from road-building to sweeping leaves.

- Public Works Administration (PWA): sponsored building projects, such as the construction of dams and bridges.
- Home Owners' Loan Corporation (HOLC): supplied loans to people unable to pay their mortgages and in danger of losing their homes.

Promoting industrial recovery

- National Recovery Administration (NRA): was set up by the National Industrial Recovery Act (NIRA). It aimed to revive industrial production by setting fair prices for goods, whilst raising workers' wages and improving conditions in the workplace. Companies taking part signed codes of practice agreed with the government, and in return were issued with a 'Blue Eagle' logo to show that they were good employers, and to encourage people to buy from them. Over 5,000 industries had decided to participate by September 1933 and the symbol became widely known.

Helping the farmers

- Farm Credit Administration (FCA): provided low-interest loans to farmers.
- Agricultural Adjustment Act (AAA): controversially rewarded farmers for cutting production levels. Many were angry to see animals slaughtered and crops ploughed back into the ground, but farm incomes doubled during 1933–1939. It did not help farm labourers and share-croppers, many of whom were replaced by new machinery.
- Tennessee Valley Authority (TVA): set up to help an area of the South 80,000 square miles in size, covering parts of seven states from Mississippi to Virginia. The region was prone to flooding and soil erosion, and there were high levels of poverty and unemployment. Tree planting helped to prevent soil from being washed away, and the building of government-funded dams created jobs, controlled the flow of the river and generated electricity with which to modernise the area's economy. This programme helped both agriculture and industry and is generally regarded as one of the New Deal's outstanding successes. To business interests, this was further government encroachment.

ACTIVITY 11.15

How far did the First New Deal achieve the aims of bringing about economic recovery and relieving poverty?

How far did the character of the New Deal change after 1933?

In 1935 the Supreme Court ruled that the NRA and the AAA were illegal because federal government had no right to interfere in states' affairs. Roosevelt had to think about how to secure re-election in 1936, and he was under pressure from radical critics who wanted more done. The Second New Deal brought a change of emphasis, in that it was concerned with longer-term plans for social justice and welfare, and establishing workers' rights. There were several major developments in 1935.

Works Progress Administration (WPA)

The WPA was a new initiative to deal with unemployment through major building projects. Examples of its work included the San Francisco Bay Bridge and New York's La Guardia airport. It also supported the work of artists and writers, helping to improve the quality of life in many communities as well as giving work to more than 8 million people. By enabling people to work in return for money it avoided the stigma attached to receiving handouts.

National Labour Relations Act

The NLRA affirmed the right of workers to form and join trade unions and to engage in **collective bargaining**. It also set up the National Labour Relations Board to protect workers who were victimised by employers.

Social Security Act

The SSA was a major move away from the idea that individuals alone should make their own provision for old age and other hazards of life. It created the first pensions for the elderly, together with benefits for orphans and victims of industrial accidents. It also set up a national system of insurance against unemployment. Although the payments were small, it marked an important change in the relationship between government and citizen.

Resettlement Administration (RA) and Farm Security Administration (FSA)

The RA helped farm workers and share-croppers move to better land. In 1937 it was replaced by the FSA, which gave loans to help these people buy their own land. Its effects on the position of the poorest people in rural areas were, however, limited.

Source 11N: A cartoon showing Roosevelt as a doctor, visiting 'Uncle Sam' (the symbol of the US), depicted as his patient, 6 May 1935.

ACTIVITY 11.16

What is the cartoon, Source 11N, saying about the way that Roosevelt approached the US's problems?

KEY TERM

Collective bargaining: negotiations between trade unions and employers on wages and conditions of work.

CHECK YOUR UNDERSTANDING 11.12

What were the similarities and differences between the First and the Second New Deal?

Why did the New Deal encounter opposition?
Opposition from the right

The New Deal faced opposition from conservatives who felt that it undermined individual initiative and excessively extended the power of the federal government. They included members of the official opposition party, the Republicans, and many business leaders. There were also some more conservative members of the Democrat Party in the South who did not support the New Deal. The short-lived American Liberty League was headed by two former Democrat Party presidential candidates.

These more traditional Americans were attached to the idea of self-help and many of them accused Roosevelt of promoting socialist or even communist ideas. They felt that Roosevelt's policies increased the power of trade unions and interfered with the right of business leaders to run their companies. Press owner William Randolph Hearst, for example, referred to 'Stalin Delano Roosevelt'. Such people resented the higher taxes they had to pay and argued that many of the New Deal schemes were a waste of money.

Although Roosevelt faced bitter hostility from the political right, it was never sufficiently well-organised to be a serious challenge to his position as president. The Republicans were divided on what they felt about the New Deal, with moderates not opposing it outright. The party's candidate for the presidency in the 1936 election, Alf Landon, found it hard to develop a distinctive policy position in opposition to Roosevelt.

Opposition from the left

At the other end of the political spectrum were those radicals who felt that the New Deal had not done enough to deal with unemployment and poverty. Three individuals in particular wanted to go further than Roosevelt in redistributing wealth to the poor: Huey Long, Dr Francis Townsend and Father Charles Coughlin (see Sources 11O, 11P and 11Q).

Long, Townsend and Coughlin appealed in different ways to different sections of the American public, and they may have indirectly influenced Roosevelt to adopt more radical policies in the Second New Deal. Like Roosevelt's right-wing critics, however, they were not able to offer a united front to oppose him. The three men's supporters came together in 1936, to form the Union Party, but their candidate, William Lemke, won only 2% of the vote in the presidential election.

Roosevelt won another term in the White House in 1936, with over 27 million votes, because victims of the Depression were grateful for what he had done to help them or decided he should be given a chance to finish the work he had started.

ACTIVITY 11.17

Study the profiles of the three radical opponents of the New Deal. Why do you think none of them in the end presented a serious challenge to Roosevelt as president?

253

Source 11O: Huey Long (1893–1935) served as state governor and then senator for Louisiana. He was a Democrat who initially supported the New Deal but called for more radical action from 1934. His 'Share the Wealth' campaign called for higher taxation of the rich to fund welfare reforms. Long was a persuasive speaker and his movement was popular, attracting 8 million supporters. FDR's supporters feared him as a possible presidential candidate in the 1936 election but he was assassinated in September 1935.

Source 11P: Dr Francis Townsend (1867–1960), pictured circa 1930, was a retired doctor who campaigned for government pensions of $200 a month for all citizens aged over 60. Recipients would be obliged to spend the money, in order to stimulate the economy. The plan would also free up jobs for younger workers. Townsend secured 20 million signatures on a petition to Congress promoting his ideas.

Source 11Q: Father Charles Coughlin (1891–1979). Like Long, he turned against the New Deal after initially supporting it. The 'radio priest' used his broadcasts to call for increased workers' rights and state control of industry. He was particularly popular in the industrial North and Mid-West and had an audience of 30 million by 1936. He lost influence after he started expressing admiration of European fascism.

Opposition from the Supreme Court

The Supreme Court consists of nine senior judges whose role is to act as a check on the president and Congress. They monitor laws to ensure that they are in line with the rules laid down in the US Constitution. Roosevelt faced difficulties with the Supreme Court because most of its members had been appointed by earlier Republican administrations. Once installed in office, they had the right to serve for life.

In two key legal cases, the Supreme Court ruled that Roosevelt had exceeded his powers in creating New Deal agencies. One of these was the 1935 'Sick Chickens Case'. The Schechter poultry firm was prosecuted under the National Industrial Recovery Act for selling chickens unfit for human consumption. The company appealed to the Supreme Court, which decided that the NIRA was unconstitutional because the federal government did not have powers to regulate businesses. In the 1936 *US* v *Butler Case* the Supreme Court ruled against the Agricultural Adjustment Act. The Court said that it was the responsibility of individual state governments, not the federal government, to support farmers.

Roosevelt's reaction

Frustrated, Roosevelt declared in 1937 that he would impose a retirement age of 70 on Supreme Court justices. He intended to appoint younger judges who would support his policies. This plan to 'pack' the Court seemed high-handed and unconstitutional. Roosevelt lost some public support and met opposition in Congress.

Although he did not get his way, some judges took voluntary retirement and their successors were more cautious in their attitude towards New Deal measures. They accepted both the National Labour Relations Act and the Social Security Act.

Source 11R: A cartoon from 14 February 1937, on the subject of Roosevelt's plan to pack the Supreme Court. The figure on the left is Uncle Sam, symbol of the US.

ACTIVITY 11.18

What view of Roosevelt do you think the cartoon in Source 11R is taking?

TOP TIP

Historians are divided about the success of the New Deal. It is important that you consider some of the arguments that have been put forward on both sides. Then you should make your own assessment of what you have been studying.

Why did unemployment persist despite the New Deal?

The case for the New Deal

Some historians argue that the New Deal played a crucial role in lifting the US out of the Depression. According to this reading of events, Roosevelt's actions in his first hundred days saved the banking system from collapse. The New Deal halted the slide of businesses into bankruptcy, which had been a feature of the early 1930s.

The New Deal saved the most vulnerable members of society from starvation and homelessness, and gave jobs and hope to millions. It was much better than the negative, limited approach of Hoover and the Republicans.

Outstanding successes of the New Deal era included the regeneration of the Tennessee Valley, the major building projects of the Public Works Administration and the employment created by the Works Progress Administration. The Second New Deal enhanced workers' rights and created a rudimentary welfare state with the Social Security Act.

Roosevelt saved the US from the extremes of fascism and communism, which ruined the lives of millions in equally desperate countries across the Atlantic. The US entered the Second World War in good shape, with its morale high.

The case against

The New Deal's critics point out that, although unemployment initially fell, it was not abolished. In 1937, concerned about government debt, Roosevelt cut public spending and there followed another slowdown in economic activity. Unemployment, which had remained stubbornly high at 7.7 million, rose to almost 11 million in 1938. The government then resumed spending on public works schemes and unemployment began to fall back.

According to this reading, it was preparing for the Second World War, not the New Deal, that was the most important cause of sustained economic recovery.

The position of certain groups in society improved only to a limited extent. Women benefited less than men since most of the jobs created by the New Deal were in traditionally male occupations involving manual labour. They continued to be paid on average less than men. Some states evaded their responsibility to provide welfare payments to women, for example by disqualifying those with children born outside marriage. Nor did black Americans gain significantly from the New Deal. Roosevelt was too fearful of the adverse reaction of southern whites in his party to tackle the continued segregation of black people.

Some critics argue that Roosevelt actually delayed economic recovery by over-regulating industry and allowing the growth of powerful trade unions. Free-market capitalism, left to its own devices, would have ended the slump. Instead. Roosevelt was the creator of an over-powerful government, which discouraged people from relying on their own efforts and initiative.

TOP TIP

Although you can check the facts, it is virtually impossible finally to prove or disprove the interpretations of them. We cannot know how much better or worse conditions would have been with alternative policies. Our assessment of the New Deal depends to some extent on the choice of a baseline figure for measuring economic performance. Are we comparing the situation in 1939 with that in 1933, at the lowest point of the Depression, or with statistics from 1928, before the Wall Street Crash?

Review your learning

Having gone through this chapter, and undertaken its tests and activities, you should be able to assess, understand and explain the following:

*   Why the 1920s saw an economic boom in the US, and how far the benefits of this prosperity were felt across American society.
*   How American society changed in the 1920s, and whether society was becoming more open and tolerant in this period.
*   The causes of the Wall Street Crash, and the impact of the crash on the US economy and society from 1929.
*   The response of Franklin Roosevelt to the Great Depression as president, and why his policies attracted opposition as well as support.
*   How far Roosevelt's New Deal was successful in dealing with the problems of the US economy.

If not, go back to the section in question and revise!

The Big Challenge

Use Table 11.3 below and the evidence in this chapter to answer the following question: Overall, do you consider the New Deal to have been at best only a partial success?

Table 11.3: Some indicators of US economic performance, 1928–1939.

	1928	1933	1939
Gross National Product ($ billion)	100	55	85
Value of consumer goods purchased ($ billion)	80	45	65
Unemployment (millions)	2.0	12.8	9.4

Summary points

*   The US experienced a remarkable economic boom in the 1920s, but not all industries, and not all American people, gained from it.
*   Inter-war US was a divided society, with great extremes of wealth and conflicts over race, culture and politics.

*   The shaky foundations of the boom were exposed by the Wall Street Crash of 1929 and the following Depression, which lasted into the mid-1930s.
*   Franklin Roosevelt's New Deal tackled a number of the US's economic and social problems without bringing about complete recovery from the Depression.

Exam-style questions

Questions in the style of Paper 1

1   The decade after the First World War in the US is sometimes called the 'Roaring 20s'.

    a   What were the main features of the 'Roaring 20s'?

    b   Why was Prohibition introduced in the US?

    c   Do you agree that for most Americans, the 1920s was a time of increasing freedom and tolerance?

2   The Wall Street Crash of 1929 was followed by a prolonged economic depression in the US.

    a   What happened in the Wall Street Crash?

    b   Why was the Great Depression in the US so severe?

    c   'The main reason why Franklin Roosevelt won the 1932 presidential election was that president Hoover's policies had failed to end the Depression.' How far do you agree with this statement? Explain your answer.

Questions in the style of Paper 4 - IGCSE only

1   How significant was the introduction of mass production as a cause of the economic boom of the 1920s in the United States?

2   How important a part did the New Deal play in bringing the United States out of depression in the 1930s?

Chapter 12
Preparing for assessment

12.1 What skills are being tested and what you need to know

There are three sets of skills which you will develop during your course. These are called 'assessment objectives' (AOs):

AO1: an ability to recall, select, organise and deploy knowledge of the syllabus content.

AO2: an ability to construct historical explanations using an understanding of:

- cause and consequence, change and continuity, similarity and difference.
- the motives, emotions, intentions and beliefs of people in the past.

AO3: an ability to understand, interpret, evaluate and use a range of sources as evidence, in their historical context.

This section will show you how you can demonstrate these skills.

12.2 The structure of the assessment

Let's begin with the format of the assessment.

Cambridge IGCSE History: There are four parts to the assessment, of which you have to do **three**. Paper 1 and Paper 2 are compulsory, and for the third part your school will opt to do *either* the coursework *or* Paper 4. Make sure you know which option you are doing.

Cambridge O Level History: There are two parts to the assessment, Paper 1 and Paper 2. Both of the papers are compulsory.

The following table shows the content of the components.

Syllabus	Assessment	Core Content	Depth Study
IGCSE and O Level	Paper 1	Yes	Yes
IGCSE and O Level	Paper 2	Yes	No
IGCSE	Coursework	No	Yes
IGCSE	Paper 4	No	Yes

Paper 1

In Paper 1 you need to answer three questions, each of which has three parts. One of these questions is on the depth study you've learned about while the other two are on core content.

TOP TIP

When sitting an assessment, it is helpful to look at the time allocated and work out how long to spend on each question. Remember that as well as writing the answer, you will also need time to read the questions carefully, choose those you will answer, and plan your answers. It is a good idea to practise this using past papers.

Paper 2

Paper 2 is unique because it is mainly based on AO3, which covers source skills. This makes it different to the other papers for two reasons:

1. You are given sources and questions which test your ability to analyse texts and pictures, as well as using your own knowledge.

2. The format of the exam paper can change, unlike the other papers. The number of sources and the marks for each question are not fixed. You'll need to think carefully about how long to spend preparing the sources and how much time you need to write each answer.

Paper 3 (Coursework) - IGCSE only

If you are taking this route, you will be expected to produce one piece of extended writing based on a depth study. It carries 40 marks – equivalent to 27% of the IGCSE qualification. Coursework is marked by your teacher and externally moderated by Cambridge. The coursework assignment can be based on one of the Cambridge depth studies or, if your school or college chooses and gets the approval of Cambridge, on a depth study devised by your own teachers.

Your completed coursework assignment must be a maximum of 2,000 words long and it should centre on the assessment of the significance of one aspect of your chosen depth study. Possible examples could be:

- Assess the significance of the use of terror in Nazi Germany.
- Assess the significance of Trotsky for the Bolsheviks in the period 1917 to 1924.

Although your teacher can give general guidance, coursework must be your own work, and you must acknowledge the source of any material you quote. Coursework tests AO1 – the ability to recall, select, organise and deploy factual knowledge. It also tests

AO2 – the ability to construct a supported explanation. In order to do really well, you must ensure that everything you write is clearly focused on the question. You need to know the topic well, so that you support your argument and conclusion about significance with accurate, relevant information.

Paper 4 (Written paper – Alternative to Coursework) - IGCSE only

This paper is one hour long and carries the same marks as Paper 3. It consists solely of essay questions on the depth studies.

As in Paper 1, each depth study will have a choice of two questions, of which you should answer one.

12.3 Tackling short answer and extended response questions

In Paper 1, all questions are in the form of structured essays, divided into three parts: **a**, **b** and **c**. Part **a** tests your ability to recall factual information, part **b** tests your ability to explain this information, and part **c** tests your ability to explain both sides of an argument and reach a supported judgement.

Look at the sample answer (written by the author) to a Paper 1-type question which follows. It is the kind of question that might be asked in **Depth Study D: The US, 1919–1941.**

In the 1920s the US experienced an economic boom.

a Describe the main economic policies of the Republican governments in the 1920s. [4]

b Why was Henry Ford successful as a businessman? [6]

c 'Almost all Americans enjoyed a rising standard of living in the 1920s.' How far do you agree with this statement? Explain your answer. [10]

a The Republican governments believed in *laissez-faire*, which meant leaving businesses alone to make profits. They helped firms by cutting taxes, which meant that people had more money to spend on the goods that they made. Businesses also had less money taken away from them in taxes.

A second policy was the use of tariffs (taxes on imported goods), which made American goods cheaper to buy than foreign products. This

protected American industries and helped them to grow. An example was the 1922 Fordney-McCumber tariff.

Guidance: This part (a) question is targeted at AO1. You should state the relevant points and any supporting detail.

Teacher comment: This is a good answer. It makes two major points and develops them, without becoming overly long – for example it does not just state that taxes were cut, but explains why this was important.

b Henry Ford made a fortune out of motor car manufacturing. The most important reason why he was successful was his introduction of the assembly line method, which made possible mass production. This involved the body of the car being passed on a conveyor belt to different workers, who each carried out a particular task such as attaching the doors or wheels. The importance of this was that it speeded up the work and therefore cut the costs of production. Another reason for Ford's success was the standardisation of parts. His factories made cars to a standard specification. For example, he famously said that his customers could have any colour car they liked as long as it was black. Again this kept the costs down. Ford believed that it was better to sell a large number of cars cheaply than a smaller number of more expensive cars. His best known car, the Model T Ford, became affordable to ordinary Americans as its price fell from almost $1,000 to under $300 between 1908 and 1927.

Guidance: This part (b) question is aimed at both AO1 and AO2. Here you should show an understanding of relevant concepts such as cause and consequence, change and continuity or similarity and difference. The motives, emotions, intentions and beliefs of people in the past may be relevant to the answer. In order to reach the highest level for this answer, TWO reasons must be explained.

Teacher comment: This answer identifies two reasons for Ford's success – assembly line production and standardisation – and explains why they were important. Ford's beliefs about what made for successful business practice are noted. There is an appropriate level of detail.

c The US was a very unequal society in which opportunities to make money varied greatly across the country. The people who benefited most were those who owned or worked in newer industries such as car manufacture, electricity generation or the new department stores which sold all kinds of consumer goods. The successful industries were linked together. For example as businesses expanded, they needed larger office premises. This meant that there were many job opportunities for those who worked in the construction industry, building the new skyscrapers in the business districts of New York. These workers, and those employed in factories which were making consumer goods which people wanted to buy, found that their wages increased and so they in turn could buy goods and perhaps shares on the stock exchange.

On the other hand people who worked in older industries such as coal and textiles, which were facing competition and losing customers in the 1920s, found that their standard of living declined. Their wages were cut as their employers made losses, and some lost their jobs. New immigrants, who usually had to take the poorest paid jobs, were affected particularly badly. Small farmers and farm workers also suffered, as agriculture was experiencing a slump long before the Wall Street Crash of 1929. Banks took over the farms of those who could not pay their mortgages, forcing them to look for work elsewhere. The most vulnerable were the share-croppers in the South, many of whom were black. They rented land and paid their landlords a proportion of what they produced, so when prices of farm produce fell they were unable to pay.

On balance it is not true to argue that almost all Americans were better off in the 1920s. Nearly half the population lived in the countryside, where the conditions were worst; for example, 90% of farms were still not connected to the electricity grid in 1930. However, until the Wall Street Crash, which wiped out fortunes on a devastating scale, life was good for many millions of people.

Guidance: This part (c) question is targeting AO1 and AO2. It requires you to consider the arguments for and against an idea, and you must examine both sides. If you focus on only one side you cannot achieve highly, even if you have provided a high level of accurate supporting detail. For a good answer, you must offer some evaluation – on balance, to what extent do you believe that the statement is correct?

Teacher comment: This is a good answer because it gives equal weight to both sides of the argument and provides a developed, fully supported explanation. The closing paragraph reaches a conclusion, explaining how far the student agrees with the statement in the question.

12.4 Tackling source-based questions

Paper 2 requires you to answer six questions on one topic from the core content. These questions require you to use source material that is provided.

Reading and preparing the sources

Under pressure of time it can be difficult to spot everything you need to in the sources. This is why you should try to read them twice – the second time round you'll notice things that you didn't see straight away. You are allowed to use highlighters to annotate the exam paper, but you can't use them on your answer script. This means you can highlight the key parts of a source if that helps you pick out the best information.

Another good tip is to label the sources with the question number it relates to. This way you think about the exact skills you need to tackle the source; for example, one question might ask what the message of Source 12C is. Write 'message' next to the source and you'll be on the right track. This also stops you making a classic exam error – writing about the wrong source in relation to a question.

Reading and answering the questions

Double-check that you're writing about the correct source (or sources) before beginning each question. Also make sure you focus on the key words in the question. In particular watch out for the command 'Use the sources and your own knowledge' – this means you have to add information which isn't given in the exam paper. Equally, do not add your own knowledge in an answer that *doesn't* require it. Don't waste time!

Three little letters to remember: **ATQ. A**nswer **T**he **Q**uestion! You must never just describe the sources or write vague answers. You have to provide an answer that is exactly on what you were asked. If the question is about the message, say 'the message of the source is …' If the question asks why the source was published, say 'this source was published because …'

Different styles of questions

When studying History, there are a variety of questions that you may come across. These can include:

- What is the message of a source?
- How far does one source support another source?
- Does one source prove that another source is lying?
- Why was this source produced when it was?
- How far do all the sources support a particular argument?

We can group these questions into the following types.

Interpretation

This means understanding what the source is saying. This is usually tested by questions which ask you about the message of the source. What is the author trying to say? Think about who the author is and when the source was produced. Then think about who the source is aimed at. If you think about these issues then the meaning of the source will become much clearer.

Purpose

Some questions will ask why a source was produced. Sources don't just appear by themselves – someone has to make them. Therefore think about who made the source and why? Use the details given to you before the source: for example, it should have information such as the author, date of the source and maybe events that had just taken place. These are all good pointers to consider in your answer. What you need to arrive at is a conclusion about what the author intended when they made the source. What was their purpose? What were they trying to achieve?

Comparison

Questions that focus on two sources are usually comparison questions. This means you need to look for similarities *and* differences. A good way to answer this question is to write two paragraphs; one that looks at the ways in which the sources agree, and one that looks at the ways in which they disagree. Then it's a simple case of ATQ – answer the question – to round it off.

Watch out for the wording of the question, for example:

- How far do these sources disagree?

This sounds like you just have to show their disagreement, but the wording at the start is 'how far'. This means you need to consider their similarity too. The same applies if

the question asks about how far they agree – look at both agree and disagree to reach your answer.

Note that you should try to compare the message or purpose of the sources, not just factual details.

Evaluation

Some questions will require you to evaluate a source. There are two main types of source evaluation questions:

- How useful is the source?
- How reliable is the source?

A few basic tips apply here. It is never a good idea to say that a source isn't useful at all. This is because all sources are useful for something, it's a question of what they can be used for. Equally, you won't be given a source that is flawless. Carefully consider the question then ask yourself what aspects of the source help you to answer it. Then think about limitations of the source. What is not ideal about the source? What else would you want to have a fuller knowledge of the issue in the question?

Questions about reliability can often prompt students to write simplistic and incorrect statements. For example: 'this is a primary source so it is reliable because they were there at the time' or 'it is a secondary source so it is not reliable because they weren't alive when it happened'. Avoid these at all costs. If a primary source is written by a liar and a secondary source is written by a world-class historian, it changes our view of the reliability. Instead, evaluate the source based on its merits. In what ways might the author be credible? Is there any reason to doubt the quality of information they present? Think about these issues and you are on the right track.

Finally, the trickiest questions require you to work out what you have to evaluate. You might be asked 'How far does source X prove that source Y is wrong?' This is a 'how far' question so that should always prompt you to think about both sides. In some aspects, source X will challenge or contradict source Y. However, it should also support it. You need to decide if, on balance, there is enough contrast to prove or disprove the issue in the question.

Testing a hypothesis

Questions that ask you to judge how far sources support a particular argument are usually found at the end of the paper and require the longest responses. You need to use all the sources to test a particular argument. A good way to prepare this is to write out a simple table like this:

262

Agree	Disagree

Go through all the sources and decide, based on the issue in the question, if they agree or disagree. You might end up with something like this:

Agree	Disagree
B	A
D	C
E	F
G	H
I	

Once you have identified which sources support and which sources challenge the hypothesis, you can start writing. The most important thing is to ensure that you explain how each source either supports or challenges the hypothesis. Make this absolutely clear: for example, you could start sentences with 'Source 12A supports the statement *because…*'. This will lead to explanation rather than description of the source.

There are two ways that you could structure your answer:

- either write about each source in turn as it appears on the paper, making sure you make a clear judgment for each one

- or write about the sources that support the hypothesis first and then the sources that disagree with it. This approach might help you to address the 'how far' element in the conclusion

You must ensure that you address each source separately and you must *explain* how each source supports or disagrees with the hypothesis.

What types of sources can you get?

There are two basic types of sources: textual and visual.

Textual sources

These are written sources, for example from a modern history book, a diary, a speech, a letter or an official document. Each type of source is slightly different so think about why. One obvious reason is that they are written for a different audience, so their purpose will be different. A diary is for personal reflection, a letter is to another person, an official document might just be for others in the government, and a speech is for a very wide audience. Think about these issues when preparing your sources.

Visual sources

The most common type is a political cartoon but photographs and posters can be used too. Cartoonists use a variety of techniques: symbolism, stereotype, humour and sign-posting. Sign-posting means inserting text to help the reader understand the meaning. Always, *always* pay attention to the text in a cartoon – it's there for a reason. Students often find photographs very hard, especially as they believe that the camera doesn't lie. The thing to consider here is that the photographer has chosen to take a picture at a specific moment, looking at a particular thing. These are both decisions that might be because they want to convey a message. This means that photographs can be biased, and perhaps misleading. The camera may not lie, but the photographer can mislead. Be on your guard.

Finally, some things to keep in mind. Too often students spend time talking about primary and secondary sources when it isn't needed. They also make pointless assumptions like 'secondary sources are unreliable because the author wasn't there at the time'. If this was true we couldn't write meaningful history. Equally, saying that a 'primary source is reliable because it was produced at the time' is also flawed. What if the author was a pathological liar? It wouldn't matter if they were present or not – they would still be unreliable. Don't waste time on these issues – deal with each source on its merits. There is no such thing as a perfect source, as all sources are limited in some way. However, all sources are useful for something – it just depends what for. Evaluate them by looking at all the positives and all the negatives, and never make snap judgements. Remember what they say about books and their covers…

ACTIVITY 12.1

Answer these three questions and then look at the advice below to see if you're on the right track.

1. Are you surprised by Source 12A? Explain your answer.
2. What is the message of the cartoon in Source 12B?
3. Why was the speech in Source 12C given in 1946?

Source 12A: The England football team giving the Hitler salute before a match in Berlin in 1938.

The Other Ascent Into The Unknown

Source 12B: A Washington Post cartoon from 1965 about increasing American involvement in Vietnam. The title is 'the other ascent into the unknown'.

Guidance

Source 12A

With 'surprise' questions, you need to identify what is unusual about the source and then try to find an explanation. In this case it's quite easy: we wouldn't expect the English football team to be giving a Hitler salute. This seems totally opposite to what British people believed and of course Hitler was the enemy in the Second World War. This makes it very surprising. However, if we know the context then we can explain

From Stettin in the Baltic to Trieste in the Adriatic, an iron curtain has descended across the Continent. Behind that line lie all the capitals of the ancient states of Central and Eastern Europe. Warsaw, Berlin, Prague, Vienna, Budapest, Belgrade, Bucharest and Sofia, all these famous cities and the populations around them lie in what I must call the Soviet sphere, and all are subject in one form or another, not only to Soviet influence but to a very high and, in many cases, increasing measure of control from Moscow.

Source 12C: A speech by Winston Churchill given on 5 March, 1946 in Fulton, Missouri (US). President Truman was in the audience when the speech was given.

why this isn't too surprising. First, it's in Berlin so the team would be under pressure to show respect for their hosts. Second, it was in 1938 before the war began and the British government was still pursuing a policy of appeasement. If the official government policy was to work with Hitler to achieve peace then we can understand why the English football team made this salute. If they hadn't it might have caused a breakdown in relations, which the British Prime Minister, Neville Chamberlain, very much wanted to avoid.

Source 12B

This cartoon is full of symbolism. The soldier represents all American servicemen, and the 'ascent into the unknown' means he has no idea what lies ahead. This is made all the more difficult by the smoke up the staircase (representing Vietnam), which makes it hard to see where the danger lies. The cartoon was drawn by an American cartoonist in 1965 just a year after president Johnson got Congress to agree to send ground troops into Vietnam after the Gulf of Tonkin incident. Clearly the cartoonist feels this is unwise and will possibly lead to disaster.

Source 12C

This speech was given in the US in 1946 by Winston Churchill. Remember, Churchill wasn't prime minister at this time as he lost the election of 1945. The speech tells us about his fear of the 'increasing measure of control from Moscow' in Eastern Europe. He calls this the 'iron curtain'. His audience is American and includes president Truman, so he is trying to influence American policy in the hope that they might take action against Stalin. By this point Stalin had control of most of Eastern Europe and even the countries outside the 'Soviet sphere' such as Czechoslovakia were under threat. Therefore, this speech was made because relations had broken down since Yalta and Potsdam and Churchill wanted the US to make a stand against the USSR to prevent the permanent loss of 'the capitals of the ancient states' to the outside world.

TOP TIP

Do quote from the sources, but make your quotations short. Anything from one to six words is fine. Avoid copying out whole chunks of the source. Focus on strong language and key evidence. Look at the way quotations are used in the guidance on Source 12C and follow this style.

12.5 Tackling essay questions

This section is relevant to IGCSE students only.

TOP TIP

Before starting to write your essay make a brief plan. Your essay needs to demonstrate your ability to select relevant evidence, and to produce a coherent argument, not just to recall facts.

In Paper 4, you will only be asked essay questions about the depth studies, and the guidance that follows applies specifically to Paper 4. These essay questions require you to assess the importance or significance of a historical event.

Here is a sample answer (written by the author) to the following question, which is similar to those which occur in **Depth Study A: The First World War, 1914–1918.**

How important was the US's entry into the First World War in bringing about the defeat of Germany? Explain your answer. [40]

The United States made an important contribution to allied victory in the First World War for several reasons. After joining the war in April 1917 it was able to provide Britain and France with additional manpower and economic resources. It entered the war when the Allies were facing major challenges and morale was low. American involvement provided psychological as well as material support.

The most obvious contribution made by US was the arrival of large numbers of new troops. The US rapidly expanded its army until by the end of the war it had over 2 million troops in France. The US entered the war at a critical time for the Allies, when there was reason to believe that Germany had a chance of winning. Thousands of tons of merchant shipping had been sunk by German U-boats in the Atlantic. Russia dropped out of the war after the Bolshevik Revolution and in March 1918 signed the Treaty of Brest-Litovsk with Germany. This freed up tens of thousands of German troops, who were transferred to take part in the Ludendorff offensive on the Western Front, where they met with strong initial success. The arrival of large numbers of American troops therefore came just at the right moment, when Britain and France were badly in need of reinforcements.

The US forces, under General John Pershing, made a crucial contribution to victory in the 'Hundred Days' campaign in the summer and autumn of 1918. In September they made a decisive assault in the Meuse-Argonne region, cutting off important German supply routes. One of the reasons why the German leaders asked for peace talks was that they knew that increasing numbers of Americans would continue to arrive, making it pointless to continue fighting.

The US also had huge industrial strength which could be brought to bear. It produced three times as much steel as Germany and Austria-Hungary combined. The US had a population of 90 million and large amounts of natural resources, making it a formidable opponent in a war which had become a slogging match between rival economies. It had provided Britain and France with loans before April 1917 and this aid was continued.

However, the US contribution should not be exaggerated. The US was slow to mobilise its manpower and its great numbers did not begin to make a decisive difference until the summer of 1918. Full US involvement was slowed down by disputes between Pershing and his French and British counterparts. He insisted on the Americans fighting as an 'associated power', largely independent of the allied armies.

Other factors were important in bringing about allied victory. The British and French had significantly improved their fighting methods by 1918. They no longer launched costly frontal attacks, after prolonged artillery bombardments which failed to disrupt the enemy defences. They had learned more flexible tactics and become more

265

accurate in directing artillery fire, using the 'creeping barrage' to cover infantry assaults. US troops were not battle-hardened as the British and French were, and they had to learn on the job. They also used large amounts of allied equipment, including French tanks and artillery.

It is also important to note that Germany was more exhausted than Britain and France by mid-1918. It was struggling to replace lost manpower and was not in a position to stage another large-scale assault after the Ludendorff offensive fizzled out. The British naval blockade was starving Germany of food and vital raw materials, imposing an unbearable strain on its economy.

Overall the US made a vital contribution to the outcome of the war. Although Britain and France successfully repelled the Ludendorff offensive, there is a question mark as to whether, on their own, they could have launched a new campaign to dislodge the Germans from the ground they already held. The arrival of US forces was certainly not the only reason for the victory but it was one of the most important, because it provided the

Allies with vital support and boosted their morale at a critical stage.

Guidance: Excellent answers should demonstrate the effective deployment of a range of skills:

- *Accurate, relevant knowledge used to support the answer and the conclusion.*
- *A good understanding of the key features that are relevant to the question.*
- *A well-argued and supported conclusion.*
- *Writing which is precise and to the point, as part of an answer which is well structured, balanced and focused.*

Teacher comment: This is an excellent answer. There is a clear structure, with an introduction which gets straight to the core of the argument, showing that the student has a clear sense of direction. A range of relevant and accurate contextual knowledge is used to support the argument. The role of the US is addressed fully but this is balanced by discussion of other factors. Finally, there is a well-reasoned conclusion which draws the argument together in a satisfying way.

Glossary

25-Point Programme: set out Hitler's early ideas. It opposed the Versailles Treaty. Only pure Germans could be German citizens; Jews could not be. It also opposed large-scale capitalism.

Abdicate (as head of state): when a king or emperor steps down or gives up the throne.

Aktion T-4: a euthanasia programme. It started at the beginning of the war and ran officially until August 1941. It involved the killing of mentally handicapped, mentally ill and terminally ill people by doctors administering lethal injections; 70,000 died.

Agency: an organisation which acts on behalf of others. Within the League different agencies focused on specific issues under the authority of the Council.

Alliance: a collection of two or more countries that agree to support the other/s if they are attacked by another country.

Amnesty: a blanket official pardon.

Anarchists: people who believe in the abolition of government.

Anarchy: a situation where no one is in control

Annihilation: complete destruction.

Appeasement: pacifying, seeking to calm down an angry opponent by giving in to some or all of their demands.

Arbitration: a method of resolving a dispute peacefully using an independent person or authority that is neutral who will listen to all the evidence like a judge and then issue a ruling.

Armistice: an end of fighting as a prelude to peace negotiations.

Attrition: A strategy where both evenly balanced sides try to wear each other down gradually, hoping that the toll on the enemy, especially in terms of casualties, will be heavier than the cost to themselves. Victory comes from exhausting the opponent rather than capturing their territory.

Autarky: complete economic self-sufficiency. A state that is autarkic has no need of imports or exports and produces everything it needs by itself. This is virtually impossible in a modern economic setting

Autocratic state: one ruled by an autocrat, someone who cannot be challenged and whose power is not limited.

Autonomy: the independence of an individual, or a group or a region to make decisions for itself without always asking permission e.g. from a central government.

Ayatollahs: are respected and influential Islamic jurists, experts on Islamic theology, philosophy and law, acting as religious judges.

Ba'ath Party: was founded in 1947 in Syria. It aimed to unite Arabs in one single state and remove western influence.

Bible belt: approximately the south-east quarter of the USA, so called because of the large number of socially-conservative evangelical Christians living there.

Blockade: a form of economic warfare where one country attempts to prevent goods being imported to its rival. The Royal Navy's blockade in the Great War also ensured that German ships could not get out of port.

Brezhnev Doctrine: this stated that Moscow had the right to interfere with military force if any country in Eastern Europe attempted to abandon communism.

Buffer zone: a group of countries that surround a major state and act as a protective barrier. The countries of Eastern Europe that shared a border with the USSR were taken over by Stalin to create a buffer zone against the West.

Bushel: a dry measure of 8 gallons, roughly equivalent to 36 litres.

Capitalism: an economic and social system in which property is privately owned, the role of the state is small and people enjoy freedom of expression, of religion and have a choice of political party to elect as the government.

Capitalists: practitioners of capitalism, in which wealth and the means of producing and distributing goods are privately owned and used for profit. Typically bankers, traders and industrialists.

Cavalry: soldiers who fought mounted on horses.

Central Powers: a term used to refer to the German and Austro-Hungarian empires at the beginning of the First World War. The Ottoman Empire joined the Central Powers later in 1914 and in 1915, the Kingdom of Bulgaria also did so.

Cheka: the Bolsheviks' political police.

CIA: Central Intelligence Agency. It was founded in 1947 by the National Security Act. Its mission statement was to collect, evaluate and share intelligence relating to national security.

Civil war: a war in *one* country between two or more sides from within that country.

Coalition government: a government made up of several different parties.

Collective bargaining: negotiations between trade unions and employers on wages and conditions of work.

Comintern: a Soviet-led organisation designed to promote communist ideology in countries outside the Soviet Union.

Commission: a kind of committee, a small group of officials who together investigate an issue or dispute and then produces a report with conclusions.

Commune: a village in which people share property, resources and labour.

Communism: an economic and social system in which property and economic activity are controlled by the state. In communist countries, people have few rights and freedoms: religion banned and the media is censored. Everyone works for the state.

Communists: believers in **communism**.

Concentration camp: prisons for political opponents up to 1939 and in the Second World War Jews were sent to them as well. The idea was that opponents would be 'purified' by hard labour, so the slogan 'Arbeit Macht Frei' ('work sets [you] free') was written above the gates.

Conference of Ambassadors: based in Paris, this group was a diplomatic body representing the Great Powers, formed at the Paris Peace Conference in order to supervise the completion of issues not resolved by the treaties. It was this body that had sent Tellini to Greece to clarify the border between Greece and Albania.

Congress: the USA's elected law-making body, which helps to govern the country. It consists of two houses: the Senate and the House of Representatives.

Conscription: compulsory military service.

Constitution: the main set of laws by which a country is governed. It sets out the powers of the government and the rights and freedoms of the individual.

Containment: keeping the USSR within certain boundaries and borders, preventing them from advancing their power and influence.

Convention: an agreement that does not have the force of law so its implementation depends on 'trust'.

Corps: a large military formation of 40–50,000 men.

Coup or Putsch: an attempt by a group to take political power through force, including violence, not by winning

an election. It puts political power into the hands of those with the power of armaments not arguments.

Creeping barrages: a line of artillery fire advancing ahead of attacking infantry, usually at a rate of 50 metres per minute.

Defect: when a person changes allegiance and physically moves across a political divide from one state to the other, they are said to have defected.

Demilitarisation: an area of land in which no soldiers and no weapons are permitted.

Democracies: societies where the government has been elected by voters in free and fair elections. Liberal democracies feature freedom of speech, freedom of religion, freedom of the press and the right to a fair trial.

Desertion: when soldiers leave their post, refuse to obey their officers and walk away from the front.

Deterrent: an action that puts off or deters a country from being aggressive towards others.

Dictatorship: one person governs a country without holding elections, and without being restrained by a parliament, keeping themself in power using the army and police.

Diktat: a treaty or other agreement which has not been negotiated but imposed, presented to the defeated without any discussions.

Disarmament: the process of destroying of some or all weapons and armed forces that could be used in fighting a war.

Dissolved: parliament is ended; elected officials are sent away.

Dolchstoss: a German word meaning 'stab in the back'.

Domino Theory: the idea that if one country fell to **communism**, so would its neighbours and their neighbours in turn – falling like a line of dominoes. The theory was first outlined by Eisenhower in 1954 at a press briefing on Vietnam. The exact phrase he used was the 'falling domino principle'.

Dreadnought: named after HMS *Dreadnought* (a British battleship launched in 1906), was a type of battleship that was so fast, and so heavily armed and armoured that no other type of battleship could match it.

Embargo: a partial or complete end to trade with a country. It is an example of a **trade sanction**.

Empire: an area of territory usually made up of more than one country, ruled by a single monarch or government.

Epidemic: an infectious disease that has spread over a wide area affecting thousands of people.

Eradicate: to abolish or get rid of.

Ex-Comm: 'the Executive Committee of the National Security Council'. It included the usual NSC people but Kennedy also invited significant non-military figures: his brother Robert Kennedy (the Attorney-General); Theodore Sorensen (White House Counsel); Truman's Secretary of State Dean Acheson; and former ambassador to the USSR Tommy Thompson who knew Khrushchev personally.

Exile: a person who has been forced out of or escaped their own country; also the process of driving out or fleeing; also the state of being in a foreign country against your will.

Exploitation: a process in which a person or group is treated unfairly at work; it may be the result of, e.g. their age or ethnicity making them weak in negotiations, leading to overwork and underpayment.

Federal: a 'federation' is a group of states; in the Federal Republic of Germany a collection of what had historically been independent German-speaking countries had a central government which sat in Bonn. In the USA the federal government is the central government, based in Washing DC, which deals with national issues such as taxation, defence and foreign policy. Each state has its own government, responsible for local matters such as education.

Five-Year Plans: the basis for communist economies. These involved the government deciding what was needed by the population and then setting targets for production. There was no private business and little incentive to create new products.

Gangrene: a medical condition caused by loss of blood supply, especially to parts of the body farthest from the heart (e.g. toes), which leads the flesh there to die.

Geneva Agreements 1954: the main points set out in the peace treaty on Indo-China.

Ghetto: an area in which a specific ethnic group is forced by law or informal threat of violence to live.

Great Powers: countries with considerable military, diplomatic and economic power and influence.

Gross National Product: the total value of all the goods and services produced by a country.

Guerrilla: 'little war' in Spanish. A guerrilla war is on in which small groups use raids, assassinations and sabotage against larger armies. Guerrilla fighters are hard for their enemies to identify; the Vietcong would use children and old people to pass messages and hide weapons. Fidel Castro and Che Guevara were also expert guerrilla fighters.

Gulf Cooperation Council (GCC): founded in 1981, and consists of six Arab states that surround the Gulf. These states had loaned substantial sums to Saddam to fight Iran.

Haemophilia: a hereditary disorder that causes bleeding and is potentially fatal.

Hobos: homeless, unemployed people travelling in search of work.

Humanitarian: taking action to promote the welfare of people.

Hyperinflation: when prices go up a lot, quickly.

Immortal: undying.

Import tariffs: taxes on goods imported into a country.

Inflation: when prices go up.

Intertribal: an activity that is carried out between tribes of people rather than different countries.

Iranian Revolutionary Guard: the Iranian Revolutionary Guards Corps ('Pasdaran' in Farsi) was founded in 1979 to protect the Islamic revolution. It is separate from the regular army so there was often tension between the two, not least because the IRGC were usually paid more and had preferential treatment. They are considered to be Iran's elite troops.

Ku Klux Klan: a white supremacist organisation founded in the southern states of the USA following its Civil-War defeat. Its aim is to ensure continued white power in part by making black people too frightened to participate in elections, strikes or demonstrations. It has also been hostile to Catholics, Jews, immigrants, communists and anarchists.

Kulak: prosperous peasant.

Kurds: mainly based in northern Iraq, are an ethnic, not a religious grouping; most Kurds are Sunni, but they include also Shias, as well as Christians and other faiths and traditions. The Kurds are the largest ethnic group in the world who do not have their own state. As well as Iraq, there are large populations in Iran, Syria and Turkey.

Laissez-faire: French term meaning 'leave alone', a policy of minimising government involvement especially in the economy.

Latrines: field toilets.

League of Nations: a membership organisation for nations (1920-1946), intended to promote international discussion, solve international disputes and so avoid war.

Leprosy: a contagious disease that affects the skin and the nervous system.

Lynchings: executions carried out by mobs, not by judicial process.

Mandates: those countries that the Paris Peace Conference had asked great powers to administer.

Minority: a recognisable group of people whose religion, language, culture or ethnicity is different from that of most people (the majority) in a country or region.

Mobilisation: all the various actions that need to be taken to prepare for war, not just by the soldiers and sailors but by the civilians as well.

Muharram: the first month of the Islamic calendar. During this period Shia Muslims remember the death of the Imam Ali at the Battle of Kerbala. It is an emotional religious period of mourning that lasts for ten days.

Multi-ethnic: made up of multiple different ethnic groups.

Mustard gas: a chemical weapon that was used during the First World War. It causes large blisters on exposed skin and lungs.

Mutiny: when a group openly rebels against or overthrows a military authority.

Mutually Assured Destruction: concept put forward by the Secretary of Defence Robert McNamara in a speech in 1962. At this point the USA had 25,000 nuclear weapons and the USSR had about half as many. His logic was that neither side would risk war due to inevitable death and destruction for all.

Napalm: a petrol-based chemical weapon. It sticks to its target and burns at a very high temperature. It is often used to clear forests (preventing the enemy from having a place to hide) but when it comes into contact with skin it causes horrific burns.

Nationalise: when a government takes possession of a business, so that it is no longer owned by private individuals but by the state.

Naval supremacy: achieved when a country has when it owns more battleships than their competitors.

No man's land: the area of contested ground between two enemy trench systems or two countries' border controls.

Nuremberg Laws: two laws called the 'Reich Citizenship Law' and the 'Law for the Protection of German Blood and German Honour'. Jews could not be citizens of the Reich and were forbidden from marrying – or having sexual relations with – a German. Jews were defined as anyone with three or four Jewish grandparents, irrespective of whether or not they were religious.

Okhrana: a Tsarist Russian policital police force formed to combat anti-government activity.

OPEC: the Organization of the Petroleum Exporting Countries was founded in 1960 and is dominated by Middle Eastern countries. Its aim is to regulate the production and supply of oil among its members to keep the price of oil stable.

Pacifism: opposition to violence and war.

Pact: a treaty, a written agreement between two or more countries to act together in a particular way.

Patriotism: having strong support for your country.

Peace treaty: a document that sets out what should happen after a war is over. It is signed by the victors and the losers.

Plebiscite: a popular vote on a specific question. These aren't usually held on the ordinary business of government (that's generally left up to a country's government and parliament to decide), but on major decisions such as rewriting the constitution. Some people use the words 'plebiscite' and 'referendum' as though they mean the same thing, others make a distinction, but both are a vote by the entire electorate of a country or region on a single important question.

Proletariat: Marxist term for the working classes.

Proportional representation: a voting system in which the proportion of assembly seats won by parties closely resembles the proportion of the votes cast in the election.

Provisional: temporary.

Punitive: intended as a punishment.

Puppet state: a state lacking all independence, being run by the government of another country. It pretends to be a real country, but does what it's told.

Quota: a strict quantity of goods that may be exported or imported under government control.

Radio Free Europe: founded in 1950 to provide radio broadcasts for people living in communist countries in

270

Eastern Europe. It was funded by the US **Congress** and assisted by the **CIA**. It reached tens of millions of people and had broadcasts in 15 different languages.

Rearmament: increasing the numbers of weapons and personnel in the navy, army and air force.

Reichstag: Germany's parliament during the imperial (Kaiser), republic (Weimar) and Nazi periods.

Reparations: a kind of fine paid by an aggressor and intended to make up for loss or damage suffered by a victim.

Repression: the use of spies and harsh punishments to crush opposition.

Republic: a state with no monarchy.

Republican Guard: formed in 1969, they were the elite troops of the Iraqi state. They were separate from the army.

Revolutionary Command Council (RCC): the main decision-making and law-making body of the Iraqi government after 1968.

Right-wing: refers to a group or an individual that believes in an ordered society where discipline and tradition are valued. In general, right-wingers are nationalist and in favour of strong government. Right-wingers oppose socialism and **communism** because they think that social inequality is natural and desirable, and because both pose a threat to private property.

Roubles: Russia's currency.

Russification: forcing Russia's ethnic and religious minorities to speak Russian and adopt Russians ways.

Sanctions: penalties or punishments imposed by some official body such as a court of law. A typical sanction in international relations is a ban on trade, which has an impact on the country targeted. The intention is to affect the country's decision-makers so that they change their policies, such as ending a war.

Sarin gas: a nerve agent which, in sufficient quantities, leads to a painful death. Victims lose control of their body and suffer convulsions, then paralysis.

SAVAK: the Iranian government's Organisation for Intelligence and Security. They used torture to obtain information and were greatly feared. The exact number of agents is not known but could have been as many as 60,000.

Scuttle: deliberately sinking a ship. In wartime navies may do this so that the enemy cannot capture a vessel and begin to use it themselves.

Secular: 'non-religious'. A secular government is one not founded on religious principles, isn't committed to a religious programme and doesn't promote religion.

Self-determination: the ability of an ethnic or other group to make their own decisions and pursue an independent course rather than be part of a larger national unit in which their wishes are subsumed or overruled.

Serfdom: a condition similar to slavery in which peasants are owned by a landowner and have few rights.

Slavs: a number of ethnic groups of people in eastern and south-eastern Europe. They and their languages – e.g. Russian, Polish, Czech, Serbian – are related and many (though not all) of them belong historically to the Orthodox Christian churches.

'**Socialism with a human face**': this term was meant to show that socialist (in this context communist) policies could and should be more about human needs than power politics.

Sortie: an aeroplane, ship or unit of troops going out on a specific mission.

Soviet Bloc: the group of east-European states that were aligned with the Soviet Union, taking their political direction from Moscow. It is also sometimes called the Communist Bloc or the Eastern Bloc.

Soviet: Russian for 'council' or 'committee'; also used as short form of Soviet Union or USSR.

Stock market: the place where stocks and shares (ownership of companies) are bought and sold.

Strategy: a plan intended to achieve an overall, long-term military aim.

Successor states: new countries formed following the break-up of an older one, as in the case of Czechoslovakia, Austria and Hungary following the break up of Austria-Hungary.

Suez Crisis: the Suez Canal, which had been built by the French, was owned by the British and lay in Egypt. When the Egyptian leader Nasser had nationalised it, Britain and France secretly planned with Israel to attack Egypt. The following Suez Crisis distracted public attention from events in Hungary which were happening at the same time.

Sunni and **Shia:** the two main branches of Islam. This goes back to a disagreement about the leadership (caliphate) in the 7th century CE. The majority of Muslims across the world are Sunni but Iran is 95% Shia. Iraq has a slight majority of Shia but the **Ba'ath Party** leadership was largely Sunni.

Tactics: manoeuvring troops and weapons in battle in order to achieve a short-term military aim.

Tariff: a tax imposed by the government that has to be paid on imports or exports.

Theory of evolution: the idea, put forward by biologist Charles Darwin in the 19th century, that life on earth developed over millions of years and that humans and apes were descended from a common ancestor.

Trade unions: organisations campaigning for increased wages and improved working conditions for members.

Tsar: Russian word for emperor.

Tsarevich: the official title of the son of the tsar.

Ulama: Muslim clerics are known collectively as the ulama. In Iran they are highly influential.

UN Resolution: a decision taken by the United Nations which is meant to be binding on its members. Twelve resolutions were passed during the Gulf War, starting with Resolution 660 which condemned the attack.

UN Security Council: the main decision-making body of the UN for military and security matters. It has 15 members in total, 5 permanent and 10 temporary. The 5 permanent members are the USA, Britain, China, France, and the USSR (later Russia). At Stalin's insistence, each permanent member had the power of veto which meant they could block any measures.

Unanimous: a decision has the support of every national representative who is voting in a decision-making process, and so no one has opposed the proposal being voted on.

UNESCO: the United Nations Educational, Scientific and Cultural Organization.

United Nations: an international membership organisation for states founded in 1946 to promote development, peace and human rights, it replaced the **League of Nations**.

USSR: Union of Soviet Socialist Republics, also known as the Soviet Union.

Veto: the right to stop a bill from becoming law.

'**Viet Minh**' and '**Viet Cong**' are both names given by western politicians and journalists to Vietnamese communist forces. The former is a contraction of 'Vietnamese' and 'Ho Chi Minh', while the latter is a contraction of a Vietnamese expression for 'Vietnamese communists'.

Vietnamisation: meant reducing USA troop levels and getting the South Vietnamese Army (ARVN) to do more of the fighting.

Violation: an action that has broken a rule or agreement made between countries or individuals.

War of the Cities: five major attacks on urban areas during the Iran-Iraq War. The aim of destroying civilian morale failed to do its job, much as in the Second World War. Instead, it only intensified hatred for the enemy on both sides and may even have prolonged the war.

Warsaw Pact: a defence treaty signed in 1955 as a response to NATO. Also the defensive military **alliance** of Eastern European states which the treaty created. Hungary, Czechoslovakia, East Germany and Poland were all members. However, the main decisions were made by the USSR.

Watergate scandal: a group of men were arrested breaking into the Watergate hotel in Washington DC to steal documents from the Democrats' offices there during the USA presidential campaign. They were caught and when it was revealed that Nixon was involved he had to resign in disgrace.

Acknowledgements

The authors and publishers acknowledge the following sources of copyright material and are grateful for the permissions granted. While every effort has been made, it has not always been possible to identify the sources of all the material used, or to trace all copyright holders. If any omissions are brought to our notice, we will be happy to include the appropriate acknowledgements on reprinting.

Cover John Parrot/Stocktrek Images/Getty Images; **Introduction Part 1.** Nick Lee / Getty Images; **Source P1A.** Matt Cardy / Stringer / Getty Images; **Source P1B.** Mr Standfast / Alamy Stock Photo; **Source P1C.** SPUTNIK / Alamy Stock Photo; **Source P1D.** Daniel Simon / Gamma-Rapho / Getty Images; **Introduction Part 2 & Source P2D.** Universal History Archive / Getty Images; **Source P2E.** Crew of 2 Gun, Royal Marine Artillery loading 'Granny', a 15 inch Howitzer (heavy artillery gun), near the Menin Road, in the Ypres sector, 5 October 1917 (b/w photo), Australian Photographer (20th century) / Australian War Memorial, Canberra, Australia / Bridgeman Images; **Source P2F.** Popperfoto / Getty Images; **Source P2G.** Horace Nicholls / IWM / Getty Images; **Source P2I.** Mediacolor's / Alamy Stock Photo; **Chapter 1 & Source 1B.** Bettmann / Getty Images; **Source 1C.** Front cover cartoon by SEM, in 'La Baionnette', 13 March 1919 / Mary Evans Picture Library; **Source 1F.** ullsteinbild / TopFoto; **Source 1H.** Return of the Guard from the War, December 1918, from 'Deutsche Gedenkhalle: Das Neue Deutschland' compiled by General Von Eisenhart Rothe, 1939 (photogravure), German Photographer (20th Century) / Private Collection / The Stapleton Collection / Bridgeman Images; **Source 1I.** Waldemar Titzenthaler / ullsteinbild / Getty Images; **Source 1J.** Bettmann / Getty Images; **Source 1M.** ullstein bild / Getty Images; **Source 1N.** Keystone / Getty Images; **Source 1O.** Based on map by AlphaCentauri and P.S.Burton, Wikimedia.org; **Source 1R.** Cartoon by Will Dyson in 'The Daily Herald' / Mary Evans Picture Library; **Source 1T.** The Reckoning / Reproduced by permission of Punch Ltd www.punch.co.uk; **Chapter 2 & Source 2A.** Central Press /Hulton Archive / Getty Images; **Source 2B.** Lewis W. Hine / Buyenlarge / Getty Images; **Source 2C.** Schomburg General Research and Reference Division, The New York Public Library. The New York Public Library Digital Collections. 1919. http://digitalcollections.nypl.org/items/510d47de-7bc8-a3d9-e040-e00a18064a99; **Source 2D.** Fine Art Images / Heritage Images / Getty Images; **Source 2E.** Keystone-France / Gamma-Keystone / Getty Images; **Source 2F.** Photo by Evans, Walker, 1936, U.S. Farm Security Administration/Office of War Information. Library of Congress, Prints & Photographs Division, FSA/OWI Collection LC-USF33- 031322-M5 [P&P]; **Source 2G.** David Low, The conference excuses itself. Evening Standard, 23 May 1934, Solo Syndication / Associated Newspapers Ltd, British Cartoon Archive; **Source 2H.** Bettmann / Getty Images; **Source 2J.** David Low, The Doormat. Evening Standard, 19 Jan 1933, Solo Syndication / Associated Newspapers Ltd, British Cartoon Archive; **Source 2K.** David Low, Trial by Geneva. Evening Standard, 24 Nov 1932, Solo Syndication / Associated Newspapers Ltd, British Cartoon Archive; **Source 2L.** Keystone-France / Gamma-Rapho / Getty Images; **Source 2N.** David Low, Self-Portrait. Evening Standard, 15 Feb 1935, Solo Syndication / Associated Newspapers Ltd, British Cartoon Archive; **Chapter 3 & Source 3F.** Bettmann / Getty Images; **Source 3A.** Galerie Bilderwelt / Getty Images; **Source 3B.** Keystone / Getty Images; **Source 3C.** Universal History Archive; **Source 3D.** German Propaganda poster, 1931 (colour litho), German School, (20th century) / Private Collection / Archives Charmet / Bridgeman Images; **Source 3E.** Fotosearch / Stringer / Getty Images; **Source 3G.** Hulton Archive / Stringer / Getty Images; **Source 3H.** Imperial War Museums / Getty Images; **Source 3I.** Universal Images Group / Getty Images; **Source 3M.** Universal History Archive / Getty Images; **Source 3N.** ullstein bild / Getty Images; **Source 3O.** Universal History Archive / Getty Images; **Source 3P.** David Low, Increasing Pressure. Evening Standard, 18 Feb 1938, Solo Syndication / Associated Newspapers Ltd, British Cartoon Archive; **Source 3Q.** ullstein bild / Getty Images; **Source 3R.** Past Pix/ SSPL / Getty Images; **Source 3S.** David Low, Stepping Stones to Glory. Evening Standard, 1936. Solo Syndication / Associated Newspapers Ltd, British Cartoon Archive; **Source 3T.** Print Collector / Getty Images; **Source 3U.** Topham Picturepoint; **Source 3W.** David Low, The End. A Cartoon History of Our Times, 1939, Solo Syndication / Associated Newspapers Ltd, British Cartoon Archive; **Source 3BB.** Fox Photos / Getty Images; **Chapter 4.** NATO / Getty Images; **Source 4B.** Soviet World War 2 poster by Kukryniksy, 1942. 'We will cut off all roads to the evil enemy, he will not escape from this noose!' Poster depicting Hitler being strangled by fabric pulled tight by Russian, British, and American hands / Photo © Everett Collection / Bridgeman Images; **Source 4C.** The Way of a Stork / Leslie Illingsworth / Reproduced by permission of

Punch Ltd; **Source 4E.** USA: US Government poster identifying a Russian soldier as a friend who 'fights for freedom'. 1942. / Pictures from History / Bridgeman Images; **Source 4G.** Trouble with some of the pieces / Reproduced by permission of Punch Ltd; **Source 4M.** Universal Images Group / Getty Images; **Source 4N.** David Low, Why can't we work together in mutual trust & confidence?. Evening Standard, 30 Nov 1945, Solo Syndication / Associated Newspapers Ltd, British Cartoon Archive; **Source 4Q.** Illingworth, Leslie Gilbert, Peep under the Iron curtain [Published caption]. Daily Mail, 6 March 1946, Solo Syndication / Associated Newspapers Ltd, British Cartoon Archive; **Source 4R.** Granger Historical Picture Archive / Alamy Stock Photo; **Source 4T.** The Granger Collection / TopFoto; **Source 4V.** Sovfoto / Getty Images; **Source 4Y.** Fototeca Gilardi / AKG-Images; **Source 4Z** The Marshall Tree / E H Shepard / Reproduced by permission of Punch Ltd; **Source 4AA.** Rival Buses / E H Shephard / Reproduced by permission of Punch Ltd; **Source 4BB.** The Bird Watcher/ E H Shephard / Reproduced by permission of Punch Ltd; **Source 4CC.** Henry Grant Compton / FPG / Getty Images; **Source 4FF.** Fototeca Gilardi / AKG-Images; **Source 4GG.** Marcus, Edwin, Artist. While the Shadow Lengthens. 1948. Image. Retrieved from the Library of Congress, <https://www.loc.gov/item/acd1996005659/PP/>, by permission of the Marcus Family; **Chapter 5 & Source 5F.** Bettmann / Getty Images; **Source 5A.** imageBROKER / Alamy Stock Photo; **Source 5C.** David Low, History Doesn't Repeat Itself. Daily Herald, 30 Jun 1950. Solo Syndication / Associated Newspapers Ltd, British Cartoon Archive; **Source 5D.** Believe it or Knout / Leslie Illingworth / Reproduced by permission of Punch Ltd; **Source 5E.** The Washington Post / Getty Images; **Source 5G.** Keystone / Getty Images; **Source 5H.** Bettmann / Getty Images; **Source 5I.** A 1962 Herblock Cartoon, © The Herb Block Foundation; **Source 5J.** Sean Pavone / Alamy Stock Photo; **Source 5K.** ITAR-TASS / TopFoto; **Source 5L.** Carl T. Gossett Jr / New York Times Co / Getty Images; **Source 5M.** Bettmann / Getty Images; **Source 5N.** Communist China Poster reads, 'U.S. imperialism, get out of South Viet Nam!' c. 1970. Poster depicts men and women soldiers of North Vietnam in heroic poses in a jungle / Photo © Everett Collection / Bridgeman Images; **Source 5O, Source 5P, Source 5Q, Source 5R.** Bettmann / Getty Images; **Chapter 6 & Source 6J.** ullstein bild / Getty Images; **Source 6A.** Ed Giorandino / NY Daily News Archive / Getty Images; **Source 6B, Source 6C.** Keystone / Getty Images; **Source 6E.** A 1968 Herblock Cartoon, © The Herb Block Foundation; **Source 6G.** Hulton Archive / Getty Images;

Source 6H. John Bryson / The LIFE Images Collection / Getty Images; **Source 6I.** Carl Mydans / The LIFE Picture Collection / Getty Images; **Source 6K.** Keystone-France / Getty Images; **Source 6L.** Wolfgang Bera / ullsteinbild / Getty Images; **Source 6M.** Topham / AP / TopFoto; **Source 6O.** Hulton Archive / Getty Images; **Source 6P.** Francois LOCHON / Gamma-Rapho / Getty Images; **Source 6Q.** Sovfoto / Getty Images; **Source 6S.** Tiit Veermae / Alamy Stock Photo; **Chapter 7 & Source 7A.** Keystone Pictures USA / Alamy Stock Photo; **Source 7B.** KARIM SAHIB / AFP / Getty Images; **Source 7D.** Riad Shehata / Hulton Archive / Getty Images; **Source 7E.** Georges Galmiche / INA /Getty Images; **Source 7F.** 2.4.7. Films / REX / Shutterstock; **Source 7H.** A 1979 Herblock Cartoon, © The Herb Block Foundation; **Source 7I.** AP/ Press Association Images / PA Photos; **Source 7J.** A 1987 Herblock Cartoon, © The Herb Block Foundation; **Source 7L.** Kaveh Kazemi / Hulton Archive / Getty Images; **Source 7N.** Saddam Hussein squeezing the world. Front cover 17 August 1990. Reproduced by permission of Punch Ltd; **Source 7O.** William Foley / The LIFE Images Collection / Getty Images; **Source 7P.** Danita Delimont / Alamy Stock Photo; **Source 7Q.** David Turnley / Corbis / VCG / Getty Images; **Chapter 8 & Source 8J.** Hulton Archive / Getty Images; **Source 8A.** Everett Collection Historical / Alamy Stock Photo; **Source 8B.** Chronical / Alamy Stock Photo; **Source 8C.** Everett Collection Historical / Alamy Stock Photo; **Source 8D.** AT History / Alamy Stock Photo; **Source 8E.** IWM / Getty Images; **Source 8G.** Universal History Archive / Getty Images; **Source 8H.** Hulton Archive / Getty Images; **Source 8I.** A Hop Over, c.1918 (gelatin silver print), Hurley, Frank (1885-1962) / National Gallery of Victoria, Melbourne, Australia / Bridgeman Images; **Source 8K.** Everett Collection Historical / Alamy Stock Photo; **Source 8L.** 2nd Lt. T K Aitken / IWM / Getty Images; **Source 8M.** John Singer Sargent / IWM / Getty Images; **Source 8N & Source 8O.** Universal History Archive / Getty Images; P**Source 8P.** Lord Price Collection / Alamy Stock Photo; **Source 8S.** Three Lions / Getty Images; **Chapter 9 & Source 9I.** ullsteinbild / TopFoto; **Source 9A.** AKG-Images; **Source 9B & Source 9C.** Hulton Archive / Getty Images; **Source 9D.** ullsteinbild / Getty Images; **Source 9E.** Hulton Archive / Getty Images; **Source 9F.** Photo by Samuel Dietz / Getty Images; **Source 9J.** Keystone-France / Gamma-Keystone / Getty Images; **Source 9M.** ullsteinbild / Getty Images; **Source 9N.** NurPhoto / Getty Images; **Source 9O.** Heinrich Hoffmann / ullsteinbild / Getty Images; **Source 9P.**Bettmann / Getty Images; **Source 9Q.** Universal History Archive / Getty Images; **Source 9R.** Chronical / Alamy Stock Photo;

Source 9T. Hugo Jaeger / Timepix / The LIFE Picture Collection / Getty Images; **Source 9U.** Fred Ramage / Keystone Features / Getty Images; **Source 9V.** INTERFOTO / Alamy Stock Photo; **Chapter 10 & Source 10M.** Bettmann / Getty Images; **Source 10A, Source 10B, Source 10C, Source 10K.** Universal History Archive / Getty Images; **Source 10G.** Fine Art Images / Heritage Images / TopFoto; **Source 10I.** Universal History Archive / Getty Images; **Source 10J.** ITAR-TASS Photo Agency / Alamy Stock photo; **Source 10L.** INTERFOTO / Alamy Stock Photo; **Source 10N & Source 10O.** Hulton Archive / Getty Images; **Source 10Q.** Fine Art Images / Heritage Images / Getty Images; **Source 10S.** SPUTNIK / Alamy Stock Photo; **Source 10T.** Bettmann / Getty Images; **Source 10U.** ITAR-TASS Photo Agency / Alamy Stock Photo; **Source 10V.** Sovfoto / Getty Images; **Source 10X.** Heritage Image Partnership Ltd / Alamy Stock Photo;

Chapter 11 & Source 11I. Keystone-France / Gamma-Keystone / Getty Images; **Source 11A & Source 11C.** Hulton Archive / Getty Images; **Source 11B.** Chronical / Alamy Stock Photo; **Source 11E.** JP Jazz Archive / Redferns / Getty Images; **Source 11F.** Topical Press Agency / Getty Images; **Source 11G.** Imagno [Der Gangsterknig Al Capone, Photographie, 3,5,1932] / Getty Images; **Source 11H.** General Photographic Agency / Getty Images; **Source 11K.** 20th Century Fox / Getty Images; **Source 11L.** Hulton Archive / Getty Images; **Source 11N.** MPI / Getty Images; **Source 11O, Source 11Q, Source 11R.** Fotosearch / Getty Images; **Source 11P.** Pictorial Parade / Getty Images; **Chapter 12.** Horace Nicholls / IWM / Getty Images; **Source 12A.** The Print Collector / Hulton Archive / Getty Images; **Source 12B.** A 1965 Herblock Cartoon, © The Herb Block Foundation

Index

278

281

283